Unwrapping Ancient Egypt

Unwrapping Ancient Egypt

Christina Riggs

BLOOMSBURY
LONDON • NEW DELHI • NEW YORK • SYDNEY

Bloomsbury Academic
An imprint of Bloomsbury Publishing Plc

50 Bedford Square
London
WC1B 3DP
UK

1385 Broadway
New York
NY 10018
USA

www.bloomsbury.com

Bloomsbury is a registered trade mark of Bloomsbury Publishing Plc

First published 2014

British Library Cataloguing-in-Publication Data
A catalogue record for this book is available from the British Library.

ISBN: HB: 978-0-85785-539-8
PB: 978-0-85785-507-7
ePub: 978-0-85785-677-7
ePDF: 978-0-85785-498-8

Library of Congress Cataloging-in-Publication Data
Riggs, Christina.
Unwrapping ancient Egypt : the shroud, the secret and the sacred / Christina Riggs.
pages cm
ISBN 978-0-85785-507-7 (pbk.) — ISBN 978-0-85785-539-8 (hardback) —
ISBN 978-0-85785-677-7 (epub)
1. Mummies—Egypt. 2. Textile fabrics, Ancient—Egypt. 3. Burial—Egypt—History—To 1500. 4. Funeral rites and ceremonies—Egypt. 5. Egypt—Civilization—To 332 B.C. I. Title.
DT62.M7R54 2014
932—dc23 2013045827

Typeset by Apex CoVantage, LLC
Printed and bound in India

CONTENTS

LIST OF ILLUSTRATIONS

ACKNOWLEDGMENTS

The opportunity to deliver the Evans-Pritchard Lectures at All Souls College, Oxford, in 2012 was pivotal in the development of this book, and I am grateful to the Warden and Fellows of the college and to the Evans-Pritchard selection committee, in particular Prof. David Gellner, Prof. Wendy James, and Prof. Sir John Vickers. The college's hospitality provided an ideal setting in which to reflect on my ideas and revise the manuscript, while responses from the lecture audience offered valuable encouragement and insight. Many other institutions and individuals have contributed to the project at every stage. A Research Fellowship from the Arts and Humanities Research Council (AHRC) of the UK, combined with study leave from the University of East Anglia (UEA), enabled me to devote the 2010–11 academic year to research and writing, without which I would never have completed a first draft. At UEA, the stimulating, cross-disciplinary environment of the School of Art History and World Art Studies has been essential to the development of my research and my approach to my subject, and I thank my colleagues and students for their interest and support throughout. At Bloomsbury, Louise Butler had faith in the book when other publishers scratched their heads, while Sophie Hodgson, Molly Beck, and the production staff have offered exemplary attention during the editorial and production process.

In preparing images for the book, I have benefitted from the wizardry of Nick Warr at UEA and from the assistance of staff at the Egypt Exploration Society, the Griffith Institute at Oxford University, the Institut Français d'Archéologie Orientale, the Metropolitan Museum of Art's Department of Egyptian Art, the Oriental Institute at the University of Chicago, the Petrie Museum of Egyptian Archaeology at University College London, and the Theban Mapping Project. Laurent Coulon, John Freed, Angela Palmer, and Martin Andreas Stadler provided images with exemplary grace and speed, and Ruth Rogers generously gave permission to use her photograph of a wrapped Osiris figure in the Metropolitan Museum of Art (see Fig. 4.8) on the cover of the book. The astonishing detail of the interleaved strips of ancient, folded linen—reconstructed by museum staff in the 1940s—was one of the winning entries in the Metropolitan Museum's 2011 "Get Closer" photography contest and conveys the intricacy of Egyptian wrapping practices in every sense.

Writing a book is a solitary activity, but the work that goes into shaping the ideas in a book is anything but. My thinking about archaeology,

Egyptology, museums, colonialism, human remains, and textiles has benefitted from conversations and exchanges with a number of individuals, including Sam Alberti, John Baines, Will Carruthers, Karen Exell, Ann French, Elizabeth Frood, Chris Gosden, George Lau, Victoria Mitchell, Sarah Monks, Robert Preucel, Gay Robins, Eleanor Robson, Alice Stevenson, Willeke Wendrich, David Wengrow, Ghislaine Widmer, and the late Dominic Montserrat. The chance to present my work at the Theoretical Archaeology Group meeting (Durham 2009) and the Visualization in Archaeology conference (Southampton 2011), and to audiences at Cambridge University, the Egypt Exploration Society, and the Norwich University of the Arts, also helped me formulate some of my ideas and respond to feedback from students, academics, and the public.

The personal and the professional are often closely linked in academic work, as this book itself demonstrates by interweaving my previous experience as a museum curator with my intellectual exploration of textiles, mummification, and the history and practice of Egyptology. My last three acknowledgments bridge the personal and the professional as well. It may be a hazard of academic life, but it so happens that I have met my closest friends in university libraries—including the archaeologist Sabine Laemmel, whose steadfast presence during a crucial summer of research on this project meant more than she can know. Armed with a sense of humor, a sharp pencil, and a sharper brain, another friend, the Egyptologist Tom Hardwick, read the entire manuscript, including early versions that could most charitably be described as unkempt. His comments and belief in the project were invaluable, and his corrections saved me from several errors, although any that escaped remain my own. My UEA colleague, the anthropologist Ferdinand de Jong, helped shape the argument and structure of the book at every stage, especially through discussions about secrecy, colonialism, and the politics of heritage. He challenged me to address issues I would not otherwise have considered and to question assumptions I had not realized I was making. His input has made this book (and my life) considerably more interesting.

Christina Riggs
Norfolk 2013

PREFACE

This book has its origins in two questions that began as discrete inquiries but gradually became inseparable. The first, which developed from my previous work on funerary art in Roman Egypt, concerns the ancient Egyptian custom of wrapping bodies and objects in linen, as well as the representation of wrapped bodies in Egyptian art. The second arose from my experience working as a museum curator in a collection full of unwrapped Egyptian bodies and half-forgotten linen textiles. Whether these material remnants of the ancient past were visible (on display) or hidden (in storage) depended on many variables that had little if anything to do with their significance in antiquity. Indeed, there was a good chance that the best-known example of Egyptian wrapping—a human mummy—would have been unwrapped in the process of being or becoming a museum object, a process that necessarily reversed the intention of the ancient actors. Thus the isolation of the two questions was misleading, for the act of unwrapping depended on the initial act of wrapping.

To understand the significance of wrapping practices in ancient Egypt, as well as its twin, the modern unwrapping of Egypt, this book adopts an unreservedly interdisciplinary approach. The core of the study is based on primary evidence from the discipline of Egyptology, set within an interpretive framework that draws on the more theorized and self-reflexive fields of anthropology, archaeology, and museum studies. Using archaeological reports, museum collections, publications of tombs and temples, and editions of core bodies of ritual texts, I have drawn together examples of material that excavators found wrapped in situ; records of linen used in mummification or otherwise associated with burials; depictions of wrapped, cloaked, or shrouded objects (including bodies); and religious practices centered on wrapping rituals. The examples range in date from the period of state formation in the Nile Valley to the Roman Period, when the adoption of Christianity began to transform the negotiation of the sacred. This expanse of time, covering more than three thousand years, is what generally defines the entity known as “ancient Egypt” because of the internal coherence of its political and religious structures as well as its territorial boundaries, encompassing the Nile delta and the river valley as far south as the First Cataract. Within this construct, whose artificiality should be acknowledged, there will have been wide variabilities in different time periods and different regions. The ancient record tends to smooth over these differences by its nature because it presents the concerns of a small elite invested in a homogeneous, unchanging state and united by a relative cultural consistency. States of preservation and the practicalities of archaeology further shape what comprises "ancient Egypt." Sites in the Nile valley survive better than those in the delta; tombs and temples survive better than domestic structures; and river and railway transport in the nineteenth and early twentieth centuries influenced where archaeologists worked, as did the system of permits controlled by the archaeological service. Important as they are to bear in mind, these caveats cannot detract from the rich range of sources that relate to wrapping in Egypt, where the dry climate has preserved organic materials—including linen, the textile specified in wrapping rituals—in remarkable quantity and quality.

Despite its cross-boundary potential, the vast data set produced by Egyptology has tended to be a closed territory, with some exceptions in recent work influenced by anthropology and archaeological theory. Egyptology also remains defined by its philological interests, stretching back to Champollion's decipherment of hieroglyphs in 1822. There is little engagement with ancient Egyptian material culture in visual studies (whether art history, anthropology of art, or museology), and even less engagement in Egyptology with how other disciplines think about visuality and the world of objects. Trained primarily as an Egyptologist, I found that the questions I wanted to ask about the use of linen wrappings in ancient Egypt could not be answered by Egyptological methods, just as those questions could not be considered in isolation from the drawers of linen, boxes of bones, and displays of mummies that I once curated. The ancient evidence pointed to a close association among Egyptian ideas about mummification, linen, and secrecy, while comparison with other cultures offered models for a parallel relationship between wrapping and the divine. In the museum context, expanding debates about the curation and display of human remains have treated Egyptian mummies as a separate category from those remains deemed to have living descendants to claim or speak for them. This distinction has received little comment, nor have the debates taken into account the myriad forms in which mummies and their wrappings survive. Although anthropological collections, especially in ethnographic museums, now incorporate indigenous or allochthonous input as a matter of course in making decisions about the care, display, and repatriation of religious objects and human remains, many museums would be reluctant to remove their most popular Egyptian exhibits from display, and repatriation requests from the Egyptian government so far concern either illegally exported antiquities or a handful of iconic objects, like the Rosetta Stone in London or the head of Nefertiti in Berlin. Without pressure from the public, from Egypt, or from its own practitioners, Egyptology operates as a discipline that has not interrogated its own histories of collecting, either in the museum or in the field. I would argue that this is detrimental not only to the academy, but also to the publics who derive their impression of ancient Egypt in part from museum exhibitions, museum-produced publications and websites, and popular media and tourist itineraries legitimized by input from museum and university experts.

I had the privilege of presenting *Unwrapping Ancient Egypt* as the Evans-Pritchard Lectures at All Souls College, Oxford, in the spring of 2012, and each of the six chapters corresponds to one of the lectures I delivered over the course of three weeks, with additional argument, discussion, and referencing incorporated for the published version. The history of archaeology and museums informs each chapter and is given particular weight in the early parts of the book. This history helps illuminate the more recent and contemporary practices discussed at the end of the volume, which I suggest have deep roots in earlier, and undisturbed, soil.

Chapter 1 introduces the overarching themes of the book, using evidence from one of Egyptology's star turns, the tomb of Tutankhamun. Entitled "Desecration," the chapter considers the practices of wrapping and unwrapping as if they were two lengths of cloth twisted and looped around each other, joining ancient Egypt to its manifestations in the modern world: the excavation, the museum, and the archive. Each subsequent chapter further traces some of these twists and loops and explores theoretical considerations relevant to its specific topic. Chapter 2, "Revelation," picks up the theme of unwrapping as a process of desacralization, examining the historical practice of "unrolling" mummies (and the less well-recorded evidence for unwrapping statues) as a form of knowledge production that helped define archaeology as a discipline. In its objectified state, the ancient Egyptian body became a focus of discourse for colonial anxieties about race, gender, and cultural heritage, but Chapter 3, "Mummification," considers what the practice might have meant in ancient Egyptian contexts. Textiles played a defining role in mummification, and the materiality of the linen used in mummy wrappings and other religious rites is the subject of Chapter 4, "Linen." Wrapping rituals were intimately connected with ideas of hiddenness and concealment, to the extent that the priests who wrapped the statues of the gods, or the bodies of the dead, were called "masters of secrets." Therefore Chapter 5, "Secrecy," takes up an issue often avoided in academic Egyptology but embraced by other Egyptologies, such as Freemasonry, theosophy, and Afrocentrism. Secrecy was an important aspect of Egyptian social organization and a necessary component of the sacred as engendered through rituals as well as art. The act of wrapping a body or a statue in linen had the power to transform mundane, or even impure, matter into something pure and godlike, and Chapter 6, "Sanctity," considers the metaphorical extension of this act, both in ancient Egypt and in the modern sphere of the museum, for instance through the use of technologies of revelation that amplify the effect (and affect) of earlier mummy unwrappings. In antiquity, Egyptian wrapping practices were a way to reveal power while concealing knowledge. Modern "wrappings" of meaning—based on our experience of ancient materiality—accomplish what is in essence the reverse, concealing power while "revealing" (that is, producing) knowledge of the past.

Because of the diversity of the subject matter and source material included in this study, and the inherently artificial, disciplinary construction of "ancient Egypt" that I have pointed out, the ancient evidence I use throughout the book ranges over some three thousand years and originates throughout the Egyptian Nile valley and the delta. Examples are drawn from sites including the cemetery and temple complexes at Saqqara, which lies just south and west of modern Cairo, and the well-documented tombs and temples in and around modern Luxor, where the West Bank region is designated as a UNESCO World Heritage Site; this area is often known by one of its ancient Greek designations, Thebes. Many of my examples date to the dominant periods, known as "kingdoms," of the pharaonic era—the Old, Middle, and New Kingdoms—as well as the Ptolemaic and Roman periods when Egypt was governed first by Hellenistic kings and then as part of the Roman Empire.[1] In using such a range of sources, my intention is not to a-historicize the material, but to suggest the richness of the evidence from different times and places and the multivalent meanings with which textiles and wrapping could be imbued.

It has also not been my intention to offer a "how-to" guide for museum professionals and academics, although some responses I received to earlier presentations of this material seemed to expect or desire exactly that—notably when the interlocutors were trained, like me, as Egyptologists. From my vantage point as a scholar seeking to understand past and present interpretations of ancient Egypt, and the relationship between them, not only would it be impertinent to set out guidelines on the display of Egyptian mummies or the content of Egyptology courses (to take two examples), but it would also be futile and counterproductive for a number of reasons. Futile, because a plurality of research interests, museological practices, and public interpretations is on the whole desirable, the more so if that plurality comes to include underrepresented voices (such as contemporary Egyptians). And counterproductive because it is up to individual practitioners and institutions to undertake their own self-critique and find their own ways forward, as those in cognate disciplines have done. Without a significant realignment of priorities and multiplicity of voices, the study and presentation of ancient Egypt increasingly risk stagnation, and that is why critical analysis—which is what I do offer here—is as urgent as it is essential.

For a country often labeled with the Orientalizing trope of timelessness, Egypt in antiquity—like Egypt today—must have been a place of diverse and dynamic experiences, on both the individual and the social level, only some of which are represented in the textual, pictorial, and archaeological records. What I have tried to characterize in this book, then, is a set of suggestive links and patterns, in the hopes of better apprehending not only the Egyptian evidence but also the archaeological and museological interventions that have shaped it. This came to seem all the more important during the three years of writing, as Egypt underwent dramatic changes that further shaped my thinking about the relationship between the country's modern history and the West's uses of its ancient past. The result is a study that follows those intertwining questions with which I began: why ancient Egyptians wrapped sacred objects and bodies in linen and what it signifies that those objects and bodies now lie bare in museum vitrines and storage drawers, their linen long forgotten. Between the present and the past, I have tried to trace the rift where the wrapping has been undone.

1

Desecration

Body broken from its legs, tail snapped clean, and shards of resin-coated wood scattered on the floor around its plinth, the leopard lay near the broken glass of a display case in the Egyptian Museum in Cairo while the Arab Spring of 2011 gathered pace outside in Tahrir (Liberation) Square. The gilded feet of Tutankhamun were nearby, splintered at the ankle and stuck fast to a smaller plinth, which had supported a standing figure of the king on top of the leopard's back. Now the king was nowhere to be seen.

After four days of peaceful protests against the Mubarak regime, leopard and king had been split into pieces, hurled, by unseen hands, out of the glazed case. Two other statues, apparently in the same vitrine, were also damaged, and Al Jazeera television footage of the smashed glass and fragmented statues seemed to confirm reports of theft or vandalism on the night of January 28, the "Friday of Anger," when protests throughout Egypt escalated. Grainy screen grabs circulated on the Internet, including an image of two mummified heads jumbled on the floor elsewhere in the Egyptian Museum. Suddenly Egyptology blogs and discussion lists outside Egypt began to pay attention to the revolution that was taking place in Egypt, and cultural heritage organizations based in Europe and America followed suit. The International Council of Museums (ICOM), the United Nations Educational, Scientific and Cultural Organization (UNESCO), the International Committee of the Blue Shield (ICBS), and, jointly, the Archaeological Institute of America (AIA), the American Anthropological Association (AAA), and the World Archaeological Congress (WAC), issued statements or appeals in the ensuing days, calling for the protection of cultural heritage in Egypt.[1] According to the ICOM statement, no less than the "collective memory of mankind" was at stake in safeguarding the collections of Egyptian museums and archaeological storerooms. A handful of academics took issue with such an emphasis on objects over people, as violent clashes erupted between protestors and the police, but most commentators insisted that politics and heritage were separate, that the protection of ancient Egyptian sites, monuments, and artifacts transcended such concerns.[2] If the treasures of Tutankhamun were not sacred, what was?

A photograph from the archives of the Tutankhamun excavation shows leopard and king united, the cat's spine curving under the level support for the royal figure dowelled into its back (Fig. 1.1). Although often described as a panther—that is, a leopard whose spotted coat is obscured by a recessive mutation that darkens the fur—the black surface does not represent the "true" color of the animal, since the same resin coating was applied to many statues of guardian animals and spirits found in royal tombs of the time. In the photograph, the light source picks out the modeled musculature of the feline legs and the mottled coat of resin on its body and both plinths. Gilding highlights the eyes, inner ears, and muzzle. Above the leopard, and entirely covered in gold leaf, stands the king, who wears a tall crown, a softly draped and pleated skirt, and sandals. He carries a walking stick and a herding flail, the latter associated with kingship and certain chthonic gods. The combination of black and gold, darkness and light, night and day, recurred throughout the tomb, as did the association of leopard and king. In ancient Egyptian cosmology, leopards were associated with the night sky; their spots were the stars. Certain priests and ritual performers wore leopard-skin robes, some made of animal hide, others of linen woven or embroidered with five-pointed stars, and fragments of three such robes were found in Tutankhamun's tomb. As news of the vandalism first broke, archive photographs provided the before shot to the screen grabs' after, documenting the significance of the statue. That significance lay not in its connections to kingship, cosmology, or materials—aspects of the ancient Egyptian worldview—but in its connections to the modern world, its place in our archive.

Public defacement, writes the anthropologist Michael Taussig, renders a "wound of sacrilege," an act of negation that can make the damaged, defaced object appear more powerful than it was when whole.[3] The attack on the Tutankhamun statues was one such act of defacement, and hence a focal point for preservationist calls to action. The attention paid to the statues, the unidentified mummies, and an assortment of other, less eye-catching antiquities feared stolen, masked what was arguably the more drastic aspect of the sacrilege—the violation of the museum itself. This defacing act represented the collapse of civic order, a breach of security and society so unspeakable that no clear explanation emerged for how the alleged break-in (or break-ins) took place. Through glass skylights, according to the first account by Egyptian antiquities officials, but the old skylights looked intact when the museum reopened. Through the gift shop, the on-site police office, the back doors, the front doors? No one could say. The glass in the smashed display cases was quickly and quietly replaced, and within a month of the incident, Egyptian Museum restorers had put the damaged Tutankhamun statues back together. The swift response downplayed the ignominy of the attack and signaled reassurance, ostensibly about the fate of Egypt's antiquities, but surely about the fate of a country that had just thrown a modern ruler out of his protected enclave, too.

The defacement of the statues unleashed an unsuspected power in these figures, which had hitherto been rather minor players in the drama of Tutankhamun's tomb, rarely discussed in scholarship and chiefly noted for

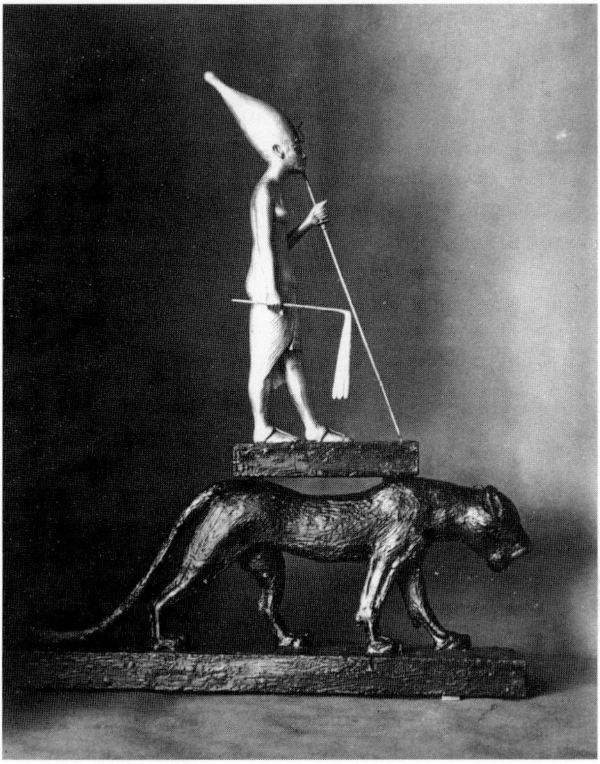

FIGURE 1.1 *Statue of Tutankhamun on a leopard, with the wrapping removed; Carter no. 289b. Photograph by Harry Burton. Copyright: Griffith Institute, University of Oxford*

the delicate features of the gilded king. In their vandalized state, however, it became evident that Egyptology held them sacred. Unlike the formal statements about the preservation of sites and objects, less formal communiques on the Internet and in email exchanges adopted an emotive tone. Images of the damaged leopard were "sad," one UK blogger wrote, "devastating" said another.[4] An accusatory air swept into the debate as well, backed by the ideological strength of the museum concept: since the Egyptians weren't taking care of the world's heritage, it was just as well that museums in Britain and Germany had fended off recent inquiries about returning the Rosetta Stone and the bust of Nefertiti to Egypt, where they might meet the same fate as the statues. The "developed" world could keep its museums secure, its powers hidden in plain sight. "Developing" nations had failed on both counts. Against such a backdrop, the blandishments of heritage professionals and discussion list moderators, with their insistence on a strict separation between antiquities and politics, rang hollow.

Some of the interlocutors seemed to feel that their opinions were apolitical, but it is difficult to imagine an institution more steeped in political symbolism than the antiquities museum in Cairo, or an archaeological find in Egypt more shaped by regime changes than the tomb of Tutankhamun. Designed in 1895 by a French architect, for the French-run antiquities service, the Egyptian Museum opened its doors in 1902 at the height of the British "veiled protectorate" overseen by Lord Cromer.[5] Egyptians were not the museum's target audience. On the façade, plaques in monumental Latin identify the founding fathers of Egyptology, all European men, and the first Arabic guidebook appeared in the 1910s, at the instigation of one of the few Egyptians trained in Egyptology.[6] As for Tutankhamun, the discovery of his tomb in 1922 came in the same year the Wafd party won nominal independence from Britain, and the fledgling Egyptian government seized on the find as a Pharaonist symbol and enforced its right to keep everything from the tomb in Egypt, rather than dividing it with Howard Carter and his sponsor, the fifth earl of Carnarvon.[7] The political repercussions of the Tutankhamun find charted the postcolonial trajectory of Egypt. In the 1970s, a blockbuster European and North American tour of the treasures marked President Sadat's realignment to Western governments and embrace of controversial free market reforms, while a highly touted tour in the 2000s, although organized by an American commercial outfit, made pointed public statements that the Egyptian government would keep the bulk of the profits this time around. Ownership not just of the revenue but of the objects from the tomb remains a point of contention. In November 2010 the Metropolitan Museum of Art in New York signed over to Egypt the ownership of nineteen objects it had received from Carter's estate that were possibly associated with the tomb, while just days before the Egyptian uprising began, antiquities officials announced that they had contacted the current earl of Carnarvon to inquire about the provenance of certain objects in the family's private collection.[8] The boy-king has been more involved in diplomacy in the modern era than he was in his own lifetime.

Only sacred objects inspire such devotion and require such exacting control, manipulation, and care. This is their defense against the "wound of sacrilege" that would reveal where power lies—not in the statue, which is, after all, a thing made of wood, resin, and gold leaf, and not even in the divine spirit that takes the statue as a body, but in the unseen hands that tend (or rend) it. In this mystery play, a museum is both sanctuary to the object and a sacred site itself. Its potency as an abstract, idealized entity and as a concrete, tangible building is proven by the seeming conundrum that its collections garner more attention and generate the loudest outcry at the instance of violation. Lamenting the defacement of an individual object—the Tutankhamun statues, the Warka vase in Baghdad, the Rokeby Venus slashed by a suffragette in London—is somehow easier than acknowledging the desecration of one of the fundamental institutions of the modern age. In other words, a museum may be a more powerful target than the objects within it, but it is the objects that bear the brunt of society's projected values and, of course, the damage.

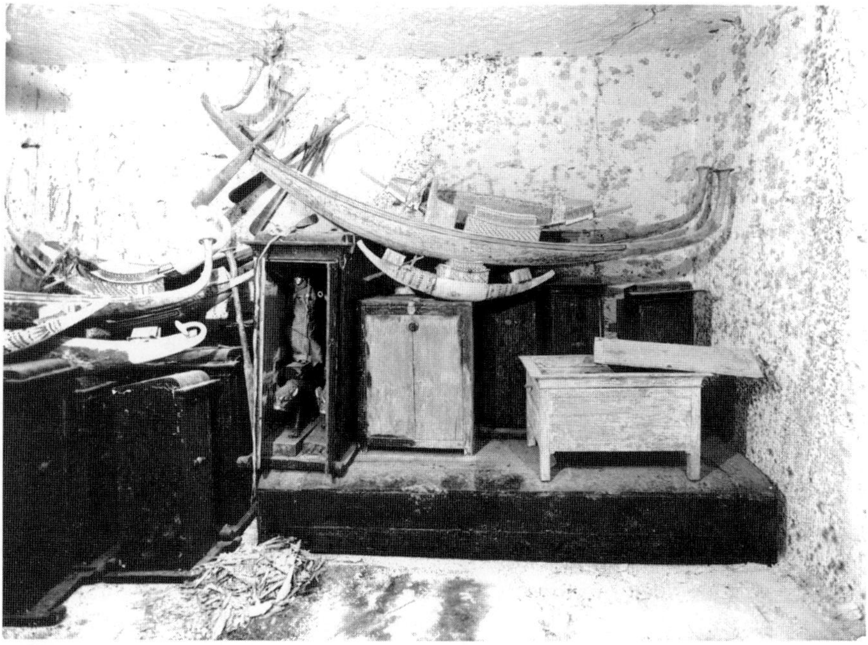

FIGURE 1.2 *View inside the Treasury of the tomb of Tutankhamun, with the doors of chest 289 open and statues 289a and b inside. Photograph by Harry Burton. Copyright: Griffith Institute, University of Oxford*

The statue of the leopard bearing a figure of Tutankhamun on its back was part of a matching pair, only one of which was on display in the Egyptian Museum that January. They had been found together in a room that excavator Howard Carter dubbed the Treasury, which was the most inaccessible part of the compact tomb. Reached only through the burial chamber, the Treasury must have been one of the first rooms filled and sealed in antiquity, and it was the last room cleared in the 1920s. When Carter entered this room, he found it jammed with boxes, boat models, the chest for the king's mummified organs, and more than two dozen wooden shrines, most with their doors bolted shut. The shrine that contained the pair of leopard statues stood against the wall, under a jumble of model boats (Fig. 1.2). As with every other statue found inside the shrines, finely woven linen wrapped the figures, in this instance draped and knotted around the body of the king like an enveloping robe. Ancient Egyptian religion operated around the care of statues, which provided the gods with a body on earth. The cult statue belonged in a shrine, kept in the most secluded part of a temple, and it was dressed in fresh linen at least once a day. With their wrapped statues neatly tucked away, the shrines in the tomb Treasury are the only physical evidence ever found in Egypt for this practice, otherwise known only from depictions on temple walls and written versions of the rite, which was conducted in seclusion by certain priests. The sealed chamber, the locking shrine, the linen covers, all marked the statues as sacred images—made them so, in fact. Shrine opened and linen lost, the leopard-borne kings and their companion statues were undone, incomplete.

In other words, lying broken on the floor of the museum was not the first desecration of the leopard and its king. They had been desanctified by the time they reached Cairo, to be resanctified when they entered the Egyptian Museum. Logged in the Museum's *Journal d'Entrée* and variously prepared for storage or display, the finds from Tutankhamun's tomb were party to a different set of rites. But being stripped of one set of meanings made it possible for them to acquire others, right up to the moment Al Jazeera filmed the fragmented leopard on the gallery floor and beyond. The resin-coated leopard and the gilded king are just one example of how the past is always created in the present. This is as true for academic scholarship in Egyptology as it is for the popular and esoteric permutations that contribute to the mainstream appeal of ancient Egypt; both embrace the narratives of discovery and preservation. Generating knowledge about the past relies on the survival of objects, monuments, buildings, even bodies, and on a culturally specific way of seeing and thinking about these survivals. Nor are the lives of all these things, which so often outlast people, fixed at the moment of creation, use, deposit, or discovery. Things are made and remade over time, both physically, like the splintered wood, and in the imagination, which is how a single thing can be, sometimes simultaneously, the body of a god-king, the focus of archaeological recording, the property of the Egyptian nation, the admired work of art in a vitrine, and the sign of a postcolonial fault line. Behind these modes of being lie hidden histories—the stories that haven't been told (and the powers that haven't been revealed) but that can be glimpsed in between those that were. Why were the statues in Tutankhamun's tomb wrapped in linen and contained in shrines or niches? Why were they unwrapped, and the linen discounted, when Carter and his expert team excavated the tomb and recorded it in minute detail? And why has it been so easy to forget that either of these events—the wrapping and the unwrapping—ever took place?

Archaeology, Museums, and the Material World

> Forgetfulness is a proof of the materiality of objects. Objects are proofs: the proof of history and the mark of others, of disparate origin and of manufacture. And a *proof* in both senses: proof as verification and testimony to material history, and proof as a first draft or first impression—simply one narrative, one history, among many possibilities.
>
> Nick Groom, "An Artists's Manual," in the Hayward Gallery catalogue for *Richard Wentworth's Thinking Aloud* (1998), p. 43

The disparate works displayed in *Thinking Aloud*, curated by sculptor Richard Wentworth, touched on themes of loss, presence, and mutability—from sketches and maquettes presaging things that might, or might not, be or have been created, to works like Francis Alÿs's *San Diego to Tijuana*, a round-the-world excursion drawing attention to the weight of a border-line drawn thinly on a map. In his essay for the exhibition catalogue, Nick Groom drew out some of the crossovers and commonalities among the works Wentworth selected and at one point refers to Derrida on Nietzsche's archive, where a note preserved in the philosopher's handwriting records only that he has forgotten his umbrella. No umbrella, no forgetting, no note, no archive. In the excerpt quoted earlier, this sequence of connections exemplifies, to Groom, how objects make histories through the fact of their material creation and existence and the possibilities that that materiality creates given that histories depend on survivals and erasures.

Where does Tutankhamun fit in here, you might wonder, and where, for that matter, do I? Without having seen *Thinking Aloud* in its first incarnation, I visited one of the show's original venues in December 2010, just a month before the Cairo uprising. I had begun writing this book, and Tutankhamun already featured in the draft of this chapter. To mark the fiftieth anniversary of the Camden Arts Centre, the artist Simon Starling curated a retrospective, *Never the Same River (Possible Futures, Probable Pasts)*, which reincarnated parts of previous exhibitions at the Centre—including *Thinking Aloud*.[9] On the same wall where they had hung twelve years previously, chosen by Wentworth, resurrected by Starling, were two framed photographs from the Tutankhamun excavation archives, one depicting jumbled boxes and baskets in the so-called Annexe and the other the model oars laid out between the wall of the burial chamber and the first of the shrines that surrounded the king's coffins (Fig. 1.3).[10] As with the image of the leopard statue and its shrine in the tomb Treasury, the photos are the work of photographer Harry Burton, whom the Metropolitan Museum of Art released from his usual duties on their excavations so that he could assist Carter with the remarkable find. Burton documented the work on the tomb in stages, in pictures that purport to present the tomb just as it was left in antiquity but in fact show the unseen hand of the archaeologist in the form of the neat, numbered placards that identify each object. Along with Carter's notes, record cards, and diaries, the Burton photographs are housed in the archives of the Griffith Institute at Oxford University.[11] When I studied there, the institute was in its original building, attached to the back of the Ashmolean Museum and reached through a narrow lane. A portrait of Howard Carter was the first thing you saw when you entered, and Burton photographs still line the corridors of the institute's new home. Seeing them, unexpectedly, in the Arts Centre was like meeting what I thought of as my own past in an unfamiliar place. It was archaeology, without the dirt.

If museums and archaeology kept bumping into each other in my personal experience, from a childhood encounter with an Egyptian statue at the Toledo Museum of Art, through my education and early museum-based

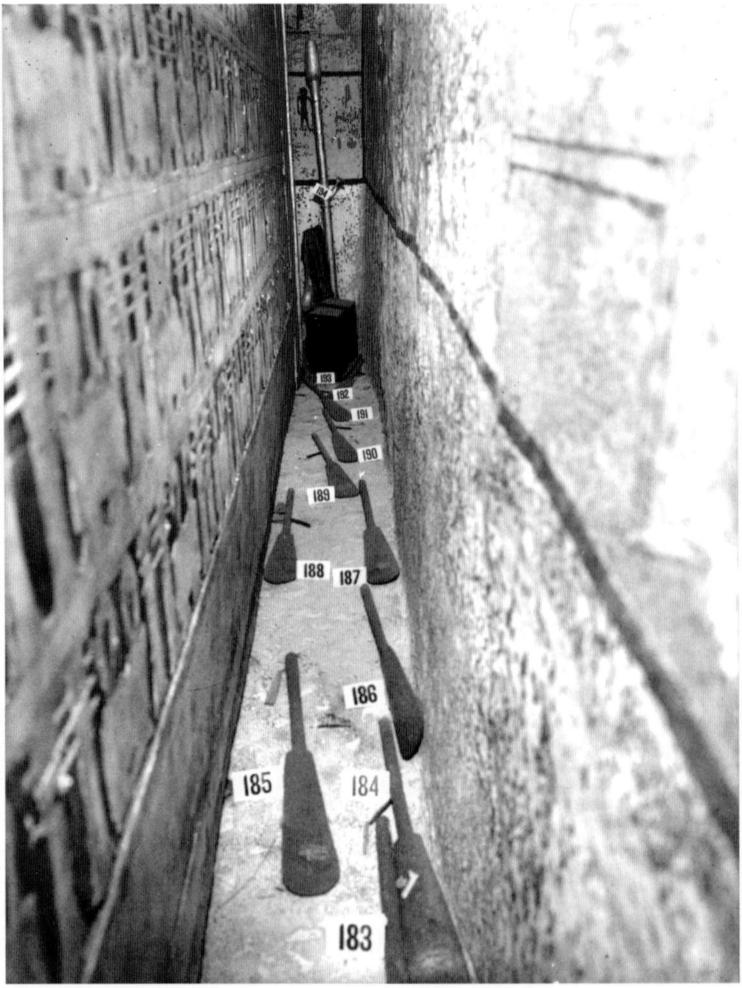

FIGURE 1.3 *Model oars between the wall of the burial chamber and the first shrine in the tomb of Tutankhamun. Photograph by Harry Burton. Copyright: Griffith Institute, University of Oxford*

career, it was no accident. Museums and archaeology have been part of a shared endeavor to locate, recover, parse, and scrutinize the material world. Their Enlightenment roots yielded explosive growth in the nineteenth century, aided by and aiding the colonial project, with the result that each became well established as academic and cultural institutions. In addition to their interrelated histories, museums and archaeology have this in common: neither could exist without the materiality of objects. And it is the material character of the object that concerns me here, together with the constitutive relationships, remembered or forgotten, that its materiality has enabled it to form over time. Attributing agency to objects and seeking out the ways in which their material properties, and the fact of their physical existence, manifest the intangible in human society (perceptions, sensations, imaginings, ideas) offers a way to fathom an object in our own cultural time as well as in its originary context. In archaeology, the concept of materiality "helps us to grant to those we study a perspicacity equivalent to that which we seek for ourselves" since artifacts speak to the immaterial, whether a social network or a cosmological system.[12] Materiality in this sense is situated in the work of Merleau-Ponty as much as Marx, and my approach owes a clear debt to Appadurai and Kopytoff, in addition to more explicit formulations of material culture and materiality—for instance in the work of archaeologists like Hodder and Meskell or anthropologists such as Gell and Miller.[13] Things, objects, do not simply express a social or cultural norm, they make that norm possible; likewise, they do not illustrate a history, but create it.[14]

Critiques of material culture studies have sounded two cautionary notes about this approach to the object. On the one hand, some scholars have asked whether materiality is too far removed from materials, too abstracted from the thing and its thing-ness.[15] On the other hand, in focusing on the object as an object, materiality may risk magnifying the subject–object/human–nonhuman dichotomy it seeks to overcome.[16] The two viewpoints are not as contradictory as they might at first seem. Instead they are complementary attempts to grapple with the challenge of thinking about the unique characteristics of the material world, of which humans, past and present, are one part. Rather than making objects behave like humans in our interpretations, Pinney argues, we should consider how objects have their own ways, and their own times. His sentiment echoes George Kubler's quiet call to expand the restricted notion of what art is, encompassing the manufactured, the mundane, and all "the useless, beautiful, and poetic things of the world."[17] Small wonder that Simon Starling named Kubler's *The Shape of Time* as an influence in preparing *Never the Same River* for the Camden Arts Centre's anniversary exhibition.

The time-depth inherent in both museums and archaeology, and at their interface, foregrounds physical endurance, one of the qualities that objects tend to enjoy more than humans. The difficulty has been to apprehend materiality as experienced *in* the ancient past, which is quite a different undertaking than understanding our experience *of* ancient materiality.[18] This is not to say that our experience of the ancient object world is unimportant. Far from it, since such an understanding is a valuable pursuit in its own right and, crucially, an essential first step toward the ancient experience, which we can only ever grasp through modeling and reconstruction. In order to recognize the uses to which we have put the useless things of the past, we must remember what we have forgotten. The sanctity ascribed to certain archaeological objects, including the treasures of Tutankhamun, is a case in point. It stems in part from the aura of the "great discovery," whereby the adventurer-archaeologist (almost always white and male) outmaneuvers the impediments of time (and the indigenous population) to recover and reveal the surviving traces of antiquity. The ancient past becomes "our" past, and the survivors, which bear witness to it, take their privileged place within the history of the discipline. As the ultimate destination of the objects, and at times the sponsor of the excavation and holder of associated archives, the museum facilitates the sacralization of all the lost things the archaeologist has found. Its role is so entrenched as to pass almost unremarked, or unremembered, in the telling and retelling of discovery.

The recovery of our experience and of the material evidence of ancient experience is made possible by the convergence of our-time and object-time in the archive, from museum records and specialist publications to the field notes and photographs of archaeological expeditions. Archaeology is based on the quandary that excavation is a destructive process, which is why the copious records that Carter and his team made of their work in the tomb of Tutankhamun exemplify the best practice of the time. Each object was numbered in situ, its position noted, and then removed to workspace provided in a nearby tomb, where measurements were taken and entered on index cards, along with descriptive notes and sketches of hieroglyphic inscriptions, in particular divine or royal names. In addition to his photographs of work in progress in the tomb, Harry Burton also photographed each object in a studio setting, often from several angles; for objects that were covered or wrapped in linen, he documented their appearance both before and after the removal of the cloth. The cards, which were handwritten in the early years, sometimes typewritten later, note the presence and position of the cloth followed by a description of the figure once the cloth has been removed (Fig. 1.4). The fact of the removal goes unmentioned so that the entire description reads as if the covered and uncovered states coexisted.

Carter's working methods epitomize what Egyptologists term "scientific" archaeology, to distinguish controlled and licensed excavations both from illicit digging and from earlier modes of excavation, which had operated with little or no reference to the surveyed plans, stratigraphic recording methods, and artifact typologies that came to characterize archaeological work from the 1880s onward. Whatever their differences, the methods had one result in common: they uncovered the material remains of the past, most of which were repurposed in museums. Before the rise of scientism, excavations and museums weren't disordered so much as differently ordered, like Borges's Chinese menagerie. But museums reciprocated the aims of archaeology; they prided themselves on their empirical approaches to artifacts and the scientific rationale behind the ordering of their collections. Although archaeology enjoyed other public venues in the late nineteenth and early twentieth centuries, such as press coverage and international exhibitions, only the museum owned and kept ancient objects, conferring on them the prestige of its own permanence, on top of the aura of miraculous survival and discovery. In museums and in the popular imagination, Egyptian objects defy time, an assumption made evident by the ubiquity of words like *immortal*

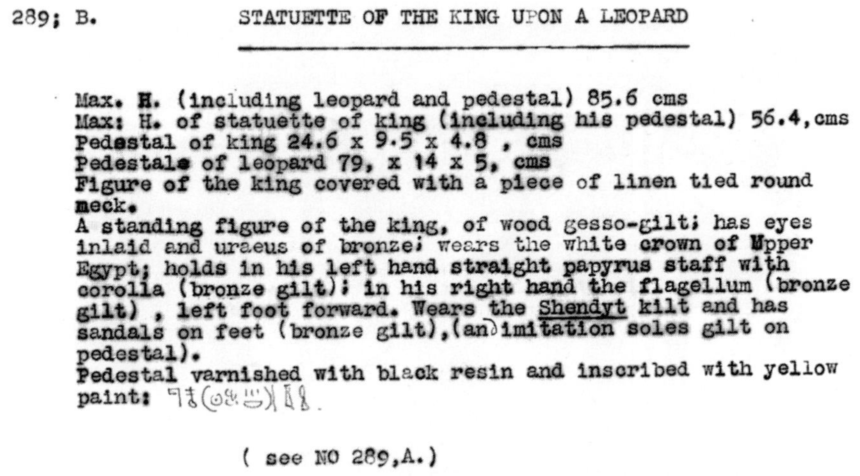
289; B. STATUETTE OF THE KING UPON A LEOPARD

Max. H. (including leopard and pedestal) 85.6 cms
Max: H. of statuette of king (including his pedestal) 56.4,cms
Pedestal of king 24.6 x 9.5 x 4.8 , cms
Pedestals of leopard 79, x 14 x 5, cms
Figure of the king covered with a piece of linen tied round meck.
A standing figure of the king, of wood gesso-gilt; has eyes inlaid and uraeus of bronze; wears the white crown of Upper Egypt; holds in his left hand straight papyrus staff with corolla (bronze gilt); in his right hand the flagellum (bronze gilt) , left foot forward. Wears the Shendyt kilt and has sandals on feet (bronze gilt),(and imitation soles gilt on pedestal).
Pedestal varnished with black resin and inscribed with yellow paint:

(see NO 289,A.)

FIGURE 1.4 *The typewritten record card for Carter no. 289b, one of the statues of Tutankhamun on a leopard. Copyright: Griffith Institute, University of Oxford*

and *eternal* in book and exhibition titles. It is an assumption that makes no allowance for another, ancient sense of time, or for the ephemera of human actions to which the enduring object testifies.

Time now to return to the example of the leopard and Tutankhamun, standing restored in a display case. The material remains through which we know (or invent) ancient Egypt are selective, in part through processes ("accidents") of preservation and discovery, but also through the material preferences of our time and our collective experience. Meskell points to pyramids, statues, and mummies as three materialities that index ancient Egypt in the modern world.[19] Other criteria can also lend an object favor, for instance an association with royalty or with certain historical periods or individuals. Yet often selectivity relates to the observable properties of the things themselves. Size: pyramids are impressive, while small statues and figurines have the benefit of being easily portable. Material: gold is good and so is well-preserved paint, as long as the colors are considered tasteful. Also good: the presence and legibility of inscriptions, on which Egyptology places such a high value. Or, more generally, aesthetic appeal and conformity to familiar types, since anything too unusual may be either fake or ugly, sometimes both. The statue of Tutankhamun carried on the back of a leopard easily meets several of these criteria: its authenticity is not in doubt, it is royal and inscribed, it is a convenient size for transport and display, it is covered in gold, and its naturalistic human and animal figures are visually appealing. Though not by any means considered the most interesting find in the tomb, its place in archaeology and thence the museum was assured from the moment of its discovery and throughout the long, slow work of reaching and emptying the Treasury.

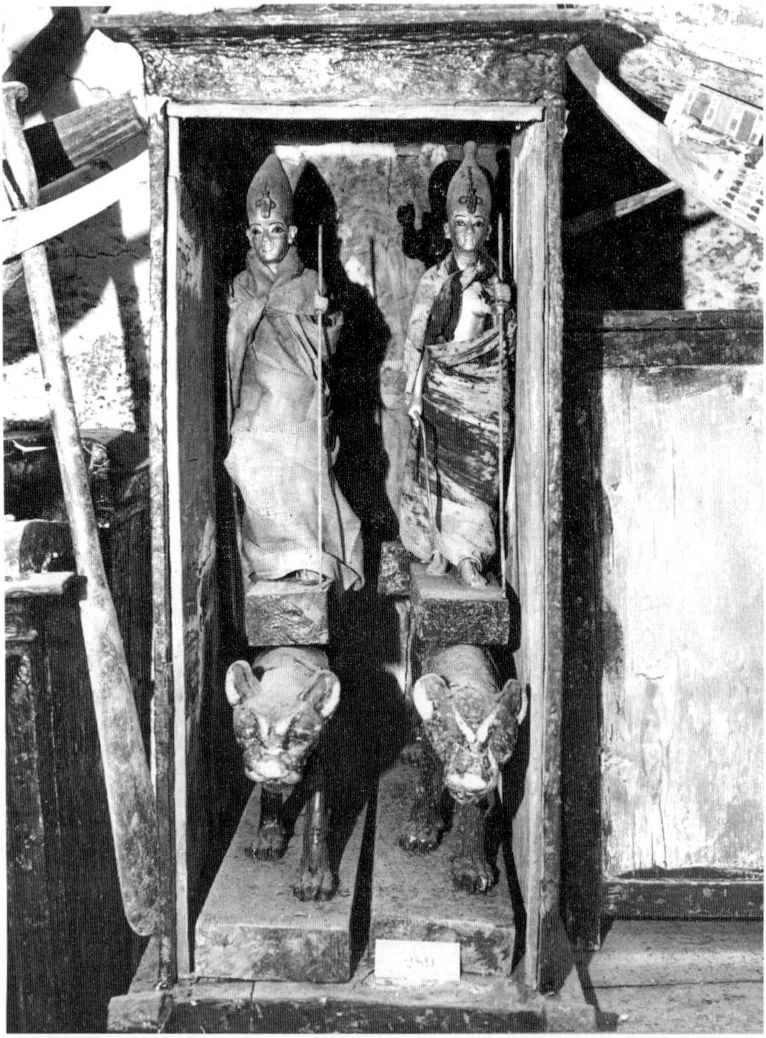

FIGURE 1.5 *Chest 289 with the pair of statues, wrappings in place. Photograph by Harry Burton. Copyright: Griffith Institute, University of Oxford*

In the end, one thing stood in the way: the fine linen wrapping knotted around the king's body when the paired statues were found in their shrine (Fig. 1.5). Dressed in their garments, the statues did not resemble what anyone, long before the 1920s, knew an Egyptian statue should look like. A piece of plain, tabby-woven textile was a clear mismatch, out of step with contemporary notions of Egyptian objects and their value; it had no quality to recommend it. The wrapping was an impediment to be removed, and so it was. Recorded for posterity, like a forgotten umbrella, the linen remains a note in an archive, and in the archive it is the last trace of the lost hands that tied the knot. This is the point where times converge, and where it becomes possible to ask what it meant from the standpoint of ancient Egyptian materiality to wrap a statue in linen, shut it into a shrine, and seal it in a tomb. If we forget the museum and the great discovery, rather than the linen, the archive stays the same, but the object world revolves.

Wrappings

The leopard statues carrying Tutankhamun were not the only wrapped objects in the tomb. In addition to the shrines with statues of the king, some two dozen other shrines in the Treasury contained statues of various gods and goddesses, each one wrapped in linen cloths. In the so-called Antechamber of the tomb, linen covered the bodies of the two near life-size statues of Tutankhamun, also coated in resin and gold leaf, that flanked the concealed, plastered-over entrance to the burial chamber. Inside the burial chamber, four concealed niches in the walls, associated with the cardinal points, each held an amulet or figure, wrapped tightly either in long, thin linen bands or a small piece of cloth (Fig. 1.6).[20] These objects—the small jackal and the human-headed figure pictured, plus an amulet called the *djed*-pillar and a figure of Osiris—accompanied a "birth brick," inscribed with magical spells from the collection known as the *Book of the Dead* and identified with the pairs of bricks placed under the feet of laboring women. Beyond the burial chamber, in the Treasury, a larger jackal statue stood guard in front of the gilded shrine that concealed the alabaster canopic chest, with its four cavities for the king's internal organs. The gleaming chest was decked with a linen pall, and the jackal positioned in front of its shrine was draped in a long, fringed tunic. Inked near the hem of the tunic was a date indicating "year 6" of a king's reign, followed by a cartouche that seems to bear the name of king Akhenaten (c. 1353–1335 B.C.E.), who was probably Tutankhamun's father.[21] Under the tunic, a rectangle of finer linen was tied around the jackal's throat, and beneath this was another length wrapped around the neck "like a leash" and covered by a wreath of flowers.[22] Among the stacked shrines full of statues lay a two-meter long, resin-coated box with a grain figure inside—a wooden frame in the outline of the god Osiris, filled with sandy silt and planted with barley that was left to sprout and grow for several days, before the whole thing was covered with fine linen and wrapped around and around in bandages.[23] Last but not least, to this list of cloth-covered objects could be added the human remains found in the tomb, which included the body of the king, his organs, a plaited lock of hair, and two fetuses.

The quantity and quality of the cloth, the care taken in the arrangement of the drapes and wrappings, and the specific choice of objects (and I include here the human remains) that received the coverings, all point to the purposefulness and importance of this treatment from the perspective of

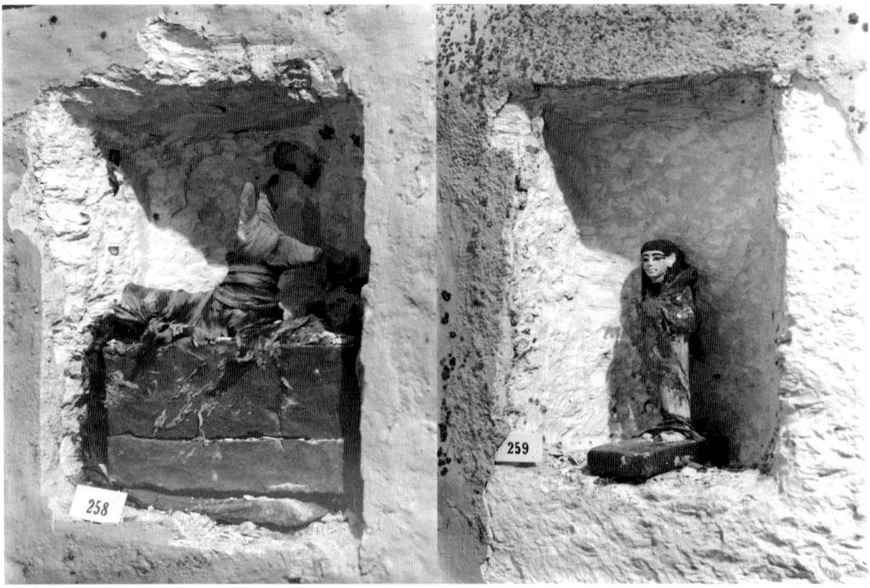

FIGURE 1.6 *Jackal and human-headed figures in the burial chamber wall niches in the tomb of Tutankhamun; Carter nos. 258 and 259, respectively. Photograph by Harry Burton. Copyright: Griffith Institute, University of Oxford*

the Egyptian actors. And in ancient Egypt, other refinements probably lent meaning to the treatment, for instance distinguishing different types of textile by size, color, weight, place of production, previous use, or ownership. The method of applying the textile to the object also suggests semantic differences. The pall draped over the top of the canopic chest, for instance, evokes a covering, as if the textile were another layer of concealment beneath the outer shrine. The pieces of linen on statues in the shrine, like the leopard statues, are gathered around the neck or shoulders and knotted in front much like the clothing worn in Egypt, where many garments were made out of rectangles of cloth folded, draped, and tied around the body rather than sewn or tailored. The tunic found on the jackal statue is a typical sewn garment, made by removing the linen from the loom, folding it in two, cutting a neck, and stitching up the sides to leave armholes, but on the jackal, it was treated like a draped cloak or robe. A third application method was the tight wrapping of narrow strips of linen, repeatedly encircling the object. This method is used on some of the niche statuettes, the grain figure, and the human remains. It is also the method that, together with the garment-like covers, evokes the physical gesture of wrapping. Unlike the draping of a pall, wrapping entails an encircling and enfolding motion, so that the person performing the action must pass his or her hands at least once, and usually many times, around the object being wrapped. The garments are held in place by knotting, and the linen strips either by a knot or by tucking in or sticking down the free end, but the end result is similar in that the object appears to be wrapped up with its contours at once outlined and concealed by the cloth.

Concealment is a concern expressed materially in the tomb, with its sealed rooms, niches, boxes, and shrines. From early in Egyptian history, spaces accessible only with difficulty were a hallmark of palace, tomb, and temple architecture. In words and images, religious texts depict the netherworld (*duat*), where the sun god is reborn, as a place of caverns, secret chambers, and confounding passageways. Canopies shielded gods and the king in pictorial representations, and the rite for clothing a cult statue first required the statue's locked shrine to be opened. The earliest written records of Egyptian cosmology, carved in royal pyramids of the fifth and sixth dynasties (c. 2465–2150 B.C.E.), refer to the dead king being clothed by the gods, as an indication of his divinity, and in later versions of these (and other) texts, the gods are said to be clothed or veiled and, more generally, hidden.[24] Among other things, then, cloth is associated with shielding and concealment, but textile coverings and wrappings operate in a different way from barriers like walls, doors, and boxes. An Egyptian shrine, for instance, is an expression of architecture on a smaller scale, with hinged doors at the front and, usually, a roofline and wall slope derived from one of two specific forms, the *per-nu* ("house of flame") and the *per-wer* ("great house"). One of the Egyptian words for a portable shrine, *ipet,* is the same word for the innermost room of a temple.[25] In the tomb of Tutankhamun, the conjunction of shrines and textiles recurs so often as to suggest that one could not replace the other. Only the largest objects, the statues of the king and jackal that seem to be guarding specific spaces, are wrapped in cloth but not placed in separate, transportable containers—a necessary distinction since the tomb itself could be thought of as a container for everything it shields inside, like the shrine and its counterpart, the temple. In a society where furniture was minimal, even in wealthier homes, containers like boxes, baskets, and jars were ubiquitous for the storage and protection of household goods and foodstuffs. In religious contexts, the use of more elaborate forms of chests and jars, made of rigid, enduring, and more prestigious materials like wood, stone, and metal, represents a scaling up of humbler objects to meet the needs of containment in temple rituals that required jars of oil or chests full of cloth. Such containers have the material quality of being impermeable as well, which may be one reason for the scarcity of references to baskets in temple scenes and rituals, despite the importance of basketry in the manufacture and skeuomorphic decoration of a wide range of Egyptian objects.[26] Containers function to protect, safeguard, and conceal. How effectively they do this depends on a range of factors, including what they are made of, what they contain, and what form of closure they incorporate, not to mention how well the human actor uses them. The boxes, shrines, and niches in Tutankhamun's tomb seem to have worked well as containers and concealers: almost all the shrines in the untouched Treasury had bolted doors, although some of the boxes, certain baskets, and a gold-leafed shrine in the Antechamber had been rifled in antiquity.[27] So far as Carter recounts, none of the textile wrappings on any objects had been disturbed by anything other than the passage of time.

Cloth also serves to protect and conceal, but not with the same functionality as a container. A textile wrapping and a container, like a shrine, are complements, not substitutes. The wrappings, or what they wrap, may require a container, while the container on its own cannot offer what the wrappings do. Here is where the materiality of textiles in ancient Egypt is of paramount importance for understanding what the actions, materials, and results of wrapping meant in Egyptian society. To touch briefly on some of these meanings, which are considered in more detail later in this book, flax production and linen manufacture were core to the Egyptian economy, and although men were sometimes identified as weavers, the responsibility of spinning and weaving had strong female connotations, which in turn associated human reproduction with the reproduction of social relations.[28] Linen bandages had magical and medical uses, connected both to the properties of the cloth and to the circular action of wrapping; a similar action would apply to swaddling infants. Wearing clothes fashioned out of draped and wrapped textiles created ways of moving, standing, sitting, and gesturing that were inseparable from the materiality of the cloth.[29] The color, texture, and heft of different kinds of linen had specific visual and tactile effects, any of which might contribute to the performance and effect of wrapping an object or a body in cloth. As a means of concealment, the obscuring quality of many textiles has much to recommend it, but ancient Egyptians also valued the aesthetic effect of sheer linen woven from fine threads, which alters the surface of what it covers in a different way, due to its lighter weight and more delicate draping as much as any transparency.

Even more than concealment, textile wrappings offer a barrier. They separate whatever is wrapped from contact with the environment external to the wrapper, affecting appearance and impeding touch. As a result, wrapping is often characterized as a form of protection for what is wrapped. This characterization emerges in Egyptology with regard to mummy wrappings, which scholars describe as protecting the dead body, and in archaeological and anthropological considerations of wrapping practice in other cultures—ancient Mesoamerica, for instance, or contemporary Japan.[30] However, wrapping affords protection to the external world as well, a point Gell and Weiner have both made with regard to wrapping rituals documented in Polynesia from the late eighteenth century to the present day.[31] In Fiji and Samoa, bark cloth wrappings have played a role in ceremonies such as the installation of a ruler, while in the Marquesas, Gell observed the wrapping of children in a ritual context, the *pahupahu*. Wrapping kept the powerful *tapu* qualities of an individual's wrapped body from affecting the outside world in an uncontrolled and dangerous manner. Dispersed *tapu* was contained by the wrapping, which in turn absorbed some of the potency of the body and itself became empowered or even sanctified. Appropriate reuse of the wrappings—placing the dead ruler's bark cloths on the new ruler—allowed the transfer of power from one entity to another. Their role as a barrier that both contained and absorbed allowed the wrappings to negotiate pivotal social encounters and to mediate between the quotidian and the divine. In Gell's words, "The functions of separation and communication are thus intrinsically connected."[32]

I cite Gell and Weiner not to suggest an equivalence between the different times, cultures, and customs of Egypt and Polynesia, but because judicious cross-cultural (and cross-temporal) comparisons can provide a useful push to move beyond the "our" of material experience and toward the array of other experiences, other significations, other materialities that are possible. In archaeology, the preoccupation with getting through the wrapping has discounted the significance of the wrapping itself, placing the focus on the internal object rather than the external sheath.[33] In museums, where today there is a rich material culture attached to wrapping for storage and transport purposes, an object on display is thought of as unwrapped and unconcealed. Its sanctity depends on its integrity as a museum object, which is predicated on a certain kind of visibility—and for ancient Egyptian objects, that visibility more often than not has precluded their containers and, above all, their wrappings.

The linen placed on statues and other religious objects in the tomb of Tutankhamun, taken together with the numerous Egyptian rites and invocations requiring linen and the myriad cosmological associations of cloth with deities, generative power, and seclusion, all seem to lead to one conclusion: the wrapping was as important as what was wrapped. Wrapping materials and practices in ancient Egypt facilitated human interaction with the divine. Moreover, wrapping encoded meaning as part of a system of restricted knowledge, which was highly developed in Egyptian society.[34] By its own nature as an erector of barriers and by the structured performance it required—somebody has to do the wrapping, after all—the practice helped mark the boundaries of what can be known, by whom, and when. The act of wrapping and the state of being wrapped operated as cultural metaphors for the hidden nature of the divine and, by extension, royal power and the social hierarchy. Knowledge designated as "secret" controlled the membership of certain groups, including priests called "masters of secrets" who were responsible for mummification or for dressing cult statues. The materiality of wrapping thus encompasses much more than the pieces of linen placed around bodies and objects. It parallels the role of restricted knowledge and space in Egyptian society and reverberates with a system of decorum that valued refinement in bodily adornment and gesture, the literal and symbolic layering of inscribed and decorated surfaces in representational art, and the creation and replication of order. Wrapping mattered.

Despite the prevalence of linen wrappings in ancient Egypt, and the wider significance of their materiality, there is almost no reference in Egyptological literature to the Egyptian conceptualization of wrapping or the use of textiles as wrapping materials.[35] In a fundamental study of ancient Egyptian perceptions of the divine, first published in 1971, Erik Hornung suggested, almost as an aside, that to wrap something in linen conveyed divinity on the wrapped item, but he did not expand on this observation, nor was it taken up by other scholars.[36] In a paper that refers in a footnote to Hornung's idea about linen wrappings and divinity, but does not otherwise consider cloth textiles or wrappings, Egyptologist Ann Macy Roth suggested that what she calls "layering" was characteristic of Egyptian cultural forms.[37] Her argument relies primarily on the idea that by working through these layers, scholars can identify the "original" in a ritual, text, or iconographic form and see what stages of their own history the Egyptians wished to preserve. Without the historicism implicit in Roth's emphasis on chronology, Assmann's analysis of how levels of the past exist in the present, as a "*Dingwelt*" (a "world of things") that contributes to cultural memory, more effectively characterizes the layering of time.[38] Furthermore, if we think of material objects occupying an object-time outside of human time, and generating their own responses and relationships through their very materiality, then the "original" can never be found. Instead, the value of Roth's insight into the symbolism of layers is not as a historical tool but as a material analysis, for some of her examples involve the use of what I characterize specifically as containers and textile covers or wraps. Even the metaphorical sense of Roth's "layering" is more akin to wrapping, with one object encircling another rather than covering it in a stratum. Ancient vocabulary also supports a correlation between circling and wrapping: the verb that means "to work magic upon" (*sheny*), for instance, has its root in the verb "to surround" or "to enclose," and these are gestures and actions that frequently appear in magical techniques.[39]

One of the examples Roth adduces fits especially well here: the wrapped and nested effect of the shrines, coffins, shrouds, and strips of linen that enclosed the mummy of Tutankhamun in the burial chamber. This is a feature surprisingly overlooked in the most famous archaeological find from Egypt.[40] Four gilded wooden shrines; a cloth pall studded with gold stars; a rectilinear, shrine-shaped stone sarcophagus; three mummiform coffins; and a gold mask surrounded the king's body. Two of the coffins were shrouded, and the embalmed body had hundreds of square meters of linen on it, although in too carbonized a state to measure. Each shrine had been disassembled to fit it into the tomb and reassembled on site; the outermost shrine was almost as large as the burial chamber. The shrines were bolted shut, and the coffins within fit tightly inside each other, resting together on a bier on the floor of the sarcophagus. Sacred images and texts covered every

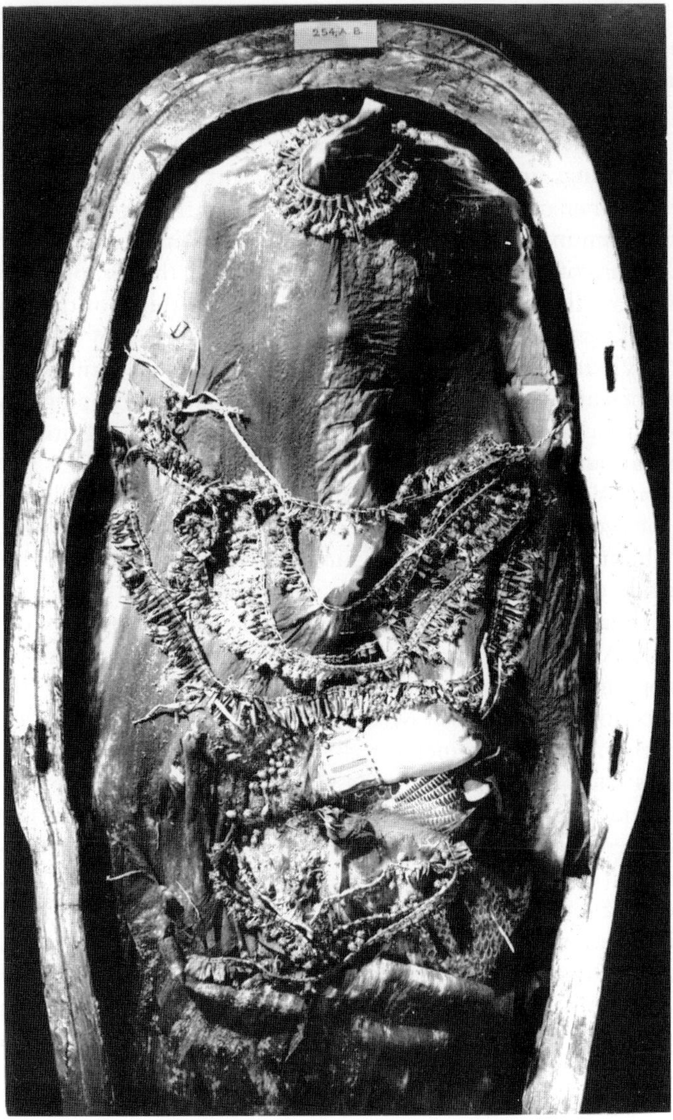

FIGURE 1.7 *Shroud and wreaths around the second of Tutankhamun's three coffins. Photograph by Harry Burton. Copyright: Griffith Institute, University of Oxford*

surface of the shrines and coffins, inside and out.[41] The two inner coffins were shrouded in linen and draped with floral wreaths (Fig. 1.7). Carter specified that the shroud over the innermost, solid gold coffin consisted of "several thicknesses" of red cloth and left the face of the mask exposed.[42] Once revealed, the mummy itself was wrapped in dozens of layers of linen in addition to almost a hundred different groups or sets of amulets, placed over the body and interleaved among the textiles. The king's body was not merely nested, like a set of Russian dolls: it was very thoroughly wrapped.

We know how many shrines, coffins, and shrouds filled Tutankhamun's burial chamber, and can estimate how much linen was wound around his body, because the shrines and coffins were opened, the shrouds removed, and the wrappings undone, reversing the ancient processes that had helped sanctify the inner core. Although Egyptian recitations for the dead sometimes refer to mummy wrappings being "loosened" in the afterlife, this loosening was part of a cyclical rebirth that required the wrappings to begin with. To violate the mummy or its casings in the earthly world was sacrilege and criminal, as documents relating to the investigation of tomb robberies recount.[43] Where wrapping has a cultural priority, the symbiosis between the wrappings and the object they wrap means that unwrapping is a fraught and critical juncture, undertaken only with the protection of ritual. Thus the daily unwrapping and rewrapping of Egyptian cult statues was the responsibility of specialist priests, and the magical unwrapping of the dead took place in the world of the divine and coexisted with their wrapped state on earth. Without such protective measures, unwrapping destroys the mediating and transformative capacity of the wrapped object. The decision to unwrap is a declaration based not merely on cultural difference, but on power differentials. Another Polynesian example points to the destructive potential of unwrapping in a context where an object changed hands, and times. Now in the collection of the British Museum, a carved wooden figure of the god A'a was originally a container for divine images, which were stored in a cavity in its back while its body was wrapped around with cords.[44] Before Rurutu islanders gave the figure to British missionaries in the 1820s, they apparently removed its binding and destroyed the figures inside as a form of desacralization. Unwrapped and emptied, the A'a lacked divine potency, and it could safely become an object of exchange between the islanders and the missionaries; the handover of such idols may also have symbolized the adoption of Christianity. The unwrapped A'a represented a cultural shift, but that shift took place within the negotiation of power, and the unwrapping marked the end of the figure's original function as it acquired other roles and other meanings.

In the tomb of Tutankhamun, containers and wrapping together produced the double effects of concealment and sanctification. The enclosing shrines and coffins helped hide Tutankhamun's mummy from view in his tomb, itself hidden underground in a remote desert wadi. The wrapping of the mummy also hallowed it so that the body of the king became a sacred, secret core, reminiscent of Polynesian figures and relic containers sacralized by their wrappings. But implicit in wrapping is its revelatory potential, even if there is no explicit intention to act upon this potential: after all, there is no secret without the tantalization, or terror, of the secret being known. If wrappings sacralize, unwrapping desacralizes—thus the stripping and gutting of the A'a before its handover to British missionaries, by which point it was no longer a powerful idol, but a hollow wooden sculpture. To be object-ified, the mummy of Tutankhamun likewise had to be rendered impotent through unwrapping. As Carter's team removed the coverings of the sealed tomb chambers, the wrapped and bundled grave goods, and the shrouded burial, one by one, the desacralization was complete. The sanctified became secular, the hidden became visible, and the past became the property of the present.

Unwrappings

Almost a century after Carter breached the tomb, Tutankhamun's mummy still makes headline news, repackaged with shifting interpretations that are variations on the themes of death, disease, and descent. Advances in scientific technologies allow for further "refinements" to competing theories about the king's short life and premature death, laying one surmise (gangrene of the leg?) over another (a blow to the head?) and reviving debates about his uncertain parentage, with its ever-present undertone of racial anxiety (Were the Egyptians black? Was his father Akhenaten deformed?).[45] At the center is the object produced by Carter's unwrapping: an embalmed body, stripped of its linen and amulets, with its head detached from the cervical vertebrae for ease of examination and to permit the removal of the solid gold mummy mask.

The unwrapping of Tutankhamun's mummy took place three years after Carter's initial discovery of the tomb, time that had been spent emptying the outer rooms and cataloguing and photographing their contents in a manner that was meticulous by the standards of the day. Dismantling and documenting the shrines was laborious work, as was the task of lifting the two inner coffins clear of the outermost coffin, and then that coffin and bier out of the shrine-shaped sarcophagus. In the nearby tomb of Seti II, which served as laboratory, workshop, and storeroom, a system of frames and pulleys winched away the coffin lids after Carter and his team prised them loose. The mummy itself was stuck with a resinous substance inside the innermost, solid gold coffin so that the unwrapping had to proceed from the top without being able to turn the body or access it from the sides. Carter had opened the lid of the inner coffin on October 28th, 1925, writing in his excavation diary:

> The penultimate scene was disclosed—a very neatly wrapped mummy of the young king, with golden mask of sad but tranquil expression, symbolizing Osiris. The similitude of the youthful Tut-ankh-Amen, until now known only by name, amid that sepulchral silence, made us realize the past.[46]

The view inside the innermost coffin was "penultimate" in expectation of the ultimate unwrapping, which commenced on November 11th. The day began with formal photographs of visiting officials standing around the coffin and mummy just inside the entrance to the tomb of Seti II. The visitors included Pierre Lacau, a Frenchman who was the long-serving director-general of the

Department of Antiquities; Tewfik Boulos, the department's chief inspector for Upper Egypt; Mohamed Shaban, assistant curator of the museum in Cairo; Sayed Fuad Bey el-Kholi, governor of the province; and the two doctors, one British and one Egyptian, who would oversee the royal autopsy, Dr. Douglas Derry, professor of anatomy in the School of Medicine at Cairo, and Dr. Saleh Bey Hamdi, previous director of the same school. During the procedure, Carter assisted, making notes and detailed drawings, and expedition photographer Harry Burton documented progress at key points. The process took more than a week, from November 11th to 19th, 1925, with a day off on November 17th. Throughout Carter's diary, the unwrapping takes place in the passive voice, with one exception crediting Derry with the first cut:

> As soon as the wax had cooled, Dr. Derry made a longitudinal incision down the centre of the outer wrappings to just below the depth to which the wax had penetrated, thus enabling the consolidated outer layers of the wrappings to be removed in large pieces.

Application of melted paraffin wax was standard in early conservation practice, both on archaeological sites and in museums. The crumbling, friable condition of the mummy wrappings was evident from the start, and Carter attributed the almost carbonized state of the linen to the oily, resinous substance that had been poured over the coffins and mummy, sticking them together as it hardened. His diary entry on October 31st, three days after he had lifted the innermost coffin lid, collected Biblical references to oil libations ("Mark 14:8. She hath done what she could: she is come aforehand to anoint my body to the burying"), and on November 1st, when the embedded inner coffins were removed from the burial chamber, his diary entry read in full:

> Removed the royal mummy to No. 15 [tomb of Seti II]. It took ten men to bring out of the tomb and carry it up. Placed in the sun for a few hours, while Lucas [the conservator], Burton & self hammered off the black coating upon the lid of the third coffin. Heat of the sun not sufficient today to make any real impression upon the pitch-like material which has stuck fast the mummy & coffins.

As the unwrapping got underway on November 11th, the problem of the state of the wrappings and the stubbornness of the libation was well established.

Carter's diary repeatedly laments the poor condition of the wrappings, which do not hinder physical progress, only the amount of information that can be gathered. November 11th: "It is to be much regretted that the wrappings were found in such critical condition—a condition preventing any reliable record of them, even their approximate system of binding.... Here & there were a number of lightly wrapped pads of linen, beyond these facts, little else could be recognized, the linen being reduced to the consistency of soot." November 12th: "Throughout these proceedings the wrappings, though much rotted and carbonized, showed evidence of having once been of fine cambric like quality." And November 15th, with the corpse almost entirely exposed from its feet to its neck: "Below this [pectoral] were alternate layers of crossed bandages passing over the shoulders and the transverse bandages holding them in place. Beneath these a sheet folded several times, under which were similar crossed and transverse bandages. Then came a great thickness (3 cms) of wrappings which came away in almost one piece revealing a large group of objects forming the 12th–16th layers before reaching the actual body." On November 16th, the team devoted the entire day to examining the head of the king, which was removed from its gold mask using heated knives to work through the resin. After a day off, removal of the multiple wrappings and amulets from the head continued on November 18th, revealing a finely worked linen cap over the crown of the head, which was left in place, and a conical pad "of linen wads and bandages wrapped in the manner of a modern surgical head bandage" between the top of the head and the mummy mask. Carter concluded, "After photographic records are made of the King's remains, these will be reverently re-wrapped and returned to the sarcophagus."[47]

Linen wrappings were essential components of the mummy from its first layer to the conical pad between the head and the mask, but the condition of the linen—and the goals of extricating amulets and revealing the body—meant that little more was ever said about the wrapping than the extracts quoted above. The whereabouts of the shrouds, pads, and bandages are unknown, and most were probably reduced to a sooty powder in the process of unwrapping. Pierre Lacau, who had been present throughout, returned to Cairo the evening after the head and mask were separated, and the next day, after measuring the skull, Derry and Hamdi followed suit. Tutankhamun was unwrapped, and their job was done.

The "reverent re-wrapping" took place at the start of the next field season in October 1926, with the mummy wrapped in unspecified (presumably modern) cloth and placed in the burial chamber inside the outermost of the three coffins and the sarcophagus. Since other royal mummies had been in the Egyptian Museum for many years, the decision was somewhat unusual, and perhaps was influenced by the plan to keep the tomb of Tutankhamun open to visitors and by the fact that the other mummies had been found in caches, reburied in antiquity after damage to their original tombs. Tutankhamun was singular for having survived intact, and the treatment accorded to his body offered an insight into what those other burials had first looked like, as Carter knew well. Years before he found Tutankhamun's tomb, he had published a papyrus on which some ancient Egyptian draughtsman had sketched the plan for the burial of Ramses IV (c. 1163–1156 B.C.E.), whose grander tomb and five shrines exceeded the provision for Tutankhamun.[48]

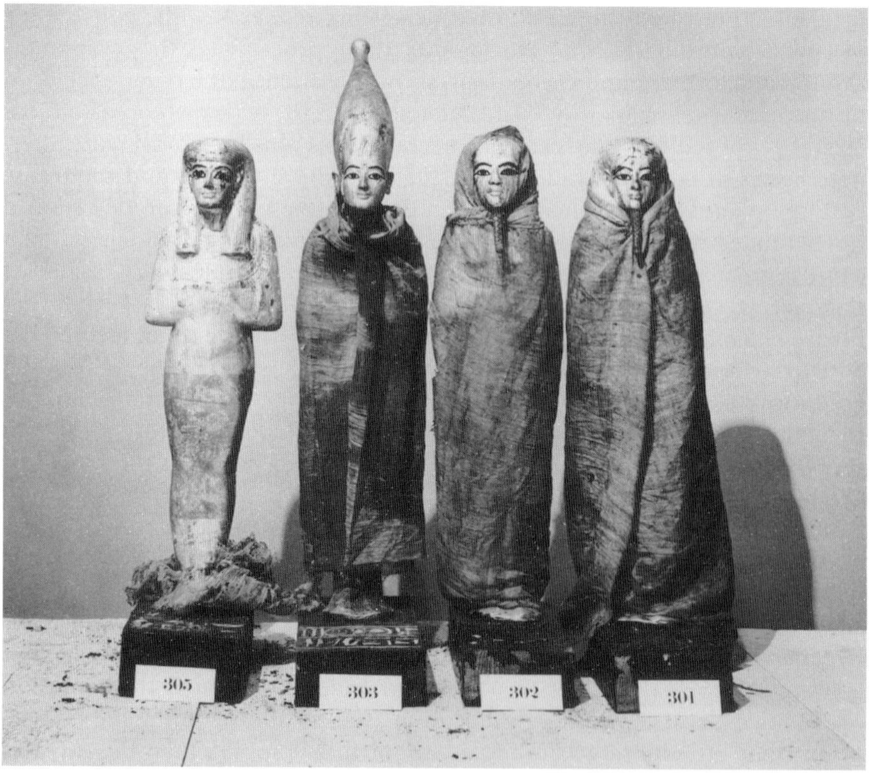

FIGURE 1.8 *Statues from four different Treasury shrines, before unwrapping. Photograph by Harry Burton. Copyright: Griffith Institute, University of Oxford*

With Tutankhamun rewrapped and lying in state in one chamber, ready for the tomb to open to the public at the New Year, Carter's team turned to the next chamber, the room known as the Treasury. Here, they proceeded to open the "sinister black chests and boxes," as Carter dubbed them—one with the leopard statues, one with the king carried aloft by a goddess (also damaged in the events of the "Friday of Anger"), and twenty containing statues of gods and goddesses, each wrapped up in linen cloths (Fig. 1.8).[49] Writing in his journal on November 17th, 1926—a year after unwrapping the royal mummy—Carter commented tersely, "Undressed, photographed and repaired the two statuettes 275b and d, from Chest 275. The wax treatment proved successful in both cases and I believe they can now be safely packed in sawdust" for shipment to Cairo.[50] Unwrapping the divine statuettes was less noteworthy than unwrapping the mummy, and the linen from the statuettes was in all likelihood discarded. Nor did Carter make any connection between the figures he had revealed beneath their linen wrappings from one season to the next, first the mummy made of embalmed flesh and bones, then the statues of gilded wood. The star-spangled pall over the second shrine (which disintegrated when it was left out in the sun during Carter's absence) and the red shrouds around the inner two coffins were reminiscent of the other cloth-covered statues and figures in the tomb, including the wrapped jackal in the Treasury and the linen drape over the canopic chest that contained the king's embalmed viscera. Several of the shrines in the Treasury, including number 289 with the leopard statues, sat on top of the long, lidded box with the grain figure inside, whose seven layers of shrouds and bandaging were unwrapped and carefully noted. At almost two meters long, the sprouted barley form of Osiris was almost a double for the royal mummy, even an improvement on it, since the Osiris figure's wrappings had no libations poured over them and could be examined in the way Carter lamented Tutankhamun's could not. None of these instances of textile coverings drew much comment, however, and the archive is all that preserves them.

More than their form, material, iconography, or placement, what linked the sacred objects (including the mummy) in the tomb of Tutankhamun was the effort the ancient Egyptians had taken to cover them in linen—an action that was integral to their sacred character and power. But as excavated objects destined for museums (or a "reburial" for tourists to view), what linked them was their unwrapping. It equalized them as things fit for collection, study, and display, ultimately turning "things" into objects, antiquities, art works, and artifacts.[51] What was wrapped was secret, set apart. What was unwrapped could be handled, documented, seen, and known, first in the site workroom and then in the museum setting. Packed in their sawdust-filled crates, the statues and their shrines traveled from a tomb that was no longer secret to a time that was never theirs. The Burton images of the statues in neat rows, first with and then without their wrappings, or of the mummy captured from above in its stages of revelation, are like passport photos by which the modern world could recognize these objects as "ours," suited to archaeological study and museological care. Although left behind in the tomb, the king's mummy nonetheless made a similar journey, blinking in the light of a camera flash. Its new wrappings were far less secure than the old ones. X-rays of the mummy were taken in the 1960s, and press photos from a CT scan in 2005, which was performed in a mobile facility next to the tomb, show that the mummy now lies cushioned on a jumble of cloth in a simple wooden tray, resolutely unwrapped.[52]

When the unwrapping of a sacred object occurs cyclically within a ritual process, the performance of the rite helps activate the object's divine qualities so that the removal of the wrappings has no desacralizing effect. The potential crisis of the unwrapping is overcome by rewrapping, and the addition of fresh wrapping materials renews or supplements the force of the object. Ancient Egyptian statues experienced a repeated sequence of dressing and undressing. The deposit of wrapped statues in the tomb of Tutankhamun ended this cycle in an earthly context, to be continued in the netherworld that Egyptian religion conceived of as a place of darkness and danger, but also of seclusion and regeneration preceding a rebirth in the light. At the time the tomb was filled and sealed, the statues, the mummies, and all the wrapped figures locked up with the king occupied this threshold of the material and immaterial words, undisturbed in their own perpetuation of time. The breach that seems to have occurred soon after the burial, when the Antechamber was rifled, could be put right, with the entrance to the tomb resealed by priests. But the second breach, by Carter, presented a more significant rupture because it took place in a schism between times and materialities. Hence the wrappings that had made and mediated divine power in the ancient Egyptian object world were discounted and, by and large, discarded. From the viewpoint of the ancient actors, this can only have been a sacrilege, an act of defacement against the object they had wrapped. To Carter and his team, it was supposedly just another day's work. But defacement reveals where power lies: thus the excavation of the tomb and the archiving of its contents reveal the power of archaeology in the early twentieth century—as a producer of knowledge, an architect of modern materiality, and a network of actors connecting Egypt, Europe, and America in a colonial enterprise whose afterlife is ongoing. The most recent defacement of Tutankhamun's treasures—the broken glass and fractured leopard, patched back together in the Arab Spring—testifies that similar powers operate today, but in a postcolonial clime. If the archive supplied the objects with a passport to modernity, then film footage and news images of the 2011 events in Cairo were the holiday snapshots proving that they had arrived.

Disciplining Egyptology

To understand the journeys that the objects in Tutankhamun's tomb have taken through time and space, materials and minds, it is necessary to interrogate the social contexts that produced them, both in antiquity and in the modern world. Elliot Colla has emphasized the "entanglement" of Egyptian antiquities and the disciplines that study them, borrowing his choice of words from Nicholas Thomas's discussion of materiality, colonial encounter, and the many facets of appropriation.[53] The work of collecting, organizing, recording, analyzing, and publishing its chosen objects of study lies at the core of a scientific discipline, and this work has never taken place in isolation. Egyptology, with its antiquarian roots, is no exception, and as the events of the Arab Spring have demonstrated, the study of ancient Egypt must still be seen in relation to both European colonialism and Egyptian nationalism. The object becomes the indexical signifier of these relationships, turned into evidence through a process that frequently transforms it into another physical state, for instance through cleaning and repair, or even erases it altogether—whether literally, as in the dismantling of a site or body, or figuratively, as in the practice of transcribing inscriptions into print and designating them with coded abbreviations ("BGU II 423") that almost make the original superfluous. Muñoz Viñas points out the flawed logic of such physical and intellectual efforts in his analysis of conservation: making an object conform to expectations, whether in a display case or (I would add) a catalogue, does not make it more "real," truthful, or authentic.[54] Despite, and because of, the transformations required of them and the freight of meaning they carry, objects of study are unstable. They seem to require continuous attempts to fix them and their extrapolated evidence into a narrative of historical development supported by truth claims. Furthermore, the embedding of Egypt in the cultural memory of Europe means that there is much at stake in such positivist endeavors, whether undertaken by professional academics, amateur enthusiasts and "pyramidiots," or indeed Egyptian nationalists. Laying claim to Egypt has been pivotal to the memory-work not only of Western heritage but also the heritage narratives of Africa, the African diaspora, and the Middle East.[55]

Unlike comparable critiques—the "new museology" or post-processual archaeology—the situated nature of Egyptology has been articulated primarily from outside the discipline (Colla is a specialist in Arabic literature) and if anything has yielded negative reactions or outright rejections rather than a paradigm shift. In studies of the ancient Near Eastern, Egyptian, and Classical pasts, the notion that scholars "just" study and interpret their evidence without "doing" or "using" any theory remains as persistent as it is widespread.[56] Given the range of methods and subject matter addressed in Egyptology, which includes philology and history alongside archaeology, some writers have been reluctant to term it a discipline, seeing it instead as a concentration of area studies that share a pool of chronologically and geographically delineated evidence.[57] Such subdivisions are much later refinements of the early nineteenth-century impetus to decipherment, discovery, and possession that first resulted in disciplinary formations, however, and those formations exert a strong epistemological influence even as they continue to develop or defend their boundaries.

One significant difference between contemporary scholarship and that of a century, or even two centuries, ago is the relative distance between scholar and object, which has fluctuated not only with patterns in collecting but also with patterns of training and professionalization. Now more than in the nineteenth or early twentieth century, it is possible to qualify as an Egyptologist without seeing an inscription, handling an artifact, or visiting Egypt. Central to early and mid-nineteenth-century ideas of what constituted Egyptology, the mummy is likewise marginalized within the field, instead subsumed into biological research of variable quality and subjected to intense, and intensely formulaic, popular regard. By focusing on the museum as a site where the object-related processes of Egyptology coalesce, the present study intervenes in order to suggest a bridge between professional and popular, ancient and modern, object and subject, discipline and critique. Colla declares himself "agnostic" about the actual evidence and interpretations put forth in Egyptology; the ancient past is not his concern, just as

Bohrer, in addressing the similarly entangled development of Assyriology, is at pains to define his interest as the reception of ancient Near Eastern antiquities, rather than the antiquities themselves.[58] Also in the field of Near Eastern art, Zainab Bahrani has taken an approach more like that adopted here, in that her book *The Graven Image* offers a reinterpretation of ancient cultural phenomena as well as a critical historiography. Specifically, Bahrani uses the work of postcolonial writers such as Frantz Fanon, Edward Said, Homi Bhabha, and Gayatri Spivak to critique art history as "a cultural discipline of empire"; she also draws on the philosophy of Derrida, whose work on representation, writing, and *différance* offers a way to rethink both disciplinary practices and ancient representational practices.[59]

Many of Bahrani's observations on disciplinary divisions and approaches could apply as well to Egyptology and archaeology as to Assyriology and art history, and foregrounding the development of self-reflexive scholarship in these academic arenas becomes all the more crucial in light of recent and ongoing events in the political arenas of North Africa and the Middle East. Analysis at the level of discourse and knowledge formation is one route for scholarship to take, but so too is the analysis of the actual practices behind such knowledge-making, in both historical and contemporary contexts. How did, and do, scholars conduct their work, whether in the field, the university, or the museum, and how were, and are, these actions connected to wider networks, whether a colonial government administration or a public for whom encounters with Egyptian mummies provide a frisson sublimated as "edutainment"? From the nineteenth to the mid-twentieth century, the operation of archaeology in Egypt was embedded in the operation of colonial power, both on site and in the imaginative exercise of scholarship and spectacle, as people, objects, and information moved from the field to the museum and back again.[60] It is significant that archaeology proved both pervasive and persuasive in Egypt and other Middle Eastern territories in the colonial era.[61] The mechanisms that enabled and facilitated the practices of archaeology—survey, excavation, and collecting—depended on the introduction of statutes and regulations, such as legislation defining certain kinds of objects as "antiquities," as well as the identification and expansion of museums as sites where those antiquities could be further defined by the post-excavation processes of study, conservation, and display.

As responses to the thefts and damage in the Cairo museum seemed to demonstrate, the academic discipline of Egyptology has barely begun to confront its colonial past or acknowledge the extent to which that past permeates both its scholarship and its public reception, up to and including the present day.[62] Politics and the ancient past are not separate, regardless of assertions by heritage organizations, museums, and academics that they are or should be. Egyptology's own nineteenth- and twentieth-century history suffuses its greatest discovery, the tomb of Tutankhamun, and its most banal terminology and tools: the titles of ancient Egyptian officeholders are still translated using terms like *vizier* and *viceroy* derived, respectively, from the Ottoman and British colonial-era regimes, while one of the editors of the standard reference dictionary of ancient Egyptian (the *Wörterbuch der ägyptischen Sprache*), Hermann Grapow, was an ardent supporter of National Socialism under the Third Reich—Egypt being both a key theater in the Second World War and, in some Fascist ideologies, an ancient example of Aryan achievement.[63] The objects of Egyptological knowledge are inscribed with modern as well as ancient significations. Seen this way, Carter's unwrappings of royal bodies and gilded statues were far from just another day's work. The cracks of history run deeper than the restorer's art admits, as the splintered statue of king and leopard now attests. But fundamental change can only occur once scholars accustomed to the myth of objectivity appreciate how much their evidence and interpretations have been governed by discourse, practice, and modalities—not least, in Joycean terms, the "ineluctable modality of the visible" through which revelation became tantamount to knowing.

This chapter has set out the core approaches used in this book to explore both the wrapping of objects in ancient Egypt and the unwrapping of Egypt in the modern world. In subsequent chapters, I return to many of the issues raised here: the impact of colonialism in Chapter 2, the materiality of mummification in Chapter 3, linen and the role of women in Egyptian society in Chapter 4, secrecy and social hierarchy in Chapter 5, and the role of the museum and scientism in Chapter 6. One aim of this book is a better understanding of the materiality of textiles and wrapping in ancient Egypt, which has fundamental implications for how we interpret a wide range of objects and images, including Egyptian mummies. At the same time, I argue that the practice of wrapping in antiquity cannot be studied in isolation from the historical practice of unwrapping. If wrappings both create and conceal the sacred, what are the implications of placing on public view that which has been revealed and thus, in some sense, destroyed? It is not a simple question of whether to display Egyptian bodies and antiquities, but rather how to generate wider recognition of the ancient intention of wrapping. Egyptian collections consist of objects overwhelmingly amassed during the long period of colonial expansion and its aftermaths, and in these circumstances, there is ample scope to interrogate the modern predilection for unwrapping and the role of collecting in disciplinary formation. Museum galleries and storerooms house an ancient Egypt created by remembering and repackaging the material past, and the encounter with that material past has been integral to the shaping of the modern world, as the recent vandalism and restoration of the Tutankhamun statues made clear. Our comprehension of ancient materialities can only be reconstructions, models, and best guesses, but to hazard them, we must first identify and acknowledge our own interference and interactions with the past. To whatever extent the useless, beautiful things of ancient Egypt have kept their secrets, or been forgotten, it is not for want of our scrutiny, but our failure to see.

2

Revelation

The pinnacle of his career brought Howard Carter face to face with a king, but a less successful juncture in his working life had also featured a royal unwrapping. In 1900, long before he would confront the sealed entrance to the tomb of Tutankhamun, Carter faced a blocked doorway at the so-called "Gate of the Horse" (Bab el-Hosan) in front of the bay of cliffs at Deir el-Bahri. Carter had been appointed at the start of that year as chief inspector of antiquities for Upper Egypt, answering to the overall head of the antiquities service, Gaston Maspero.[1] His appointment, alongside James Quibell as chief inspector for Lower Egypt, was the result of delicate negotiations between Maspero; leading British figures like Flinders Petrie, who by then had been appointed to the chair of Egyptian archaeology at UCL; and Evelyn Baring, Lord Cromer, the first consul-general in charge of the British "veiled protectorate" in Egypt. Established in the 1850s by Maspero's predecessor, Auguste Mariette, the antiquities service was a French domain and depended on a system of specially trained Egyptian inspectors throughout the country. The addition of the chief inspectors—both British—was something of a diplomatic feat.[2]

In his published report, Carter recounted the story in a tone somewhere between academic dispassion and Rider Haggard adventure: in 1898, while working at Deir el-Bahri for the Egypt Exploration Fund, Carter had been out on his horse when it stumbled in a depression. The spot lay outside the team's concession, however, so it was only when he became inspector that Carter had the authority to go back and dig at the locations, which turned out to cover a wide passageway sloping underground for seventeen meters toward the Deir el-Bahri cliffs. At the end, the passage was blocked by a mud-brick "door" covered by seal impressions. The "door" consisted of solid mud bricks stacked almost four meters deep. Beyond lay the remains of a sacrificial calf and then the rest of the passage, descending toward the cliffs at a gradient of 1:5 for a length of 150 meters. It ended in a spacious chamber, where

> in the left hand corner, lying on its side, there was a seated statue about two metres high, completely wrapped in linen of a very fine quality: beside it lay a long wooden coffin which was inscribed but bore no name.[3]

Sealed pots, a number of ceramic saucers, and more animal offerings were distributed around the chamber. In the gloom, and with field photography still rudimentary, Carter relied on his skill as a draughtsman to record the scene (Fig. 2.1). His account, as quoted earlier, is preemptive in describing the large, swathed object as a seated statue, for although he could have determined its basic shape and material through the linen wrapping, Carter only saw the statue on Christmas Day, 1900, when it was "unrolled" in the presence of Maspero.[4] The choice of words is hardly accidental: the statue was wrapped like a body, and the chamber resembled the burial he hoped to find, with the food offerings and empty, expectant coffin.

Given its location in relation to the eleventh-dynasty mortuary temple of king Nebhepetre Mentuhotep (now conventionally numbered Mentuhotep II, c. 2061–2010 B.C.E.), Carter thought it possible that he had stumbled onto a royal burial complex, and his hopes were buoyed by the presence of another shaft some thirty meters deep, again ending in a sealed doorway. Carter opened this doorway on New Year's Day, 1901, in the presence of both Maspero and Cromer, whose presence was a sign of the high expectations Carter had for what might lie beyond. Holiday spirit perhaps made up for the disappointment, for the doorway led to a small room full of "rubbish," containing three wooden boats and more pots. A third side shaft, only two meters long, yielded a shallow wooden box inscribed with the name Mentuhotep, and possibly Nebhepetre; it was empty.[5] The following week, Maspero wrote to the chief inspector for Lower Egypt, Quibell, and

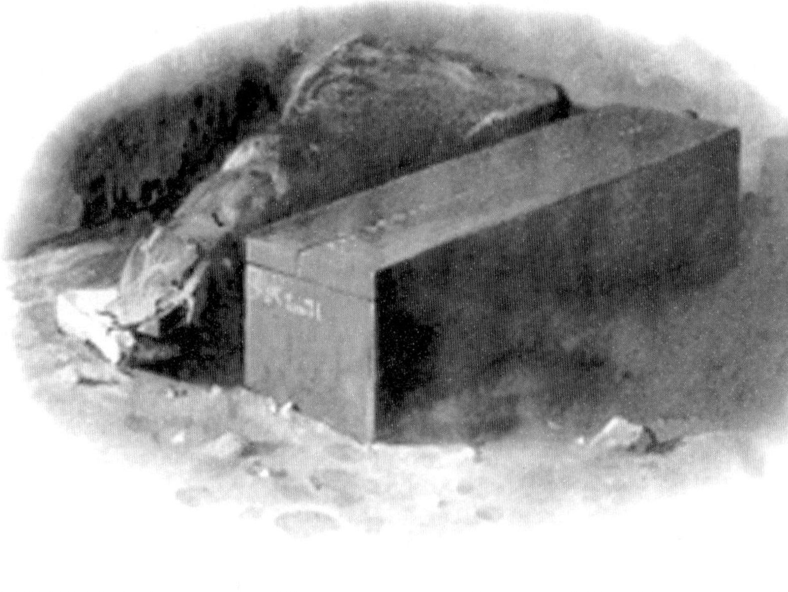

FIGURE 2.1 *An empty coffin next to a seated statue of king Mentuhotep II, placed on its side and wrapped in linen. Drawing by Howard Carter. After Carter, "Report on the Tomb of Mentuhotep Ist," pl. ii*

lamented Carter's haste in notifying Cromer of the find.[6] Model boats and empty boxes were hardly worth the consul-general's time.

As for the painted sandstone statue that had been wrapped so carefully in linen, once "unrolled" it was shipped downriver to Cairo together with other material from the tomb. Wooden rollers, a stonemason's mallet, and lengths of rope in the debris of the chamber attest to the physical effort of creating the space and dragging the statue down to it, efforts the local workforce in Carter's day repeated in the other direction. Identified as Mentuhotep II, founder of the Middle Kingdom and builder of the earliest temple complex at the site, the statue became the best-known example of royal sculpture from this period, and its striking appearance and coloration—black skin (painted over a layer of red), white cloak, red crown—has since seen it reproduced in numerous surveys of Egyptian art and guidebooks to the Cairo museum (Fig. 2.2).[7] It also figures frequently in Afrocentric interpretations of ancient Egypt as a black African state, including the seminal work of Senegalese scholar Cheikh Anta Diop.[8]

The Bab el-Hosan find was a precursor to the small, wrapped figures Carter would later bring to light in the tomb of Tutankhamun, but neither Carter nor other Egyptologists drew a comparison between the shrouded statues. Frequently presented as a substitute burial for the king, whose actual burial site is unknown, the Mentuhotep II statue has come to stand for many things—kingship, renewal, the distinctive artistic style of the early Middle Kingdom, even race—but its lost wrappings are scarcely mentioned in the literature after Carter's original report.[9] Any human body, real or represented, that had been wrapped up by ancient Egyptians could easily be unwrapped by archaeologists. But represented bodies were easier to classify, for statues were art objects and belonged in museums. Real bodies were more complicated.

In this chapter, I explore the historical trajectories of ancient Egyptian mummies and how the study of mummies developed in tandem with the colonial project over the course of the long nineteenth century and reflected the era's concern with its constructed Others, especially around questions of race and sex. Following a discussion of Egyptology, colonialism, and early modern encounters with Egyptian mummies, I focus on two case studies, first the 1822 unwrapping of a mummy in London by Dr. Augustus Bozzi Granville, and second the unwrappings conducted in Cairo of royal and priestly mummies buried in caches, which were discovered in the late nineteenth century—and to which we will return in Chapter 6, to consider some of the subsequent debates surrounding their study and display. What was done to the ancient body in many ways paralleled the cataloguing and control of the colonized body in Egypt and other contact zones. To restore the discovery and appropriation of the object, and thus enable an assessment of archaeological and museological practice from a postcolonial vantage point, requires historical grounding, which is the proviso recently put forward by Burke and Prochaska in their reevaluation of colonial discourse analysis structured around the concept of Orientalism.[10] From discovery

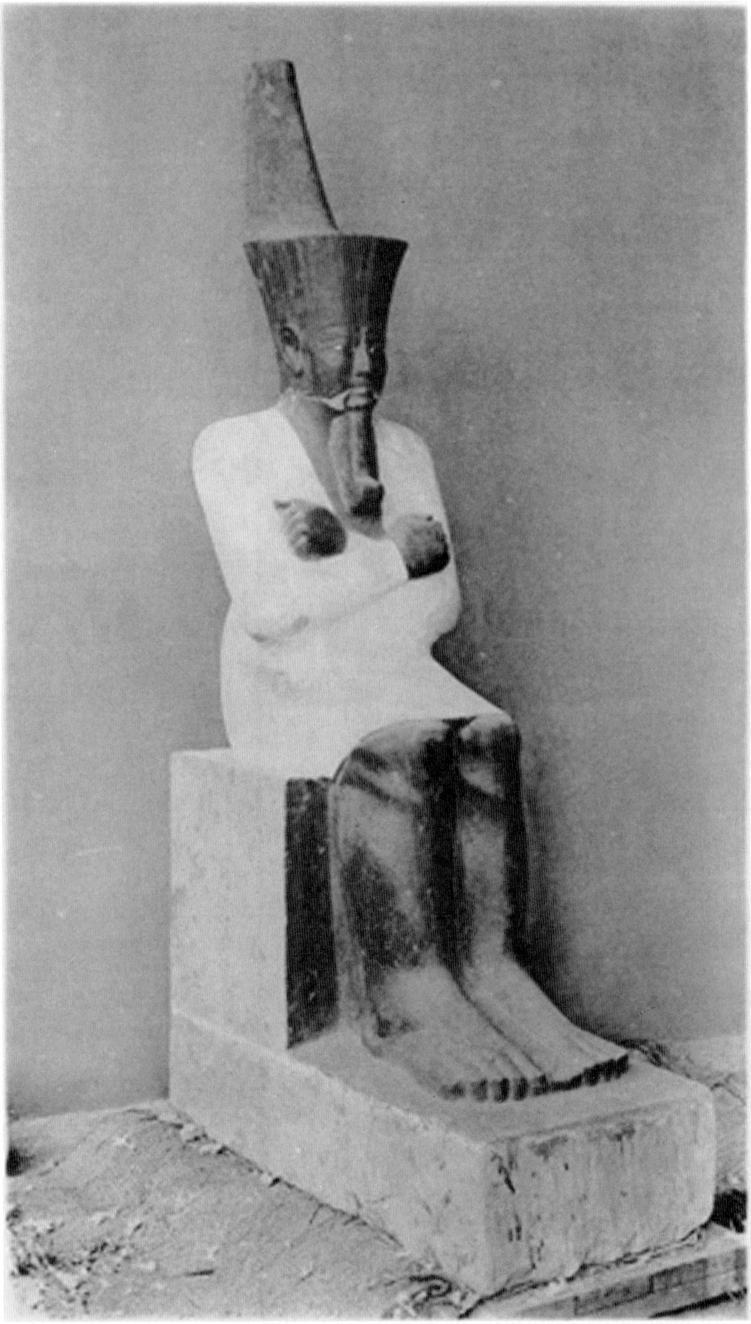

FIGURE 2.2 *Painted sandstone statue of Mentuhotep II, from the Bab el-Hosan at Deir el-Bahri, 11th dynasty (c. 2020 B.C.E.). H. 138.0 cm, W. 47.0 cm. Cairo, Egyptian Museum, JE 36195. After Maspero,* Le Musée Égyptien, *pl. ix*

to desecration, mummified bodies and other once-wrapped objects were part of a network of personal and institutional relationships, cemented and replicated through visual and textual representations and enmeshed in the colonial relationship between Europe and Egypt.

Colonialism, Egyptology, and the Object(ive) Other

The impact of Edward Said's *Orientalism,* which first appeared in 1978, cannot be underestimated, though it was just one of several influential critiques that appeared around this time and addressed the relationship between imperialism and Western thought.[11] Over the following ten to fifteen years, momentum built toward a paradigm shift that would take place in several humanities and social science subjects, in particular literary studies, history, anthropology, and the history of art. Not, however, Egyptology: in 1995, I bought a copy of *Orientalism* at a bookshop in Luxor, prompting the professor with whom I was traveling to remark, without sarcasm, that it was a "very trendy" book. Using Foucault's insights into the interrelationship of power and knowledge, Said analyzed the Western construction of the Orient as a discursive strategy of colonial systems. His evidence was textual and related chiefly to the British empire, two points that were springboards for both negative and positive responses to his work.[12] The role of the visual in colonial relations was the subject of Linda Nochlin's influential essay on the Orientalist genre of art, while Timothy Mitchell's *Colonising Egypt* used the broader Heideggerian concept of the "world as picture" to similar effect. Works like these provided the starting point for a range of studies demonstrating that images were fundamental to the production of the Other.[13]

Antiquities and the museums created to house them were part of this production as well. Like Orientalist paintings, ancient objects offered a powerful means of messing about with time—for instance, by reestablishing the presumed historical and intellectual link between Europe and ancient Egypt (via Greece and the Bible) while presenting Islam and the Ottoman empire as the invidious cause of the rupture in the first place. The political use of ancient Egyptian monuments in France predated the Napoleonic campaign and helped create a geographic locale to reclaim and recover through conquest. Subsequently, elegiac paintings, the *Description* project, and the development of an Egyptian museum in the Louvre all served to justify ongoing French colonial efforts in Africa and the East—yet there is a persistent assumption, in both scholarship and in popular interfaces, that fervent interest in ancient Egypt from the late eighteenth century to today can be explained by "the tautology that Egypt was a subject of fascination because it was so inherently fascinating."[14]

Underlying this fervor was, and is, an element of projected fantasy and desire, which is to do not so much with the one-directional, instrumentalist flow of power that Said emphasized, but rather with the relational exchange between metropole and colony, "West" and "Other."[15] That the "Other" did exist, and did not passively receive the colonial project, is a counterargument developed in Homi Bhabha's work, which posits a range of ambivalent and ambiguous responses on the part of the colonized (and in the postcolony).[16] Frustrations, adaptations, complicities, and duplicities characterize the colonial relationship, with several effects: for the colonized, such equivocations yielded fractured identities but also created forms of counter-knowledge and resistance, while for the colonizer, the reactions of their interlocutors variously confirmed the worst stereotypes, demonstrated the positive impact of Western modernization, or fed the complementary fantasies of "obélisques and odalisques."[17]

In anthropology, scholarship from the 1970s onward has been concerned with realigning and refocusing the discipline through what amounts to postcolonial critique, but incorporating such approaches into archaeology has been a slower process, perhaps attributable in part to the thoroughness with which the archaeological object (often turned museum object) has been cut off from the circumstances of its discovery.[18] But the representation of the Other—through scholarship, art, writing, and display—was a prerequisite of first establishing and then justifying authority over it, for, in Elleke Boehmer's words, "to assume control over a territory or a nation was not only to exert political or economic power; it was also to have imaginative command."[19] Undertakings like archaeological excavation and the formation of museum collections were not mere reflections of imperial endeavors. They were part of the process of colonization itself, a term I use here not in the sense of settler colonialism or government annexation, since Egypt remained part of the Ottoman empire, but in the sense of one country being subject to the political, military, economic, and cultural domination of another. Besides which, by the 1880s, there were some 90,000 foreign residents in Egypt, connected in various ways to the development of the country's infrastructure.[20]

Representations of ancient Egypt, both through archaeology and in the museum, created a simulacrum, an imaginary Egypt that was variously timeless, long past, or contemporary with what the "West"—and I use this term while acknowledging its shortcomings—encountered whether in Egypt or at home. These temporalities could be opposed to each other—reconciling the splendors of the imaginary ancient Egypt with the (perceived) grime, disorder, and laziness of colonial Egypt was a struggle often remarked upon in nineteenth-century travel or archaeological accounts—or they could mingle together—for instance, as travelers imagined that their Nile views and the picturesque *fellahin* had remained unchanged over the millennia.[21] The "ancient Egypt" that stood in for the historical and modern actualities of Egypt, whether through contrast or commingling, was so effective a substitute that it still has sway in both popular and academic perceptions. This jaundiced holdover continues to shape the experience of tourists to the (neocolonial) Egypt of today and the expectations of museum visitors and other public audiences interested in Egyptian antiquities. In a survey conducted in 2000 for the Petrie Museum of Egyptian Archaeology at University College London, one visitor, who had holidayed in Egypt, clearly preferred the simulacrum, asserting that the Egyptians of the past had created so many wonders but "now they can't even fix your toaster."[22]

Like other forms of archaeological exploration and representation, the (figurative) unwrapping of ancient Egypt through the (literal) unwrapping of its antiquities cannot be set apart from that colonial history and its postcolonial ramifications. Yet critiques of the relationship between Egyptology and colonialism are in their infancy and, thus far, originate outside Egyptology itself. Academic training in the subject includes little or no consideration of its history and methodologies, aside from a creation myth involving the Napoleonic expedition and the decipherment of hieroglyphs. Popular engagement, for instance through books, magazines, and membership societies that attract "armchair Egyptologists," likewise presents accounts of Western "discovery" and derring-do.

Museum exhibits are complicit, offering an ancient Egypt that ends well before the Islamic era and credits Western collectors and archaeologists with the marvels on display. Growing public awareness of repatriation debates, such as the high-profile case of the Parthenon Marbles, has led some museums in the United Kingdom and North America to incorporate information about the role of division of finds in earlier excavations, albeit without reference to the geopolitics that encouraged the practice throughout the Middle East.[23] My own experience, having met hundreds of museum visitors over the years, confirms an alarming disconnect between what British and American audiences recognize from ancient Egypt and what they know of Egypt's modern history and culture. "Do the Egyptians still speak hieroglyphics?" was not an uncommon question to field, even in a decade that started with an Egyptian piloting a plane into the World Trade Center and ended with the overthrow of Hosni Mubarak.

Thus the interpretive framework of postcolonial studies offers one way of looking more critically at the archaeological and museological drive to reveal what the ancient Egyptians wrapped up. The urgent desire to know more (how mummies were made, what the Egyptians looked like, how they died, etc.) and to photograph, quantify, collect, and record the past meant removing all the layers, locks, and wrappings that the ancient actors had put in place. For European rationality to triumph, there could be little regard for what other, lesser cultures, living or dead, considered sacred. In many ways, unwrapping a mummy is homologous with the derogation of indigenous autonomy and action. Western accounts of acquiring and despoiling mummies, whether contemporary to the event or written as a retrospective history, often venture the justification that Arab Egyptians of the seventeenth, eighteenth, and nineteenth centuries were prying apart mummies anyway. By intervening in or copying such indigenous efforts, the Western collector was saving the mummy, a view that, among other things, ignores the fact that the aim of such "native plunder" was to obtain pulverized *mumia* and portable antiquities to sell to European markets. Usually, as with the unwrapping of Tutankhamun, archaeologists and scientists offered no specific justification for their actions. The implicit or explicit aim was to acquire (that is, create) knowledge, and the value of that aim was self-evident. The construction of one Egypt was the destruction of another.

In this endeavor, mummies have occupied an unusual and uncanny position. Their materiality exerted (and continues to exert) a strong physical and imaginative pull, but it is to some extent a selective or manipulated materiality, having been determined by the removal of their wrappings. Although contemporary debates in museum ethics often argue that mummies have been treated like objects (and, by implication, should not be), it is in many ways the humanity of the mummy that has shaped its fate. On the one hand, discussions of race, sex, and pathology—a heady mix of archaeological, anthropological, and medical science—were a means of "othering" the mummy, while on the other hand, historical or fictional biographies attached to individual mummies, like famous pharaohs, emphasized the West's connection to the ancient Orient and helped make the exotic seem familiar, as did the display of mummies in museums and international exhibitions.

Complete mummies were scarce and desirable curiosities in Europe until well into the eighteenth century. Travel to Egypt was difficult, and mummies and coffins were unwieldy to transport; there were also superstitions attached to transporting dead bodies by ship.[24] The exception was the trade in powdered *mumia,* which flourished in the late sixteenth and early seventeenth centuries when powdered mummy gained popularity as a health tonic. Fragmented mummy parts were ideal for the purpose, and although the quantity of exports are no doubt exaggerated, *mumia* was considered a potent product. It was also a potent metaphor, associated in English literature with crime, blame, and guilt. Concern about the commodification of mummies—as in Thomas Browne's lament that "Mumie is become merchandise"—stood for concern about the emergence of a market economy where even the human body would have a price. Through the trope of *mumia* consumption, which entailed an unspoken cannibalism, early modern writers used antiquity to apprehend a timely problem.[25]

The Italian traveler Pietro Della Valle offered a firsthand account of the mummy fields at Saqqara, outside Cairo. He kept whole two shrouded mummies he acquired there in 1615 and intended to send home, but when he spotted a broken mummy replete with resin or bitumen, he hammered at the hard black substance with stones and iron tools. As he recounted,

> Of the broken pieces of this mummy, I wanted for myself the completely intact head, and a fair piece of bitumen, with a handful of those bandages; the rest of it, since I felt I had been recompensed over and above what I had spent, I left entirely to those poor peasants.[26]

Della Valle's trophies satisfied the curiosity value that was uppermost in the mind of early modern collectors, to whom Egyptian antiquities were both "naturalia" and "artificialia," God-formed and man-made.

Before the emergence of what we now think of as "science," knowledge was pursued and ordered differently, and to a polymath like Athanasius Kircher, the surfaces of a mummy were as interesting and informative as what might lie inside. An engraving from his work *Oedipus Aegyptiacus,* published in 1652, shows the before and after pictures of a mummy in the collection of Giovanni Nardi, court physician to the Grand Duke of Tuscany (Fig. 2.3). As an eminent surgeon and antiquarian, Nardi had apparently unwrapped the mummy's outer layers but gone no further, perhaps considering such work, essentially a dissection, to be beneath him.[27] Both drawings convey in detail the numerous narrow bandages that comprise the wrapping, from the rolled horizontal passes crossed by an x-shaped arrangement on the chest—on the left, "before" example—to the narrow plaits and dizzying, layered rhomboids that are so striking on the right-hand figure.

Given the rarity of mummies in Europe at the time, and the wide dissemination of Kircher's work, this depiction of a mummy was influential and frequently reproduced. It inspired, among others, the surgeon Thomas Greenhill, who printed it (in reverse) in his own work, *Nekrokedeia,* published in 1705 (Fig. 2.4). Greenhill collected Greek and Biblical sources on the ancient practice. He knew the astronomer John Greaves's account of seeing stripped mummies near Cairo, but otherwise he made no mention of the interior of mummified bodies. Instead, he devoted copious attention to descriptions of the linen bandages and shrouds in which mummies were wrapped:

> With these they bound and swath'd the dead Body, beginning at the Head and ending with the Feet. Over these again they wound others, so often one upon another, that there could not be less than 1000 ells upon one Body. They interwove these Roulers so artificially and in such manner, says Kircher, as would puzzle the ingenuity and tire the Industry of our Modern Surgeons to find out, yet, with submission to him, it may not be so difficult to perform by any one tollerably skill'd in the Art of Bandage as he imagines, for, as I take it, they began with the Feet and Hands, and ended with the Head, contrary to what Greaves asserts, tho' I cannot say this of my own Knowledge, having never had the opportunity of unrouling such Bodies, but only offer the Consideration thereof, according to the appearance of the following Figures, of which the first shows

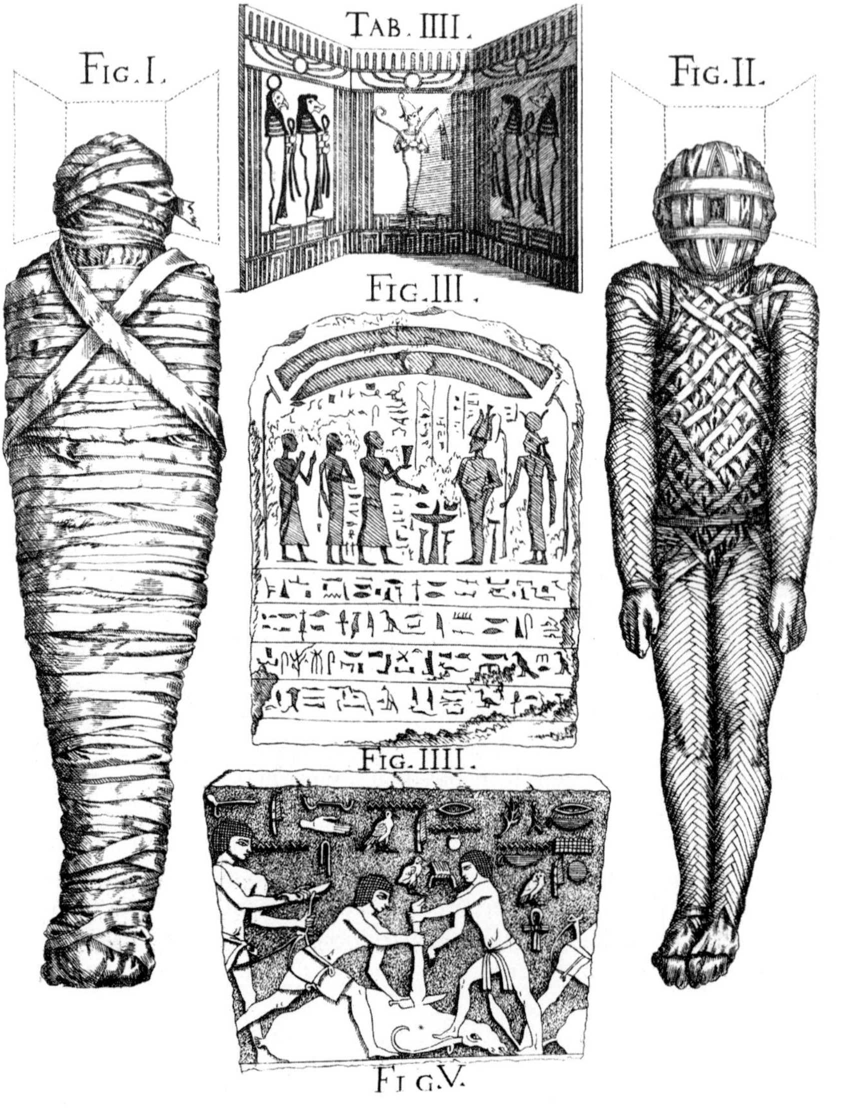

FIGURE 2.3 *Athanasius Kircher, plate from* Oedipus Aegyptiacus *(1652). Courtesy of the New York Public Library*

> the interior artificial circumvolutions of the Roulers, the Body being first wrapp'd in fine Linnen, wherein Egypt excell'd, as the Holy Scriptures testifie, Prov. 7.16 etc. [all spellings original][28]

Greenhill was keen to promote embalming among the English aristocracy, but the practice was falling out of favor—in part because people feared they might be dissected while still alive.

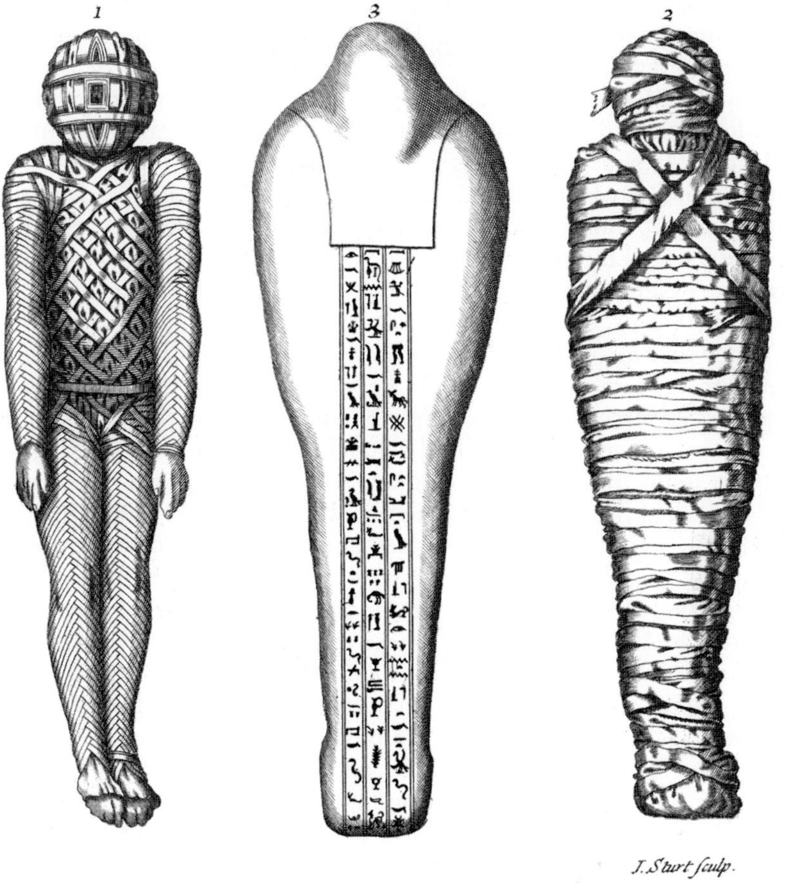

FIGURE 2.4 *Thomas Greenhill,* [Nekrokedeia] or, the Art of Embalming *(1705), plate opposite p. 290 (Classmark Rare Books L.3.51). Reproduced by kind permission of the Syndics of Cambridge University Library*

In the early modern era, up to the early eighteenth century, anatomy was something to be practiced on the recently dead, not the ancient dead. Executed criminals, "othered" within their own society, supplied fresh corpses to well-known anatomy theaters like that in Leiden, where the theater was located in a church. Images of these early anatomy theaters are rich with symbolism: the dissecting table is like an altar and the anatomist like a priest, gesturing in benediction toward his reference book with one hand and the Christ-like corpse with the other. This was anatomy made sacrosanct, cleansing the surgeon from the taint of handling a criminal body (a decomposing one at that) and imparting to the gathered crowds that the human body was the work of God and worthy of such study.[29]

In the course of the eighteenth century, however, the perception and performance of anatomy changed. For one thing, the Enlightenment separation of theology and knowledge meant that anatomists held their own sacred ground. Medical thinking had reconceptualized the interior of the body as the location of disease, making rigorous dissection paramount for training doctors. As Foucault observed, this development coincided with changes in penal practice, which favored imprisonment and surveillance over torture and public execution. Foucault read power relations onto, or into, the human body, whose interiority had been realized through the penetrating gaze cultivated by anatomy.[30] The change also meant that corpses were much harder to come by.

The dissection of Egyptian mummies in late eighteenth- and early nineteenth-century England should be viewed against the background of controversies surrounding the supply of corpses for anatomical dissection. Since no one owned a corpse, body snatching was not in itself illegal, unless other items from the body or grave were taken as well. "Resurrection men" exploited this loophole, selling unclaimed corpses and pauper burials. In the 1810s and 1820s, as the demand for cadavers to supply medical students increased, so too did public outrage over both the practice of dissection and the threat to human bodies, alive and dead. The murders committed in 1827 and 1828 by Burke and Hare, who provided cadavers for Edinburgh anatomist Dr. Robert Knox, were a catalyst to the Anatomy Act of 1832, which licensed anatomy instructors and made it easier for medical schools to acquire unclaimed corpses for dissection or accept donated bodies for the purpose. The parallel between body snatching in England and the opening of tombs in Egypt was not lost on contemporary observers: in describing how he came to purchase the coffin and mummy of a man named Soter at Thebes, Sir Frederick Henniker wrote that he was "standing by when the resurrection men found a sepulchre," a witticism that cast the Arab Egyptians (not Europeans like himself) as the grave robbers.[31]

Prior to the paradigm shift of the Enlightenment gaze and its quest for interiority, the disinclination to unwrap Egyptian mummies had made a simple fraud possible. In the 1750s, the founding Egyptian collection of the British Museum included small, intact mummies collected by Sir Hans Sloane and Sir William Hamilton. These were revealed to be false only in 1792, when they were unwrapped by Johann Blumenbach, professor of medicine at Göttingen.[32] Composed of ancient linen neatly arranged around a core of animal or human bones, linen scraps, and debris, such mummies had been acquired in good faith as examples of mummification because their external appearance matched what Europeans had come to think of as "a mummy," thanks in part to images like Kircher's.

The absence of human remains inside these mummies was a particular disappointment because Blumenbach's chief aim was to make detailed measurements of skulls. His work laid down the fundamental principles of what would become physical anthropology, including the use of craniometry to develop the new concept of race, and the results of his research on mummies contributed to his major publications on natural history, which appeared throughout the 1790s and early 1800s. Blumenbach's doctoral thesis had characterized human "variety" through five races, identified by skull shape and skin color—in his terms, Caucasoid, Mongolian, Ethiopian, American, and Malayan.[33] Blumenbach's work was both product and promoter of prevailing ideologies, which used race as one way of examining the bewildering differences that confronted Europeans in colonial contact zones and pulsed beneath the slavery debate. In addition to whatever antiquarian or anatomical insights might be gained from examining mummies more closely, there was now another incentive for unwrapping Egyptian mummies, whose preserved skin and bones held the promise of further data for the scientific classification of humankind.

The Body Laid Bare: "Dr. Granville's Mummy"

> These observations respecting the art of bandaging among the ancient inhabitants of Egypt, as displayed in their best class of mummies, have not, as far as I recollect, been made before to the extent here alluded to, and will throw a new light on the history of that branch of practical surgery.
>
> Augustus Bozzi Granville,
> *An Essay on Egyptian Mummies* (1825), p. 6

During his visit to England, Blumenbach presented his research to the Royal Society, of which he was a foreign member. At the time, the Royal Society met in an elegant set of rooms in the government building complex of Somerset House, which is now home to the Courtauld Gallery. They shared an anteroom with the Society of Antiquaries, whose own meeting room was adjacent, while the Royal Academy had study and exhibition space upstairs.

In April 1825, the Royal Society heard a paper delivered by Dr. Augustus Bozzi Granville, a proponent of the new field of obstetrics, or "male midwifery." His unwrapping of a mummy was a fillip in an eventful life.[34] Although "Dr. Granville's mummy," as it has come to be known, is routinely mentioned in Egyptological histories of research on mummies, and recently reappeared in news headlines when DNA analysis of extant tissue identified tuberculosis, the meanings created by the unwrapping, publication, and subsequent history of the mummy have gone without comment.[35] "Mummy studies" narratives, which extol the "scientific" study of mummies as a linear route to knowledge, single out the Granville unwrapping for its empirical results, and in particular the ovarian tumor identified by his dissection. But a critical reading of Granville's text reveals the extent of its engagement with the concerns that were at the heart of the new interiority, including race, gender, and disease.

Granville received the mummy and its coffin in 1821 from one of his patients, Archibald Edmonstone, the son of a baronet, who had traveled through Egypt in 1819—one of a number of British aristocrats to do so after the end of the Napoleonic Wars. The painted wooden coffin, fastened with pegs, had already been opened by Edmonstone, but the mummy was untouched, "covered with cerecloth and bandages most skilfully arranged, and applied with a neatness and precision, that would baffle even the imitative power of the most adroit surgeon of the present day" (Fig. 2.5).[36] Over the course of six weeks, Granville undertook the unwrapping and dissection of the mummy at his London home. In total, more than a hundred medical colleagues and acquaintances, including Edmonstone, visited to witness this display of surgical skill in what one imagines was a convivial but learned atmosphere. Granville referred to his task as a dissection and conducted further experiments as part of his investigation, testing the textiles and embalming a human fetus presumably obtained through his professional practice.[37] His essay for the *Philosophical Transactions* of the society, also published as a pamphlet, included drawings by London-based painter Henry Perry, which Granville singled out for their "great precision" and the "scrupulous accuracy" of their representation.[38] The skill and authority of the medical profession were complemented by the skill and authenticity of Perry's drawings, engraved for publication by the established antiquarian studio of James Basire.

The unwrapping took more than an hour, yielding cloth that weighed twenty-eight pounds. The process of unwrapping, apparently with little impediment from resin, gave Granville the opportunity to observe the system of wrappings in some detail, and what struck him was their resemblance to surgical bandages. The purpose of the wrapping, he ventured, was "securing the surface of the mummy from external air," and in between the "rollers" were folded pads "placed like compresses" in the hollows of the body to create a smooth surface and thus facilitate the "firm and steady application of the bandages." He identified the wrappings with the bandaging techniques familiar to a surgeon of his own day: "the circular, the spiral, the uniting, the retaining, the expellent, and the creeping roller," and "the *couvrechef*, the scapularium, the 18-tailed bandage, the T-bandage, as well as the *linteum scissum*, and *capistrum*."[39] The outermost surface of the mummy was wrapped in a bandage eleven yards long, which spiraled from the feet to the head and then back down to the chest, where its fringed end bore an inscription in ink. In addition, Granville observed that a single bandage was drawn back and forth around the body, crossing the front three times, and that on top of the face lay "a thick mass of linen, by no means neatly folded

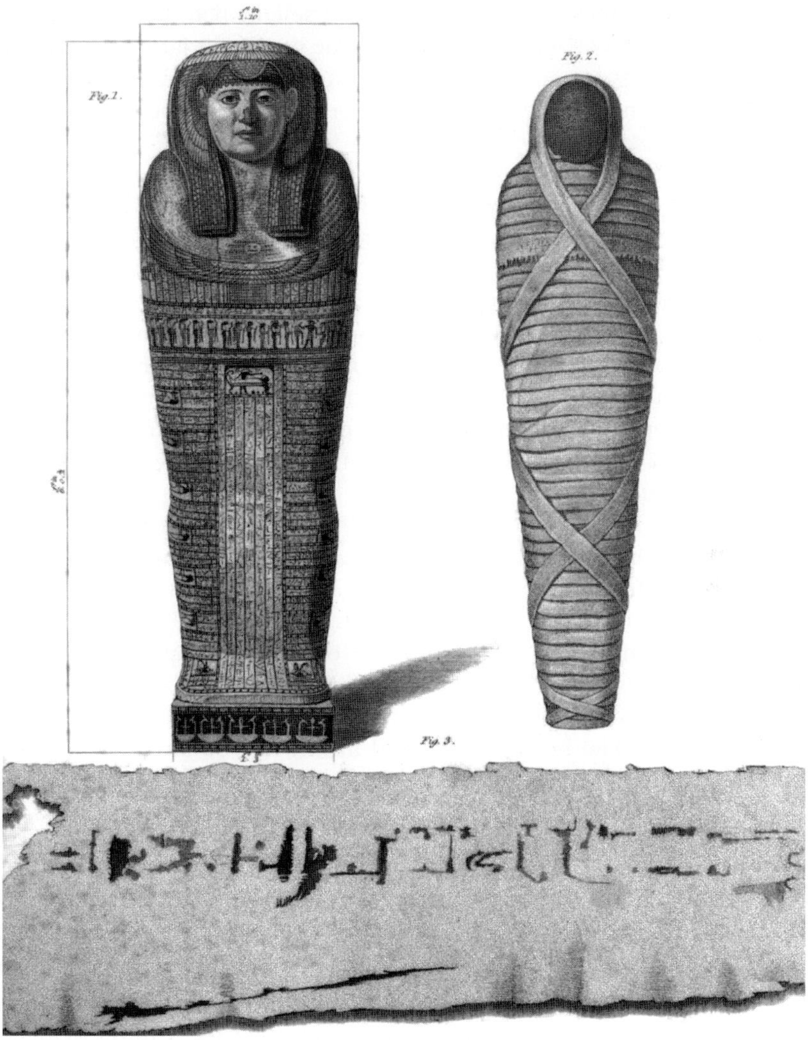

FIGURE 2.5 *Coffin (left) and wrapped mummy (right) studied by Augustus Bozzi Granville; at the bottom of the plate is a copy of the Egyptian inscription inked on the wrappings. Drawing by Henry Perry, engraved by James Basire. After Granville,* Essay on Egyptian Mummies, *pl. xviii*

up, covered by a considerable layer of a black bituminous substance."[40] The inner layers of wrapping included at least twenty repetitions of the rolling bandages, which were made of "a very compact, yet elastic linen," and four interspersed instances where squares of cloth "of a less elastic texture" had been placed around the head, throat, and abdomen. Granville observed that none of the cloth had any stitches. The cloth itself, he believed (erroneously), was both linen and cotton, and to confirm the use of the latter, he submitted samples to the "inspection of an experienced manufacturer."[41] The expertise of medicine and industry were brought to bear in the scrupulous analysis of the mummy's wrappings.

Even more care was expended in examining the embalmed corpse revealed by the unwrapping, which was female, and Granville's first comments are directed at the body's secondary sexual characteristics:

> The external parts of generation, on which not a vestige of hair was found, had been brought in close contact, and notwithstanding their shrivelled condition, were readily recognised. The mammae must have been large during life, for they were found to extend as low down as the 7th rib, against which they are closely pressed by the arms passing over them. But on lifting the latter, the breasts themselves were raised with little exertion.[42]

Examining the unwrapped mummy was a tactile, not just optical, experience: short hair on the shaved head "can be felt by passing the hand over it; and on close inspection, may be distinctly seen," wrote Granville. The nose was bent to the right from the force of the bandages—which, I would add, suggests the direction of the bandaging, since tilting the nose to the right would result from a right-handed embalmer working from behind the head. The body was that of an older woman, posed with the hands crossed on the chest; the left hand was clenched and held a resin-soaked wad of textile (Fig. 2.6). The surface of the body was creased with deep wrinkles, which Granville took to indicate that the subject had been overweight.

Granville proceeded to measure the unwrapped body "with precision," as he put it, and several measurements are duly recorded on Perry's drawing. The reason for measuring this "really perfect female mummy" was to determine her race, for, quoting Granville again, "it is well known, that the Egyptian form has been assumed as the type of a specific variety of the Ethiopian race, particularly by the venerable Blumenbach, from certain supposed peculiarities of outward conformation."[43] Granville compared the proportions of the mummy to two strikingly different sources: the Venus de'Medici and "the most perfect pelvis of a well grown Negro girl, which I prepared some years ago"—possibly from the body of someone he treated, and possibly the body of someone who was, or had been, a slave. As for the Medici Venus, this "Aphrodite of Knidos" type had been held up by Winckelmann as the Greek ideal of female beauty and had also been used by the eighteenth-century Dutch anatomist Pieter Camper to demonstrate "perfect beauty" in comparative anatomy. Granville referred to both authors as authorities and concluded that the stature and limb ratios of the mummy corresponded almost exactly to the Venus, while its pelvis was quite different from that of the "Negro girl."

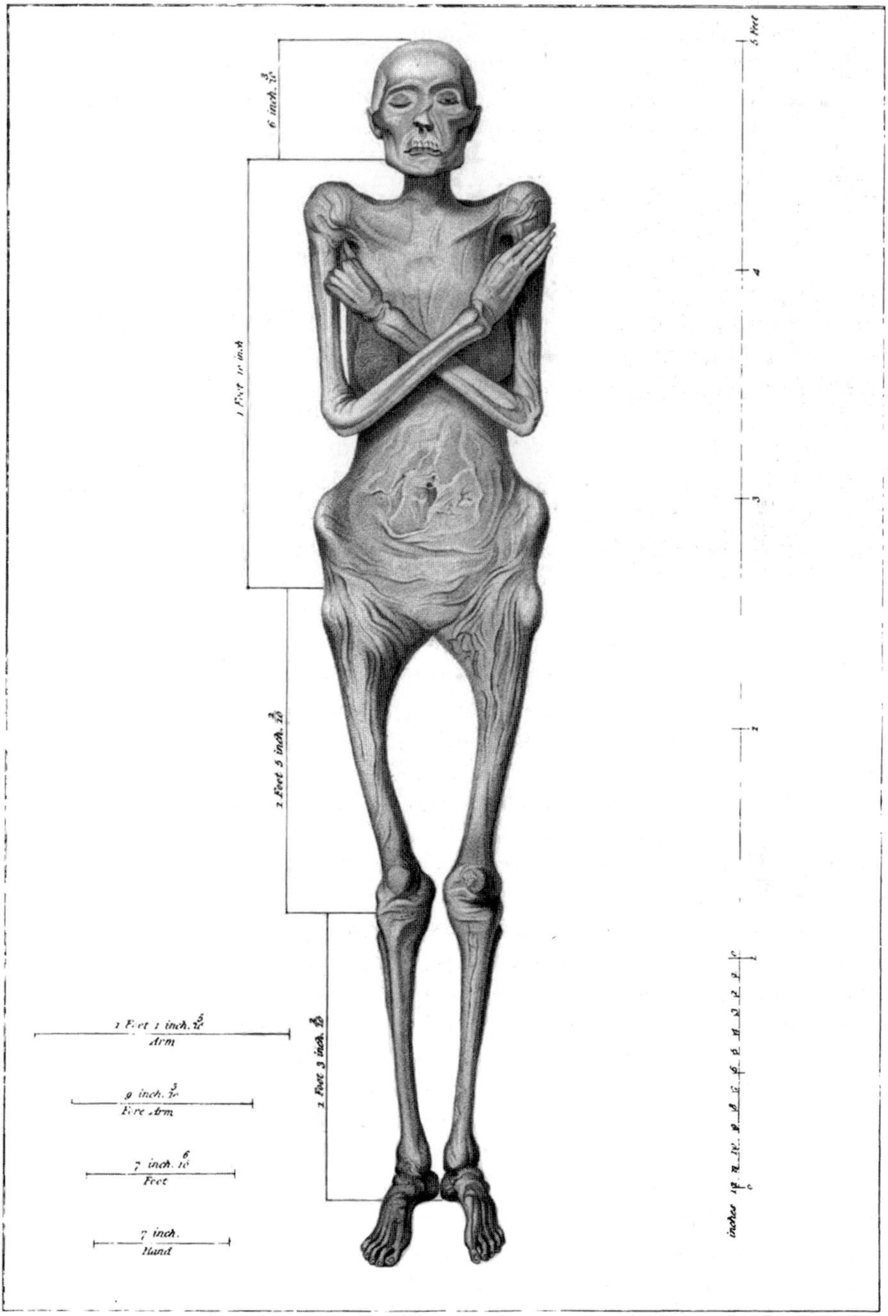

FIGURE 2.6 *"Dr. Granville's mummy," after unwrapping. Drawing by Henry Perry, engraved by James Basire. After Granville,* Essay on Egyptian Mummies, *pl. xix*

Granville was ready for the next stage of his examination, which he implicitly acknowledged as a destructive act:

> Having proceeded thus far in my inquiry into the state of preservation of the mummy before me, I determined, perfect, and beautiful as it was, to make it the object of further research by subjecting it to the anatomical knife, and thus to sacrifice a most complete specimen of the Egyptian art of embalming.[44]

The mummy's perfection was its destruction, and the second half of Granville's account deals with the dissection of the body and its organs. After emptying the abdomen, he was able to extricate the pelvis, having "sawed off the thighs a few inches from the hip" and divided the body at the first lumbar vertebra (Fig. 2.7). Where the removal of the mummy's wrappings had taken one hour, the dissection of the pelvis required two hours a day for almost a week, "some medical or scientific friends being present at each sitting."[45] In female skeletons, he explained, the pelvis "presents the most striking difference in different races," and the pelvis of the mummy "comes nearer to the *beau idéal* of the Caucasian structure." To prove the point to the Royal Society spectators, he had the dissected pelvis of the "Negro girl" ready for inspection.[46]

The mummy's head offered confirmation that it was European rather than Ethiopian and that it specifically resembled the Georgian female type in Blumenbach's "very instructive" work on skulls.[47] The drawing of the skull (Fig. 2.8) demonstrates the "Cuvier facial angle," the diagnostic tool that the most famous French scientist of the day, Georges Cuvier, had devised for his own studies on the anatomy of race. It was Cuvier who, just a few years earlier, had published the autopsy of Saartjie Baartman, the so-called "Hottentot Venus" whose skeleton, preserved genitals, and brain were displayed in the Musée de l'Homme in Paris until the 1970s.

The mummy's place on the anatomist's dissecting table was secure—more so, at this point, than its place in the museum. Mummies, which had crossed between categories of the artificial and the natural in earlier cabinets of curiosities, still resisted comfortable classification. Were they antiquities or medical specimens? Were they suitable for museum collections, and if so, in what form? Granville turned the physical remnants of his mummy into its own cabinet of curiosities, using a wooden chest with subdivided drawers to keep the pieces in his home. In 1853, he sold the chest, the battered coffin lid, and assorted textile rolls, pads, and fragments to the British Museum. The remains in the wooden chest, with some of the contents labeled in a nineteenth-century hand, include the fetuses he had experimentally embalmed, a dissected arm said to be from "North Africa," and fragments of the female mummy—a sliver of femur, a ball of "bitumen" (a mixture of animal or vegetable fat and conifer resin), and a leathery brown patch identified

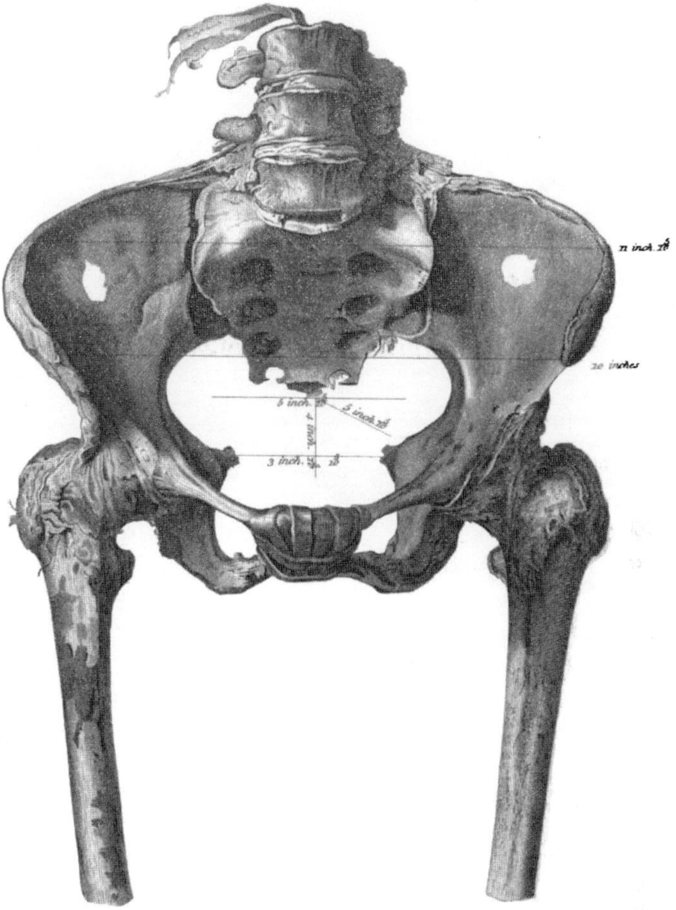

FIGURE 2.7 *Dissected pelvis from "Dr. Granville's mummy." Drawing by Henry Perry, engraved by James Basire. After Granville,* Essay on Egyptian Mummies, *pl. xx*

as the "peritoneum." In his autobiography, Granville criticized the museum for not doing more to disseminate his work to visitors, as he himself had done through public lectures at the Royal Institution in the 1830s. There, he said, his evening talk had been lit by candles that were made up from the crumbly white substance he had found around the mummy's skin.[48] Granville took the substance to be beeswax, which he believed the Egyptians had used in mummification, to seal the body from decay. It was, in fact, adipocere—the saponified body fat of an individual who, as Granville had correctly observed, must have been overweight in life. Granville was burning human flesh.

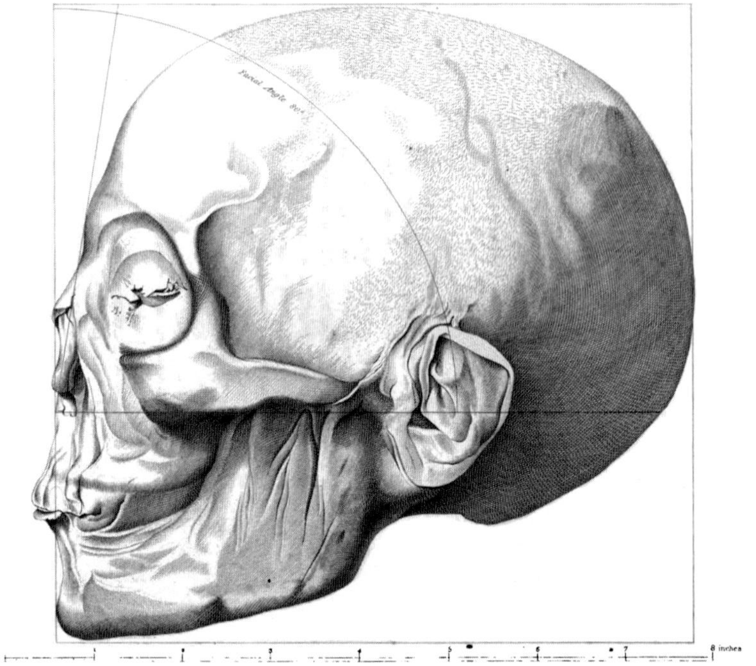

FIGURE 2.8 *The skull from "Dr. Granville's mummy," with an indication of the Cuvier facial angle. Drawing by Henry Perry, engraved by James Basire. After Granville,* Essay on Egyptian Mummies, *pl. xxi*

The Mummy in the Archaeological Age

The 1830s saw a spate of mummy unwrappings, in particular by Thomas Pettigrew, who turned his unwrappings into staged spectacles. Pettigrew published an authoritative book on Egyptian mummies in 1834 for which his childhood friend, the satirical cartoonist George Cruikshank, prepared the illustrations.[49] By the 1840s, newspapers were growing tired of unwrappings, which had become too predictable; not much new or different ever happened.[50] Public "unrollings" continued through mid-century, however, and were popularized in America by the British-born, one-time U.S. consul in Egypt, George Robbins Gliddon, who gained a reputation for the grandiloquent lectures that accompanied his unwrappings of mummified bodies.[51]

Although discomfiture with such investigations of mummies was rarely hinted at in the reports of journalists or practitioners, fiction of the time suggests both fascination and dismay. Literary scholarship interprets the nineteenth-century vogue for mummy fantasies and romances, in which mummies come back to life to haunt or seek revenge, as an expression of European anxieties about the struggle to control the colonized Other and order its material world.[52] Added to this were contemporary preoccupations with race, and in the antebellum United States with slavery, with the result that in terms of the consumption of mummies and other ancient Egyptian tropes, "the mummy slipped its yoke and began to run amok."[53] The unwrapping and anatomical probing of mummies, normalized earlier in the century by practitioners like Granville and Pettigrew, was nonetheless fraught with dangerous intimacies. Gliddon was lampooned in Edgar Allan Poe's short story "Some Words with a Mummy," which satirized the authoritative claims of Egyptology and medical science established by mummy unwrappings. Written in 1845, after Gliddon had unwrapped a mummy in Poe's home city of Baltimore, the story recounts an investigation that goes awry when the corpse comes back to life, jolted awake by the experimental application of electricity. The mummy—named Allamistakeo—admonishes the men who, having spirited it away from a museum in the dead of night, have gathered at the home of a Dr. Ponnonner to "unroll" it. Spying Gliddon, the mummy exclaims,

> But you, Mr. Gliddon...you, whom I have always been led to regard as the firm friend of the mummies—I really did anticipate more gentlemanly conduct from *you* [emphasis original].[54]

In the story, Gliddon calmly explains to the revivified Egyptian the "vast benefits accruing to science from the unrolling and disemboweling of mummies," but the mummy is unconvinced.

Fanciful fictions like Poe's are clearly indebted to the commodification of the mummy in the course of the nineteenth century. The public spectacle of staged unwrappings, together with reports in the press that combined scientific information and romanticized attributions (every other mummy was a princess, it seemed), confirmed the imagination of Egypt as a source of exoticism, wonder, and danger. Personalizing a mummy, calling it by name, and envisaging either its past life or its reactions to the present day were all ways of making the ancient past familiar and strange at the same time, and claiming that past for the Western audience.[55] The ostensibly disinterested voice of scholarship employed similar formulations. Granville, for instance, "could not help experiencing a degree of enthusiasm" when he "beheld before me the heart of an Egyptian female, whom imagination, aided by historical records, may fancy to have been contemporary with the great Sesostris."[56]

With the expansion of museums and museum collections, however, a subtle shift in the cultural position of antiquities, including mummies, occurred. The more such objects were understood to belong in museums, the less commodity value they appeared to have, for the museum removed objects from the cycle of selling and buying as part of its resacralization (and recontextualization) of them.[57] For objects other than mummies, like the Mentuhotep II statue and the coffin found next to it, the conceptual trip to the museum was straightforward. It involved an established set of processes (transport, registration, cataloguing, and so on) and an assumption of preservation. Mummies discovered through organized excavations enjoyed a less direct route to the museum, and many never made it. So fundamental had the evidence of unwrapped mummies become to one of the overriding concerns of the colonial project—the differences written on the bodies of the West and its others—that investigation of the mummy was imperative.

The mid-nineteenth century marked a turning point in the development of Egyptology, in terms of increasingly ambitious collecting habits and museum displays as well as the emergence of disciplinary apparatuses for the academic study of ancient Egypt. Specialist journals and university chairs in the subject were established from the 1860s onward, with the name of the oldest journal in the field, the *Zeitschrift für Ägyptische Sprache und Altertumskunde* (founded in 1863), reflecting the primacy awarded to philological studies in the nascent discipline. Not by accident, this period coincided with heightened European influence in Egyptian affairs of state and economics, in part exploiting differences between the ruling khedives and the Sublime Porte.[58] European influence in Egyptian affairs of state and economics heightened in the 1850s and 1860s, as Khedive Ismail negotiated with France and Britain, in particular, to attract foreign investment and expertise. Opened in 1869, the Suez Canal was the culmination of a long and close involvement between Egyptian and French concerns, to British consternation. But Britain benefitted from its overtures to Egypt as well. Egyptian cotton fed the textile mills of northern England when the American Civil War interrupted supplies in the 1860s—a financial boom that eventually went bust. In the short term, however, newfound wealth allowed the Egyptian government to hire European and American specialists, ranging from engineers, to teachers, to military advisors—including, rather ironically, former officers of the defeated Confederate army. Population growth, which had stalled in the early eighteenth century, more than doubled.[59]

On the back of the colonial infrastructure came tourism and archaeology, two different but related ways of representing Egypt to audiences "back home." Organizing trips from the British Midlands to London to view the Crystal Palace Exhibition of 1851 led Thomas Cook to launch his successful tours to Egypt, opening up the adventure of travel to a less adventurous, and somewhat less moneyed, class. Egypt's developing infrastructure, engineered and financed by European interests, made organized tourism and archaeology possible, overcoming a host of practical obstacles. For example, the opening of the Alexandria to Cairo railway in 1858 reduced the journey time between the Mediterranean port and the capital city from four days to eight hours.[60]

Even with increased comfort and convenience, travelers embraced the idea of exploration, as did archaeologists. It is enshrined in the name of the Egypt Exploration Fund (EEF), established in London in April 1882—just months before the British bombardment of Alexandria—to sponsor excavations in Egypt. The organization changed *Fund* to *Society* in 1919 but retains the Victorian conceit of *Exploration* in its name today. *Exploration* implied the unknown, an alien territory in which European ingenuity and energy could "discover" the ancient civilization beneath the unsatisfactory veneer of modern society. As ever, the explorers were male hero figures who recounted their discoveries with little reference to the indigenous men, women, and children who carried out the physical work or acted as intermediaries with the local population as well as the Egyptian government.[61]

Large-scale archaeological work in Egypt radically altered the information and artifacts available for scholarly study and the types and numbers of objects available for museums to collect. Although there had been attempts already under Muhammad Ali to found an antiquities museum in Cairo and make the export of antiquities illegal, it was the impetus of the French Egyptologist Auguste Mariette and his successor, Gaston Maspero, that created an effective system for licensing excavations and established a fully fledged museum in the Egyptian capital, albeit as an institution run by Europeans, for Europeans.[62] The antiquities service operated under a principle of division of finds, whereby approximately half (often a much larger portion) of whatever objects an expedition found became the property of the expedition's sponsor, whether that was an organization, a university, a museum, or a wealthy individual. The remaining portion belonged to the Egyptian state and was destined for the antiquities museum in Cairo, although regional museums and site storerooms were eventually created to deal with the sheer amount of material that archaeology generated.

Thus, museum collections outside of Egypt expanded with finds, and archaeologists like British pioneer W. M. Flinders Petrie made their initial decisions in the field, thinking ahead to an object's institutional destination. The trajectory from the field to the museum depended on ideas of quality and typicality (how rare or representative was it?), as well as concerns about condition and transport. The methodology of the archaeologist also created an archive alongside the excavated features and artifacts, with field notes, drawings, maps, and photographs to record the context and catalogue the finds. Since the entire premise of archaeology rested on discovery and revelation, the implication for wrapped, sealed, or otherwise concealed objects was self-evident. Archaeologists opened ancient boxes, jars, and coffins; unrolled papyri or prised them out of the *papier mâche*–like layers of mummy masks; and unwrapped votive objects and statues. Such interventions were so commonplace that archaeological reports do not mention every instance and record only a few with a drawing or photograph. Even less often were the wrapping materials preserved, though sealings, on jars for instance, might be kept if they were inscribed, since inscriptions were considered to have potential historical value.

Archaeology created a larger context for individual finds, which might be part of a burial assemblage or an entire cemetery. The discovery of a hundred *shabti*-figures, for instance, allowed each *shabti* to stand for the whole, while the hundred were split first between Egypt and the archaeological sponsor, and then perhaps divided again among European and North American collections. Collecting multiple objects, or multiples of a defined type or class of object, akin to the "type specimen" in natural history, allowed specialist distinctions to be made in the service of scholarship. The disciplinary regimes of field archaeology and museum curation subjected the artifact to measures, such as cataloguing, cleaning, and photography, that were essential to defining it as an object of study and potentially—though by no means always—for display. Once incorporated into a museum collection, the object perceived as being the best quality, and thus most representative and informative for the type, could be put on display, while objects deemed to be poorer quality, incomplete, damaged, or otherwise less informative (for instance, lacking inscription) were "duplicates" to be kept in "reserve" collections for recording and research.

In terms of collecting human remains, the excavation of a cemetery might yield hundreds of bodies, but it proceeded at a speedy pace by later standards of archaeology. Excavators numbered the graves and listed the contents, often sketching the position of the body and the arrangement of goods around it. But what happened to the bodies is a point of silence. Select examples were destined for museums, chosen for the beauty or rarity of their surface decoration, and an unusual anatomical feature might also deserve recording and sometimes preservation, such as a hydrocephalic skull photographed at the site of Shurafa.[63] But there is no explicit mention of what happened to the hundreds of other bodies found, or how they were disposed of. Petrie's work in the Roman period necropolis at Hawara was typical in this respect. He collected the famous painted portraits, along with several mummy masks and painted shrouds, chiefly by removing them from the mummies. Only about a dozen or so mummies were kept intact, for museums in Cairo and Europe, while hundreds of skulls from Hawara, and from other sites, met a different fate. Extracted from their wrappings and separated from their bodies, these skulls were destined for craniometric study—notably Francis Galton's work on eugenics at University College London.[64] Following a line of descent from Camper and Cuvier, to Granville and Gliddon, the study of ancient Egyptian skulls continued to underpin the development of racialist theory and legitimize Western authority over Egypt, past and present. But where the early nineteenth-century performance of mummy unwrapping and anatomical scrutiny had been set in the drawing room, or the public lecture hall, the late Victorian and Edwardian heyday of archaeological collecting placed unwrapping back at the source, in an Egypt that lay open for inspection.

In the Presence of Kings

> Twenty years have elapsed since he was brought back to the light, this master of the world. He was wrapped *thousands of times* in a marvellous winding-sheet, woven of aloe fibres, finer than the muslin of India, which must have taken years in the making and measured more than 400 yards in length. The unswathing, done in the presence of the Khedive Tewfik and the great personages of Egypt, lasted two hours, and after the last turn, when the illustrious figure appeared, the emotion amongst the audience was such that they stampeded like a herd of cattle, and the Pharaoh was overturned.
>
> Pierre Loti,
> *Egypt (Le mort de Philae)* (1909), Chapter 4

The 1870s and early 1880s were a time of crisis in Egypt. The proceeds of the 1860s cotton boom had been spent several times over, and the opening of the Suez Canal in 1869—a French initiative opposed by Britain—at first contributed to financial instabilities, forcing Khedive Ismail to sell Egypt's shares in the canal to the British government in 1875. The use of corvée labor in the construction of the canal exemplified the gulf between the Ottoman elite and the Egyptian populace. An emerging middle class was stymied in between, thanks in large part to the influence of European powers and the influx of foreign professionals, not only from Europe and North America, but also from elsewhere in the Ottoman Empire (including Greece, Turkey, Armenia, and the Levant). From 1879, Egyptian dissatisfaction manifested itself in the series of political and military clashes known as the Urabi Revolt, after the Egyptian general Urabi Pasha. Urabi organized an opposition government, challenging colonial support for Khedive Tewfik, who had replaced his father Ismail in 1879 as part of the deal by which Britain, France, and Italy stepped in to restore Egypt's finances. It required British military intervention to suppress the revolt in 1882, with Urabi's subsequent trial—he was spared the death penalty in lieu of exile—covered extensively in popular outlets like the *Illustrated London News*.[65]

In the spring of 1881, however, Gaston Maspero—the newly appointed head of the antiquities service—had other things on his mind. For some time, he had been trying to identify the source of several rare antiquities being offered for sale in Egypt, all linked to the twenty-first-dynasty high priests of Amun who had ruled as kings at Luxor, the site of ancient Thebes.[66] Like a detective in one of Poe's other short stories, Maspero had pieced together enough clues to narrow the suspects to two antiquities dealers operating in Luxor, one of whom—Mustafa Ayyad—had diplomatic immunity because he was a vice-consul for Britain. The other dealer was Ahmed Abd er-Rassul, of the West Bank village of Sheikh abd el-Gurna.

With the appropriate authorization from the governor (*mudir*) of the province, a man named Daoud Pasha, and from the Egyptian Ministry of Public Works, which oversaw the antiquities service, Maspero had the Luxor police arrest Abd er-Rassul on the 4th of April, 1881. Maspero and two assistants from the antiquities service, Emil Brugsch and Maxence de Rochemontaix, personally questioned the suspect, who maintained his innocence and invited a search of his house. Two days later, when the official government order for the investigation arrived, Maspero had Ahmed Abd er-Rassul and one of his brothers sent to the *mudir*'s offices in Qena, where they were interrogated and tortured, this time not in the presence of the Europeans but of their delegate, an Egyptian inspector for the service based nearby at Dendera. Ahmed spent two months in prison before being released without charge.

Meanwhile, Maspero had informed the khedive and secured his permission to do whatever was necessary to find the source of the suspected thefts. The case was soon cracked: in early July, a third Abd er-Rassul brother confessed to the *mudir* that he knew the location of the tomb. Maspero had returned to France for the summer, but his deputy, Emil Brugsch, and another member of staff from the Cairo museum, the Egyptian Egyptologist Ahmed Kamal, immediately went to Luxor, where the confessant, Mohammed Abd er-Rassul, led them to a concealed opening high in the cliff face between Deir el-Bahri and Gurna. By candlelight, Brugsch made his way into the shaft and through a corridor that twisted more than sixty meters into the cliff. Everywhere were coffins, mummies, pottery and metal vessels, and boxes of *shabti*-figures. The tomb contained not just a handful of minor twenty-first-dynasty rulers, but the burials of earlier, New Kingdom kings whose names covered temples and colossi up and down the Nile. As Maspero later recalled:

> Monsieur Emil Brugsch, coming so suddenly into such an assemblage, thought that he must be the victim of a dream, and like him, I still wonder if I am not dreaming when I see and touch what were the bodies of so many famous personages of whom we never expected to know more than the names.[67]

The dream of this archaeological find, with its cache of kingly bodies, matched any mummy fiction. What the Abd er-Rassuls had found was a tomb complex (now numbered DB 320 or TT 320) that contained royal mummies from the eighteenth, nineteenth, and twentieth dynasties (c. 1550–1070 B.C.E.). Apparently having been robbed and vandalized, the mummies had then been carefully rewrapped in the twenty-first dynasty (c. 1070–945 B.C.E.), placed in recycled coffins, and buried in the deepest recesses of a sixty-meter tomb shaft, while the burials of the twenty-first-dynasty high priests of Amun (who ruled the southern part of the country) and their family members lined the entrance corridor. Inscriptions on the mummies' new linen shrouds or coffins recorded the date when the reburial took place, which in at least three instances was timed to coincide with the burial of the high priest Pinudjem II (c. 968 B.C.E.).[68]

Within forty-eight hours, Brugsch, Kamal, and Tadros Moutafian, who was antiquities inspector for the Giza pyramids, had overseen the clearance of the entire tomb, standing guard outside the shaft while a *reis* in the museum's employ managed the work inside. It took another three days for three hundred local men, conscripted by the *mudir,* to move approximately six thousand objects from the foot of the cliffs across the valley to the river bank. In the heat of early July, several of the coffins needed more than a dozen men to lift them, and the overland journey to the river took up to eight hours. At the Nile, the mummies and coffins, wrapped protectively in fabric, awaited the arrival of the museum's steamboat for their journey downstream to Cairo. With its "freight of kings," the boat set off for Cairo, and Maspero reported that from Luxor downriver to Quft, peasant women came to the riverbank, howling and disheveled as if in mourning, while men fired rifles in the air as was the custom at local funerals.[69]

Like the Tutankhamun find, the story of how the antiquities service foiled the thieving Abd er-Rassuls became the stuff of Egyptological legend, but the legend glosses over the darker social and political implications. Maspero's account makes the influence of European powers quite plain, as well as the role and tactics of the Ottoman elite, from the khedive to regional administrators and antiquities inspectors.[70] In fact, Daoud Pasha, the *mudir* who had obliged Maspero by interrogating the Abd er-Rassuls, backed Urabi and was targeted as anti-European in consular reports made by Mustafa Ayyad—the Luxor dealer who could not be pursued for the Deir el-Bahri thefts because he was a British agent. According to Ayyad, the *mudir* encouraged village leaders in the region to support Urabi, using "the most seditious and frightful language" to threaten that if Urabi lost, European powers would occupy Egypt.[71] That part of the threat came true: the British fleet bombarded Alexandria in July 1882, and a British force advanced from the Suez Canal zone to defeat Urabi at Tel el-Kebir on September 13th. The "veiled protectorate" dropped into place.

The Urabi revolt and the interruption to Tewfik's reign did not stop work relating to the Deir el-Bahri cache. By the end of 1882, the royal mummies were on display in a dedicated gallery that was added to the Boulaq Museum on the khedive's order, because the existing museum had no space to accommodate them. For a time, visitors were only allowed inside the entrance of the new gallery, where they could see two of the best-known and best-preserved mummies, Seti I (c. 1306–1290 B.C.E.) and Ramses II (c. 1290–1224 B.C.E.).[72] Maspero delayed investigation of the mummies until 1886, put off not by political developments but by an initial, exploratory examination of the mummy of Thutmose III (c. 1479–1425 B.C.E.) that suggested it was in poor condition.[73] That summer, though, all but two of the mummies from the cache were unwrapped; the exceptions were the mummies of a twenty-first-dynasty priestess and of king Amenhotep I (c. 1525–1504 B.C.E.), which were considered especially attractive examples and were left intact. The unwrapping of the mummies was one of his last official acts before he left the directorship of the antiquities service, although he would return to the post in 1899, and for the four deemed most interesting (Seqenenre Ta'o, Seti I, Ramses II, and Ramses III), Maspero published a full description in the form of a "procès-verbal," framing the encounter in legalistic terms.[74]

The Coptic room of the museum, where material from Byzantine Egypt was on display, was the setting for the unwrappings, which took place before invited audiences on June 1st, 9th, 27th, and 28th, ending on July 1st. Maspero was assisted by Brugsch (who also made photographs), Urbain Bouriant (another museum employee and the first director of the Institut Français d'Archéologie Orientale), and Daniel Marie Fouquet, a French medical doctor working in Cairo. The invited audience included European consuls and Egyptologists, as well as British and Ottoman representatives. At the June 9th unwrapping of Seqenenre Ta'o and Seti I, General Stephenson, the commander of the British army of occupation, was present. On the first day of the unwrappings, Khedive Tewfik himself attended.

The first mummy to be unwrapped was that of Ramses II "the Great," whom Shelley had immortalized under a version of his throne name, Ozymandias. The mummy typified the care that the priests of the twenty-first dynasty had taken with the reburials. It lay in a rather plain wooden coffin that may originally have been made for an earlier pharaoh, and a hieratic inscription inked on the surface recorded how Ramses II had in fact been reburied twice. In year 10 of Pinudjem II (around 968 B.C.E., some 250 years after Ramses's death), the mummy was moved to the "high place"—the Deir el-Bahri shaft—from the tomb of Ramses's father, Seti I, where it had been for at least a few years. The long text credits the two priests in charge and records an official statement that no injury occurred in the removal; Egyptologists refer to these texts by the legalistic term "dockets."[75] The docket for Ramses II referred to the day of his second reburial as "the day of taking the god to his resting place."

Once Maspero had shown this text to the khedive and other eminent members of the audience, the unwrapping began. Beneath the inscribed shroud, a band of linen twenty centimeters wide encircled the body, followed by a second shroud strapped with narrow bands. Next was another encircling cloth band whose removal revealed a fine-quality linen cloth laid over the body from head to foot, on which was a red ink drawing of the sky goddess Nut. Under this were pieces of linen, folded into squares and drenched with resin or bitumen, after which, as Maspero put it, "Ramses appeared."

Next, Maspero turned to the mummy of the twentieth-dynasty pharaoh Ramses III (c. 1194–1163 B.C.E.), which had been in a coffin inscribed for an earlier queen. This mummy had an outer shroud dyed red, with no inscription, and around its head was a linen fillet with divine figures in black ink (Fig. 2.9, right). Beneath the red shroud was a white shroud inscribed for "the Osiris, the king," Ramses III, below a drawing of the sun god in the form of a ram-headed falcon (Fig. 2.9, left).[76] The royal identity confirmed, Maspero paused proceedings so that the mummy could be set on its feet and photographed with the outer wrappings in place, a break made longer than necessary because the audience left their seats and crowded around. When the unwrapping resumed amid an air of impatience, progress was rapid: "The mummy seemed to melt and give way under our fingers," Maspero wrote, as if the removal of several layers of linen were so inevitable that it happened of its own accord.[77] He noted in passing that some individual pieces of linen bore drawings of gods, and one was inscribed with a priestess's dedication to Amun. After the last shroud was removed, the audience was disappointed that a layer of resin obscured the king's face, and at 11:20 a.m., the khedive took his leave. The unwrapping resumed in the afternoon and continued two days later, aided by the museum's sculptor, an architect named Alessandro Barsanti, who chipped away the resin with a chisel. Maspero could then go on to describe the corpse and its face, reading noble character traits into the royal physiognomy. He closed the procès-verbal by confirming that the mummies of Ramses II and Ramses III would be returned to their stands, uncovered, for display.

Coming as they did in the early years of "scientific" archaeology, and of the British occupation, the Maspero unwrappings bear a number of comparisons with earlier unwrappings, particularly in the way the reports combine demonstrations of discovery and fact with comments on the audience's barely controlled reactions, and remarks on the obstacles the practitioner had to overcome. Like passages of Granville's account, too, Maspero's reports convey the up-close experience of handling and observing the mummy: the face and head of Ramses III were so closely shaven that Maspero could detect "no trace of hair or beard," recalling the fresh stubble Granville identified with a pass of his hand over the head of the mummy he investigated. Within a decade or two of the unwrapping of the Deir el-Bahri cache, archaeologists had further refined their recording techniques in the field and the museum and adopted an increasingly detached and dispassionate tone in their written reports. Moreover, the application of anatomical expertise to both living and dead bodies throughout the colonized world saw the emergence of a new specialism, physical anthropology.[78] Suitable application of its methods to archaeologically recovered remains would, it was thought, yield more and

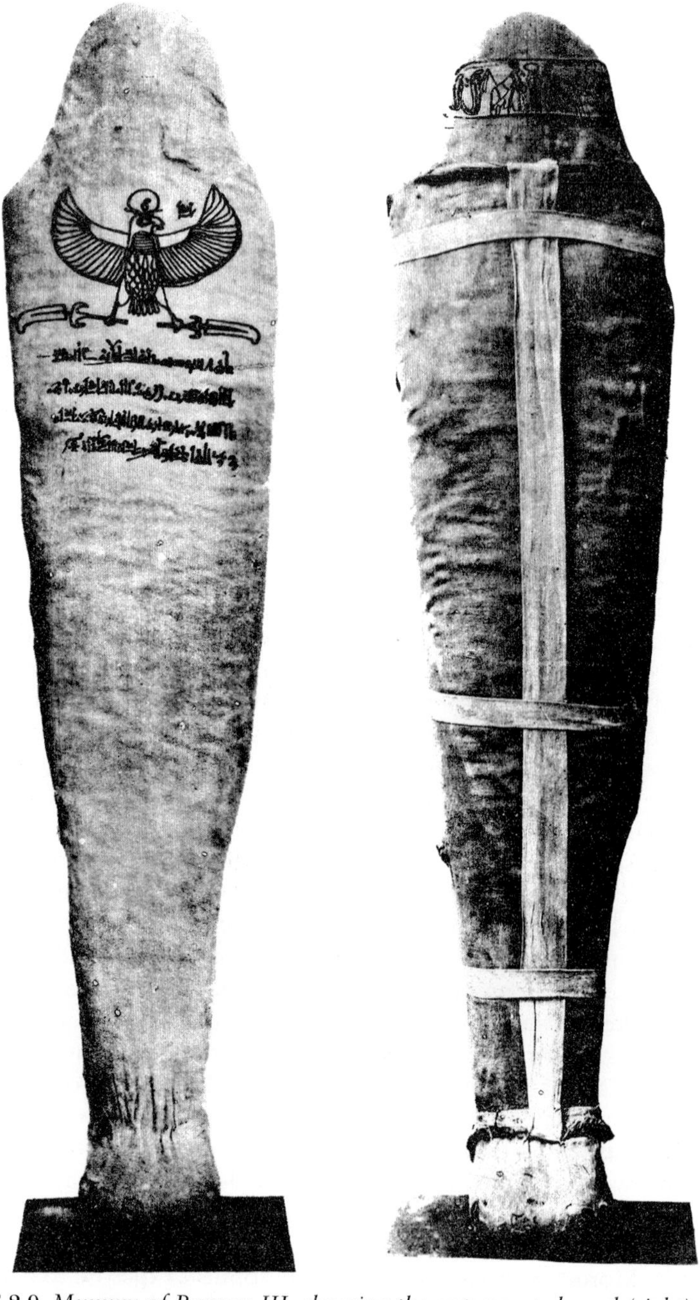

FIGURE 2.9 *Mummy of Ramses III, showing the outermost shroud (right) and the next layer of wrapping (left). Photograph by Emil Brugsch. After Maspero,* Momies royales, *pl. xvii*

better knowledge of the ancient world through the study of the human body, just as was being done among the indigenous populations of the Andaman Islands, Indonesia, New Zealand, South Africa, and elsewhere.

All that was needed was a supply of mummies to unwrap—and archaeology obliged. In 1891, Eugène Grébaut discovered another shaft at Deir el-Bahri, containing more mummies belonging to the high priests of the twenty-first dynasty, and in 1898, Victor Loret found an unexpected second cache of royal mummies, this time gathered in the tomb of the eighteenth-dynasty ruler Amenhotep II (KV 35). All the coffins, mummies, and associated objects were transported as before to the antiquities museum, which had moved from Boulaq to Giza in the interim. The unwrapping of excavated mummies was by then established practice at the museum, but the second group of royal mummies was left aside until Maspero, who had spent several years in France, returned to head the antiquities service at the turn of the century. Among the mummies in the second royal cache was a body labeled as eighteenth-dynasty ruler Thutmose IV, whose own tomb was discovered in early 1903 by Theodore Davis, a wealthy American licensed to excavate in the Valley of the Kings. Davis's discovery spurred Maspero into action, making plans to examine the newly found mummies and reexamine those he had previously unwrapped.

As before, the staging of the royal unwrappings mirrored the power structure of Egypt, only this time, Maspero invited Lord and Lady Cromer to the unwrapping of Thutmose IV on the 16th of March in 1903; the khedive, Abbas Hilmi II, was absent. Brugsch and Georges Daressy conducted the unwrapping in a room at the museum before the Barings, Theodore Davis, and an audience of European Egyptologists—Wilhelm Spiegelberg, Pierre Lacau, Percy Newberry, James Quibell, and Howard Carter.[79] Also in the audience was the Australian-born anatomist Grafton Elliot Smith, who had arrived in Egypt from Cambridge in October 1900 to become professor of anatomy at the Cairo Medical School.

Elliot Smith had already started to work on excavated human remains at the invitation of the methodical American archaeologist George Reisner, and observing the Thutmose IV unwrapping seems to have piqued his interest further. He convinced Maspero to x-ray the king's body at a private nursing home, one of the first times the technique was used on a mummified body.[80] Duly impressed, Maspero asked Elliot Smith to study all the royal mummies, and Smith agreed to start by practicing, as it were, on the twenty-first-dynasty mummies of high priests and their families found by Grébaut. Elliot Smith and museum curator Georges Daressy unwrapped a selection of these at the museum, inviting Sir Eldon Gorst, Cromer's second-in-command (and eventual successor), and Lady Gorst.[81] The established propriety of public unwrapping acknowledged the hierarchy of the colonial administration: Cromer attended the unwrapping of royal mummies, while Gorst witnessed the unwrapping of mere aristocracy.

Although the goal was the same—to reveal the corpse and study its physical features, embalming method, and pathology—the method Elliot Smith adopted set his work apart from previous unwrappings. For a start, he spent days rather than hours on each mummy, and he also paid conscientious attention to the wrapping methods and textiles used, enlisting the help of Arthur Mace, who later assisted Carter at the tomb of Tutankhamun. When Elliot Smith, with Brugsch and Daressy, unwrapped a twenty-first-dynasty priestess in July 1905, "kindly placed at my disposal by Maspero," Mace "undertook the very laborious task of writing the account of the bandages used and the texture of the linen of which they were composed."[82] The wrappings of the twenty-first-dynasty mummies were similar to the outer wrappings Maspero had found on the restored royal mummies from Deir el-Bahri, giving Elliot Smith some idea of what to expect when he began unwrapping the mummies from the KV 35 cache that same year. He also performed further investigations into the mummies Maspero had already examined and summarized the results, mummy by mummy, in a volume of the museum's *Catalogue général* that appeared after he had returned to England to take up a chair in anatomy at Manchester University.[83] The mummies were assigned new catalogue numbers, and Brugsch documented the bodies, faces, hands, and hair in photographs that benefitted from technological advances since the 1880s (Fig. 2.10).

The catalogue entries indicate in some detail the linen that Elliot Smith removed from the KV 35 mummies: spiral bandages, figures-of-eight, folded pads, and sheets as long as four meters. The mummy of Seti II, which Elliot Smith started to unwrap on September 5th, 1905, was a rich source of textile evidence. The unwrapping took several days and occupied a series of assistants, including the ever-present Brugsch.[84] The corpse itself had been badly damaged before its rewrapping: the head and arms were disjointed, several fingers were missing, and the skin had been slashed by an adze or similar tool. Near the body, folded into packets, were "two perfectly intact shirts of very fine muslin"—one embroidered with the name of Seti II's father, Merneptah—but the shirts had disappeared in the museum by the time Elliot Smith finished the catalogue. Fragments of further, fine-quality tunics were part of a bundle of "loose rags" on the mummy's chest. In total, Elliot Smith counted twenty-six individual bandages or sheets wrapped around the body, underneath which the corpse lay in "a large mass of pieces of exquisitely fine muslin (many pieces with elaborately fringed and coloured—red and blue—borders) and clothes." The legs were individually wrapped in eight distinct layers of thin linen bandages, each alternating with a layer of resin. Elliot Smith judged that the rewrapping included much of the original linen, salvaged for reuse despite the ancient vandalism.

The chronicle of the royal mummies was a chronicle of violence aimed at Egyptian bodies. Glancing, slicing blows cut into the mummies in antiquity and wrenched apart their wrappings and limbs, but violence also attended their unwrappings—not just Maspero's knife and Barsanti's chisel, but the damage done to those other Egyptian bodies, the Abd er-Rassul brothers

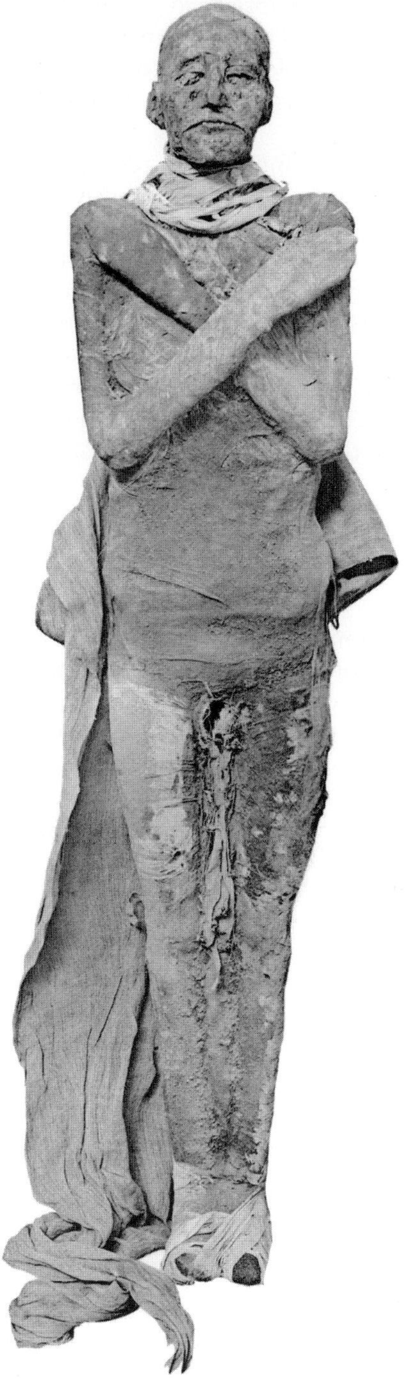

FIGURE 2.10 *Mummy of Ramses III, unwrapped. Photograph by Emil Brugsch. After Elliot Smith,* Royal Mummies, *pl. l*

interrogated, tortured, and imprisoned at the behest of the antiquities service. Neither the ancient nor the modern violence could really be lamented, however, for it made possible the work of Egyptology, which had by then been resolutely reconfigured as an academic discipline steeped in scientific endeavor.

The study of the royal mummies also took place at a crucial historical juncture: colonial power was at its most extensive, but also its most vulnerable, in terms of anxieties about the cultural, and biological, hybridity that colonialism might produce. Knowing where things, and people, fit in the scheme of things was important work, and mummy unwrappings contributed to it. Coming face to face with mighty pharaohs brought a thrill as well as a quiet relief: the kings of the New Kingdom had high foreheads, aquiline noses, and fine cheekbones. In the discourse of race that shaped and shadowed the colonial project, ancient Egypt—or at least its ruling class—fell on the comfortable side of the color line.

Race, Sex, and Disease in Colonial Egypt

> The making of mummies and the strange and rather beastly makeshifts resorted to by the professional embalmers became important questions. The preservation of the intestinal contents of mummies led to inquiries into the food supplies of the period: and rescuing the textiles and preservative of their wrappings opened up another field of archaeological research. And, above all, it was not enough that a record be made of the anthropological measurements for future reference. The archaeologists needed to know the racial characters of the skeletons in graves as they were opened up.
>
> Prof. Frederic Wood Jones, in Dawson, *Sir Grafton Elliot Smith* (1938), p. 145

Alongside his work on the royal mummies, Elliot Smith continued to work with Reisner, who became director of the Archaeological Survey of Nubia formed by the British administration.[85] Instigated by plans for a new dam at Aswan, the rescue work of the Survey aimed to establish the ancient character of the region and how it related to sites downriver in the Nile valley. Elliot Smith joined the survey in 1907, assisted by the young anthropologist Wood Jones, whose quote above makes clear the importance of identifying the race of the ancient, exhumed skeletons and mummies that were excavated, sometimes hundreds at a time. The question was of particular concern in the region of Nubia, where the natural barrier of the Nile cataracts marked an intellectual barrier between "Egypt" and "Africa." In political terms, especially for the British, the region was a liminal zone between a known entity and a new, potentially problematic, venture: the Anglo-Egyptian Sudan established in 1899.

Questions about the race of the ancient Egyptians had informed the unwrapping of mummies since the efforts of Blumenbach, who agreed with Herodotus that the Egyptians had an "Ethiopian" countenance and used this term as his category for a black or African race. The leading French scientist of the era, Georges Cuvier, considered the Egyptians to be Caucasian instead, and it was with Cuvier that Granville sided in the dissection of his "perfect" mummy. As formulated in the late eighteenth and early nineteenth centuries, theories of race had helped defend the slave trade, but as the institution of slavery was challenged and eventually abandoned, the racialist line of argument broadened its scope. From the 1840s onward, race-based science reemerged in a subtly different and more potent form, focused on a taxonomy of races that judged their character, degree of "civilization," and intellectual capacity.[86] "Race" was a far-reaching tool of categorization and was broadly understood to encompass any group thought to be defined by lineage and to bear physical manifestations of difference, which included prostitutes, criminals, Jews, and the Irish.[87] Museums and universities played a key role in the development and promulgation of racial theory, and by Elliot Smith's day, it cut across disciplinary formations in the humanities, social sciences, and biological sciences. Racism had become the default stance of Western rationality.

The race of the ancient Egyptians had long been a sensitive question with unstable answers. The same George Gliddon sent up by Poe had a keen interest in the subject, and while U.S. consul in Egypt in the 1830s he had sent ancient skulls to Dr. Samuel Morton in Philadelphia. In his work *Crania Aegyptiaca,* published to acclaim in 1844, Morton classified the ancient Egyptians as a subtype of the Caucasian race, contradicting Blumenbach's earlier classification of the Egyptians as an "Ethiopian" type (Fig. 2.11). In contrast, the British physician James Cowles Prichard, working in Bristol in the 1840s, agreed with Blumenbach and concluded that the ancient Egyptians were Ethiopian types with some "negroid" features.[88]

After Morton's death, Gliddon sought to continue his work and went on to coauthor the best-selling *Types of Mankind* with the Alabama doctor, and slave owner, Josiah Clark Nott—a treatise that argued for the separate origins of different races (Fig. 2.12).[89] Recognized as the earliest advanced civilization, Egypt could not be African. It had to be "white" in order to share the stage with ancient Greece, Rome, and modern Europe. *Types of Mankind* treated ancient Egypt as a mirror of the American south: a white society where blacks were slaves and servants. In Nott's view, immigration from India into the Nile valley had been responsible for the rise of Egyptian civilization, and the eventual intermingling of races led to its decline; Egypt could never recover from this blood taint, making modern Egypt no threat to the Western world.[90]

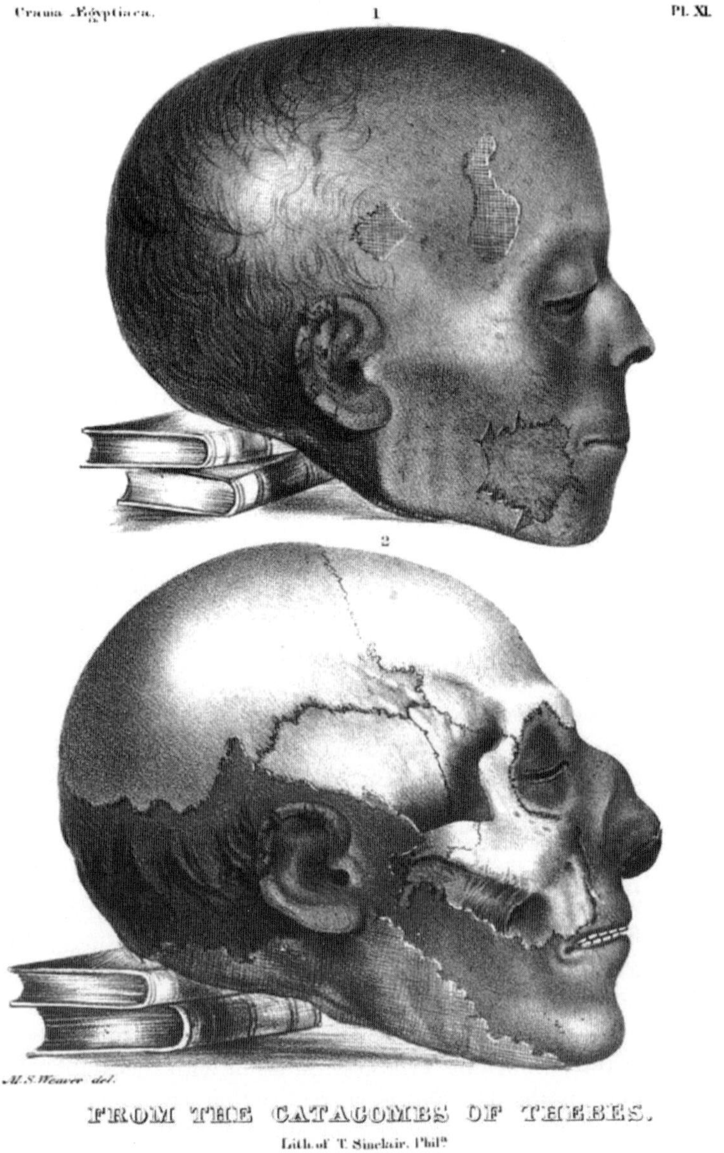

FIGURE 2.11 *Ancient Egyptian skulls, from Samuel Morton's* Crania Aegyptiaca *(1844)*

If the unwrapping of mummies offered an intimate, romanticized, even eroticized confrontation with the past, it also made it possible to observe Egyptian phenotypes, including facial features and skull structure, hair texture and shade, and skin color. All of these formed a diagnostic vocabulary of race in which contemporary viewers were fluent. Minute variations in

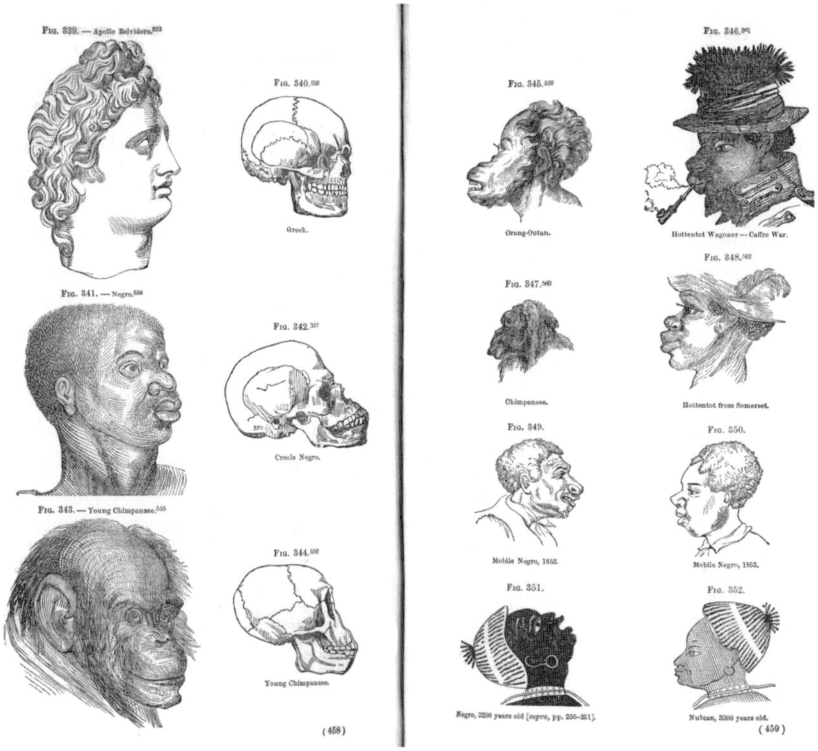

FIGURE 2.12 *Comparative chart of "racial types" from Josiah Nott and George R. Gliddon's* Types of Mankind *(1854). Courtesy of the New York Public Library*

skin color were read as signs that could reveal even remote black ancestry, and Victorian viewers made subtle distinctions of race in physiognomy that viewers today find difficult to discern.[91] Such scrutiny informed anatomical approaches to mummies. From the earliest unwrappings, with their frustrated attacks on hardened resin, investigators realized that some brown or black substance, whether resin or bitumen, had been applied to the skin of many mummies. Investigators were aware that such applications, as well as the dehydration process, altered the external appearance of the mummy, but they remarked on skin color as a matter of course, purporting to describe the present state of the corpse. In the race-aware atmosphere of the long nineteenth century, however, any comment on skin color echoed the wider discourse of race. "The skin is of a dark brown colour, soft, moist and tough, like oiled leather," wrote Elliot Smith of a mummy in Cairo, while pale color was worthy of note as well: Maspero described the skin of Ramses II's mummy as "yellow earth."[92]

The hair of Egyptian mummies became similarly weighted with meanings, and Elliot Smith drew on contemporary comparisons to describe female mummies in particular. One mummy had hair "enclosed in cloths tied like those of modern Egyptian girls," while the "numerous tight plaits" tied to the thinning hair of an older female mummy were like "modern Nubian women's hair."[93] Maspero had observed that the short face and scalp hair on the mummy of the elderly Ramses II was white, and the beard bristly, but by the time Elliot Smith examined the body, the hair had turned yellow and was "silky."[94] The observations that Elliot Smith made on the skin, hair, and physiognomy of the royal mummies were inevitably embedded in the discursive strategy of race, though his generation of scientists might not have been able to predict the ends to which their research would be put. Toward the end of his life, Elliot Smith was dismayed to see race science used to promote the idea of a superior "Aryan" race.[95]

Questions of race were also closely tied to questions of gender, in mummy studies as in colonial contact zones. Couched as a masculine enterprise, colonialism attributed feminine, and thus weak, qualities to the colonized male and led to what has been characterized as the double colonization of indigenous women; it also produced deep-seated worries, from a Western perspective, about the biological hybridity that would result from sexual relations between the races. Observing sexual characteristics was important, though, because they were thought to be another way of identifying race. Gilman cites a claim from the 1860s that the hymens of African women were in a different position than those of white women, while the "steatopygous" buttocks and "Hottentot apron" of Saartjie Baartman were well-rehearsed signs of black female difference and libido.[96]

Both male and female bodies were analyzed for their sexual characteristics, but for the male mummies, it was the perception of abnormality that prompted the record; for female mummies, the probing of breasts and genitals served as standard description instead, even down to measuring the length of the labial cleft.[97] All females could be denoted by their genitals, which stood for the pathological state of not being male. Working for Reisner at the Naga-ed-Dêr cemetery, north of Luxor, Elliot Smith commented on a Predynastic burial said to be that of a young girl: "Vulva kept. Good photos. of hair wanted. Girl with long auburn wavy hair down her back. Ear. Long pendulous breasts."[98] Breast size also featured in Elliot Smith's catalogue of the royal mummies, where he mentioned the breasts of two-thirds of the female examples. They were "small or only moderately full," "large and pendulous," "enormously enlarged" on a mummy he presumed to have been lactating, or suffering from "senile atrophy" in the bodies of older women.[99]

Scrutiny of the mummified male body chiefly recorded the absence or invisibility of sexual characteristics. Elliot Smith referred to the genitals of just over half the male mummies from the royal caches. Several had the penis and scrotum pushed back against the perineum or pressed against an upper thigh, at first sight rendering it invisible; hence a body ascribed to Thutmose I had the "appearance of being that of a eunuch."[100] Others had no extant genitals, perhaps because the embalmed parts had broken off during the ancient vandalism. Some cases were more puzzling. The body of Merneptah was "very curious" in that the penis was intact but the scrotum had been cut away, leading to speculation that the king had been castrated at some point before his death.[101] Elliot Smith examined the penis of the body of Ramses IV by thin-slicing skin from the glans, to determine whether the king had been circumcised (yes, he thought), and supplied measurements for the penis and scrotum.[102]

Regardless of gender, all unwrapped mummies were also inspected for signs of disease or deformity, and a new field of study, known as palaeopathology, owed its existence to the British administration of Egypt, since the term was coined by Marc Armand Ruffer, one of Elliot Smith's colleagues at the Cairo Medical School. Ruffer was president of the Sanitary, Maritime and Quarantine Council of Egypt from 1901 to 1917 and, in the words of a biographer, "enjoyed the confidence and support of both Lord Cromer and Lord Kitchener."[103] The focus of his work was to rehydrate skin, muscle, and organ tissues for histological study, a further step "inside" the unwrapped body in pursuit of ancient disease. In a number of publications, Ruffer diagnosed spondylitis, arterial disease, kidney stones, cirrhosis, pneumonia, and schistosomiasis. His method, "adopted after many failures," involved soaking the whole mummy or detached limbs in a water and sodium carbonate solution and then stripping away the muscles to reach the "remarkably elastic" arteries.[104] Ruffer sourced mummies and fragments of mummies, especially internal organs, from Petrie, Maspero, and Elliot Smith, among others—and was careful to note that the fragments he used for his research "were of no possible use as museum specimens, and I had no hesitation, therefore, in dissecting them."[105]

Ruffer's work took rational scientism as far inside a mummy as it was possible to go, stripping not only the textiles from the body, and the organs from the abdomen, but the fibers of flesh and skin to their cellular constituents. Nonetheless, preservation was a cherished tenet of Ruffer and other specialists working on mummified remains at the time. In publishing their work on skeletal material from the Archaeological Survey of Nubia, Ruffer and his coauthor Rietti made a plea for action to preserve ancient remains for further research:

> Before entering into the main part of our paper, we should like to add that surely the time has come when a check should be put on the wholesale destruction of the pathological specimens of the past, which has been going on for over one thousand years. Hundreds of mummies and dried human corpses have been removed from Egyptian tombs, and...there exist only a few very imperfect records of the state of these bodies. We hope and urge that the authorities will prohibit the exportation of skeletons, dried remains, or mummies until these have been examined by experts.

> Unless this is done soon, the present waste of scientific material will continue, only to be bitterly regretted before long.[106]

They envisioned that the Medical School would maintain its own museum, to keep examples of "diseased bones" that could be sent to "any recognized pathological Institute" to compare with contemporary bones exhibiting the same disease.[107] Ancient bodies would again bridge past and present, and reduced to its bare bones, the mummy would be "preserved"—as museum object, pathological specimen, and diagnostic tool.

The materiality of Egyptian mummies was their undoing, whether as powdered *mumia* or as human bodies to which all the techniques of science could be applied. As this chapter has shown, processes of discovery, cataloguing, measurement, unwrapping, dissection, and representation produced the mummy as an object that might ultimately be archived in the museum. Unlike objects made of pottery, metal, stone, or wood, however, the mummy fell under the peculiar, post-Enlightenment medical gaze that could—and would—see beneath the surface.

What lay beneath the wrappings was the crucial thing: Carter lost face for having no mummy to show Cromer because a massive statue was no fit substitute, no matter how much linen was wrapped around it. But what lay beneath a mummy's wrappings was a larger question as well, to which the inscriptions on the royal mummies gave one answer, and to which I turn in the next chapter. According to the text inked on the shroud of Ramses II, which Maspero had proudly shown to the khedive, what lay beneath the wrappings was a god.

3

Mummification

The nearest thing to an instruction manual for mummification that has survived from ancient Egypt includes directions for how to wrap the mummy's horns, tail, and all four of its legs—because the procedure described is to be performed not on a human, but on a bull. The "manual" in question is a papyrus roll inscribed on both sides, the recto alternating Demotic and hieratic scripts, and the verso written in Demotic with a few hieratic words interspersed. The two scripts correspond to different stages of the Egyptian language, hieratic reflecting the grammar and vocabulary in use since the second or third millennium B.C.E., and Demotic approximating what was spoken around the time the papyrus was written out in the late Ptolemaic or early Roman periods (late first century B.C.E. or early first century C.E.).

The papyrus, which Egyptologists refer to as the *Apis Embalming Ritual,* or P. Vindob. 3873, is in the collection of the Austrian National Library in Vienna. Its ancient Egyptian title is lost because the beginning of the papyrus, which formed the outer layer when it was rolled up, has not survived, meaning that approximately the first column of writing is missing. The text appears to be an incomplete copy of another, perhaps earlier manuscript; the scribe has left blank spaces where illustrations would go.[1] In ancient Egypt, ritual handbooks and other manuscripts were kept in the "house of life" (*per-ankh*) of temples, which was a library for priests and a training place for scribes. At the time this copy was made, Egyptian priests were engaged in studying, recording, and revising centuries of knowledge and practices contained in these scriptoria, with the aim of shoring up the temple as an institution under Greek and Roman rule and adapting the priesthood to the needs of a changing society.[2] How to wrap a mummy was vital knowledge for the temple to preserve.

The cult of the Apis bull was based at the ancient capital of Memphis, near Cairo. Only one Apis was alive at any time, and when it died, the priests installed a new calf whose sacred identity was revealed through its special markings and auspicious birth. The dead Apis was mummified and buried in an underground complex at Saqqara, in an area known as the Serapeum (after the related cult of the anthropomorphic god Serapis).[3] Since

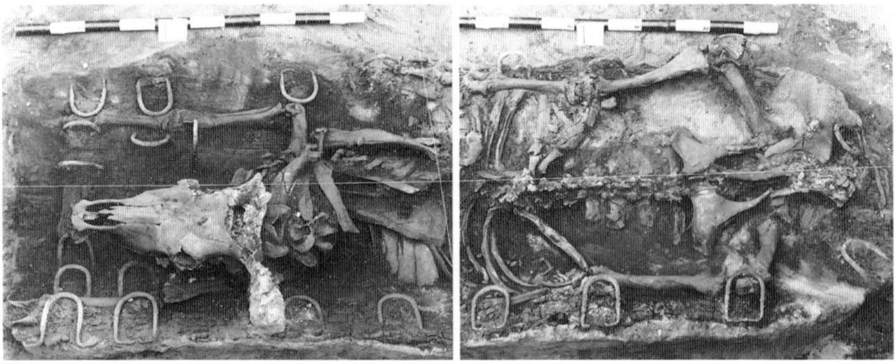

FIGURE 3.1 *Mummified bull from the Bucheum, with fixings to attach it to a carrying board. Roman period, 1st or 2nd century* C.E. *Copyright: The Egypt Exploration Society*

a bull can live for thirty years, embalming the Apis might well have been a once-in-a-lifetime event, and the ritual is remarkably precise in the guidance it gives to the practitioners. One practical difficulty they faced was the sheer size of the animal, as the Dutch editor of the papyrus discovered when he tried to recreate the procedural conditions in an Amsterdam abattoir using a carcass weighing nine hundred kilos.[4] Part of the instructions are therefore concerned with fixing the bull to a board with metal clamps, examples of which were found at the site of another bull cult, the Buchis at Armant (Fig. 3.1). The bull was placed on its abdomen with its forelegs and rear legs tucked under, its head upright and forward, and its tail wrapped around its right flank.

A closer consideration of this ritual text and its weighty carcass makes a good starting point for this chapter, but my interest lies in what the text does not include as much as what it does. Egyptological discussions of mummification exemplify what is sometimes referred to as the "whiggish" approach to history, "transplanting into the past the hidden or potential existence of the future," in the words of Latour.[5] With regard to Egyptian mummification, this happens in two ways—first by assuming a trajectory of development based on the assumption that the Egyptian embalmers' main aim was to keep the corpse in a lifelike state, and second by projecting into the ancient past the medical and scientific knowledge developed in the present, as if medical science were immune to time. In the last chapter, I explored the latter of these points in the context of the colonial era, and I will return to it again in Chapter 6. In this chapter, I tackle the first point, using textual and visual evidence from ancient Egypt to challenge the assumption that mummification developed in a linear fashion that can somehow be judged by the appearance of an unwrapped corpse. Instead, I argue that mummification is about materials and processes rather than preservation, and that thinking about mummification in this way offers an entirely different perspective on the ancient Egyptian worldview.

To return to the *Apis Embalming Ritual,* what it doesn't cover, and could not have addressed in the initial lost column, is the actual embalming of the body—that is, the removal of internal organs, desiccation in natron salt, and treatment with resins and oils, inside and out. These tasks required around fifty days, give or take a brief initial period of mourning and bathing the corpse, and took place in a structure called the "house of purification", according to information pieced together from other sources and suggested by the text itself. The so-called embalming ritual in the Vienna papyrus begins with the wrapping of the already prepared and preserved carcass. The wrapping required up to sixteen days and brought the total elapsed time since the bull's death to sixty-eight days. On Day 68, the bull was placed in its coffin and a cloth was torn outside of the embalming house, signaling the start of the final lamentations. Allowing another two days for the elaborate funeral rites, which included a procession around the temple's sacred lake, yielded seventy days from death to burial—an ideal number that was associated with the reappearance and disappearance of the decanal star groups on the horizon in the ancient Egyptian calendar.[6]

Rather than eviscerating, desiccating, and perfuming the corpse, what the *Apis Embalming Ritual* actually details is the elaborate process of wrapping it. This takes place in something called "the wrapping room," whose floor was covered with a two- by three-meter bank of pure desert sand. Over the sand, the most junior workers spread a papyrus mat and a sheet of linen, and only then did they fetch the priest who would oversee the wrapping. He is called the "master of secrets" (Egyptian *hery-seshta, ḥrỉ-sšt3,* which can also be translated as "overseer of the mysteries" or, in Greek, *stolistes,* "stolist"), and his four assistants are what Egyptologists call "lector-priests" (Egyptian *khery-heb, ẖrỉ-ḥb*), who are often shown in pictorial representations as if they are reading from a papyrus. All the men involved in the wrapping made themselves pure before undertaking the work—shaved, washed, censed, and dressed in fresh linen garments and papyrus sandals, and when they enter the wrapping room, they add a long, narrow band of linen, called the *pir,* around their necks.[7]

The list of materials required for the work was vast, comprising some three hundred jars, presumably containing oils and other salves or liquids for the process, plus an array of cloths, bandages, and small pads (six digits diameter, one and one-half digits thick), much of which the workers made or formed out of the supplies of textiles they had to hand. The text instructs the junior workers to rip sheets of linen in a continuous motion to make bandages measuring two fingers wide and two hundred cubits (more than a hundred meters) long; these were rolled onto pieces of wood in preparation for use. Linen chests, whose dimensions are specified in the text, held cloths called *nemes*-cloths required for the wrapping, and all the materials gathered were set on papyrus mats, keeping them separate even from the cloth-covered mat over the sand floor.[8] While the workers prepared these materials, two lengths of the finest quality "royal" linen, dyed blue, covered the carcass and the coffin.

The wrapping of the bull proceeded from head to tail. One of the *khery-heb* priests was responsible for dealing with the anal cavity, which he did while a large cloth entirely draped and covered both him and the carcass's rear end. For an animal that the ancient Egyptians identified with sexual virility, it is remarkable that no mention of the bull's sexual organs appears in the main version of the text, and only a possible reference to the scrotum and testicles, but not the penis, appears in the versions on the reverse.[9] Wrapping the face and the sensory organs was a priority, reiterated in both the hieratic and Demotic versions with slight alterations. The *hery-seshta* himself performed this stage of wrapping, which involved the application of ointment-soaked pads and up to sixteen passes of different cloths and bandages around the head, horns, neck, and chest.[10]

Different verbs distinguish the actions used to apply textiles. The action of wrapping, as in wrapping the bandages, is conveyed in the papyrus by the verb *wety* and, in one instance unique to this text, the verb *neten,* while the action of covering, used for the application of larger textiles or pads, uses the verb *djem* or *tjam.*[11] The same verbs appear in Egyptian medical texts concerned with bandaging wounds or limbs, and the verb *tjam* can also be translated as "to clothe" or "to veil." The word for fastening with a knot, *tjestjes,* occurs just once, in connection with *seben*-bandages used to secure other layers at the end of one wrapping stage. Otherwise the bandages are stretched taut and presumably held in place by gum, resinous oil, or the next bandage. The number of layers and revolutions prescribed may be significant as multiples of three (perfect plurality, in Egyptian thought) and four (associated, among other things, with the cardinal points). The finest quality of linen, including linen from the temple workshops of the goddess Neith, in the delta city of Sais, was always the first layer applied in contact with the body.

I have chosen this bull ritual as an introduction to mummification not only because it is the most extensive Egyptian source on the subject, but also because dealing with something other than a human body makes it easier to think about what mummification actually does. First, what was mummified? A sacred animal—an animal that was inherently special and that embodied the god on earth. Why was it mummified? Because it was sacred—the nature of the animal during its earthly existence made it fit for mummification, an explanation that most Egyptologists would be comfortable in putting forward. And what part of the mummification process has been written down at such length? The wrapping and anointing of what, in the text, is always referred to as "the god."

As we saw in Chapter 2, from the eighteenth century to the present day, Western responses to human mummies have been predicated on their human-ness. Thus the questions scholars have asked about mummification have either been questions related to the human sciences, such as race, gender, cause of death, and so on, or else have been questions framed around lifelikeness and preservation, clearly inspired by that direct confrontation with the unwrapped corpse in its often—though by no means always—uncanny state, familiar and strange at the same time. The concerns of a text like the Apis ritual, with its emphasis on what happens to the animal *after* its body has been emptied, dried, and "preserved," run counter to modern preoccupations with what happened to a human body immediately after death and what signs might be read from, or into, the body in its preserved state.

There are comparable papyri, preserved as three fragmentary rolls, that deal with human, rather than animal, bodies. They were written in hieratic with some Demotic notations and are of a similar date to the Apis papyrus, in the early first century C.E.[12] Like the Apis papyrus, these texts are known in English and other scholarly languages as the *Ritual of Embalming* or *Embalming Ritual*. They provide much less detail about the provision of materials involved in the rite, focusing instead on eleven acts of anointing and wrapping the corpse, including an instruction to wrap the internal organs and place them in canopic jars—one of many indications that these are copies of earlier texts since such jars were not used in the Roman period. The ritual combines two modes of expression: a brief instruction or description of how to anoint and wrap a specific body part, followed by a longer recitation or discussion that couches the action in the language of metaphor and myth. Like the Apis text, the *Ritual of Embalming* is written in the present tense; proceeds from head to foot, with the head being wrapped twice; and specifies linen from Sais for the first layer next to the skin. The practitioners involved were also similar, with some variation perhaps due to regional difference (the Apis text is from Saqqara, while the "human" versions seem to be from Thebes). The *hery-seshta* was once again in charge of the process, followed in rank by a priest known as the *hetemu-netjer* (*ḫtmw-nṯr*), translated as the "god's chancellor" or "god's seal-bearer." Next in rank was the *khery-heb* present in the Apis rite, and finally the workers known as the *wetiu*, the wrappers or bandagers.[13]

The most remarkable similarity between the human and the Apis embalming rituals is absence: what the texts do not say, rather than what they do. What happened to the corpse in the days and weeks between the moment of death and the commencement of the wrapping is not included, even if one allows for some missing space at the beginning of the scrolls. An argument from silence could assume the existence of some missing prequel, but it is just as likely that the absence is intentional, based on a difference, broadly speaking, between orality and literacy, and a range of forms that were used for transmitting knowledge within the bounds of cultural decorum. What seems significant is, first, that there are so few written sources that deal with any aspect of mummification at all, and second, that those that do are concerned not with the postmortem treatment and handling of the corpse, but with the wrapping. Egyptologists may have titled these papyri "embalming rituals," but the actual "embalming" is what the ancient sources seem to have remembered to forget.

Making Mummies, Making Gods

The ancient Egyptian silence in matters of mummification extends to pictorial representations as well. The process of wrapping a mummy is the subject of only two surviving depictions, both from Theban tombs of a similar date. The better of the two recorded scenes, rendered in a rather sketchy line drawing by the British Egyptologist Norman de Garis Davies, comes from a tomb made for the scribe Tjay in the nineteenth dynasty, around 1220 B.C.E. (Fig. 3.2).[14] The four equally sized scenes are half-height subdivisions of a register headed "Entering of the West by the scribe [Tjay]"; in Egyptian, the word for "entering" can also be read as "opening," and "the West," *Imentet,* was the land of the dead and the setting sun. Question marks in Davies's line drawing indicate the poor state of the scenes when he copied them, but the main elements are discernible. In each scene, a priest holding a rolled papyrus supervises men who are working on a supine form. The priest gestures with one hand in each scene, a sign that he is speaking, and this together with the papyrus identify him as the *khery-heb.*[15] The interior setting is suggested by a doorway in the bottom left corner. The presence of a linen chest, with its distinctive peaked roof, in three of the scenes indicates that textiles are involved, and in one scene, at top left, workers pass a narrow bandage around the supine form. The scene at the bottom left shows a cauldron for heating aromatic, resinated oil (labeled *merhet, mrḥt* in the hieroglyphs), which the workers brush onto the surface of the form from the small pots they hold in their hands.

The supine form takes the shape of what Egyptologists often call a "mummiform figure." It has smooth contours, without any separate limbs, and the head and face are shown with a beard, which is an iconographic feature worn by many gods and referred to in scholarship as a "divine" beard. The form also wears a wig or hair covering, which in Egyptian art is often painted solid blue, associating it with lapis lazuli, the substance that makes up the hair of the gods. This divine hair covering is described in Egyptology as "tripartite" because it has two blunt-ended, straight sides (lappets) that fall onto the chest, on either side of the neck, and a third section that hangs over the shoulders and down the back. If there is a sequence of action implied by the position of the four scenes relative to each other, it is difficult to establish with certainty since the decoration of a tomb or temple wall could read from left to right, like Egyptian writing, and depended on the orientation within a given room, the significance of a particular wall or feature, and sometimes, in the spaces of cramped tombs, happenstance. Together, the four scenes represent aspects or stages of preparing the corpse for burial—but the corpse itself is never shown. The work the men carry out, as they apply resin-rich oil and wrap the figure in linen, is depicted as

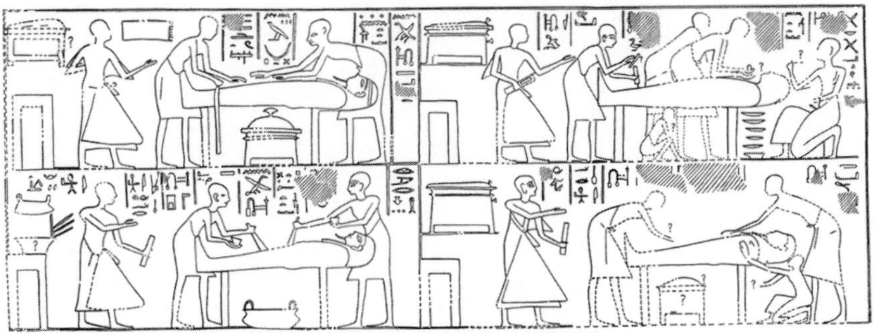

FIGURE 3.2 *Norman de Garis Davies, line drawing of wrapping scenes from the tomb of Tjay, Thebes (TT 23), 19th dynasty (c. 1220* B.C.E.*). After Dawson, "Making a Mummy," pl. xvii*

if it were being performed on the finished product. They are wrapping what is already wrapped.

The Tjay scenes make a stark contrast to the depiction of mummy unwrappings, used to commemorate or publicize these events in the late nineteenth century and beyond. Perhaps the most monumental of such images is a large-scale oil canvas painted in 1891 and said once to have been in the collection of the last ruler of the khedival line, King Fuad II (Fig. 3.3).[16] Titled *Examen d'une momie,* the painting presents the investigation of one of the twenty-first-dynasty mummies found by Eugène Grébaut at Deir el-Bahri during the years between the discoveries of the two royal caches. The artist was Paul Dominique Philippoteaux, who, like his father Henri Felix Philippoteaux, was a successful French painter of military and historical scenes. The younger Philippoteaux had been based for many years in the United States, where he created a vast panorama of the Battle of Gettysburg in 1883. The Gettysburg Cyclorama brought Philippoteaux such renown in the United States that the *New York Times* devoted half a column to his return to the country on November 14th, 1892, after two years spent in Egypt.[17]

Set in a gallery of the antiquities museum at Giza, *Examen d'une momie* shows the unwrapping of the mummy of a priestess named Ta-udja-ra, whose stiff corpse reclines on a wooden plank propped on trestles, like some parody of an odalisque. Wisps of cloth trail over her hip and thigh to hang in swathes over the edge of the plank, and her hands curve modestly over her pubic area. At the far left of the scene, the constrained and covered bodies of European women form a demure contrast; one wields a fan in the heat. Around the body of the priestess are eight European men whose active gestures, clear delineation, and bright colors contrast with the passive, hazy, grey and brown form of the mummy. In keeping with the Orientalist gaze, and genre of painting, indigenous figures occupy positions of distance and disinterest. An elderly man sits at the remote right edge of the painting, his view blocked by the backs of the European men in the foreground and his placid,

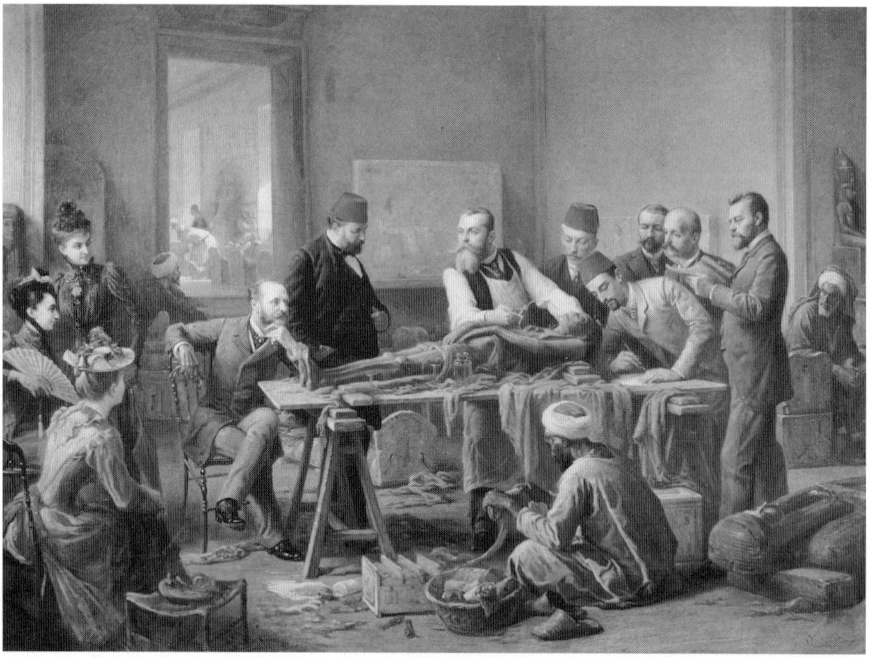

FIGURE 3.3 *Paul Dominique Philippoteaux,* Examen d'une momie *(1891). Oil on canvas, H. 183.0 cm, W. 274.5 cm. Private collection. Copyright: Peter Nahum at The Leicester Galleries, London/The Bridgeman Art Library*

seated pose a corruption of the royal statue just behind him. Cross-legged on the floor, his back to the viewer, another man in Arab gown and turban rolls up the unwrapped mummy bandages to store in the basket on his left. He shows no interest in what is happening on the wooden plank and, by extension, in the knowledge being generated there. Tidying away the ancient strips of linen, his work is the opposite of the Europeans', in every way.

The examination of Ta-udja-ra is the ostensible subject of the painting, but it would be more accurate to call it a group portrait of the men gathered around the table, who are identified by name and title on a plaque affixed to the painting's frame. The seated man at the far left is the Marquis de Reversaux, French consul to Egypt, and standing next to him is the discoverer Grébaut himself, then director of the antiquities service (while Maspero was back in France for family reasons). In a white apron and shirtsleeves is Dr. Daniel Marie Fouquet, who turns toward the seated women as if explaining a point while his hands hover over the body of the priestess. Next to Fouquet are Brugsch and Daressy, who, like Grébaut, wear the fez as signs of their employ in the Ottoman government. The three bare-headed men clustered at the right, around the head end of the mummy, are Bazil, secretary *complable* to the museum; Barois, French advisor to the Ministry of Public Works; and Egyptologist Urbain Bouriant, director of the French archaeological institute.

There are certain similarities between this painting and the Tjay tomb scenes: the inert passivity of the supine figure, the male activity and attention focused on it, the oratorial performance of the most authoritative man—the priest, or Dr. Fouquet—and, of course, the sacred space where each procedure takes place, one in a museum gallery, and the other perhaps in a wrapping room or what Egyptian funerary texts often term the *wabet,* or "pure place," where the process of creating a mummy took place. But the contrast between the rare tomb scene of wrapping a divine figure, and the rather ubiquitous representation of mummies in various states of unwrapping, exemplifies the gulf between ancient and modern ideas of what a mummy was and what it was for.

Over the course of the nineteenth and early twentieth centuries, examinations of mummies like Ta-udja-ra's had given scholars a pretty good idea of how the Egyptians embalmed and wrapped their dead. Mummies veered between predictability—a ten- to fifteen-millimeter incision in the left abdomen, plugs in the bodily orifices, and the alternation of narrow, wound bandages and large, covering shrouds—and uncertainty, which required further study and exemplification in order for empirical scholarship to progress. Were corpses packed dry in salt or brined in a salt bath? How to explain different positions of the limbs, the presence or absence of body hair, the quantity and character of resin, amulets, or linen? Each unwrapping held two possibilities: first, that it would add to the grander scheme of knowledge, and second, that it would yield information unique to that specimen, revealing the individual's sex, age at death, measurements, health, and treatment at the hands of the embalmers. Always uneasily categorized, the mummy was at once singular and generic.

Even the word *mummy* was, and is, unstable. Derived in medieval times from the Persian word *mūmiyā'ī* for bitumen—hence *mumia,* in most European languages—the word *mummy* applies equally to wrapped and unwrapped bodies and all the stages in between—and, as we have seen, to both humans and animals. Although mummification primarily refers to an artificial embalming method through which the dead body was dehydrated, there are "natural" mummies as well, desiccated through the dryness of an environment. This yields a certain ontological confusion, whereby a mummy might not be mummified after all.

A coffin in the shape of a smooth-contoured figure, with a "tripartite" head covering (or "divine headdress") and sometimes a "divine beard," can also evoke the category "mummy," and museum visitors often refer to such coffins as mummies whether or not they conceal a body. The old "mummy rooms" at the British Museum, uninstalled in the late 1990s, contained many more coffins than mummies, which is even more true of the same galleries today, and even museum staff can slip into category confusion. At the Manchester Museum, I noticed that education and conservation staff had long referred to one coffin lid, which was used for visiting school groups, as "the child mummy" even though they knew (and were relieved) that there was no body underneath it.

In medieval Egypt, the black coating on ancient, preserved bodies became associated with bitumen imported from the environs of the Dead Sea and, especially, Iraq. Bitumen was used to waterproof ships and was also thought to have medicinal properties, hence the grinding up of ancient bodies for this purpose in both Middle Eastern and European contexts.[18] The term *mumia*, or *mummy*, was metonymical, using a part to designate the whole, and since the "bitumen"—in fact, the black coating was usually resin-imbued oils—was on both the skin and the wrappings of the ancient bodies, what "whole" the part referred to was indistinct, whether corpse, wrappings, both, or neither. The word *mummification* likewise has ambiguous meanings, often within the same discussion or publication.[19] It refers to the drying and preservation of the corpse and also operates as a blanket term for all the processes carried out on the dead body, up to and including its anointing, wrapping, and adornment. *Embalming* and *mummification* are frequently interchanged, although the former refers in a strict sense only to the treatment of the corpse with spices or scented balms to preserve it, a meaning attested in English since the fourteenth century. Common use of the word *mummy* today has strong connotations of the embalmed corpse on its own, divested partially or completely of its wrappings. In nineteenth-century literature and twentieth-century films, this is the state in which the ancient creature terrorizes or seduces, and museum visitors confronted with wrapped mummies sometimes ask why they "can't see the mummy," by which they must mean the corpse. Hence my own use of the phrases "wrapped mummy" or "intact mummy" is an attempt to differentiate these from "unwrapped mummy," "corpse," or "embalmed body" in this book.

The ancient Egyptian language was considerably more precise. From at least the eighteenth dynasty (around 1500 B.C.E.), and almost certainly with earlier roots, the word *sah* (*sʿḥ*) applied to a wrapped figure wearing the divine head covering and beard. This is the word Egyptologists generally translate as "mummy." *Sah* did not apply to a corpse, whether embalmed or not. Instead, the dead body was the *khat* (*ẖ3t*) or, once it had been embalmed, the *djet* (*ḏt*), which was a homonym for "eternity."[20] Thus the supine figure in the Tjay tomb scenes, which superficially resembles a style of coffin, is better understood as the wrapped mummy, or *sah*, to which workmen applied linen and oil while the *khery-heb* presided. The shrouded contours and masked head of the *sah* are associated with divinity in Egyptian art—and the use of textiles, wrapping, and padding all helped produce this outer form. Where modern, "scientific" approaches to the mummy have needed to strip away the exterior, at any cost, to reach the inner core, the original Egyptian practice was the reverse, swaddling a larva-like body to generate the *sah*. What the anatomists and archaeologists had sliced, unpeeled, and chiseled away was its cocoon.

To modern, Western ways of thinking, the notion that a "human" body can be a god, or god-like, is uncomfortable, even improbable. That there was something inherently special about the individuals who were mummified, as there was for the Apis bull, is suggested by the fact that only a small portion of the population received such treatment and that it is best attested among royalty, priests, and high officials. Membership of certain social groups, whether based on kinship, rank, or other factors, was a prerequisite for mummification, more so than any cost implications—social strictures are as effective a check on action as is expense. Those individuals who were elaborately embalmed and wrapped were in some sense god-like, supra-human, in their own lifetimes—an aristocracy or higher caste, so to speak. Care taken over the mummification of children and young adults at some time periods (the Roman period, for instance) suggests that untimely death may have been an additional factor in meriting special treatment, but the deceased in these instances seem already to have been members of an elite.[21] The mass of the population experienced much humbler treatment, in burials that have not survived or have gone unremarked—for instance, as mixed skeletal remains in larger cemeteries.[22]

Ancient Egypt was not an egalitarian society, and the lives of its poor are as lost to us as their deaths. "Daily life" along the Nile has been a favored theme of late twentieth- and early twenty-first-century museum displays, often paired with "Death and the afterlife," yet the material used to exemplify the everyday often derives from elite burials, with the exception of tools, implements, and pottery found in a few settlement or construction sites. The reverence in which a privileged class might be held, without question, may seem alien in our own era of easy "celebrity"; however, parallels in our own and other societies exist, from the "blue blood" aristocracy of prewar Europe, to the Brahmins of the Indian subcontinent, to the spiritual leaders, and their descendants, honored by Sufi brotherhoods in Mali and Senegal.[23]

If the living can be sacred, so can the dead. Still, scholarship has tended to downplay or deny the embodied divinity of the mummy itself, for instance by reasoning that it is a shell to which the spirit periodically returns in the form of the *ba*-soul, represented as a bird with a head that is variously "human" or divine (that is, wearing the divine head covering), suggesting that the iconographic distinction Egyptologists make here was not necessarily made in antiquity. But the Egyptian evidence seems quite clear in its own reasoning that the mummy was a god, and that wrapping was an integral part of making and keeping it sacred.

Having removed all the wrapping, investigators were left with what seemed to be a remarkably well-preserved corpse, at least for certain bodies, at certain periods of Egyptian history. Fascination with the method of embalming, and its eerie results, has led Egyptologists, and others, to focus on the efficacy of preservation and the perceived simulation of lifelikeness.[24] The usual interpretation of mummification, which has been offered ad nauseum in books, in museum displays, and now on the Internet and television, is that the aim of the process was to preserve the body in a lifelike manner so that the soul could recognize and return to it. If we adhere to this interpretation, we are faced with a number of issues that remain unarticulated and unexplored. We are also faced with serious methodological problems, in particular the creation of a chronological narrative of evolution whereby the technique of mummification was born, developed, flourished, and declined.

According to the usual interpretation, mummification was "discovered" in prehistory when people somehow noticed that bodies buried in the desert sand had dried out. People then developed techniques that "improved" over nearly two thousand years, experimenting through trial and, usually, error, since very few fleshed bodies have been found prior to the Middle Kingdom (around 1800 B.C.E.). Mummification then "peaked" when the "best," most "lifelike" mummies were created around the New Kingdom and twenty-first dynasty. According to one version of this narrative, mummification then fell into a "decline" sometime in the Late Period before dying out altogether in Roman times—exactly when documentary evidence of the mummification industry survives, as well as the papyri with wrapping instructions.[25] The supposed decline of mummification and other cultural expressions in the Late Period is a holdover from late nineteenth- and early twentieth-century historiography, which held that indigenous Egyptian culture (and the population) became diluted by foreign contact and invasions, echoing a deeply ingrained fear in contemporaneous colonial discourse.

This narrative depends entirely on modern perceptions of what the bared corpse looks like. The scholarly literature does, of course, recognize that the application of embalming techniques depended on a range of factors, and different techniques existed at any given time period. Not everyone was embalmed, for one thing—not by any means—nor is it unusual to find wrappings that contain skeletonized remains buried alongside well-mummified bodies.[26] Still, the narrative I have traced here has been influential not only in popular treatments of ancient Egypt, but in academic resources as well: the authoritative 1970s *Lexikon der Ägyptologie* and a new online *Encyclopedia of Egyptology* both interpret the practice of mummification primarily as an exercise in preservation and resemblance.[27]

The difficulty lies in just how much evidence this interpretation excludes. It offers no way of thinking about other manipulations of the corpse, such as elite burials in the Predynastic and Early Dynastic periods that display decapitation, dismembering, and de-fleshing.[28] Even at the purported high-point of mummification in the twenty-first dynasty, a carefully wrapped body might show little or no trace of intervention with the corpse: if lifelike preservation was the goal, then the fact that the mummy of princess Henattawy was "just wrapped in bandages" becomes "difficult to explain, given the very high quality of her coffins."[29] To fit the accepted interpretation of mummification, any sign of decomposition must be taken as anomalous. Bodies that are rearranged, incomplete, skeletonized, or that turn out to be bundles of mixed bones and other materials are read as signs of error, incompetence, or dishonesty, with the ancient embalmers Orientalized as lazy, greedy opportunists. It is the European fascination with unwrapped mummies that has prioritized the encounter with ancient, fleshed bodies, particularly those in an extended position, which lent themselves so well to anatomical investigation.

From the marvel of such preservation, scholarship has deduced that maintaining the "lifelike" appearance of an individual human body was the goal.

However, viewing mummification as a performative, materials-based process suggests quite a different interpretation, and a more open-ended result—namely, a fundamental transformation of the human body's own materiality. From Egyptian prehistory to late antiquity, the action of wrapping, the use of linen as a wrapping material, and the application of natron salt and resin provide a common denominator, although I would emphasize that no discussion of such a complex and long-lived cultural phenomenon should assume any kind of fixed, unchanging idea. My point is that focusing on the state of the corpse is a modern, not an ancient, proclivity.

The mummification of animals, like the Apis, again may make it easier to see why resemblance to a living creature was not the be-all and end-all of the technique. Many animal mummies had the tendons in their hind legs cut so that they could be posed like a recumbent statue, right down to having the tail curled, sphinx-like, around the proper right side of the body. In other words, the mummy was carefully crafted not so much to "look like" a bull, but to look like an image of a bull, inside, in terms of the posing of the body, and outside, with its wraps in place, like any sacred image needed (Fig. 3.4). Other animal mummies had their limbs, wings, or heads tucked in to form a compact bundle, which was then wrapped with exquisite care, while a number of mummified falcons were wrapped to resemble upright humans, recalling the composite falcon-human form of the sun god Re.[30]

The mimetic effect of mummification is what we might think of as "magical mimesis," to borrow another phrase from Taussig.[31] The copy or simulacrum exists to fulfill a magical and spiritual role, and its effectiveness as a copy needs to be judged accordingly. The fidelity of a mummy's replication is not in its resemblance to a human, but its resemblance to what the human had become: an image fit for veneration.

In Egyptian religion, gods had multiple manifestations, and the more powerful the god, the greater the number of visible and invisible forms in which he or she could be detected by the human senses. Egyptian art represented the gods in human, animal, or hybrid form, not because they "looked" that way, but as one convention for materializing the immaterial.[32] Their splendid difference was signaled by shining skin, blue-black hair, kohl-rimmed eyes, feathered wings and garments, multicolored linen wraps and sashes, handheld attributes, and hieroglyphs incorporated into or surrounding them like emblems. Many of these same features appear on coffins and masks, manifesting the god-like status of the dead, but godliness was more than skin deep. Here is a way to rotate the object world constituted by the Egyptian mummy: suppose that the state of preservation that characterizes many mummified bodies, especially those dating from the New Kingdom to the Roman period, was not so much the goal but the by-product of processes that were carried out on the body to make it less human, more divine.

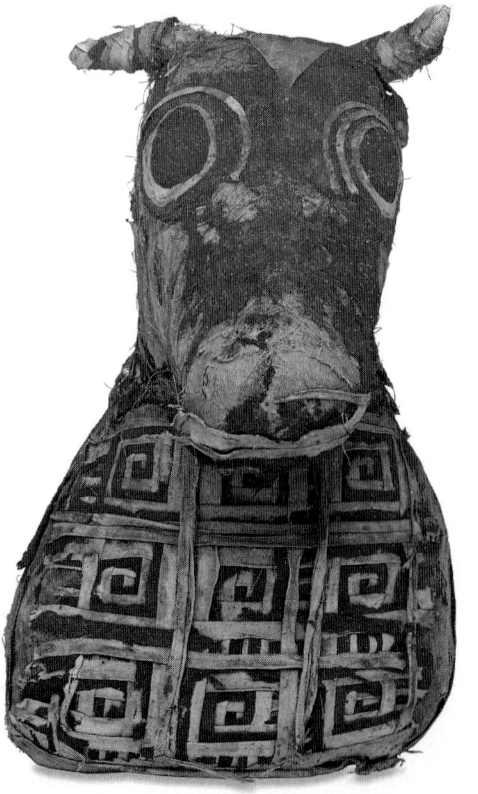

FIGURE 3.4 *Wrapped mummy of a bull calf, acquired at Thebes by Henry Salt in 1821. H. 45.7 cm, L. 73.7 cm. Roman Period, 1st or 2nd century* C.E. *British Museum, EA 6773. Copyright: The Trustees of the British Museum*

Purity and Perfection

Your purity is the purity of the gods.
Purify your limbs. You will be purified.
Pure, pure, pure, pure.

Opening of the Mouth, Scenes 4 and 6 (extracts), after E. Otto, *Das ägyptische Mundöffnungsritual* (1960), pp. 44–50

The aforementioned lines are typical passages from the long textual tradition attached to the rite of *Opening the Mouth,* spoken by the leopard-skin priest, or *sem,* as he fumigates the mummy with incense, anoints it with oil, and daubs it with natron salt and holy water. Purity was clearly a concern.

As the anthropologist Mary Douglas demonstrated almost half a century ago, in her classic study *Purity and Danger,* notions of purity and pollution operate on several levels within a given cultural system, defining group membership, encouraging social cohesion, and articulating values and structures that might otherwise operate unseen. In response to Douglas, other anthropologists, like Valeri, have emphasized that ideas about pollution arise out of social needs in the first instance, which is why taxonomies of pollutants may be inconsistent and methods of purification symbolic, rather than functional.[33] To those outside the system, what is required for purity or condemned as taboo can seem strange and thus noteworthy—and Greek and Roman writers had plenty to say about Egyptian practices related to cleanliness or pollution. In the fifth century B.C.E., Herodotus claimed that "almost all Egyptian customs and practices are the opposite of those of everywhere else." He was struck in particular by dietary laws, circumcision (which he thought was universal), and the regulations attached to the priesthood. Priests wore linen garments and papyrus sandals, shaved their body hair, abstained from eating fish and beans, washed in cold water twice a day and twice in the night, and, he wrote, "practice thousands upon thousands of other religious observances" (*Histories* II.35–37).

To Herodotus, mummification was one oddity among many others he witnessed in Egyptian society. His description of what was done to embalm a corpse is frequently cited and complements the evidence yielded by investigations of mummified bodies. He described three methods based on cost, the most expensive of which entailed excerebrating and eviscerating the corpse, cleaning it with palm wine and spices, filling the abdomen with myrrh, packing the body in natron for seventy days, and wrapping it in gummed linen bandages, about which he had nothing more to say. In the second procedure Herodotus described, a wood oil—often said to be cedar but probably a form of turpentine—was injected into the corpse through the anus and was retained for several days to dissolve the internal organs, while natron desiccated the flesh. For this and the third method, which involved flushing the abdominal cavity with myrrh, Herodotus made no mention of wrappings.

Writing in the first century B.C.E., and familiar with Herodotus's account, Diodorus Siculus offered a similar, three-tiered version of embalming and marveled at the result of the best-preserved bodies, which he said left the corpse so "unchanged" that "even the hair on the eyelids and brows remains." Diodorus also characterized the embalmers as "skilled artisans who have received this professional knowledge as a family tradition. [They] are considered worthy of every honor and consideration, associating with the priests and even coming and going in the temples without hindrance, as being undefiled" (*Bibliotheca Historica* I.91). Among the embalmers, Diodorus singled out two men whose task was first to draw and then to cut the abdominal incision in the body with a flint or obsidian knife. The man who made the first cut in the abdomen was the "slitter" (*paraschistes* in Greek, from a verb meaning to rip lengthwise, tear, or rend), and once he had made the incision, he performed a flight from the scene while the others hurled stones and curses after him "to turn the profanation on his head," as Diodorus puts it. Violence towards a body, he explained, was anathema to the Egyptians.

Herodotus and Diodorus identified two of the key ingredients used in embalming, traces of which have been found in mummified remains—natron and myrrh. But neither author commented on the cultural significance of these materials, which were purposefully chosen and culturally weighted. Myrrh is the resin of the *Commiphora myrrha* tree native to Yemen, Somalia, and Ethiopia.[34] Myrrh and other resins were rare and expensive imports used extensively in religious ritual. Temples employed perfumers, that is, resin-preparers, whose title derived from the Egyptian word for myrrh, *antu*.[35] The incense burned to cleanse the air was often frankincense, the resin of the *Boswellia* shrub (*Boswellia sacra* or *papyrifera,* found in Somalia, Arabia, Ethiopia, and Sudan), and the Egyptian word for incense, *senetjer,* has the literal translation, "to make divine."[36]

Natron likewise has the word for "god" or "divine," *netjer,* at its root: the Egyptian name for it was *netjery,* whose vocalized consonants n-t-r are preserved in ancient Greek (*nitron*), Arabic (*natrun*), and thence English and other European languages. Natron occurs in depressions in the Wadi Natrun, northwest of Cairo, and is also found in Ethiopia, Niger, and the shores of Lake Chad. Natron is a hydrous sodium carbonate consisting of sodium bicarbonate, sodium carbonate, sodium sulphate, and sodium chloride. It makes an effective preservative for foodstuffs and was also used as a detergent and mild bleaching agent. Its desiccating, cleansing, and whitening properties can all be said to contribute to its purifying character.

Like living bodies, dead bodies were washed and sometimes shaved to remove pollution, and for some, the cleansing and purging of the corpse extended to the removal of the brain and internal organs. Often explained in Egyptology as a way to stave off decomposition, the removal of the brain and organs was not performed, or was not performed completely, on every mummified body that survives. This suggests evisceration was not essential for effective preservation. The practice only became widespread in the late Middle Kingdom, and the earliest evidence for it is unclear, since Old Kingdom boxes or recesses often identified as canopic—that is, precursors of the four headed jars later associated with the internal organs—in fact are either empty or contain linen packets with traces of resin or other ritually significant materials.[37] When it was practiced, the value of evisceration lay instead in removing a source of pollution, an effect that could be obtained symbolically by other methods—for instance, by removing only part of the contents, extracting them through the rectum, or doing nothing at all.

Cutting into the body was a dangerous operation because it breached the boundary between internal and external, pure and impure: thus Diodorus's anecdote about the treatment doled out to the "slitter" who made the first cut. The knife used to make the incision was obsidian or flint, materials that had magical, otherworldly powers in addition to being suitably sharp.[38] Also significant was the consistent position of the slit on the left side of the body, angled downward, which may have forced the embalmer to favor his left hand when extracting the organs.[39] Mummies dating from the New Kingdom to the Late Period sometimes have an obsidian or dark stone amulet in the form of two fingers extended together; placed among the wrappings, usually near the site of the abdominal incision, the fingers may represent the fingers of the embalmer, converting the mode of intrusion into a protective device.[40]

The brain was removed by piercing the ethmoid bone through the left nostril as well—thus, the left side of the body was the site for invasive procedures and was probably considered inferior to the right. To complete the embalming process, before the wrapping could begin, the embalmers washed the body inside and out and sealed every orifice—eyes, nose, mouth, ears, and anus—with wax or linen plugs; a thin gold (or gilded) plate sometimes covered the abdominal incision. On female mummies, manipulations of the genitals, such as stitching or pulling together the labia, also represent an attempt to close off the purified interior of the body.[41]

The embalming rituals preserved on papyri pick up, as it were, where Herodotus and Diodorus left off—with the wrapping of the body, or, as the texts put it, the wrapping of the god. In the Apis ritual, the priests and bandagers must first remove plugs and packing materials from the animal's body, replacing these with fresh plugs and covers of pure linen soaked in resinous oil. The first stage of the treatment of the bull, after the priests have brought it into the wrapping room, reads as follows:

> The lector-priest sits before the master of secrets. He [apparently the master of secrets] opens the mouth of the god. He puts his hand in its [the bull's] mouth as far as it can reach; he takes away the *hebes*-cloths and everything he may find in the mouth, and he covers the inside of the mouth thoroughly with *hebes*-cloth.... He puts a big bag filled with myrrh under its tongue. He covers its tongue with *hebes*-cloth soaked in *segen*-ointment, and he swathes it at its front with three *pir*-bandages. One goes up, and another is directed upwards over it.[42]

The passage continues, describing how six other *hebes*-cloths were wrapped around the upper and lower jaw. The whole sequence was then repeated before the embalmers moved on to the eye sockets; nose; horns; the "mysterious face," which required especial care; and finally the limbs, anus, and tail.

In the Apis text, *hebes* (Egyptian *ḥbs*), which is one of the most widely used words for cloth, seems to denote a more substantial, rectangular piece of textile, while the *pir*-bandages are narrow bands, but not the same as the long strips torn from larger sheets that were part of the initial preparations, which are called *nebty* bandages. Other bandages mentioned in the text are the *seben,* the *geba,* and the *seker.* The *seweh* (*swḥ*), *benet,* and *kheret* (*ḫrt*) cloths complete the repertoire of larger pieces or pads, whose quality is sometimes specified. For instance, a *kheret*-cloth of best-quality "royal" linen was added as a final layer over the wrapped mummy before it was carefully lowered into its coffin.[43]

In the *Ritual of Embalming* concerned with human mummies, some of the same terms occur, including the word *hebes* to refer to lengths or sheets of cloth, and the *pir*-bandages, which are the first layer applied to the hands and legs and are accordingly made of royal linen. The workers who assist the priests are termed the *wetiu,* or bandagers, from the generic word for a bandage, *wet.* The word *wet* designates a bandage in magical-medical prescriptions, which give instructions for the use of salves and incantations to accompany the circular, smoothing motion of wrapping the bandages, all of which contributed to the restorative process. The parallel between wrapping the embalmed corpse and wrapping a wound echoes the observations of surgeons like Greenhill, Granville, and Pettigrew, and there are certain conceptual links between mummification and magical-medical care. Healing was a compelling metaphor for the rebirth of the dead: just as something new (fresh skin or a set bone) appeared out of something damaged or disrupted after a healer's treatment, so too did the embalmed and wrapped body appear whole and healthy—but to make it godlike, not lifelike. The perfection of the corpse was the result of its purification and its material transformation, completed by its layers of textiles and other adornments. Other terms derived from *wet,* and distinguished in writing by different classifier signs at the end of each word, referred variously to the wrapped body or (with a "wood" classifier) the contoured, so-called mummiform coffins that began to be produced in the late Middle Kingdom.[44] The terms based on *wet* differed from the word *sah* in that they had a concrete, physical origin in the bandages through which the outer, bundled form was produced. The body or image at its core could not exist in isolation. It was, in a literal sense, "that which is bandaged", or simply "the wrapped."

The Mummy and the Statue

> Speech of the lector-priest: *Sem,* take the *nemes*-cloth, dress [the mummy] with the *nemes*-cloth, sweep out the mouth and the eyes, open the mouth and the eyes of [name of the deceased] once with it. Speech: Oh, [name of the deceased]! The *nemes* comes, the *nemes* comes. The whiteness comes, the whiteness comes. The Horus-eye comes, the whiteness comes, which comes forth from el-Kab. It dresses the gods in its name "*nemes.*" It dresses you, it adorns you, in its name "whiteness, which comes forth from el-Kab." Oh [name of the deceased]! Take to yourself the Horus-eye. Things harmful to you on the earth will be swept out.
>
> *Opening of the Mouth*, Scene 48, after E. Otto, *Das ägyptische Mundöffnungsritual* (1960), pp. 110–11

To find a parallel for purifying, anointing, and wrapping a body, we need only look to the treatment of cult statues, which lay at the heart of Egyptian religious practice. The similarity between mummies and cult statues has been often remarked upon but little discussed.[45] The similarity is no accident, nor a subsidiary development from the ostensible quest to preserve the body. Rather, the synergy between the mummy and the statue is the most significant factor in mummification, which in turn demonstrates the centrality of statue cults in ancient Egyptian society.[46] Throughout its effective existence, the cult statue received daily rites to clean, perfume, feed, dress, and entertain it. Statues made the gods manifest: the statue was the god, yet this belief is so alien, or abhorrent, to Judeo-Christian tradition that scholarship has skirted around it, speaking instead of the divine spirit inhabiting an image, or retreating to the (seemingly) safer ground of mimetic resemblance.[47] This ambivalence toward statues being not just divine, but active and alive, echoes the resistance to seeing mummies, or at least human mummies, as in any way sacred or divine as well.

But statues led busy lives: they were born, not made, and eventually, they might die and require a proper burial themselves as their physical substance wore out and their powers waned. Statues came into existence wholly formed, not manufactured by craftsmen. The act of sculpting was known as "causing" or "giving" life, subsuming the skill of chiseling, carving, and polishing into a metaphor of birth. Ancient sources refer rather obliquely to the physical processes involved in making images, in the same way that embalming the body was a point of silence.

Thought of in terms of smoothness, density, surface, and sheen, the bare, embalmed body in fact shares a number of physical characteristics with sculpted wood—the core material of cult statues, which were then encased in a metal "skin" and adorned with their clothing, crowns, and jewelry. The dowelling of limbs onto wooden statue bodies may be analogous to the piecing together of body parts that concerns so many Egyptian funerary texts, raising the possibility that the very idea of what constitutes a body, human or divine, owed some debt to the practice of manipulating and wrapping either a statue or a corpse. Egyptologists have interpreted such texts as part of the mythology of Osiris, the murdered god-king whose dismembered body parts were reassembled by Isis and mummified by Anubis.[48] The dismembering of Osiris, however, is another absence in Egyptian sources. Although Egyptian rituals and recitations from the Old Kingdom onward describe various bodies—king, god, deceased—being rejoined, head to neck and limbs to torso, Plutarch's *De Iside et Osiride,* written in the early second century C.E., is the only narrative version of the myth, and projecting it backward in time has yielded the teleology that the mummification of the dead apes the mummification of Osiris. But myths come after human behavior, not before, and a more productive way of thinking about the resonances between mummification, cult images, and the mythic body of Osiris is to think of them all as part of a continuum of statue worship, which used the material world to conjure the immaterial. Since the gods have bodies made (on earth) of metal-covered wood, then the body of the deceased, who becomes a god, must also be durable in its earthly form, made to share the material qualities of the cult statue.

During the embalming process, desiccation changed the texture, color, and flexibility of the body. The dehydrated skin, flesh, and underlying bones were lighter in weight and denser in feel, like soft woods. Unless they are packed solid with resin, unwrapped mummies weigh very little, and the incorporation of packing materials helped give both shape and heft to the prepared corpse, perhaps mimicking harder woods and other sculptural materials. Among the New Kingdom royal mummies, Amenhotep III had a subcutaneous layer of resin in his limbs and along his neck, creating a "stony hardness," while the twenty-first-dynasty mummy of an elderly woman named Nesit-khonsu, emaciated at the time of death, had its thighs plumped with sand that had been introduced through the abdominal cavity and under the skin, as well as linen padding in the chest to round out the breasts, a practice Elliot Smith attributed to "the vanity of the deceased."[49]

To the firm, dry, and stiffened texture of the embalmed body, the applications of resin and oils—the *mumia*—gave the skin a shine or gloss, emphasizing its smoothness, color, and fresh, shining quality. In the Roman period, gold leaf was applied to the surface, making it gold like the skin of the gods, while earlier mummies, like the twenty-first-dynasty rulers and priestly families buried at Deir el-Bahri, had layers of pigment coating the skin, down to the genitals of the male mummies. In keeping with the conventions of Egyptian art, the male mummies were coated in red pigment, and the female mummies in yellow, both of which derived from ochre.[50]

The arm positions and hand gestures of mummies sometimes echoed those observed in sculpture, too. The single or double cross-arm posture of the royal, male mummies echoed sculptural depictions of kings, and of the god-king Osiris, holding royal insignia. On the mummy of the nineteenth-dynasty ruler Siptah (c. 1204–1198 B.C.E.), the bandages and resin over its damaged right forearm had a depression with traces of gilding, which Elliot Smith surmised was the impression left by just such an item, seized by thieves.[51] Some female mummies had one bent and one extended arm, corresponding to the "fly whisk" pose that came into wider use for images of women after the New Kingdom.[52] The Late Period mummy that Granville unwrapped had the arms crossed right over left, with the left hand clenched in a fist around a twist of resin-soaked linen—an instruction given in the *Ritual of Embalming* and a gesture that evokes sculptural and pictorial representations in which the subject holds a piece of cloth in one hand, usually by the side of the body or resting on one knee. On a mummy, the cloth may be a substitute for other handheld attributes, but the fact that it is a piece of textile, and hence identical to the cloth that appears in sculpture and painting, may also suggest that all these images (including the posed corpse) refer to the role of textiles as signs of the sacred.

The clearest indication that ancient Egyptian religion equated the mummy and the cult statue is the rite of *Opening of the Mouth*, which was performed on both. The title is a translation of its Egyptian name, *wepet-re,* and the symbolic "opening" of the image was depicted pictorially when the ritualist, dressed in a leopard skin, touched the mummy or statue with a carpenter's adze, representing the manufacturing process that could not be represented. Like the wrapping, the *Opening of the Mouth* took place in a state of purity and on a bed of sand—indicated in some pictorial representations, such as the *Book of the Dead* made for Hunefer, by the stippled texture under the upright mummy and its bright white tomb and stela (Fig. 3.5).

Attested in nonroyal tomb inscriptions from at least the fourth dynasty (around 2500 B.C.E.), the *Opening of the Mouth* likely had even earlier origins.[53] Much academic ink has been spilled over whether the *Opening of the Mouth* was a statue rite or a funerary rite, but the identification of statue with mummy and vice versa makes this a moot point. At the core of the rite are the processes and recitations that the statue and the mummy receive: its purification with incense, water, and natron; the presentation of offerings, including the heart and leg of a slaughtered calf; and adorning the image with scented oils and linen textiles. Versions of the ceremony were performed on a range of sacred objects and buildings, as well, because the ritual "opens" the sensory organs, and hence magical efficacy, of whatever it is performed upon.

Otto's edition, based primarily on a long, illustrated version in the eighteenth-dynasty tomb of a high-ranking official named Rekhmire, divided the ritual into seventy-five individual components, which he termed "scenes."[54] Whether these scenes imply any kind of order, or even represent a single ritual, is far from clear, and in any case, actual performances would have entailed overlaps, elisions, and adaptations based on the circumstances and the expertise of the ritualist. In addition to the adze, the rite makes use of a flint knife called the *pesesh-kef,* whose distinctive forked end was used to cut the umbilical cord of newborn babies, and two slim stone blades, the *netjerwy*-knives, perhaps referring to the use of a little finger to clear a newborn's mouth.[55] Interpreting the *Opening of the Mouth* as a ritual that evokes birth and infancy, and that brings the quotidian into the realm of the divine, complements the use of the rite at the "birth" of statues, mummies, or other sacred objects.

In the *Opening of the Mouth,* the lead ritualist is the *sem*-priest, whom the ritual structure designates as the son of the rite's recipient. The father-son relationship was a structuring metaphor in a number of Egyptian rites and occurs in several priestly titles, such as the "god's father," *it-netjer.* Although Egyptologists refer to the *sem* as a priest, the role appears to be situational, rather than part of an established priesthood, and as such may sometimes have been taken on by nonspecialists, with appropriate guidance—hence passages in the rite concerned with dressing the image call for the lector-priest (*khery-heb*) to instruct the *sem.*[56] Tomb scenes and

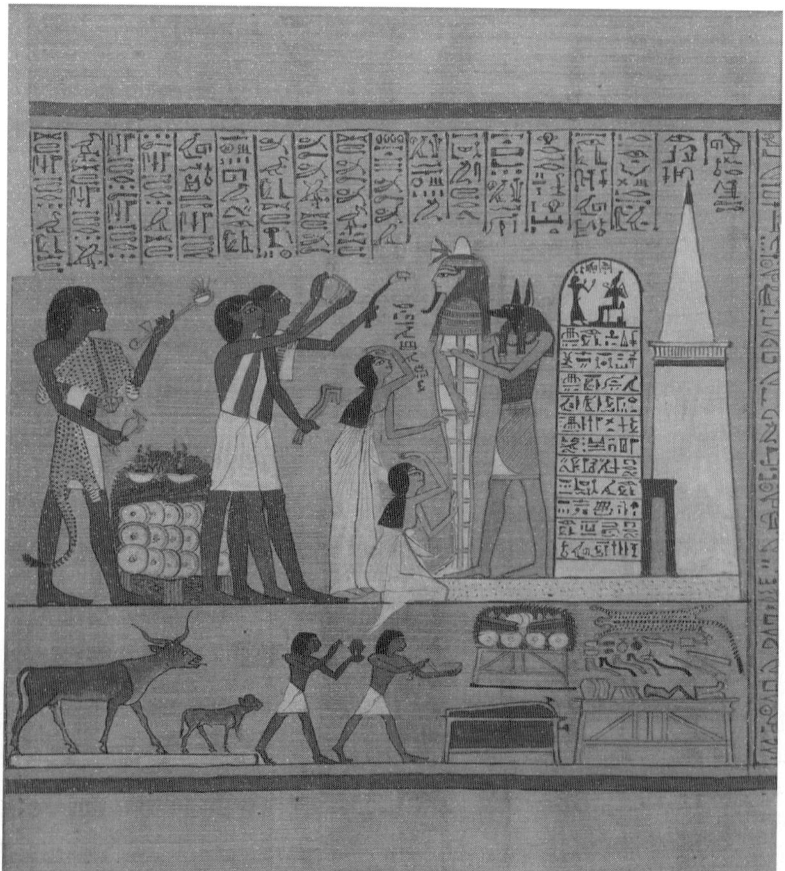

FIGURE 3.5 Opening of the Mouth *ritual from the* Book of the Dead *papyrus made for Hunefer, from Thebes, 19th Dynasty (c. 1285* B.C.E.*). H. 40.0 cm. British Museum, EA 9901, Sheet 5. Copyright: The Trustees of the British Museum*

commemorative stelae depict male subordinates of the deceased carrying out the role of *sem*, and in the tomb of Tutankhamun, it is his successor, Ay, who was not a kinsman, who performs the *Opening of the Mouth* on the dead king (Fig. 3.6).[57] The *sem* is one of a handful of Egyptian ritualists who wears a leopard skin, with its connotations of magical birth and rebirth.[58] For statue and mummy alike, the *Opening of the Mouth* marked a birth: the appearance in the world of something that had not existed before in that particular form. This newly extant form embodied the divine and took physical shape—dry, stiff, sound, and shining—amid the sanctity of perfumed resin and incense, cleansing water and natron, and the all-enveloping linen that gathered together its limbs like the swaddling clothes that soothed and stilled a newborn.

Mimesis and Mummification

Much of the evidence used to discuss embalming and wrapping techniques dates from the mid-second millennium B.C.E. up to the Roman period. This is a time span that encompasses not only the most well-preserved bodies, which have captured popular and scientific attention, but also those bodies finished in a consistent outer form and depicted in all pictorial representation, including hieroglyphic writing, like the central figure in the Hunefer papyrus (see Fig. 3.5)—the form that seems to be known as the *sah,* or sometimes the *wet.*

In written sources, the first use of the word *sah* to refer to the cocoon-like outer form dates to the beginning of the New Kingdom but almost certainly has more ancient roots, although how ancient is impossible to say. The word occurs in the Theban tomb of Puyemre in a text whose style suggests that it predates this early eighteenth-dynasty prayer, where it was inserted into the usual list of offerings for the dead: "May he [that is, the god] cause the *sah* to be *akh,* together with his monument."[59] To be *akh* was to be transformed into a being of light and power, variously translated as "glorified," "honored," or "venerated," and in the Puyemre prayer, the *sah* and other manifestations of the deceased (his "monument," or offering stela) are to be imbued with this divine quality.[60] Much later usages likewise identify the *sah* as a form to be venerated and receive offerings. In the late fourth-century B.C.E. tomb of Petosiris, who was an important priest of Thoth at Hermopolis, the deceased declares:

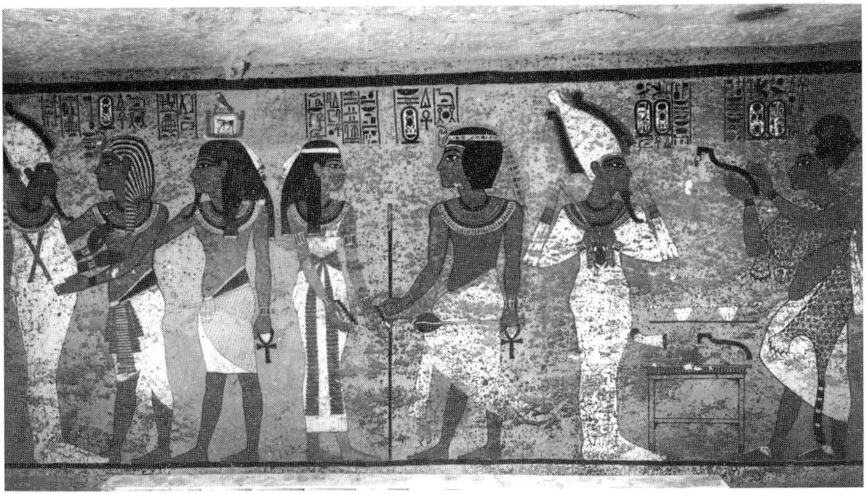

FIGURE 3.6 *Wall painting in the burial chamber of the tomb of Tutankhamun, with Ay at far right performing the* Opening of the Mouth *before the king. Photograph by Harry Burton. Copyright: Griffith Institute, University of Oxford*

> I am a *sah* who merits the making of sacrifices...so that my name will be pronounced after my death....I am a *sah* who merits veneration, because I have not done ill to men, I have not stolen, I am true of heart.[61]

The *sah* could also intercede between supplicants and temple gods, hence inscriptions on a Late Period statue, originally set up in the temple of the ram god of Mendes, describe the subject as "a *sah* for him who offers to him, who speaks (a prayer) for him," encouraging viewers to pray to the sculpture.[62]

The final, silent hieroglyph in the writing of *sah* is a wrapped body with a human face and divine headdress and beard, drawn in profile: . This "mummiform" hieroglyph first appeared as a classifier for the earlier word *tut (twt)*, meaning statue or image—the name Tutankhamun, for instance, reads "living image of Amun." *Tut* is a very old word, used in the Old Kingdom to designate any male statue, whether a king, a male deity, or a human, regardless of the size, material, pose, or setting of the statue. In its early use, the classifier of the word *tut* was an articulated, rather than wrapped, male figure, either seated or standing.[63] In the Middle Kingdom, the "mummiform" hieroglyph became the standard classifier for *tut,* and remained that way, but how to relate these two developments to each other has been a matter of debate.[64] The same sign was a classifier for the word *sah* as well as *tut,* and in later periods for other words meaning statue or image, like *sedjed, ky (ḳi͗),* or *ked* (*ḳd*); it is also attested in the expression *akh ikr,* "effective *akh*."[65] But whether the "mummiform" classifier was first associated with *tut* and then with *sah,* or the other way around, is to my mind less significant than the fact that both words are concerned with divine images.

Tut referred to the quality of being godlike. It conveyed beauty and perfection, the sense in which it could be used variously to describe incense, a temple full of offerings, and Ptah, the creator god identified with artists and craftsmen.[66] *Tut* implies resemblance—but resemblance is not merely visual. Mimesis in its broadest sense is at stake, and the chicken-and-egg question of which came first, the cocoon-shaped, *sah*-form mummy or the hieroglyph classifying *tut,* is rendered rhetorical if a "human" figure bundled up in compact, limbless form means "image" when "image" means "divine."

The resonance between sacred images and wrapped forms may help elucidate the treatment of bodies from earlier periods of Egyptian history, which scholarship has tended to dismiss either as "imperfect" examples of mummification or else has described as straightforward attempts to preserve the appearance of the dead even where embalming techniques had "failed" or had not yet "evolved." Both these interpretations can be challenged using evidence from the Old Kingdom pyramid fields west and southwest of Cairo.

Archaeologists working further south in the Nile valley have found a combination of linen and resin used to wrap the dead from as early as the fourth millennium B.C.E. The bodies were sometimes resting on or covered by reed mats as well, and key sites with textile evidence include the

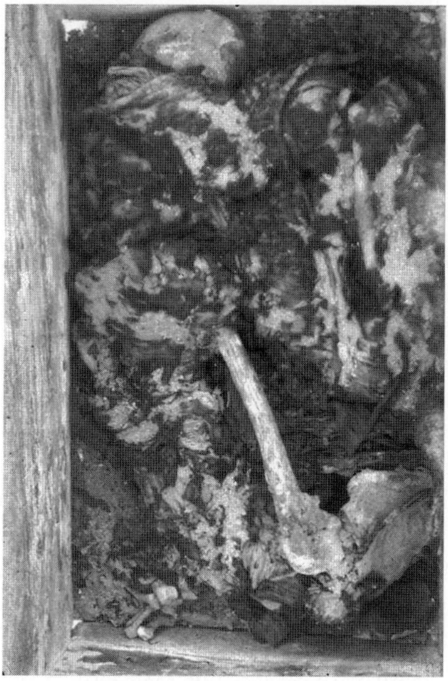

FIGURE 3.7 *Box with contracted burial found east of the pyramid of Snefru, Meidum, early 4th dynasty (c. 2575 B.C.E.). Copyright: Petrie Museum of Egyptian Archaeology, University College London*

cemeteries at Badari, Mostagedda, Naga-ed-Dêr, and Hierakonpolis, where excavation is ongoing.[67] Traces of natron have also been identified, whether applied to the body or as a bleaching agent for the linen; for instance, Elliot Smith suggested that on a second-dynasty (c. 2770–2649 B.C.E.) burial from Saqqara, which had multiple layers of linen wrapped around each limb and further linen laid over and under the body in its coffin, natron had corroded the textiles in direct contact with the body.[68] However, burials in flexed or contracted positions, or where the corpse was in a skeletal state, did not fit the assumptions that mummies were simulacra of the living. Bones elicit a different response than preserved soft tissue and were even categorized differently when collected for museums, with skeletal material from Egypt destined for ethnographic or anatomical collections while material with preserved soft tissue, deemed "mummified," was classed with Egyptian antiquities.

On the northern side of the pyramid of king Snefru at Meidum, dating to around 2550 B.C.E., the archaeologist Ernest Mackay, a protégé of Flinders Petrie, found a simple, small burial chamber at the end of a stone-lined passageway. Inside, a wooden box-shaped coffin contained a tightly contracted burial, filled almost solid with resin-soaked linen that largely concealed the body within (Fig. 3.7). Pottery in the chamber included two jars filled with "a solid mass of resin and cloth, but no signs of any human organ," as the excavators put it, revealing their own expectation that a burial should contain viscera stored in jars. The body, which was a skeleton, revealed "distinct evidence of attempted mummification"—but "how the resinous packing was placed inside the mandible is not easy to understand, unless the flesh was first stripped from the bone."[69] In other words, the resin-soaked linen packed around the body was packed inside the body as well, and in fact adhered to the inside of the lower jawbone, with linen and resin in direct contact with bone, and no skin, muscle, or tissue in between. The linen and its resin coating replaced the flesh that had been stripped from the body before burial, presumably by first burying the corpse for several weeks, or even months, in conditions that would allow the soft tissues to decompose.

The contracted body in the box was not the only burial at Meidum to feature a de-fleshed body. The two largest tombs on the more prestigious eastern side of the pyramid contained bodies that had been treated in a similar way, although rather than contracted, these were extended. The tombs were numbered 16 and 17 and are known as *mastaba* tombs, using an Arabic word referring to the low, bench-like profile of the structures. Tomb 16 belonged to an official named Nefermaat and his wife Atet (distinctive reliefs from which were distributed to museums), while tomb 17 was anonymous, its shafts robbed and disturbed by the time the excavators entered it. Inside number 17, Mackay and his team found a skeleton lying in an articulated position on its back inside a massive sarcophagus of red granite imported from Aswan, which confirmed the extraordinarily high status of the tomb and its owner. Wooden objects found near the body suggest emblems of rank to be worn on the body or carried in the hands, here placed around the dead body in the sarcophagus: a carved wooden knot, as if to fasten a kilt; a painted piece that resembled the end of a sash; and several walking sticks.

On the skeleton from tomb 17, linen wrapped not just each bone, but many of the joint faces, up to a thickness of two and a half centimeters. The cloth was described by the excavators as "fine gauze, soft and smooth as silk," with warp:weft counts per inch of 155:60, 102:68, 140:60, 128:73, and 123:62. The hollows of the wrist, the elbow joint, the edges and processes of the vertebrae, and every surface of the sacrum bore traces of linen; there was linen on both sides of the shoulder blade and in the hollow of the left shoulder socket, and the sternum likewise had linen on its inner and outer surfaces. One kneecap had linen on the inside, likewise a dozen of the ribs. The penis, the excavators thought, had been severed and bandaged separately, while the skull had a full head of hair and skin left in place on the cheeks but not the forehead. The eye sockets were empty, as was the skull cavity, and the intact ethmoid bone indicated that the brain had been removed while the head was detached from the spine. The lower jaw had been wrapped "round and round," teeth and all, and a twisted hank of linen filled the mouth, as in the contracted box burial.[70] All these de-fleshed, linen-wrapped bones had then been reassembled into a coherent whole.

Petrie donated this skeleton and what he called "critical examples of the wrappings" to the recently established department of ethnography at the British Museum—not to the antiquities department. Excavation of the Nefermaat mastaba, tomb 16, suggested that the male body there had received a similar treatment, although an influx of mud in the burial chamber partly encased it. "But as in the candlelight the magnifying glass did not shew any sign of flesh or skin," the excavators reported, "we removed samples of the wrappings, taking care to see that nothing but clean bone was left, and submitted them to Dr Ruffer for examination." Ruffer confirmed that there were no traces of skin to be seen.

If early burials of de-fleshed or skeletonized bodies have been conceived in scholarship as imperfect, not-yet-realized stages in the grand evolutionary scheme of mummification—"distinct evidence of attempted mummification," in the words of Petrie, Mackay, and G. A. Wainwright—then the next stage of this projected timeline dates to later in the Old Kingdom and includes bodies that have been taken to exemplify a drive to preserve the corpse in a "lifelike" manner, as if arresting or denying death.

In January 1933, a team led by American archaeologist George Reisner cleared a shaft in one of the *mastaba* tombs arranged around the pyramids at Giza. At the end of a shaft was a rectangular, flat-lidded wooden coffin, inside of which lay the wrapped body of a woman covered by a large sheet of cloth "showing regular folds as if taken from a box (newly laundered)."[71] Reisner thought the cloth had probably slipped while the coffin was lowered into the shaft, something difficult to judge from the photographs (Fig. 3.8). In his diary, Reisner recorded that the coffin was opened on January 15th, the eighteenth day of Ramadan. Within a week, the body had been carefully lifted out of the coffin and moved to the camp so that it could be examined—that is, unwrapped—by Dr. Douglas Derry, the same surgeon who had opened and examined the mummy of Tutankhamun.

The arms of the body were separate and along its sides, the legs were close together, and the feet were bandaged separately and positioned side by side (Fig. 3.9). Each limb had been wrapped in a ten-centimeter-wide bandage, to a thickness of one centimeter, and over this Derry counted thirty-seven layers of different widths of cloth wound around the body. Pads were sometimes interspersed to smooth the hollows, and two of the pieces of linen folded into pads were inked with a label referring to the quality of the cloth as "fine linen" (*shemat neferet, šmꜣ.t nfr.t*). In addition, linen soaked in resin had been molded to the face and around the breasts, complete with little plugs to indicate nipples, and the uppermost wrappings took the shape of a dress in the same sleeveless, v-necked style observed in sculpture of the period. Eyes and eyebrows had been painted on the face as well. It looked, Derry said, like a statue. When he had finished with it, it looked not unlike a pile of rags (Fig. 3.10).

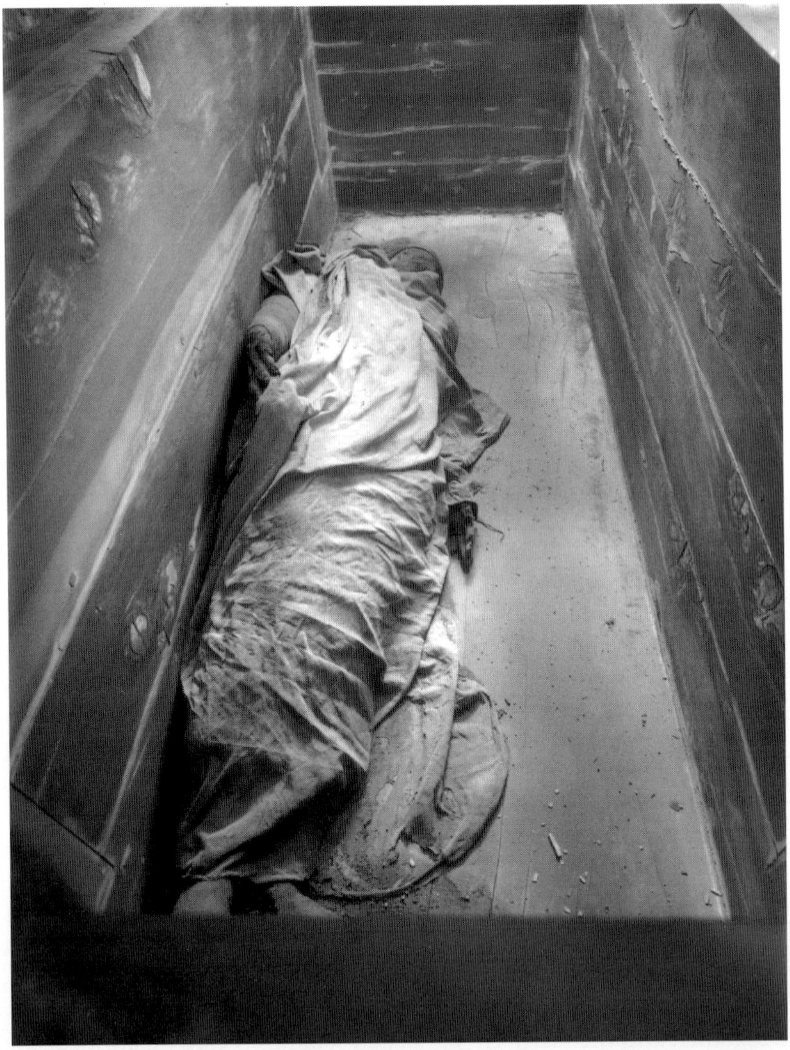

FIGURE 3.8 *Mummy in wooden coffin, from mastaba G2220 B I at Giza, late 4th to early 5th dynasty (c. 2450 B.C.E.). Photographer: Dahi Ahmed. Harvard University–Boston Museum of Fine Arts Expedition, Giza Archives. Courtesy Museum of Fine Arts, Boston*

Making the body look like a statue was just one potential outcome of wrapping a body in textiles. The statue-like effect that Derry commented on was a visual effect, primarily in response to the v-neck "dress" created by the wrappings. But other features of the body were statue-like as well. Its posture—feet together, arms at sides—corresponded to Old Kingdom statues of women, likewise the application of pigment to the eyes and brows, which were highlighted in malachite on some statues. Other Old

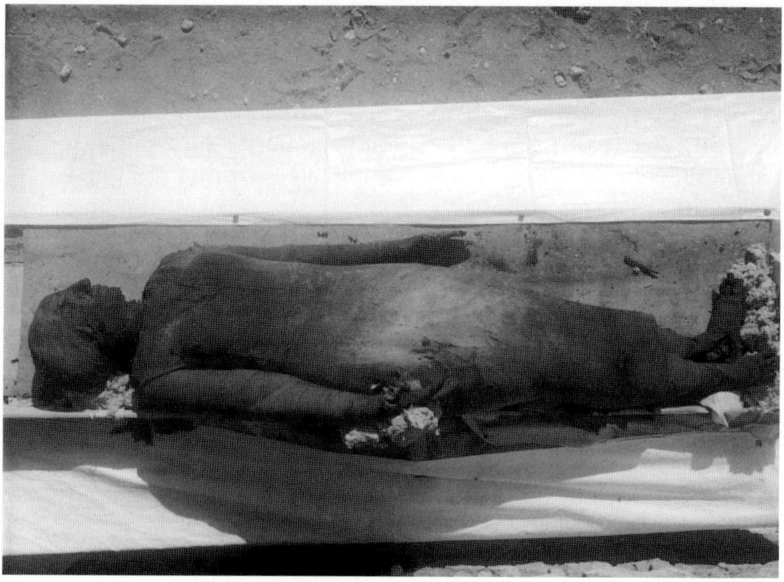

FIGURE 3.9 *The mummy from mastaba G2220 B I at Giza, in dress-shaped wrappings. Photographer: Dahi Ahmed. Harvard University–Boston Museum of Fine Arts Expedition, Giza Archives. Courtesy Museum of Fine Arts, Boston*

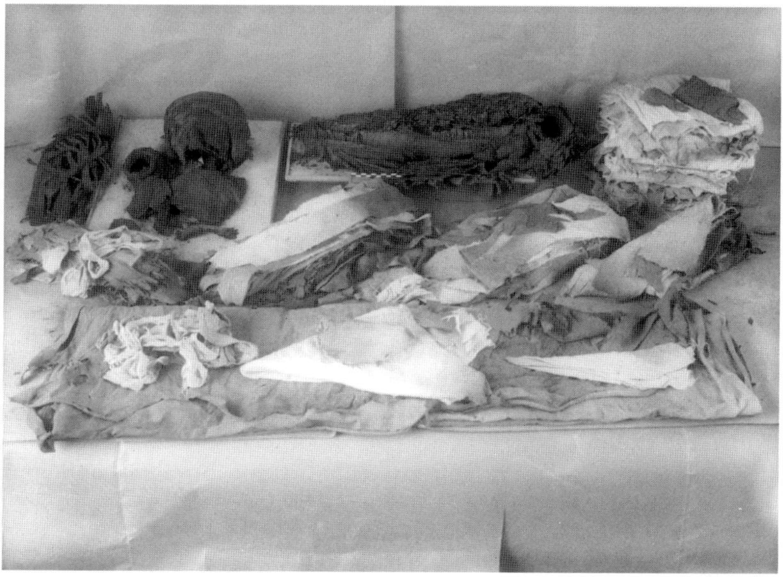

FIGURE 3.10 *Linen wrappings from the mummy from mastaba G2220 B I at Giza. Photographer: Dahi Ahmed. Harvard University–Boston Museum of Fine Arts Expedition, Giza Archives. Courtesy Museum of Fine Arts, Boston*

Kingdom bodies were treated in a similar way, such as a fifth-dynasty (c. 2400 B.C.E.) burial from an earlier season of Petrie's work at Meidum, usually attributed (with scant evidence) to a man named Ranefer. The outer wrappings of the body were disturbed, but over the initial wrappings next to the skin, a coat of resin had molded the linen "into the natural form and plumpness of the living figure, completely restoring the fulness [sic] of the form, and this was wrapped round in a few turns of the finest gauze," which had the eyes and eyebrows painted on the surface with a green pigment.[72] On that occasion, Petrie donated the poorly preserved remains to the Royal College of Surgeons, and they were subsequently destroyed in a World War II bombing.

Even the wrappings of a single foot, discovered inside the "great pit" of the third-dynasty Step Pyramid of king Djoser (c. 2630–2611 B.C.E.) at Saqqara, suggested to archaeologists the statue-like character of early mummification, though this became subsumed into the idea that the body became an effigy or likeness of the deceased, rather than a sacred image in itself. Douglas Derry was again called on to investigate the remains, which some argued were the remains of Djoser himself. Derry theorized that resin-soaked linen had been molded into the precise shape of the foot, down to its toes and tendons—but that this had been done in a separate stage from the initial wrapping because the layer incorporating the impression (an "effigy of the tendons," as Derry described it) was separated from the skin and flesh of the foot by layers of fine linen.[73] Only when the linen had been wrapped around the foot, in direct contact with the skin, was the dried and set layer of molded linen put in place, and then the whole body was wrapped again with a layer of coarser linen.

On its own, the molded linen of the Djoser pyramid remains would have resembled a sculpted shell of the supine corpse, a doubling of the human form in "practically imperishable" hardened cloth.[74] Later Old Kingdom mummies achieved a similar effect when plaster was spread over the outermost layer of linen wrappings, molding the white, malleable material over the textile-covered face, chest, and sometimes limbs of the deceased. Such plaster covers have survived better than the remains beneath them. The plaster surface was often gilded as well, so that the plaster "wrapping," like the textiles, became another layer, like a new skin, and another scintillating, physical manifestation of the divine.[75]

The layering of materials freighted with meaning—wood, metal, and cloth for cult statues; bones, flesh (real or otherwise), and wrappings for the dead—made an image that represented a god on earth and that required all the attendant care of ritual and seclusion. What the *sah-*, *wet-*, or *tut*-shaped mummies that appear in the early Middle Kingdom seem to express most strongly is the state of having-been-wrapped, formalizing the appearance many cult statues must have had in their consecrated garments, bundled up like cocoons, as a wrapped tomb statue from an eleventh- or twelfth-dynasty (c. 2000–1800 B.C.E.) burial at Asyut suggests (Fig. 3.11).

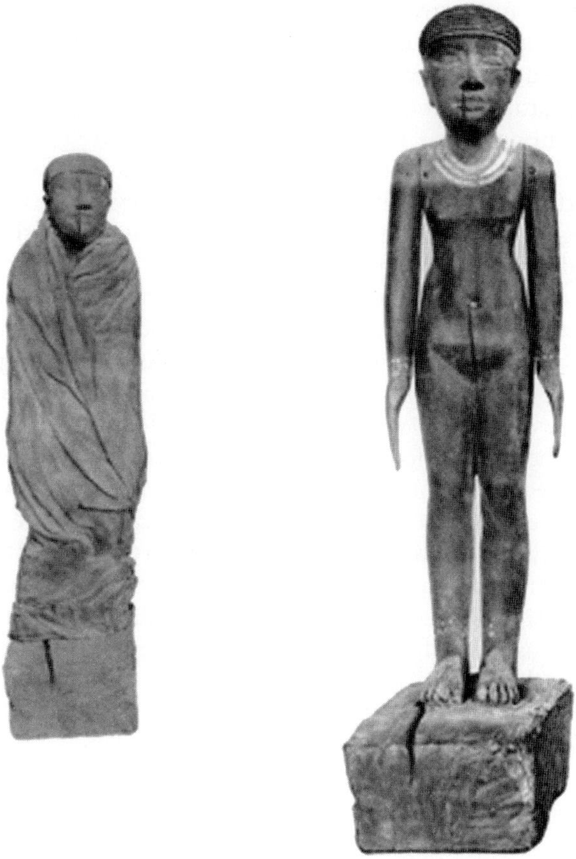

FIGURE 3.11 *Wooden statue found in a burial at Asyut, wrapped and after unwrapping; 11th or 12th dynasty (c. 2000–1800 B.C.E.). After Chassinat and Palanque,* Une campagne de fouilles, *pl. xxxii. Copyright: Institut Français d'Archéologie Orientale (IFAO)*

Since few people in ancient Egypt knew, or were supposed to know, what a wrapped-up cult statue, or a wrapped-up mummy, looked like, to have a pictorial form that conveyed the myriad associations of the two, whether in hieroglyphs, sculpture, or magical objects like *shabti*-figures, was elegantly concise and remained virtually unchanged into Roman times. Arguably, this "mummiform," wrapped figure offered a permissible way to represent a state of being that fell within the purview of a sacred, secret world.

It was the process, as much as any end result, that made a suitable body into a sacred image, a "magical mimesis" of the deceased as divine. The various treatments and wrappings that are attested over time both materially and conceptually transformed the body into another form of existence, whose resemblance was not to the human we might think we see, but rather to the divine we cannot grasp. Looking primarily at the treatment of the corpse, and its perceived state of preservation, means that the questions Egyptology has asked about mummification stem from modern valuations of materiality, not ancient ones.

To substitute one monolithic, evolutionary narrative about mummification for another is not my intention. For a start, evidence for the practice is astonishingly rich and diverse and spans more than four thousand years, from the Predynastic era to the Roman and Byzantine periods. But one question that has not been asked before offers a way into this evidence: did wrapping matter as much, or more, to the ancient actors than the treatments applied to the corpse itself? If the answer is yes, the implications are vast, for to accept the importance of textile wrappings means reevaluating what we think a mummy was—and is. Archaeological evidence will never cooperate to the satisfaction of a discipline convinced that new discoveries will yield more "facts" or that some kind of perfect knowledge can, and must, be obtained. The archive is incomplete and can never be anything else: there will always be another mummy to open, probe, or scan. Meanwhile, in the hundreds upon hundreds of meters of cloth that investigators have "unrolled," or simply sliced through, lies one of the most costly and culturally significant aspects of an Egyptian burial: fine linen, just as the ancient scribes had marked it.

4

Linen

Flinders Petrie knew cloth. Warp, weft, spin direction, thread counts: as a subject of the British Empire, whose wealth derived in no small part from textile manufacture and trade, Petrie spoke a language of materials now lost on twenty-first-century consumers of fast fashion. It was cotton that made Petrie's work possible, both through the colonial infrastructure that had fostered cotton agriculture in Egypt in the nineteenth century and through the wealth generated in the mill towns of Lancashire, whose textile tycoons were key sponsors of Petrie's excavations. Moreover, the Museums Act of 1845 had established funding for local authority museums throughout the United Kingdom, offering provincial burghers a setting for collecting and learning in the interest of civic good.

So when Petrie unwrapped three mummies in the Roman period cemetery at Hawara—each requiring "half a day's hard work for two or three observers" to unwrap and record—he paid close attention to the cloth. From one mummy fitted with a gilded mask, Petrie measured 196 individual pieces of linen and took a sample from nearly every one, for which he calculated the "gauge" by counting the threads per inch (tpi), presenting the results in tabular form in the final publication.[1] Some were what he identified as a basket weave, rather than the usual plain tabby with equal numbers of warp to weft threads, and the qualities ranged from a coarse 36 tpi to a finer 88 tpi, by Petrie's counting. Several of the textile pieces were similar enough, he thought, that they must have been torn from the same length of cloth. Moreover, the quantity of linen explained why the mummies were so bulky and "often over a hundredweight" (112 pounds), much of which came from the cloth.

The textiles that Petrie and other archaeologists found in Egypt were a product for which the Egyptians were renowned in antiquity. In the Old Testament, Ezekiel prophesied the downfall of Tyre by lamenting the seaport's lost glories, including ship sails of "fine linen with broidered work from Egypt" (Ezekiel 27:7). Flax cultivation and linen production were essential to the Egyptian economy and embedded in a system of cultural values linked to their manufacture, their material properties, and the function of the finished cloth. Linen clothed bodies, whether human or divine, living or dead. It swaddled infants and held them to their mothers in slings. It covered wounds, splinted broken bones, and absorbed menstrual blood. In mummification, it soaked up the last liquid drawn out of a corpse and smeared slick oils and sticky resin over the embalmed body. In temples and shrines, it signaled, demarcated, and concealed sacred spaces. It was graded, labeled, traded, and stored; darned, reversed, cut down, and restitched. Circulated between domestic and temple (state) economies, linen led a rich life that might end on a rag pile, around a statue, on a mummy, or neatly folded and boxed in a tomb.

This chapter considers the cultural significance of linen textiles in ancient Egypt, which is essential to understanding their use in the wrapping of dead bodies and other sacred objects. Although archaeologists readily reversed such wrappings, and although textiles lacked the cachet of archaeological objects like statues or coffins, they nonetheless caught the attention of late nineteenth- and early twentieth-century excavators such as Petrie, who saw these fragile cloth survivors as evidence of ancient technology and craft. Historically, the study of Egyptian textiles grew out of mummy unwrappings conducted mainly in the field, as with Petrie's work. The categorization of archaeological objects enforced a strict separation between "textile" and "body," however, and collecting priorities meant that excavators often cut textiles down into samples deemed to have technical or aesthetic interest, such as the tapestry panels on late antique clothing.[2] Textiles were thus at risk of being separated not only from the bodies they wrapped or dressed, but also from their own, original length of cloth or garment, and the first part of this chapter looks at the ramifications of this approach on the way museums and scholarship dealt with ancient textiles.

The deposition of linen in Egyptian funerary contexts, including the large quantities wrapped around mummified bodies, facilitated the preservation of textiles, but why cloth had been used in these contexts drew far less comment than technical considerations of how the cloth had been made. The two questions of use and manufacture are in fact closely entwined, for the production and circulation of linen textiles was not only a core activity in ancient Egypt, but also, as in many societies, an activity to which women made a substantial contribution. Female agency, both human and divine, was crucial to the way cloth functioned in Egyptian religious practice and means that women played a role in Egyptian economic and political life that has otherwise been overlooked, or discounted as "mere" symbolism, as if symbolic meanings come into being independent of social relations. The textiles employed in Egyptian wrapping rituals were "inalienable possessions," to use anthropologist Annette Weiner's term for material goods whose symbolic significance makes them "transcendent treasures" to be guarded against loss, for instance by restricting their exchange.[3] Weiner's work on textiles informs the argument I develop in the remainder of the chapter, which links the making and materiality of ancient Egyptian linen with its symbolism, expressed through patterns of ownership and the ritual performance of wrapping as well as the artistic representation of wrapped bodies.

Linen was the primary textile used in ancient Egypt throughout the pharaonic era, but its ubiquity was no hindrance to its potential as a carrier of cultural value—quite the opposite, perhaps. Where regular, intensive labor goes into making a product that is prone to wear and tear, both the labor and the product may take on meanings and associations beyond the monetary value assigned to manufactured goods in industrialized, capitalist societies. But it was the monetary value of another textile—cotton—that made the study of ancient Egyptian textiles possible, which is where this chapter picks up its thread.

King Cotton

At the time excavators like Petrie were working in Egypt, flax cultivation had long since given way to cotton farming in the Nile valley and delta, with yield-expanding methods developed in part to feed the mills of northern England. Attempts to cultivate cotton, rather than flax, may date back to at least the Roman period in Egypt; in southwestern Iran, cotton fiber has been identified as early as the eighth century B.C.E., and by the Roman period, it was well established in the southern reaches of the Nile valley.[4] Before the Napoleonic invasion, however, cotton remained a small-scale concern, with a poor-quality yield. After a French botanist identified a long-staple variety suited to the Egyptian climate, cotton began to attract the attention of Muhammad Ali and the West. In the 1830s, when George Gliddon was the American consul in Cairo, he was asked by the U.S. Treasury department to keep an eye on the Egyptian competition, mindful of the cotton economy of the southern states.[5] American cotton produced on slave plantations was the finest raw material available, and the southern states were keen to protect their interests. In March 1858, Senator James Henry Hammond, from South Carolina, delivered a rousing speech to the assembly:

> What would happen if no cotton was furnished for three years? I will not stop to depict what everyone can imagine, but this is certain: England would topple headlong and carry the whole civilized world with her.…No, you dare not make war on cotton! No power on earth dares to make war upon it. Cotton is King.[6]

Hammond might have been scaremongering, but his concern was prescient, for when the American civil war broke out three years later, disrupted production and the Union blockade of southern ports deprived Britain of 80 percent of its raw cotton supply. Egyptian cotton boomed. Foreign, and especially British, investment throughout the 1850s had improved both the quality and quantity of cotton grown in Egypt, and production increased fourfold between 1861 and 1866.[7] In 1862, Khedive Sa'id visited Manchester to tour the mills and meet with members of the city's Chamber of

Commerce, who urged him to improve the Egyptian cotton industry still further since concerns about how finely Egyptian cotton could be spun were a recurrent problem.

Elizabeth Gaskell's *North and South,* published in 1855, conveys the extent to which the industry ruled Manchester, dubbed "Milton North" in the novel and "Cottonopolis" in popular parlance. The denizens quite literally breathed and ate cotton, the fluff of the raw bolls filling the mouths and lungs of workers in the city's mills.[8] In a city that owed both its wealth and its poverty to the cotton industry, it was no surprise that textile money flowed into its galleries and museums—and gave it a collection of Egyptian antiquities. In 1880, Manchester cotton merchant Jesse Haworth combined a business trip to Egypt with a tour of its antiquities, inspired in part by reading Amelia Edwards's best-selling account of her own Nile excursion, *A Thousand Miles up the Nile.* Edwards founded the Egypt Exploration Fund in the spring of 1882 to raise subscriptions for archaeological work in Egypt. At her encouragement, Haworth began sponsoring Petrie's work independent of the Fund in the late 1880s, receiving a share of the finds in return. He pressed Manchester University to accept donations of his Egyptian antiquities for its museum collection (which they were at first reluctant to do), and to build an extension with dedicated space for an Egyptology department, including galleries, offices, and storage. The extension opened in 1912, and when Haworth died in 1920, he left £30,000 to the university specifically for the maintenance of the Egyptian collection.[9] Cotton grown in Egypt and processed in Manchester thus generated the money to procure and import that other Egyptian commodity—antiquities, including mummies wrapped in yard after yard of linen.

Howarth also helped raise £500 to secure a stellar find that Petrie offered to Manchester in 1907 with the promised new wing in mind: the complete contents of an undisturbed, twelfth-dynasty tomb at Deir Rifa in Middle Egypt, comprising two sets of double coffins, their mummies, a chest of canopic jars, two model boats, two figures of offering bearers, and three small statues of the deceased, who were brothers and priests in the local cult of Khnum. Known as the "Tomb of Two Brothers," the find became the subject of a study by Petrie's protégée, Dr. Margaret Murray of University College London. Murray had been delivering a course of lectures in Manchester at the time and cataloguing the museum collection, which as yet had no dedicated member of staff in charge of it. She arranged to return to Manchester in May 1908 in order to unwrap one of the mummies—the one whose coffin bore the name Khnum-nakht—before a public audience; the second mummy was unwrapped at some point thereafter.[10] At the public part of the unwrapping, snippets of Khnum-nakht's linen wrappings were distributed to members of the audience, who included "the learned, the curious, and…the uncultured student," as the *Manchester Courier* reported. Undergraduates sniggered in the back rows of the large chemistry theater as the somber performance got underway.

When Murray published the contents of the tomb, including the unwrapped mummies, in 1910, her introduction declared to "the general reader" that objections to the archaeologist's practice of opening tombs and mummies were "purely sentimental." Archaeology was a new science, "which contains within itself all other sciences," including ethnology and comparative anatomy.[11] As if to demonstrate this assertion, the publication included chapters by the university's professor of chemistry, on the composition of salt found with the mummies; by a local physician, on the anatomy of the bodies; and by textile and dye experts from Manchester's technical college, on the linen. The expert findings confirmed what archaeologists and other mummy unwrappers had often surmised. For instance, the finest linen, with counts up to 151 tpi, occurred in two distinct places, first in direct contact with the body and, second, as the last, large shroud forming the outermost layer of the wrappings.[12] Extensive darning indicated that the textiles were well worn before being used as wrappings, and nearly half the linen from Khnum-nakht's mummy—and all the linen from his brother Nakht-ankh's mummy—had been dyed yellow using safflower and an alum-based mordant. Armed with this scientific analysis, museum staff cut square samples from the cloth wrappings, which were mounted on cardboard and framed under glass for display in the new galleries. Neat captions explained the different weights and colors of the linen samples, for in a city like Manchester, staff must have reasoned that visitors were interested in—and conversant with—the details of textile weaves and dyes. The rest of the linen from both mummies was carefully laundered, folded, and pressed for storage.

Applying analytical methods to the linen, rather than only the bodies, paralleled the taxonomic approach that archaeology had begun to take toward its finds and the self-conscious way in which it styled itself as a science. From the late nineteenth century, museums accommodated ancient textiles in their collections, whether as samples mounted for reference or whole pieces, but they were often defined as being of technical, rather than cultural or antiquarian, interest, a distinction mapped onto the organization of museums and collections. For example, the South Kensington Museum (from 1899, the Victoria and Albert Museum) collected Egyptian textiles in keeping with its founding emphasis on improving industrial design and manufacturing, while other Egyptian antiquities largely remained within the remit of the British Museum in Bloomsbury. As with the study of the Two Brothers linen, expertise developed in the British textile industry informed the study of ancient textiles: in Bolton, another Lancashire mill town that acquired Egyptian antiquities, museum curator W. W. Midgley had a professional background in weaving and applied himself to studying textiles from a number of excavations, as did his son Thomas Midgley. The elder Midgley prepared samples of linen from Early Dynastic graves at Tarkhan by sandwiching them between sheets of glass for protection and for ease of use, since the different gauges of textile selected for mounting were potential comparanda for other textiles, including those still to be discovered.[13]

Cutting textiles into pieces and framing them in glass—as was also done for papyri—facilitated storage and display as well as visual scrutiny for the purpose of study and demonstration. Like the linen from the Two Brothers, or the Deir el-Bahri cache, almost all the Egyptian textiles that museums and individuals collected came from burials, whether they had wrapped the body or had been stored separately. Their use in the past seemed to be something to forget, however, washed and ironed out of the object's history like the stains and creases on Khnum-nakht's shrouds. "A mere wrapping," was how the archaeologist John Garstang described the treatment of nearly nine hundred bodies in a Middle Kingdom cemetery he excavated at Abydos, which baffled him because he could detect no trace of embalming salts or spices on the eviscerated bodies.[14] He could not consider them to have been mummified, and Murray had been similarly struck by the poor state of preservation of the Two Brothers corpses, whose flesh crumbled away from the bone. To these British scholars in the Edwardian era, when textiles were an industrialized commodity, the value of ancient textiles lay in their evidence of preindustrial handiwork. For the bodies they enfolded to disappoint, like factory seconds passed off in the same packaging, thwarted Egyptology's expectation that corpse outranked cloth. But if cotton helped make the Empire, linen had helped make Egypt.

Spun Gold: Linen Production in Ancient Egypt

> But the flax springs from the earth, which is immortal; it yields edible seeds, and supplies a plain and cleanly clothing, which does not oppress by the weight required for warmth.
>
> Plutarch, *De Iside et Osiride section,* 4

To understand the "mere wrapping" in linen, and what it might have meant in an ancient worldview, we might as well start at the beginning, with the brilliant blue flowers of a flax field in bloom—a blue "which is like to the heavenly azure which enfolds the universe," as Plutarch wrote, to help explain why Egyptian priests favored linen garments. The flax attested in Egypt, from Predynastic times onward, was *Linum usitatissimum,* and although there were other kinds of textile in use, notably goat or sheep wool, linen differed in an important way: it was a plant product, not an animal one, and thus was associated with the agricultural cycle of renewal and return.

Turning flax into linen is painstaking, if routine, work. Flax was a winter crop, sown in the alluvial soil deposited by the annual flood and harvested at different stages of growth depending on the desired end result. Plants mature in around three months. Young, green plants, harvested just after the blue flowers faded, yielded fine fibers to be spun into the sheerest, best-quality linen, whereas plants left to develop in the field until their stalks were yellow produced coarse fibers suited only for sackcloth, matting, or rope. Although grown throughout the Nile valley, flax was especially suited to the humid climate of the delta, which is where the best linen was made. The association of fine-quality linen with the delta city of Sais, home to the cult of the goddess Neith, reflects the distinctiveness of the region's linen products in Egyptian thought.

Processing began in the field.[15] Pulled out of the ground, rather than cut (since the bast fibers in the stems extend into the plant's roots), and with their seed heads removed, the stalks of flax were submerged, or retted, for about two weeks in water, perhaps pools created from irrigation channels in the fields. Retting gives off a foul odor, after which the soaked plants were stripped of the softened outer hull and the stalks left to dry. These were then beaten with sticks or mallets in a process known as scutching, to extract the bast fibers from the woody core of the stem. In their study of textile production at the eighteenth-dynasty site of Amarna, Kemp and Vogelsang-Eastwood suggest that the Egyptians may also have used an alternative to retting whereby the plants were left drying in the sun rather than soaked, after which the stems were beaten and the bast extracted in a similar way.[16]

The agricultural labor of sowing, harvesting, and decortifying flax was group work in which men, women, and children could all participate to some degree, but visual and written evidence suggests that the next stage, yarn production, was performed only by women and girls, a gendered division of labor observed in other cultures as well. Unlike cotton bolls, flax fibers cannot be spun directly but first have to be spliced together in bundles called roves, which the worker does by rubbing the flax fiber between her fingers, hands, or one hand and a thigh. This process coarsens the flax worker's hands, which in turn facilitates the repetitive motion.[17] One bundle of fibers was spliced to the next by moistening the two ends, activating the gluey cellulose in the flax.

The next stage was spinning the long, continuous yarn. Wool and cotton are spun to lengthen the yarn, but flax is spun to add twist to the spliced fibers and turn them into a finer, stronger, less elastic thread. Spinning is in some ways a misnomer, but it is the most widespread term for this stage of processing, following on from the splicing.[18] Adding twist to the flax fibers was done by placing the spliced roves in a spinning bowl, or something similar, with water in the bottom to keep them moist. The fibers could be passed through loops in the bottom of the bowl to increase the tension on them, and were then wound around a spindle.[19] Two methods—drop-spinning and grasped spindle (either hand to hand or against the spinner's thigh)—are attested in ancient Egypt, and both use the force of the spindle to draw out a few of the flax fibers from the rove and twist them more and more tightly. It was straightforward work, conducive to interruptions—multi-tasking, in today's terms—and to working in a group, since it allowed for companionable conversation and benefitted from collaborative efforts.

Wound into balls, or around the shaft of the spindle, the twisted thread could then be fed directly onto the fixed (warp) beams of a loom. Until the New Kingdom, only the horizontal loom is depicted in Egyptian art, but even after the vertical loom was introduced, around 1500 B.C.E., the horizontal loom would have continued to be used for its ease of assembly and disassembly.[20] Although men may occasionally be shown operating looms, there is a distinct preference in the visual evidence towards women weavers (Fig. 4.1). Egyptian vertical looms did not use weights at the bottom of the warp threads, like ancient Greek looms, but instead attached them to a fixed beam. To produce long sheets of cloth on either type of loom, the weaver wrapped the excess around a beam (an upper, moveable beam, on a vertical loom) and continued work. Large looms required at least two people to operate them, an operation depicted in the tomb of a man named Neferenpet, who was an "overseer of weavers" in the mortuary temple of Ramses II.[21] The circular action of winding woven cloth around the loom beam, like the circular action of spinning, may have helped create or reinforce cosmological links between textile production and the cyclical pattern of human and agricultural production as well.

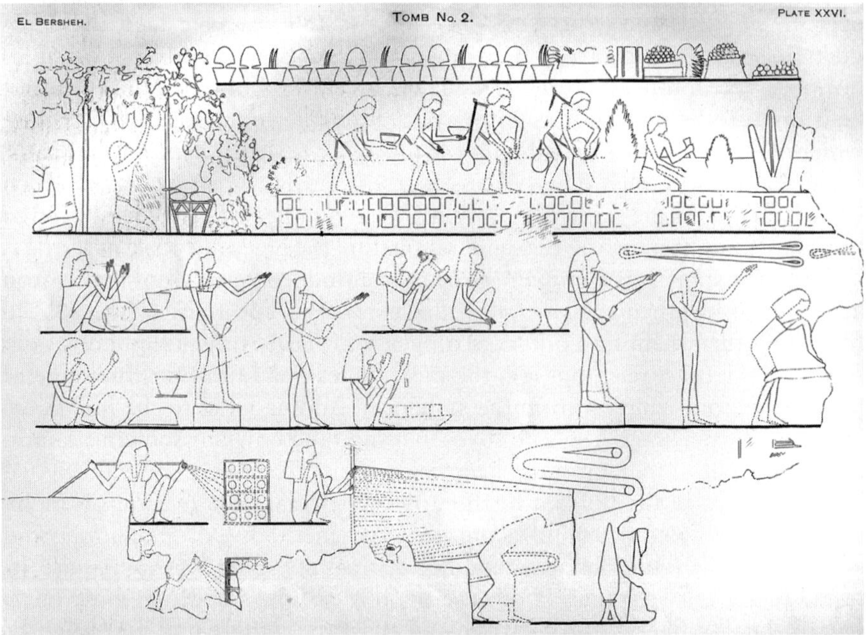

FIGURE 4.1 *Drawing of a workshop with women spinning and weaving, from the tomb of Djehuty-hotep, el-Bersheh, 12th dynasty (c. 1850 B.C.E.). After Newberry,* El Bersheh *I, pl. xxvi. Copyright: The Egypt Exploration Society*

The final stage in cloth manufacture was dying or bleaching the fabric. The natural color of linen is a pale, yellowish tan or ecru, and the cellulose in flax makes linen difficult to dye. For anything other than indigotin, which was probably available in Egypt through the woad plant, the process required an alum-based mordant, imported from southern Turkey. But as Murray found with the Two Brothers, whole lengths of linen could be dyed yellow with safflower, while iron oxides or madder yielded shades of orange and red, like the shrouds found around Tutankhamun's inner coffins. In the Middle Kingdom burial of a "king's daughter" named Itaweret at Dahshur, the mummy was surrounded by dark red cloth.[22] The wrappings, and re-wrappings, of the New Kingdom royal mummies included dark and pale red linen, as well as blue textiles dyed with an indigo-based stuff.[23] What seems to have been the most favored color for linen, though, was the palest color possible, a creamy white attained by laundering linen with natron and bleaching it in the sun.[24] White (Egyptian *hedj*) was the color of purity, cleanliness, and bright, gleaming metals and light. In hieroglyphic writing, the classifier written at the end of *hedj* was the sun disk itself.

The materiality of linen extends far beyond the visual, however. The cellular structure of flax helps moisture evaporate quickly, which is what gives linen its cooling properties. As Plutarch observed, linen could also be layered without adding weight or bulk in cool weather, and although sheep and goat husbandry almost certainly supplied wool textiles for extra warmth, only linen is ever found in funerary contexts, at least until the Roman era or late antiquity. Herodotus (*Histories,* II.81) made the same observation, which he said applied to temples as well, in the fifth century B.C.E. The texture of linen softens with repeated use and laundering, meaning that the freshness and relative age of clothing and other textiles would be evident to the touch, and both newness and age-value were appreciable qualities.[25] The finest linen, known as "royal linen," was almost sheer and is sometimes erroneously translated as byssus, after the Greek word for a thread spun from mollusk secretions, whose miraculous, gossamer quality the finest woven flax may have resembled.[26] A length of linen in the Metropolitan Museum of Art, from the eighteenth-dynasty burial of a woman named Hatnofer, measures 1.6 meters wide and some 5 meters long but weighs a mere 140 grams.[27] Sheer or lightweight cloth would gather, drape, and flow with ease, and the intimate interplay between cloth garments and the contours of the body was a frequent concern of Egyptian art.

The relationship between artistic representation and the archaeological evidence is not straightforward, and some of the tailored garments found in burial contexts have no equivalent in art. Many of the garments are more modest and subdued than their pictorial counterparts, but no less remarkable both for the workmanship and for the fact that they are included in the wrappings or coffin of the deceased. A dress now in the Louvre is one of about half a dozen similar dresses folded up and placed in the coffin of a female burial in an early Middle Kingdom cemetery at Asyut (Fig. 4.2, the same burial in which a wrapped wooden statue of the deceased was found: see Fig. 3.11).[28] Its long sleeves and straight skirt both bear horizontal pleating. The style of the dress has no exact parallel in artistic representation, but pleats were a frequent feature of elite dress for both men and women, especially in New Kingdom and Third Intermediate Period images. The same cellulose structure that makes it difficult to dye also makes linen resistant to

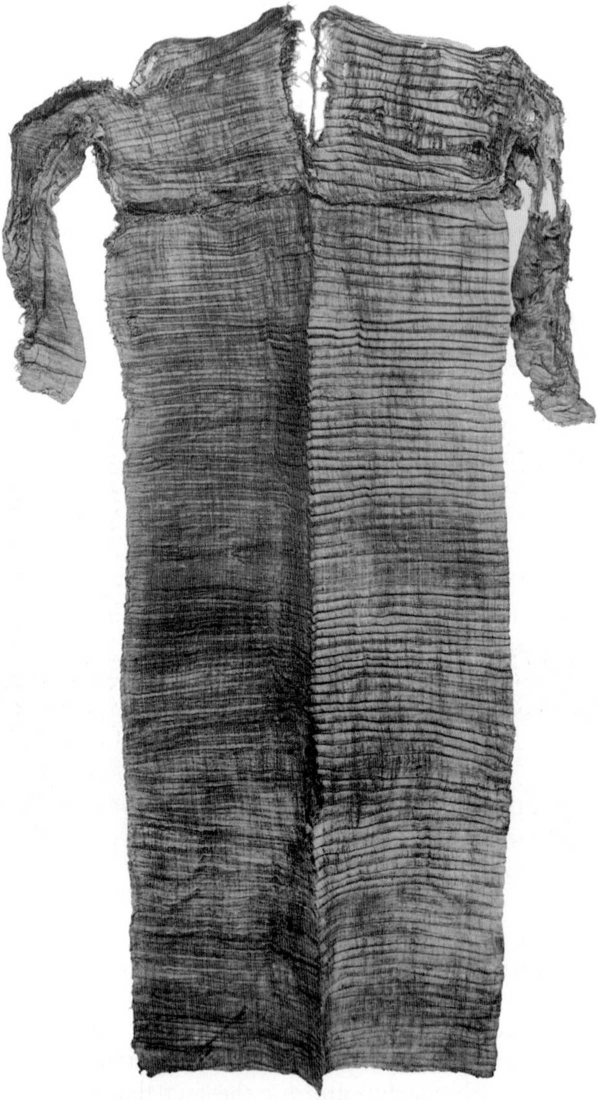

FIGURE 4.2 *One of the dresses found folded up in a coffin in a burial at Asyut, 11th or 12th dynasty (c. 2100–1900 B.C.E.). L. 121.0 cm, W. 47.0 cm. Louvre, E 12026. After Chassinat and Palanque,* Une campagne de fouilles, *pl. xxxiii. Copyright: Institut Français d'Archéologie Orientale (IFAO)*

keeping a pleat, although a zigzag weaving technique helped create pleated effects.[29] Even so, pleating required additional effort and expense, in some cases doubling the quantity of textile required for a garment.[30]

Smoothing textiles completely flat was another desirable treatment, not just for the storage of textiles, but for garments as well. Instead of or in addition to pleating, a number of depictions of clothing show deep, rectilinear fold lines, indicating the garment was fresh and unworn.[31] A particular type of wooden chest was often used to store linen; with a gabled lid and bosses on one end, the chest could be closed by looping a cord around them, and potentially the cord could be sealed to monitor access (Fig. 4.3). Several similar linen chests in the tomb of Tutankhamun had inscriptions inside the lid, recording what kinds of cloth and clothing were inside. Keeping such an inventory and securing the chest were not just tidy housekeeping: the suggestion of surveillance and control within a well-to-do household is indicative of linen's value as a commodity, central to the economics of both household and state, the latter operating in the pharaonic period largely through temples. The value of linen textiles lay not only in their financial worth but also in their cultural and symbolic worth, which cloth and

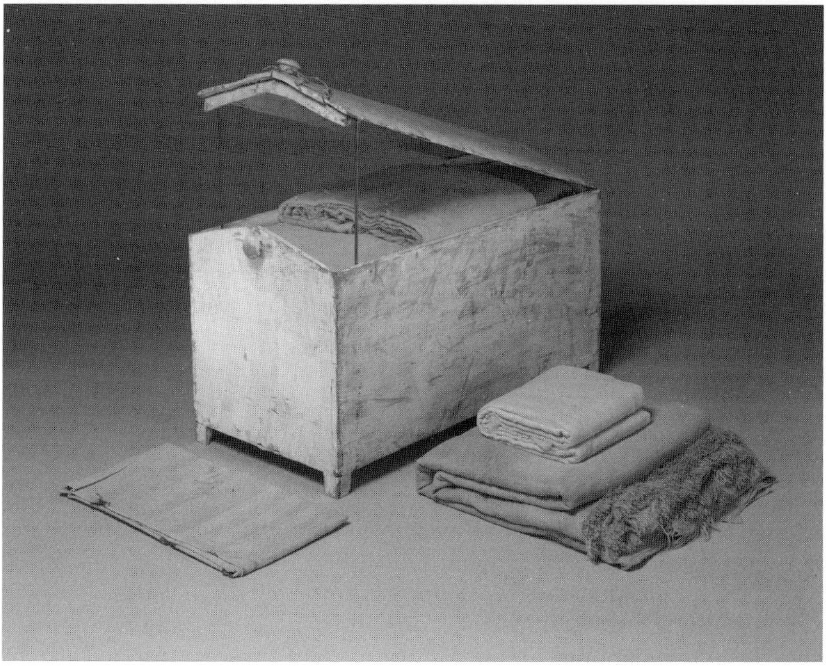

FIGURE 4.3 *Gable-topped wooden chest and linens from the tomb of Hatnofer at Thebes, 18th dynasty (c. 1492–1473 B.C.E.). The Metropolitan Museum of Art, Rogers Fund, 1936 (36.3.54, 36.3.56a-b, 36.3.111, 36.3.140). Image © The Metropolitan Museum of Art*

clothing accrued through their materiality, their manufacture, and, as the next section of this chapter explores, their association with the individuals who owned and wore them.

Cloth, Commodities, and Cultural Value

To use Appadurai's influential formulation, the "social life" of an ancient Egyptian textile encompassed its manufacture and its subsequent chain of ownership and functionality, which might culminate in its use as a mummy wrapping.[32] Separating the mortuary use of a textile from its other functions would be misleading: textiles were deployed in burials because of, not despite, the social lives they had led. As Weiner observed in her anthropological analysis of cloth wealth and social relations, textiles function in many cultures as "a kind of symbolic skin" used as a wrapping or covering for human bodies, living or dead:

> It is not accidental that the very physicality of cloth, its woven-ness, and its potential for fraying and unraveling denote the vulnerability in acts of connectedness and tying, in human and cultural reproduction, and in decay and death.[33]

Created, like life itself, through the physical labor of the female body, textiles entered into networks of exchange with certain distinct characteristics, imbued as they were with the potential symbolic significance of birth. The fact that cloth could be replicated, though, made it possible to vary the significance attached to specific cloths so that some textiles were available as commodities to buy, sell, or stockpile, while others were reserved for sacred or ritual use, inalienable possessions too powerful to relinquish to commerce. This latter use of textiles goes some way to understanding their role in ancient Egypt as temple offerings, as the clothing (or wrapping) of statues, and in mummification and burial.

The textiles used for kingship ceremonies and temple rites were probably produced with these functions in mind in workshops linked to the royal household and to local temples. Both temple inscriptions and the *Ritual of Embalming*, discussed in the previous chapter, make repeated references to the ritual value of cloth woven in the temple of Neith at Sais, but many, if not all, temples would have had their own linen workshops or else (or in addition) acquired linen from local producers, who would have met certain criteria of social status and skill. In terms of wrapping the dead, the most elaborate mummifications, like those performed for royalty, may have had recourse to linen that had a specific provenance and perhaps had been specially created for the purpose, such as the rare assortment of bandages cached near Tutankhamun's tomb that had been woven to widths between 1.8 and 11 centimeters, or two highly unusual pieces found folded into packets in the tomb of the early eighteenth-dynasty queen Ahmose-Meritamun, each piece woven in the form of a human body with squared-off heads and limbs. Ink inscriptions on linen used in the twenty-first-dynasty rewrapping of the mummy of Ramses III specify that the cloth had been woven by the daughter of the high priest of Amun Piankh, for the temple of Amun at Medinet Habu; this was the largest temple in the vicinity of the royal necropolis, and the cloth would have been roughly contemporary with the rewrapping of the body.[34] However, most of the textiles used in mummification or otherwise buried with the dead comprise a form of cloth wealth accrued during an individual's lifetime—clothing the deceased had worn; garments or textiles associated with preceding generations, other kin, or dependents; and cloth produced by his or her household, which for deceased women might mean the cloth was their own handiwork or part of a dowry linked to their maternal line. In some instances, the cloth used in mummification originated from a temple workshop or was used to wrap a statue before being passed on to the embalmers. Seen in light of Weiner's observations, this was not (or not only) opportunistic recycling, but a symbolically significant transfer from one inalienable mode of ownership to another, with the exchange of cloth tying the deceased to social institutions like the temple, not to mention the gods themselves.

The processing of flax and production of linen linked the agricultural cycle, female agency, and social organization, including the cosmological ideas that underpinned Egyptian religion and kingship. The material qualities of linen as a textile—its color, texture, and physical properties—further informed, and were informed by, this complex web of metaphor and association. In addition, linen had a material resonance with another important Egyptian product, papyrus.[35] Both linen and papyrus are made up of strands that cross perpendicular to each other, and like flax, papyrus was processed by stripping out the fibers from the stalk of a plant. Sheets of papyrus were made by spreading the sliced and dampened fibers in layers, alternating the horizontal and vertical, and pressing them flat. Although it is not actually woven, papyrus has a surface appearance based on perpendicular, enmeshed strands, and it also shares the natural yellowy color of unbleached linen—moreover, the finest papyrus, like the finest linen, had a brighter, whiter hue than standard versions of the product.

The resonance of linen and papyrus comes through in the fact that both were used as writing surfaces, and writing had a special significance in magical and devotional practice. At first or even second glance, and in person or in a photograph, the object reproduced in Fig. 4.4 might look like a papyrus inscribed with hieroglyphic texts, specifically a version of the texts known today as the *Book of the Dead*. Instead, it is a 1.5-meter length of what was originally a shroud more than 5 meters long wrapping the body of king Thutmose III, one of the mummies opened by Maspero from the Deir el-Bahri cache. There are rare examples of the reverse, with inscribed papyrus being used as a layer of wrapping on the body, as on a Ptolemaic mummy of a priest from Akhmim, now in the collection of the Musée d'Yverdon in Switzerland.[36] But what was more usual was writing or drawing on the linen used as mummy wrappings. A common practice seen on mummies from the first millennium B.C.E., in particular, was the use of inked inscriptions on bandages, wrapping the body in the magic of ritual knowledge and performance. Some inscribed bandages are numbered, suggesting that they were part of a set and perhaps were intended to wrap specific parts of the body, and considerable quantities of bandages could be created for a specific corpse. A Ptolemaic period mummy acquired by Giovanni d'Athanasi in the early nineteenth century yielded inscribed bandages totaling more than fifty meters in length when it was unwrapped by Pettigrew before a public audience in London in April 1837, having failed to sell at auction as d'Athanasi had hoped.[37]

A more mundane use of an inscription on linen was to mark its owner or user, its origin, or its quality. Marking cloth in this way was not simply a record of ownership, distinguishing one person's kilt from another in the laundryman's basket. It was also a way of inserting the owner, and the cloth, into a circle of exchange with both cosmological and social significance, as discussed earlier. Marks that indicate the place of manufacture, or originating source, had similar symbolic values, especially given that the places named seem to be temples or royal storehouses. Hence, linen from a single burial might give what are probably the dead person's name and titles, as well as the name of a local temple or part of the titulary of the reigning

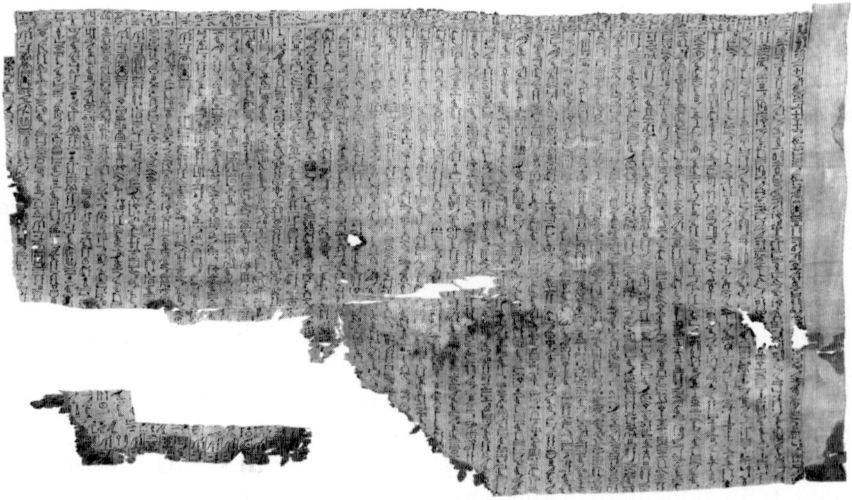

FIGURE 4.4 *Fragment from the shroud of Thutmose III, 18th dynasty (c. 1479–1425 B.C.E.). H. 63.5 cm, W. 111.0 cm. Museum of Fine Arts, Boston 60.1472; Gift of Horace L. Mayer. Courtesy Museum of Fine Arts, Boston*

king. Other marks on textiles refer to their quality, distinguishing grades of linen and pointing to a measure of control or standardization in the market. Although various scholars have suggested translations of the grades—such as *shemat neferet* as "good" or "fine" (seen on the female mummy Derry unwrapped at Giza), and *naa (nʿʿ)* as "smooth"—it is difficult to know exactly what characteristics each grade had, and archaeological reports have tended to give subjective assessments, such as fine versus coarse, heavy versus light.[38] Modern judgments may not correlate to ancient standards, but thread counts offer a more objective, though still imprecise, approximation of the ancient grades.[39] As its name implies, royal linen (*sesher nesu, sšr nsw*) was the most prized cloth in ancient Egypt, and the sheer length labeled as such from the burial of Hatnofer gives an indication of the type of cloth that could fall under this rubric.

The only personal name marked on the linen in Hatnofer's tomb is Boki, which is not attested anywhere else among the burials. This person may have been a relative, colleague, or retainer, as appears to be the case with other examples of mummy linen marked with a name different than the deceased's. Linen from the late Old Kingdom burial of Idu, at Giza, which was excavated by a German team before World War I, included his mummy wrappings, a mattress and pillow of folded linen, and a balled-up bundle of cloth in the foot end of the coffin.[40] Now in the collection of the Roemer-Pelizaeus Museum, Hildesheim, the bundle was relaxed by conservators in the late 1980s, yielding twelve sheets of three different qualities, haphazardly rolled up together with the finest quality on the outside, and the coarsest on the inside, perhaps reversing the order in which they had covered the body or coffin.[41] All the sheets of cloth, from the mummy and the coffin, had been darned and frequently laundered, and two bore inscriptions in red ochre that name men other than the deceased. One may be the name of his father, Nefer Idu, while the other gives the full name and title of a man named Pepi-ankh who, like Idu, was a priest serving in a royal funerary cult.[42] Pepi-ankh was a junior rank to Idu, however, which may suggest that he supplied linen to his social superior in a similar way that lower ranks of priests might organize offerings and perform as "sons" (the leopard-skin *sem*-priests) for the funerals of their senior colleagues.[43]

The names of older male family members on wrappings indicate that these textiles came from a household supply, assuming that the name was a mark of ownership. Some may represent heirlooms whose use on the mummy reinforces the continuation of a paternal family line. As earlier chapters have mentioned, a number of textiles used as mummy wrappings or to wrap tomb goods in a royal context have been marked with the name of that king's father—thus the jackal statue in Tutankhamun's tomb was draped with a tunic inscribed for Akhenaten, and a tunic found among the wrappings of Seti II's mummy bore the name of his father, Merneptah. At the same time, however, the cloth itself was a product closely associated with women, who played a significant role in spinning and weaving. Thus cloth used in burial contexts, such as mummy wrappings, also evoked the maternal line and the role played by women in human reproduction as well as the reproduction of social relationships, for instance through marriage and in the legitimation of kingship.[44]

Most of the names marked on mummy linen appear to refer to the deceased, but these too may also have had a longer history, embedded in the lifecycle of an individual and his kin: the twelfth-dynasty mummy of a man named Wah, from Thebes, included a sheet bearing a date in the year of his birth, making it, like him, about thirty years old. The case of Wah is also one of the best examples of just how much linen could be incorporated into a burial—and how much it could be disregarded by archaeologists. Excavated in 1920 by the Metropolitan Museum of Art, the tomb was a small offshoot of a complex belonging to the man for whom Wah was employed as an estate manager.[45] The fact that the tomb contained nothing much except the coffin led the excavator, Herbert Winlock, to describe it as quite poor—an opinion that has since been revised given that in addition to some 375 square meters of linen used in the wrappings, not to mention the copious resin, there were about another 500 square meters of linen supplied inside and on top of the coffin (Fig. 4.5). One of the sheets measured twenty-six meters long and a remarkable two meters wide (a vast loom width), and in addition, the excavators found a linen pall on the floor of the tomb, presumably used to cover the coffin during transport.

Another burial richly supplied with linen, and coincidentally also excavated by the Metropolitan Museum, is that of the elderly woman named Hatnofer, source of the long, sheer piece of "royal linen" and the sheet inscribed with the name of Boki. Hatnofer had lived long enough to see her son Senenmut rise through the ranks to become the most powerful official in Egypt during the reign of the female ruler Hatshepsut. In a tomb near Senenmut's own in western Thebes, the best coffin and the canopic chest were inscribed for Hatnofer, whose body had been carefully mummified and wrapped, while the body of her husband Ramose, who had died in his thirties, and of six other individuals were in a skeletal state and jumbled together with sand, dirt, and gravel; it is possible that these remains had been rewrapped, for instance if the family's improved fortunes had enabled a new, collective burial at the end of Hatnofer's long life.[46] The supply of textiles in the tomb constituted a personal history and identity formed not only through family and household relationships (depending on the identity of Boki), but also through connections with institutions of state power. The sheer piece of royal linen also has a mark woven into it which refers to the storehouse of a royal estate in the vicinity, as do several of the other lengths of cloth in the tomb. Whether the linen was supplied from the royal estate specifically for the burial, or belonged to the deceased during her lifetime, is difficult to say, but this cloth in particular bears signs of laundering and repair, as if it were a well-loved piece.

The marks of royal estates and, on other linen, temples point to the role of these institutions as producers and distributors of cloth. A group burial at Thebes known as the "Slain Soldiers," dating to the twelfth dynasty,

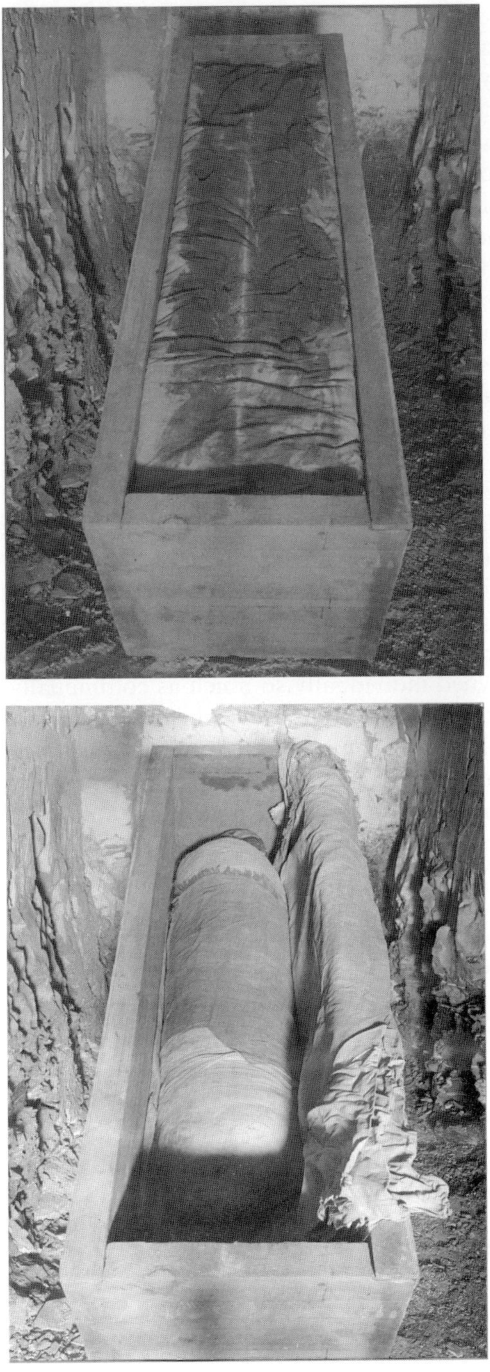

FIGURE 4.5 *The coffin of Wah, filled to the top with folded linen and after removing thirty-eight sheets. From his tomb at Deir el-Bahri, 12th dynasty (c. 1950 B.C.E.). The Metropolitan Museum of Art, photograph by Egyptian Expedition, 1918–20. Image © The Metropolitan Museum of Art*

comprises the remains of at least sixty adult males who had died violent deaths, probably in battle since there are arrowheads embedded in some of the bones. The bodies had been wrapped in textiles inscribed with their names and patronymics, and some of the linen was also marked with a symbol found on cloth from the eleventh-dynasty burials of royal women and girls at the nearby funerary temple of king Mentuhotep II at Deir el-Bahri.[47] The symbol is thought to refer to this temple or another royal estate and, by association, to the workshop or storeroom from which the linen originated. A range of goods produced on temple estates and used in temple ceremonies was redistributed in the local economy, with members of the priesthood probably given shares—for instance of bread, beer, and meat offerings—proportionate to their rank.

The mechanics of this system are poorly understood, despite the important role it must have played in the supply of foodstuffs, textiles, and other goods and services.[48] The redistribution of products and offerings from the temple throughout local communities, and thence households, can be related to Weiner's concept of "keeping-while-giving," whereby certain goods—characterized, for instance, by their association with temple cult—have a value beyond the economic confines of the commodity because they have a talisman-like effect.[49] As transmitters of social and cultural mores, such goods are not owned individually so much as communally in the sense that they are transmitted as gifts or largesse rather than through sale or exchange. Enduring goods like the linen used in temple rites, as opposed to linen produced as a surplus, exemplify the character of Weiner's "inalienable possessions" because they either cannot circulate at all (and one imagines the most special ceremonial cloths did not) or can only circulate in a limited way, for instance to be deployed in mummification and burial. Though not necessarily exclusive, women's significant involvement in the production of cloth for the temple and its rites means that women were "agents of transfer" between humans and gods, even if men had pride of place in the ritual performance.[50] Institutions that appear to be predominantly male spheres of activity, such as the temple and its priesthoods, thus relied on the input of female producers, whose role in exchange has often been overlooked in scholarship.

The interface between personhood, social institutions, and linen production is nowhere more apparent than in the codified "linen lists" that appear on stone reliefs in Early Dynastic and Old Kingdom *mastaba* tombs commemorating both men and women.[51] The Old Kingdom examples take a distinctive, tabular form arranged in rows and columns within a rectangular frame, similar to the format in which royal events were recorded, while the earlier reliefs are more loosely organized (Fig. 4.6). The lists dominate a scene that depicts the deceased receiving funerary offerings, and each list provides an inventory of textiles, designating the kind or quality of linen as well as the quantity, usually expressed in terms of surface area.[52] In some cases, the quantity is a generic expression like "a thousand," representing an ideal, almost infinite number, but in others, specific measurements tally the different types of textile or garment. The inscriptions include indications of a textile's structure—that is, whether it had a short weft fringe, which was created on the left side of the textile, or a longer warp fringe, where the textile was trimmed from the beam, or both. Warp fringes could be finished for decorative effect by twisting the yarns together at regular intervals, and these twists were the hieroglyphic sign for linen.[53] The terminology also reveals certain associations between the qualities of linen and its connections with the gods and with magico-medical practice: royal linen, written as *idmy* in this period, was marked by a falcon hieroglyph indicating "divine," while another variety, *sheser,* may relate to Egyptian words for a male medical practitioner, linking this type of linen to bandages and healing.[54] In all, at least twenty-six different terms describe the varieties of linen—a rich vocabulary indicating the precision with which different types of cloth could be differentiated from each other.[55]

Scholars have tended to assume that linen enumerated in these lists was an offering, perhaps for storage in the tomb—but the lists may well refer to, or at least include, cloth supplied for wrapping the body. Equipping the dead with linen both through symbolic means, on the reliefs, and through actual supplies in the tomb or on the mummy, attests to the commodity value of textiles in Egyptian society, and in that sense, the linen is part of

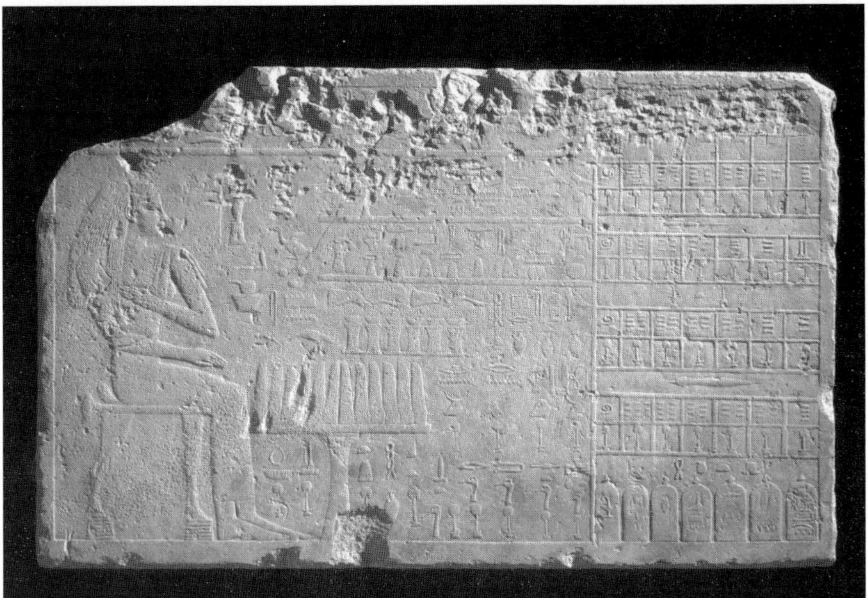

FIGURE 4.6 *Limestone slab stela of a woman named Meretites, from tomb G 4140 at Giza, 4th dynasty (c. 2500 B.C.E.). H. 53.0 cm, W. 82.5 cm. Harvard University–Boston Museum of Fine Arts Expedition, 12.1510. Courtesy Museum of Fine Arts, Boston*

a display of wealth and privilege. But it served another function as well: depositing linen owned and especially worn by the deceased in life removed from circulation garments that were imbued with an individual, embodied identity, while linen donated by others, or gathered from heirloom sources, also contributed to making and remaking the personhood of the deceased. Some garments may have been so closely associated with an individual that death made them unsuitable, or even dangerous, for others to use. Moreover, the very act of supplying cloth helped align the dead with the gods, who consumed a steady diet of linen alongside their temple offerings of wine and choice meats. Although the formal linen list fell out of use after the Old Kingdom, the presentation of textiles remained a constant concern of art and funerary ritual. Textiles helped bridge the gap between gods and humans, but they also marked gaps between humans of different status—thanks to the distinctions of quality, cost, and source, as well as the ways in which textiles were cared for and worn. The dress of the gods, including the dead, had its origin in the dress of day-to-day life.

Cloth and Clothing

Like representations of cloth and clothing in art, archaeological textiles also present issues of interpretation. One issue is the identification of clothing among archaeologically recovered textiles, especially those found used as mummy wrappings. Some pieces of clothing were obvious to excavators because they were fully or partly tailored. In the Old and Middle Kingdoms, long-sleeved, v-necked dresses were found folded up and placed in the coffins of female burials, for instance at Tarkhan, Deshasheh, Gebelein, and Asyut (see Fig. 4.2).[56] A similar practice is observed in New Kingdom burials, where the tunics and triangular kilts that formed the basis of elite male attire have been found folded neatly and stored in chests, for instance in the Deir el-Medina tomb of Kha (with his name stitched or inked on the garments) and in the tomb of Tutankhamun, which contained some two dozen matched sets alongside an entire wardrobe's worth of garments, from gloves, to head wraps, to tunics adorned with the finest tapestry and sequin-like disks.[57]

Linen tunics were also folded up and placed like padding within the layers of mummy wrappings, not only in royal burials like that of Seti II, but also at regional sites such as el-Lahun in the Faiyum, where Petrie discovered three or four folded tunics on a single male mummy of New Kingdom date.[58] In an anonymous adult burial at Sheikh abd el-Gurna, dating to the early eighteenth dynasty, three tunics of fine linen found among the wrappings have such a short length and narrow neck openings that they could only have fit a child, raising the possibility that they were garments the deceased had worn earlier in life, or perhaps belonging to young children in the deceased's family.[59] The use of shaped garments in mummy wrapping was an enduring phenomenon; for example, a tunic was identifiable among the poorly preserved wrappings of a Ptolemaic mummy "autopsied" at the Manchester Museum in the 1970s.[60] The small dimensions of this tunic corresponded to the small stature of the preadolescent remains, again suggesting a link between the garments reused as wrappings and the individual whose body was being wrapped.

By far the bulk of the textiles found either stored in the tomb or wrapped around the body are medium- to large-sized rectangles of cloth—typically around one to one and a half meters wide by two or three meters long. The original function of these lengths of cloth was not self-evident to archaeologists, who settled for descriptions such as "sheet" or "household linen." But what looks like a bed sheet to a nineteenth- or twentieth-century archaeologist might have had very different uses in antiquity, none of which had much to do with sleeping. Working at the New Kingdom village and cemetery at Deir el-Medina, the French archaeologist Bernard Bruyère was an exception and recognized that the fine, rectangular pieces of linen he found in burials, often fringed on at least one side, were garments just as much as the shaped tunics and loincloths he found spread between the shrouded layers of mummy wrappings at the site.[61]

In a culture where wrapping was a fundamental use of cloth, and where many garments—from skirts to dresses to mantles—were made by wrapping cloth around the wearer, what archaeologists termed a "sheet" may well have been an article of clothing. The qualities and dimensions of the textile would have governed its specific function in a way that may elude us now, but an ancient actor was unlikely to mistake an actual piece of bedding for a mantle or a dress. As Kemp and Vogelsang-Eastwood have pointed out,

> where the modern study of Egyptian dress misleads is in the desire to identify strict categories amongst the various ways of wearing or draping an untailored cloth length, something which is, by its nature, adaptable to more than one style.[62]

A rectangular textile could be wrapped and knotted into a short or long skirt for men and different types of dress for women. Some fabrics suited cloaks and mantles, and others head scarves, shawls, or aprons. Any number of variations—color, decoration, density of weave, finished texture—might have distinguished garments for different sexes, age groups, or social ranks, and these are some of the distinctions that can make words for cloth and clothing difficult to translate.

Moreover, the difference between tailored and draped clothing bears a cultural weight, no less so when the two were used in combination with each other, as seems to have been the case in ancient Egypt. A general preference for draped clothing can rest in part on reluctance to cut into whole cloth, as tailoring requires.[63] To reduce a piece of cloth to smaller sizes, tearing along the weft is more efficient than the slicing action of ancient bronze or flint knives, and prevents unraveling, but cutting actions were used elsewhere, for instance to trim the warp threads of a textile upon removal from the loom. Where the Egyptians did tailor cloth into clothing, they did so by minimizing the amount of tearing, trimming, or cutting needed, which reduced both waste and labor since less sewing was required.

When garments are created in part through wrapping techniques, the distinction between cloth and clothing becomes especially blurred in one key area—the ancient terminology relating to items of dress and the state of either dressing or being dressed. One of the most widely used words for cloth or the action of clothing and wrapping was *hebes,* attested since the Old Kingdom and written with a hieroglyph indicating a bolt of cloth with a fringed end.[64] *Hebes* is one of the words for a textile used in the Apis and human embalming rituals. The more generic *menkhet (mnḫ.t)*, meaning cloth or clothing, also had wide use, from everyday lengths of cloth, to cloth used in temple rites, to the "noble cloth" used to wrap the dead, as inscribed on a fragmentary shroud for "the Osiris, the mistress of the house, Ta-iry," recorded by Bruyère.[65] This is the word used in temple offering scenes where the gods are presented with their wrappings: *henek menkhet* (*ḥnk mnḫ.t,* "presenting the clothes") or sometimes *djeba menkhet (ḏbꜣ mnḫ.t,* "clothing with clothes").[66] All these words, and more, comprise a vocabulary of textiles used in ritual contexts as well as the "everyday," reinforcing the link between cloth and clothing, human and divine, and art and object in the material world of Egyptian antiquity.

Cloth and Cult

> Your face is illumined with this white linen. Your body is blooming with the green linen. You unite with the *seshed*-linen and overthrow your foe. You hold the red linen in its moment. It is the inundation that washes away your sweat. The sunshine illumines your face. These clothes woven by Isis and spun by Nephthys, they fit you, they cover your body, they remove your opponents from you.
>
> Offering inscription, Temple of Horus, Edfu, first century B.C.E., after A. Egberts, *In Quest of Meaning* (1995), p. 180

In 1902, the French Egyptologist Alexandre Moret published his study of the cult ritual carried out in temples each morning and sometimes at noon and sunset as well.[67] His chief sources were the temple complex of king Seti I at Abydos and a papyrus in Berlin, dating to the twenty-second dynasty, whose long Egyptian title can be summarized as "the daily ritual" performed for the god Amun-Re, which is divided into sixty-six "chapters," or ritual actions. Although now more than a century old, Moret's study is a useful reminder of how close Egyptology, archaeology, and anthropology once were, for he refers to Mauss's work on sacrifice to formulate a typical argument for the time, theorizing that the daily ritual replaced a "primitive" sacrifice of the god in earlier Egyptian practice by reconstituting the god's dismembered body through the application of incense, oils, and linen wrappings.[68]

The Abydos temple has seven shrine rooms that depict the rite being performed on the six gods of the temple, plus the deified king Seti I himself. The rite always follows the same general order: the purification of the participants and the chamber through the burning of incense and the

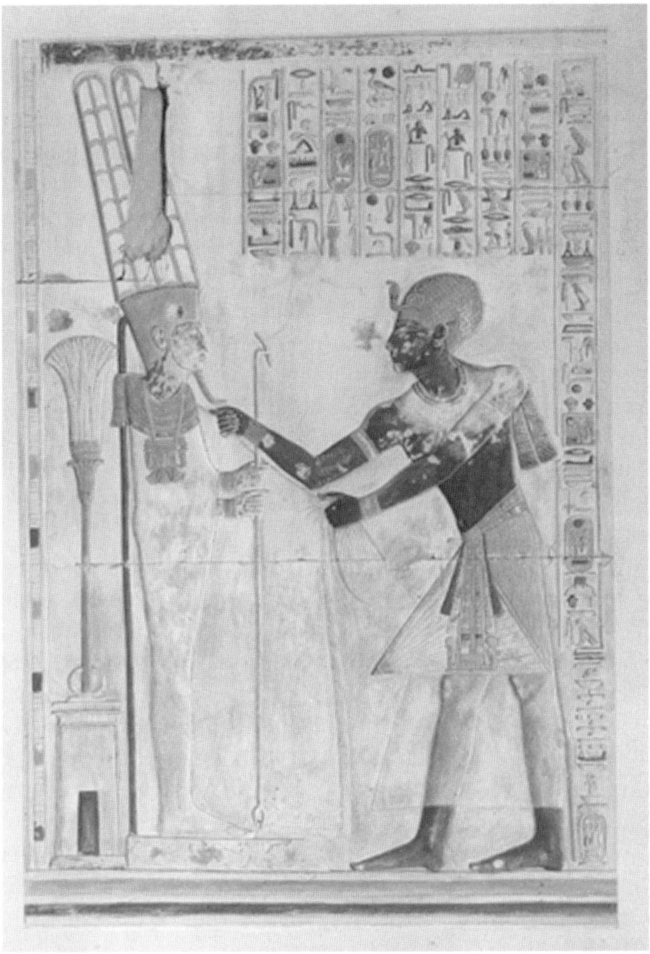

FIGURE 4.7 *Seti I wrapping the statue of the god Amun-Re, in the temple of Seti I at Abydos, 19th dynasty (c. 1306–1290 B.C.E.). After a watercolor by Amice Calverley. Copyright: The Egypt Exploration Society*

sprinkling of water and natron around the shrine; the opening of the shrine; prayers and prostrations before the statue; the undressing of the statue; the application of oils to the statue; fitting the statue with new clothing and other adornments, like collars and necklaces (Fig. 4.7); more prayers and purification; the sealing of the shrine; and finally the retreat and closure of the chamber.[69] The statue might have had to be removed from its shrine temporarily, to facilitate the unwrapping and rewrapping, but this action is never mentioned in the texts. The papyrus version of the rite even avoids mentioning the removal of the wrapping, which is said to have simply "fallen away" as if it could no longer contain the divine power.[70] The ritualist credits the god with the act of wrapping that he himself is about to perform, ceding any human agency to the divine: as he removes the bolt from the statue's shrine, he recites an exhortation to the god, who appears in all his beauty: "You who are naked, clothe yourself! You who should be wrapped, wrap yourself!"

The regime of care for the god's earthly body equipped a statue of wood and metal with the physical and spiritual qualities it needed not only to be a manifestation of the divine, but also to enable the god's cyclical rebirth, in line with the rebirth of the sun. These processes—both the care regime and the divine regeneration—had to take place in a pure and hidden place, accessed only by ritual practitioners who were themselves in a pure state and entrusted with the required, and restricted, knowledge. Incense, sacred water, and the ritual purity of the practitioners were essential, as were the oils, linen, and amuletic adornments applied to the image. That the wrapping action had to be undone and redone each day, or even at different times in the day, suggests that repetitive performance was integral to the rite. The list of linen produced for the temple of Amun in the reign of Ramses IV (P. Harris I) numbers tens of thousands of different kinds of garments and cloths, so supply was not an issue.[71]

The cloth removed from the statue had absorbed some of the power emanating from the image—and would have to be reused or disposed of appropriately, either in other temple rituals or for mummification. The inscriptions on some bandages and small pieces of linen indicate that they had first been dedicated to a certain god, perhaps used to make an intercessory request or as part of a votive offering.[72] Although examples preserved in Lille and Brussels have no archaeological provenance, the textiles are more likely to have survived if they had subsequently been used in a burial. One of the pieces in Brussels, inscribed in hieratic, reads "noble cloth of the temple of Amun," while the other is labeled as a cloth dedicated by "...-en-Khonsu [a proper name], for his master Osiris, the prince, the great, to beseech for life, integrity, and health, a long lasting life." Either of these inscriptions, and the size of the first cloth (14.5 × 63.5 centimeters), would have been suited to use as a statue's wrapped garment, if those were its dimensions at the time; the second cloth, at almost 4.5 meters long, would have had to be wound like a bandage around any statue it might have dressed. From as early as the *Pyramid Texts,* which are themselves written versions of earlier literary forms, the wrappings of the dead are referred to as the "cast-off clothing" of the gods.[73] In this way, the power of the god was redistributed—not to mention the social and economic power of the temple and its priesthood.

Other temple rites and religious practices also depended on the use of linen textiles, for instance in the wrapping and deposition of votive objects or as a support for writing in order to communicate a request to the god. A rare survival from a temple, rather than burial, context is a linen petition fixed to two wooden sticks, perhaps to allow its insertion into a mud brick niche or wall near a shrine.[74] This petition, inscribed in Demotic, was found among rubble at the Sacred Animal Necropolis in North Saqqara, a complex of temples and cemeteries for mummified animals that flourished in the late and early Ptolemaic periods. The inscription asks the god Osorapis to intervene in a legal case—not uncommon in Egyptian practice, where prayers and votive offerings bridged what we might consider the sacred and the quotidian, but which were inseparable in the Egyptian context. More significant is the use of linen as the medium for this kind of message. The editor of the petition has suggested that linen was too closely associated with the dead, and too impractical as a writing surface, for it to have had widespread use in other religious contexts. However, the rarity of survivals like this one makes this an argument from silence; instead, the cultural values ascribed to linen would have made it more, not less, appropriate for use as an intercessory object in every kind of religious and magical context.

The cults at specific sites, or for certain gods, had their own rites related to the clothing of the cult statue and the pivotal role that wrapping played in this. Cults of Hathor, for instance, incorporated a procession of linen chests to "unite" the cloth with the goddess, attested from the late eighteenth dynasty to the Ptolemaic period.[75] A rite in which the king consecrates—makes sacred, *djeser*—four chests of linen called *meret*-chests is attested in tombs and temples from the seventeenth dynasty to the Roman period.[76] This rite focused on the king as an intercessor in the supply of textiles for sacred use, perhaps similar to his role as the ritual actor who supplied temple offerings in general. At Kom Ombo, linen was offered to a number of deities but is particularly prominent in offering scenes to Neith, the goddess whose temple at Sais was credited with producing the best-quality cloth, in a reciprocal relationship.[77] Linen also featured prominently in offerings to Osiris, who epitomized the wrapped body in artistic representation. On a monumental gateway at Karnak, erected by Ptolemy III, the king offers linen and *medjat*-ointment to Osiris-Wennefer, who appears in royal form. Ptolemy enjoins the god to accept these items from the temple workshops of Neith as a "secret" or "mysterious" wrapping *(djeba sheta)* for his body.[78] Secret—*sheta*—is here written with the classifier of a linen bandage.

In temples from the Ptolemaic period, an entire sequence of rooms was devoted to versions of the *Opening of the Mouth* ritual performed on statues in the temple throughout the year, and in particular at the new year, which corresponded to the start of the annual Nile flood.[79] Existing statues were taken from underground crypts in the temple, carried through the linen chamber and an open-air court called the *wabet,* through a space called the "house of gold" (*per-nebu*)—an area where the *Opening of the Mouth* was performed and which is also mentioned in connection with priestly initiation rites. On New Year's Day, the statues would then be carried upstairs to the roof of the temple to be reinvigorated in the light of the rising sun.

The *wabet,* or "pure place," was the same term used for the place where embalming or wrapping a mummy took place, but as Coppens observes, the distinction between a temple *wabet* and the *wabet* as a mortuary workshop is a distinction made by modern scholarship and not one the ancient priesthood would have recognized.[80] Adjoining the *wabet* was the linen room, or the "chamber of cloth," which was accessible from the central axis of the temple. Its decoration was oriented toward the *wabet,* suggesting the line of movement and the focus of the offerings of linen and ointment depicted in its reliefs. At the temples of Philae and Dendera, fecundity figures—emblematic offering bearers of quasi-divine status—appear at the bottom of the wall reliefs and carry the linen, each piece identified by a particular name or color.[81] Part of the relief decoration of the linen rooms featured Tait, the goddess most frequently credited with weaving clothes and dressing the gods, the king, and the dead.[82] She was also often paired with two male deities, a god of resin and ointment, Shesmu, and the only male god associated with linen, Hedjhotep, who often functioned like a stolist priest or *hery-seshta* ("master of secrets"), dressing the gods with the linen that Tait produced.[83] Tait is described as bright and gleaming, like the cloth she weaves, and as one temple inscription put it, she was "the mother of the gods, the mistress of the goddesses, who arrays the empowered images in her handiwork, gives sweetness to their flesh, clothes their bodies, and gives health to their frames." When the king is shown offering linen to the gods at Dendera, he is said to be the "image [*tut*] of Tait," and she in turn weaves swaddling clothes for newborn gods and the newborn king.[84]

Other goddesses were also invoked to describe the production or the qualities of linen, in much the same way that spinning and weaving were associated with women and girls in Egyptian society. Neith oversaw the weaving of the very finest linen at the workshops of her temple at Sais, where the "two houses of the north" were the house of Resnet and the house of Mehnet, weaver goddesses who also appear in the entourage of the sun god.[85] The houses or weaver goddesses could be represented as young crocodiles suckled by Neith, and to be "united with the two crocodiles" was to be shrouded in fine linen.[86] The wrappings placed on mummies or statues were also sometimes called the dress of the goddess Hathor, or the dress of Renenutet, a goddess associated with agricultural fertility—especially fitting for a product made from flax. In the *Pyramid Texts,* the deceased receives the "dress [*djeba*] of Renenutet" to wear, as does the statue in the *Opening of the Mouth* ritual, and the phrase reappears more than two thousand years later in the temple of Hathor at Dendera, where the linen god Hedjhotep dresses Osiris in the "dress of Renenutet"—his bandages or shroud.[87]

The close relationship between women and cloth in human life found its parallel in the divine sphere, especially in the mythology of the sister goddesses Isis and Nephthys. Associated with spinning and weaving cloth and with the care of the dead, Isis and Nephthys were the sisters of Osiris, the god-king whose own death and divine transfiguration offered a mythical parallel for death and rebirth. The importance of these sister goddesses in sustaining kingship recalls Weiner's observation that a sister is in some ways an inalienable possession of her brother, too valuable to relinquish entirely, and therefore she continues to assert influence over his lineage and property.[88] As the most powerful and enduring of Egyptian goddesses, Isis had powers that in many ways overshadowed those of her brother Osiris, but in combination with her sister Nephthys, the sisters consistently took on the role of spinning or weaving women with the power to nurture and protect. Like Tait, Isis and Nephthys could be invoked in magical-medical spells when the healer prepared a linen poultice or tampon, for instance against a burn or vaginal bleeding.[89] Isis and Nephthys were variously said to spin and splice yarn or to weave cloth, their roles overlapping with those of the other goddesses associated with the production of textiles. As one passage from the *Coffin Texts* characterizes the textiles provided to clothe the deceased, what Isis twisted (*sšn*), what Nephthys pulled (*sṯꜣ*), what Neith spun (*msn*), what the two *rekhty* wove, was the work of Ptah, the creator god.[90] Isis and Nephthys are probably also the deities referred to on an Osiris-figured shroud dated to the Roman period at Thebes. Sized for a child, the shroud bears an inscription in which the textile "speaks" to identify itself as "the cloth of the two goddesses," whose "two arms" envelop the boy named as the deceased.[91]

The motif of a linen wrapping as two enfolding arms seems to conflate the action of wrapping and the material used for it—reminiscent of the scenes of Seti I extending his arms to dress the gods at Abydos (see Fig 4.7). Other representations of the statue clothing rite do not depict the actual textile being wrapped or unwrapped. Instead, the deity appears in its conventional form while the king extends his arms toward the god's upper body, "placing his hands" on it, as the accompanying inscriptions describe the action.[92] Another metaphorical image of wrapping as a pair of arms is found in the *Book of Caverns* in late New Kingdom royal tombs, a composition that concerns the dovetailing cycles of Osiris's and the sun god's death and rebirth, in the most secret and remote reaches of the cosmos. When the sun god passes through the cavern of the Weaver-goddess, she places her hands on his body, which at this juncture of the gods' union can be designated as "that which is in Osiris."[93] The sun god addresses the cavern, acknowledging what has taken place: "Behold, the Weaver has received me. You have given me my two arms"—in other words, his wrapping.

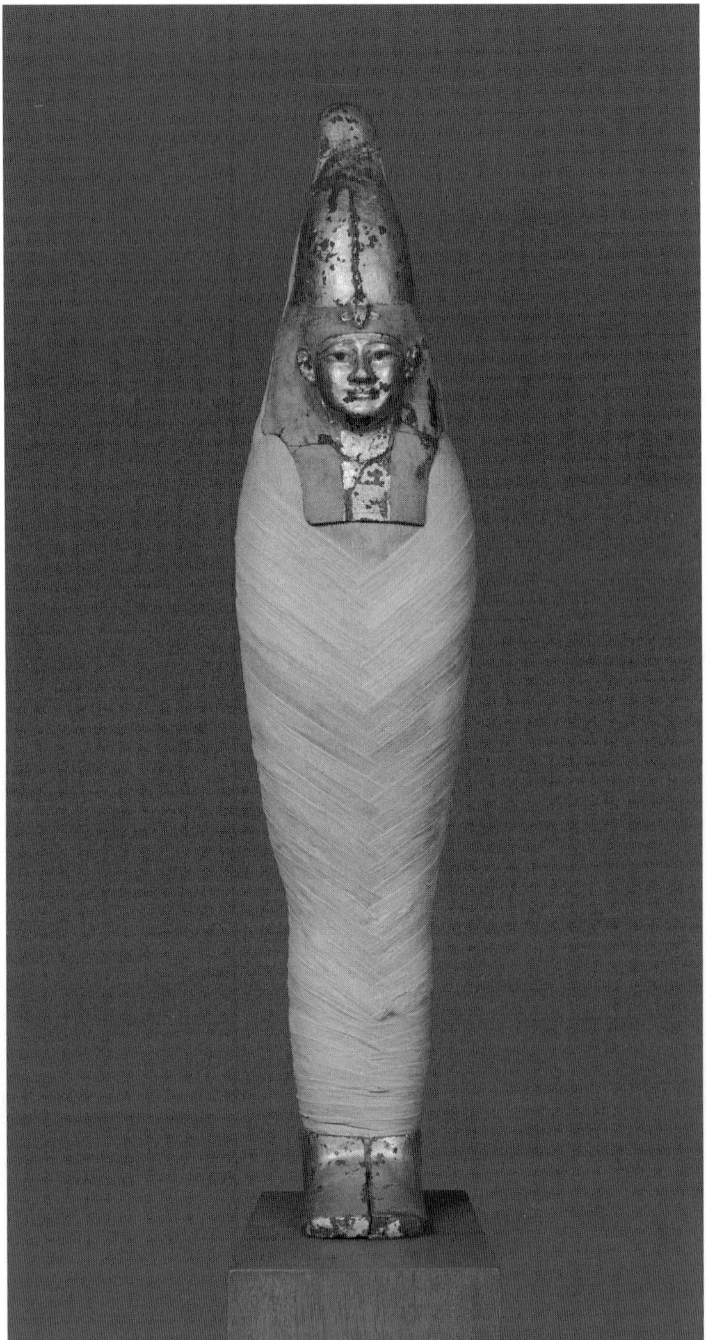

FIGURE 4.8 *Figure of Osiris with gilded cartonnage mask and foot cover; the linen is ancient, but was reconstructed in the 1940s, based on the wrapping of animal mummies of the same period. Provenance unknown; Ptolemaic period (c. 305–30 B.C.E.). The Metropolitan Museum of Art, Gift of Mrs. Goddard DuBois, 1942, 1944 (44.6.1). Image © The Metropolitan Museum of Art*

The recondite proclamations of the underworld and the cultic rites of the temple may seem to place textile wrappings on an elevated plane, a practice so out of the ordinary that it had no relevance outside the lives of a narrow elite. But archaeological finds of objects wrapped in linen point to a much wider sphere of activity in which the wrapping of sacred images was applied in magical practice, the deposition of burial goods, and votive offerings. On a quotidian level, linen was incorporated into the sealing of some containers, especially stone vessels, but pottery as well. As a permeable material, however, linen was not the seal itself, but a means of establishing that the seal was intact, and great care could be taken in creating the textile cover: for example, linen seals on food and wine vessels deposited in the tomb of Kha at Deir el-Medina wove strips of linen in different colors together to form a geometric pattern, reminiscent of the geometric patterns used on animal mummies and votive figures in the Ptolemaic and Roman periods, as well as human mummies (Fig. 4.8, reconstructed on the basis of animal mummy wrappings, and see Fig. 3.4).[94] The elaborate interweaving of linen strips, which were sometimes dyed in shades of brown and purple and folded to create a clean edge on each side, created an optical effect of depth and detail and may well have been construed as repelling harmful forces, much as net or knot patterns do in other cultural contexts. Knots themselves were not necessarily avoided, or at least not consistently, either in mummy wrappings or the wrapping of statues; knots could also have positive benefits, for instance in magical practices where they were the material evidence of the actions and vocalizations performed.[95]

The layered effect of plaited or net-patterned bindings recalls the tight, circular wrapping of objects like the jackal figure placed in a niche in Tutankhamun's burial chamber, which was part of the magical performance described in *Book of the Dead* spell 151 (see Fig. 1.6, left).[96] A similar motivation may lie behind the taut bandaging of several objects used as votive deposits or in tombs (Fig. 4.9).[97] *Shabti*-figures, which served both functions, have been found wrapped in linen, and a pair excavated by Bruyère at Deir el-Medina displayed the dexterous spiraling of a single linen strip from head to foot end of each figure—the same direction observed in the wrapping of mummified bodies.[98] Other miniaturized figures of humans, kings, or gods received a similar treatment, deposited on their own at pilgrimage sites or in remote valleys, where they populated the actual and the spiritual landscape contained in scraps of textile gathered to their shapes.[99] Not all votive figures wore bandages, though: small clay fertility figures found in a mining settlement at Gebel Zeit on the Red Sea were wrapped in a square of linen and adorned with strings of beads.[100]

The difference between such cloth "garments" and the wound bandages on many objects hints at a variety of wrapping practices that might well have had different kinds of significance, as observed in the different effects of textile drapes, bandages, and wraps in the tomb of Tutankhamun. But one common feature is the close interrelationship of wrapped objects and bodies, so much so that any gap between nonhuman and human (that is, flesh and bone) appears negligible. The wrapping of wooden tomb statues representing the deceased offers a close parallel to the wrapping of temple statues, but other tomb goods wrapped or bandaged in linen were also representations of the deceased as well, extensions of the person that related

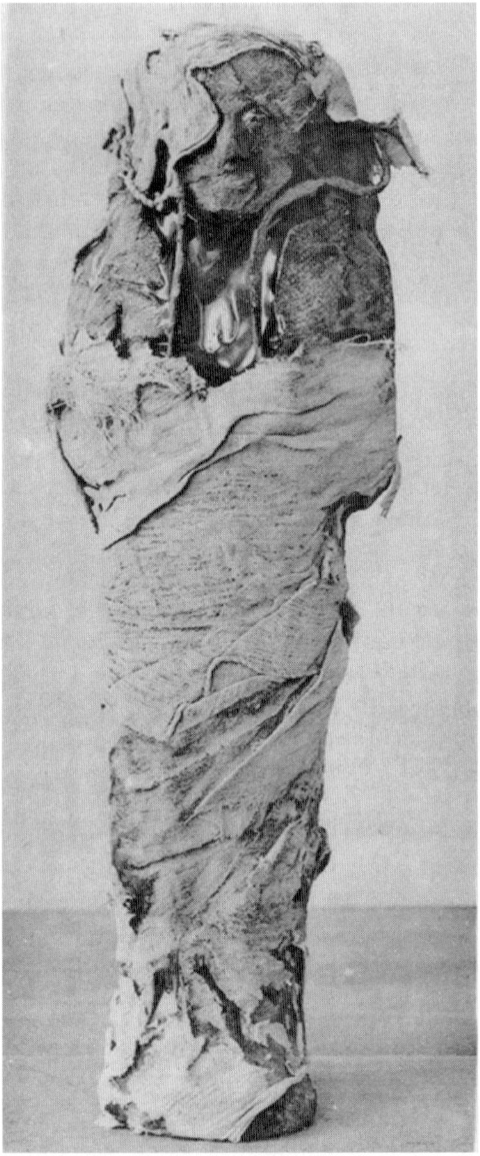

FIGURE 4.9 *Wooden* shabti *holding a copper crook and flail, anointed with resin and wrapped in linen. After Carnarvon and Carter,* Five Years' Exploration, *pl. xlii.1*

to a regime of bodily care both during life and after death.[101] For instance, the wrapping of mirrors placed in graves, which is especially well attested in female burials, must concern the distinctive characteristic of the mirror's reflecting surface, which became identified with the individual whose image appeared within it.[102] The canopic jars, used to contain wrapped, resin-coated remnants of the deceased's inner organs, were also part of the body of the deceased, and the human (later also animal) heads that form their lids or stoppers stand in relation to the smooth shape of the jar in much the same way that a head (the "mysterious face") framed by the divine headdress related to the smooth contours of the wrapped mummy. Fine travertine jars in the eighteenth-dynasty burial of Tjuya, the mother of queen Tiye, duplicated this effect because the remains inside them were formed into a

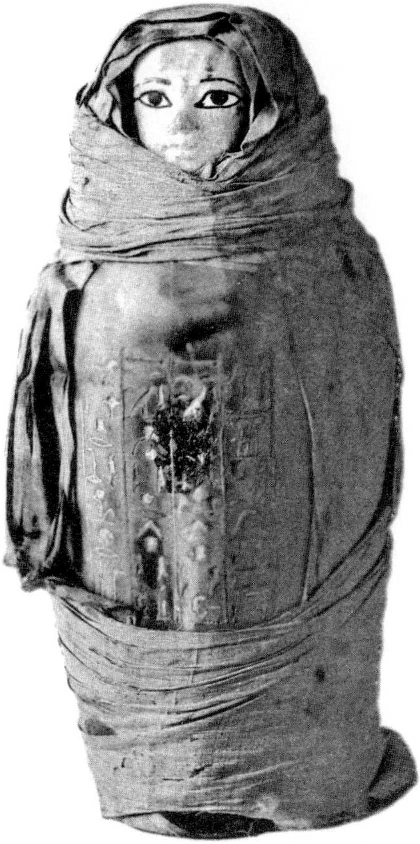

FIGURE 4.10 *Wrapped canopic jar from the burial of Maiherperi in the Valley of the Kings, 18th dynasty (c. 1450* B.C.E.*). H. 28.0 cm. Cairo, Egyptian Museum CG 24006B. After Daressy,* Fouilles de la Vallée des Rois, *pl. iv*

mummy-shaped, linen-wrapped package fitted with its own miniature mask.[103] Two elite burials of the New Kingdom also used wrapping around the head and body of the canopic jars themselves, reminiscent of the wrapping of the mummy and other images of the deceased: in the eighteenth-dynasty tomb of Maiherperi, a childhood companion of Thutmose III given a privileged burial in the Valley of the Kings, carefully arranged bandages revealed the face of each jar lid and the panel of inscription on the front, but encircled the body of the jar and covered the headdress of the lid (Fig. 4.10). Similarly, the canopic jars in the twentieth-dynasty tomb of Sennedjem, at Deir el-Medina, were also individually wrapped in linen.[104] Excavators left one jar unopened, but the other three were unwrapped to reveal the contents inside—in each case, a packet of human organ encased in resin and more linen. Like the arms of cloth that embraced the sun god in the underworld, or the mummy of a boy in Roman Thebes, the contents of canopic jars demonstrated once again that the cloth and the body were one and the same, inseparable.

The Wrapped Body in Egyptian Art

The arms of Tait are your flesh.

Opening of the Mouth, Scene 53, preserved on a Roman period papyrus, after J. Quack, "Fragmente des Mundöffnungsrituals" (2006), p. 100

The cloth that wrapped the sacred image was its new skin, muscle, and tissue, so that textile and object—or textile and body—became a unity. Where one stopped and the other began may have been a point of material demarcation, but conceptually, the demarcation was immaterial. Wrapping bodies and objects in linen created a range of visual and verbal metaphors whose multivalent symbolism, and social significance, is lost if the textile is seen as separate from or additional to the body/object. The fact that textiles have tended to be sidelined in interpretations of ancient Egyptian material culture only compounds this loss.

In Egyptian art, the depiction of wrapped or minimally tailored garments sought to engage with the tactile and visual qualities of high-grade linen, such as its color, draping, transparency, fringing, pleating, and, in some cases, fold lines. Representational art is often cited in studies of Egyptian textiles to try to illustrate what ancient clothing looked like, but how an artist drew or carved the arrangement of clothing, and what kind of clothing was represented, depended on symbolism and visual conventions, especially in two-dimensional images. The skintight dresses on some female figures—elite women at certain periods, goddesses always—owe more to artistic imagination than to linen, as does the contrasting fullness of men's aprons and skirts, which can appear to project in straight lines in front of the wearer's legs as if the cloth were starched and boned. Either way, clothing conveyed messages about social status, gender, or divine beauty, among other things, and the surface effects and tactility of the linen were intrinsic to such meanings.

The different wrapped skirts on a series of four wooden statues made for the scribe Merer show the artistic possibilities that even this most simple, and scanty, of garments offered (Fig. 4.11).[105] Dated to the Middle Kingdom and probably from Asyut, the statues show Merer in two versions of male dress, one a skirt that wraps right over left, and the other a *shendjet*-skirt (*šnḏy.t*), with a shaped "tab" visible under the wrapping, probably formed by a short apron-like undergarment underneath.[106] The *shendjet* is one of the rare garments whose name is securely known since it is clearly depicted and identified in friezes that show objects and amuletic adornments supplied for the dead.[107] All the skirts on the Merer statues were created by layering gesso over the wood, which was painted bright white to represent the brightness and fineness of the cloth. Hieroglyphic texts were then incised into the smooth, white surface and painted black, further "wrapping" the wrapped skirt in inscriptions derived from the *Coffin Texts,* which hail Merer as *imakh (îm3ḫ)*, "revered" or "honored," with the gods. Garment, figure, and inscription work together, elevating an item of what might seem to be basic attire—the male skirt or kilt—to a feature of beauty and brilliance, for body and textile alike.

The more substantial, concealing wrapping applied to statues and similar objects was also evoked in representational forms, with a subtlety that can be attributed to the system of decorum that governed the design, execution, and placement of images.[108] The cloth covering of some statues echoes the depiction of cloaks or mantles on men, a visual trope that recurs in Egyptian art as an alternative to the more usual bare-torsoed figure associated with images of the male elite like the Merer figures. Stone statues in particular suited such depictions of smooth expanses of linen over the contours of the body, sometimes incorporating small details of the textile such as the drape and crease lines where the subject grasps a corner of his cloak, or the short weft fringe worn uppermost to frame his chest (Fig. 4.12). The cloak offered a way to suggest wrapping, and hence veneration, without trespassing on representational decorum. Some Egyptologists have suggested that the preference for cloak-wearing statues relates to economy, arguing that they were less labor intensive to produce, or to sturdiness, supposing that such statues would stand up better to open-air exposure in a temple courtyard.[109] However, examples of cloaked statues range from a few centimeters high to more than life-size and can be finished with such detail, including inscriptions carved over the "surface" of the cloak, that any savings of labor or material would have been slight.

If their form suited temple dedication in particular, then it is just as likely that their subjects' wrapped appearance, rather than sculptural

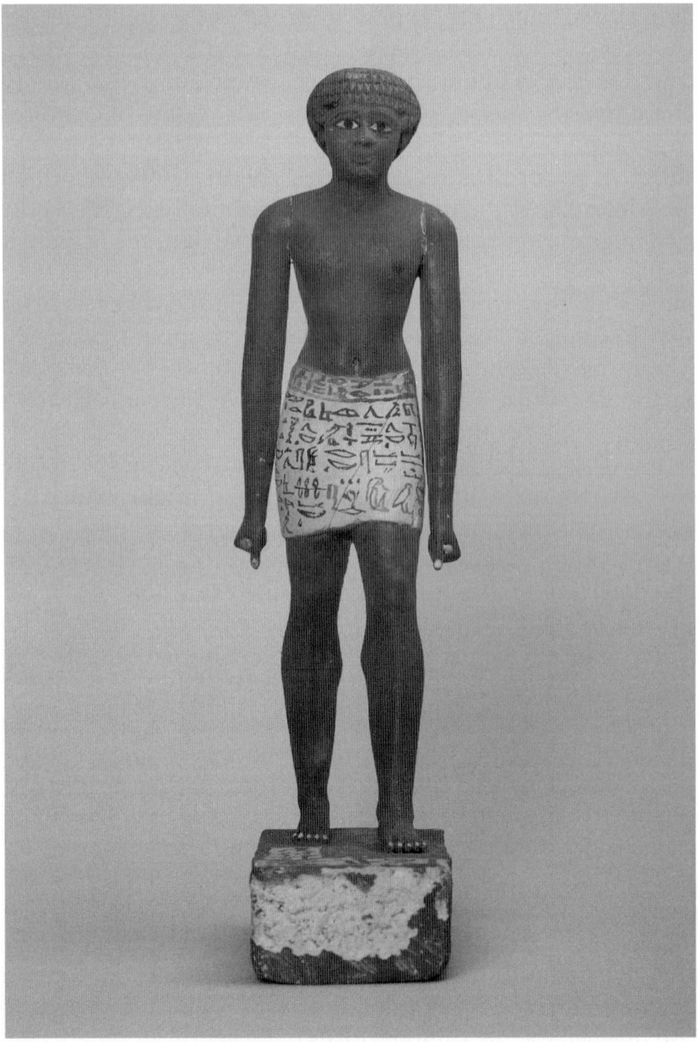

FIGURE 4.11 *Wooden statuette of Merer, with inscriptions on the skirt. Attributed to Asyut, 12th dynasty (c. 2000–1800 B.C.E.). H. 35.3 cm. The Metropolitan Museum of Art, Rogers Fund, 1910 (10.176.59). Image © The Metropolitan Museum of Art*

ergonomics, was the reason, especially given the hand and arm postures that cloaked figures often adopt. The arms of cloak-wearing figures lie crossed or bent beside each other, hands either flat, in fists, or grasping an edge or corner of the wrap. One or both arms may be bent or crossed on statues without any cloak as well, which were by far the majority at any period, but these arm positions occur most frequently in conjunction with a wrapped garment. The different variations of bent arms and hand

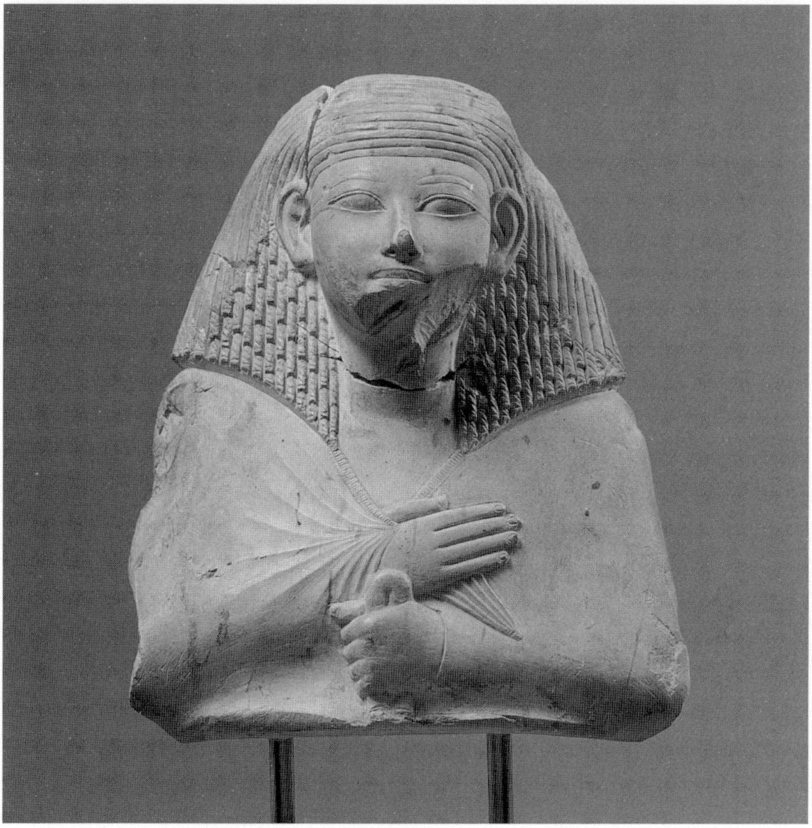

FIGURE 4.12 *Upper part of a limestone statuette, 18th dynasty (c. 1450–1400* B.C.E.*). H. 19.0 cm. Photograph by Ole Haupt. Copenhagen, Ny Carlsberg Glyptotek, ÆIN 655A. Courtesy of the Ny Carlsberg Glyptotek*

positions play with the possibilities of the cloak and seem to convey qualities such as bodily restraint, patience, dignity, or humility, as well as the subject's readiness to receive food and drink offerings with the dominant, right hand that emerges from the garment.[110] Although often characterized as a posture related to the god Osiris, bent arms appear in Egyptian art as early as the Old Kingdom, more than a thousand years before the earliest secure representation of Osiris. The argument may work better in reverse: Osiris comes to be represented with crossed arms, in a white shroud, because an association between wrapped textiles and this gestural language already existed.

Images of kings wearing cloaks or shroud-like wrappings were more explicit than nonroyal images in using the statue itself to represent the coexistence of the human and divine. A painted limestone statue of the third-dynasty king Djoser, found walled up in a chamber abutting his monumental tomb at Saqqara, the Step Pyramid, uses distinctive iconography to manifest Djoser's divine qualities, especially in his transformation after death: his hair is arranged in the three-part form, barely covered by a scarf draped over his head; he has a long, blunt-ended beard not normally attested in royal iconography; and he is wrapped in a white cloak that bares his feet and hands so that the right is in a fist on his chest and the left lies flat on his lap (Fig. 4.13).[111] Similar knee- or ankle-length cloaks were part of the *sed* festival, a key ritual that renewed the power of the reigning king.[112] The Djoser statue's longer version, along with the wig and beard, may emphasize the king's divine qualities overtaking his human form, as if the transformative power of the textile were exerting itself in stone. A *sed* cloak was made of *idmy*-linen, the fine-quality cloth equivalent to royal linen on the Old Kingdom linen lists. Later temple inscriptions specify red, green, or white *idmy*-linen for the clothing of the gods, all aspects of multicolored light, and the cloth is also associated with the magic, healing eye of Horus.[113] During the *sed* rites, the king was censed, anointed with oil, and wrapped in the cloak under the protection of a tented structure called the *seh-netjer (sḥ-nṯr)*—identical to the tent some early sources identify as the location for embalming and wrapping the dead. Thus at the heart of the *sed* festival was the same explicit connection between fine linen, renewal, and the divine that was expressed through mummification rites and the dressing of cult statues as well.

To avoid the implication that bodies covered in smooth, white cloaks, mantles, or shrouds referred in any way to mummification, the Egyptologist Erik Hornung used the word *undifferentiated* to describe them, especially when discussing gods like Osiris; Hornung also wished to avoid the impulse to call such figures "Osiriform" or "Osirian," given the tautology this creates between the god and the act of mummification. Similarly, the term *anthropoid,* applied to contoured coffins with human faces, and sometimes hands, is an Egyptological non sequitur, for rather than representing the deceased as *anthropos,* "man" or "human," such coffins manifest a sacred image in its wrappings, their smooth surfaces frequently covered with further imagery and inscriptions. They are the ancient Egyptian *wet,* literally "the wrapped," and wrapping was a key feature not only of mummification but also of other rites, including the daily statue cult and the *sed* festival. The representation of a body seemingly enclosed in a shroud or bandages thus takes on a meaning far beyond the treatment of the dead corpse.

Certain gods, especially gods with creative or regenerative powers, were almost exclusively depicted in the state of being wrapped: Osiris, the slain and rejuvenated king; Ptah of Memphis, a creator god associated with art and craft production; and Min of Akhmim, a primordial creator god usually depicted with an erection and with his right arm free of the wrapping and raised in a threatening posture. Some manifestations of another virile creator god, Amun of Thebes, also took wrapped form, as on occasion did the young moon god Khonsu, whose waxing and waning involved generative force. The

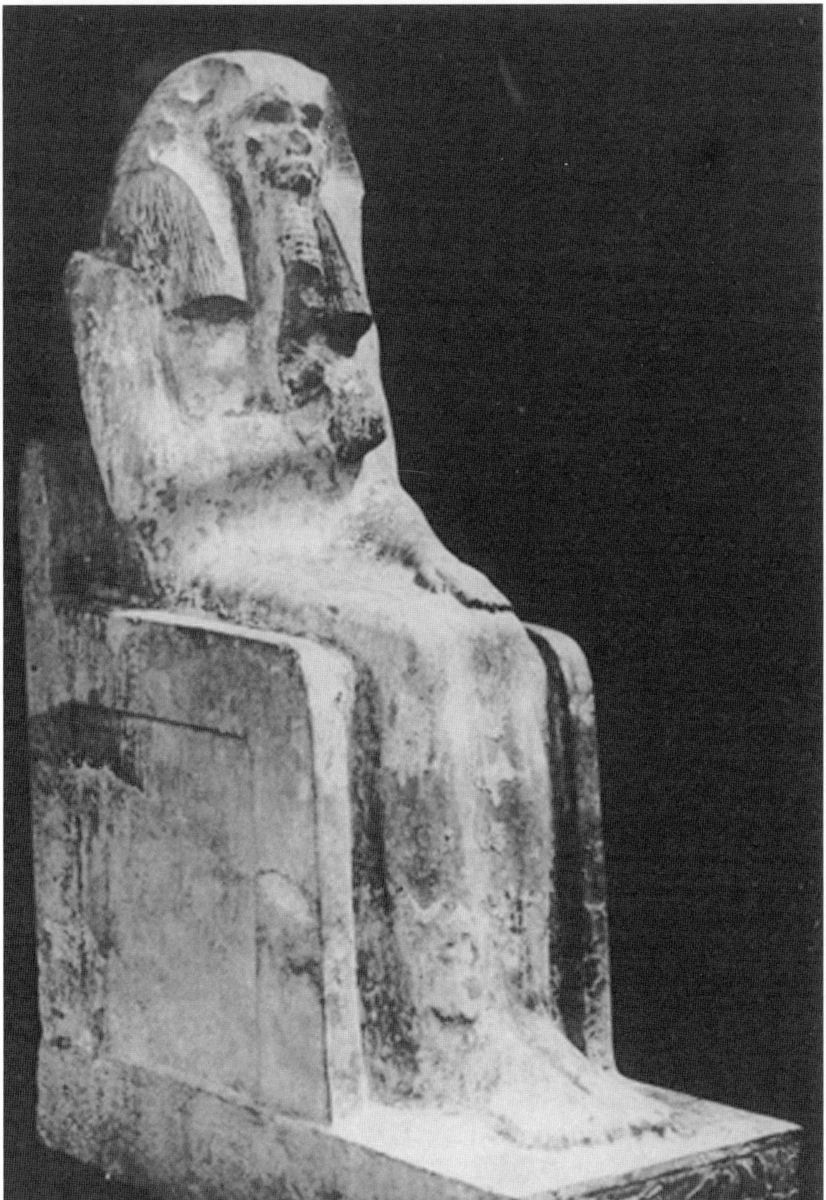

FIGURE 4.13 *Limestone statue of king Djoser, discovered in a chamber abutting the Step Pyramid at Saqqara. H. 142.0 cm, W. 45.3 cm, L. 95.5 cm. Cairo, Egyptian Museum JE 49158. After Quibell and Firth,* Step Pyramid Complex, *pl. 29.2*

creation and ritual burial (with wrapping) of smooth-contoured figures identified with Osiris, Sokar, or the composite god Ptah-Sokar-Osiris featured in religious rites during the month of Khoiak, but the wrapping and burial of the figures is not a "mummification" to enact rebirth; rather, mummification is one wrapping ritual among many, concerned with mutual protection (of and from divine power) and with the seclusion gods required to nurture and restore themselves through their images.[114] Because of its significance beyond the funerary realm, the wrapped body was a form in which nearly any god could be represented—in the appropriate context.

As a sign of veneration, the wrapped form was particularly suited to the representation of ancestors—not only of the gods, but of humans, too. The primeval gods of Thebes, known as "the Eight" (in Egyptology, the "Ogdoad"), and the four generations of male-female pairs from whom Osiris and Isis, and their son Horus, trace descent ("the Nine," or "Ennead"), are often depicted with contoured or wrapped bodies.[115] Kings and queens honored with cults can also appear in wrapped form in statuary (such as a queen of Thutmose III, depicted in a pink granite statue found near Tod) or in scenes of commemoration, for instance in the hypostyle hall of the Ptolemaic temple at Kom Ombo or the tomb of Anherkhawy at Deir el-Medina, where this "overseer of works" under the twentieth-dynasty king Ramses III (c. 1194–1163 B.C.E.) dons a leopard skin to perform cult rituals for the kings and queens who had established and benefitted the village for workmen in the Valley of the Kings.[116]

Depicted on the same plane as the honored kings and queens, the sole deified human in the Anherkhawy scene—a renowned priest and official named Amenhotep son of Hapu (eighteenth dynasty, c. 1380 B.C.E.)—wears flowing white robes; here, he is called by his familiar name, Huy, and identified as "justified among the gods." But elsewhere, the representation of human ancestors and other venerated figures—we might think of them like saints or sheikhs, the latter being derived, after all, from the Arabic for "elder" or "noble"—was likewise realized through forms that gave them a wrapped, or in some cases almost lump-like, form.[117] A nineteenth-dynasty fragment of relief, now lost, likely comes from an elite tomb at Saqqara and preserves three registers of venerated figures (Fig. 4.14).[118] Known as the "Daressy fragment" after Georges Daressy, who first recorded it, the relief depicts deified, enthroned kings in the topmost register, with wrapped bodies, long beards, and a *nemes*-like head scarf over the three-part headdress, much like the Djoser statue. The figures hold the crook and flail, corresponding to representations of the dead king on New Kingdom royal coffins. In the two lower registers, a series of upright, wrapped figures represents priests and scribes extending back to the Old Kingdom, including high priests of Ptah (who wear their characteristic sidelock of hair instead of the three-part headdress), lector-priests, overseers of embalmers, and semi-historical sages whose wise sayings are preserved in ancient literary works.

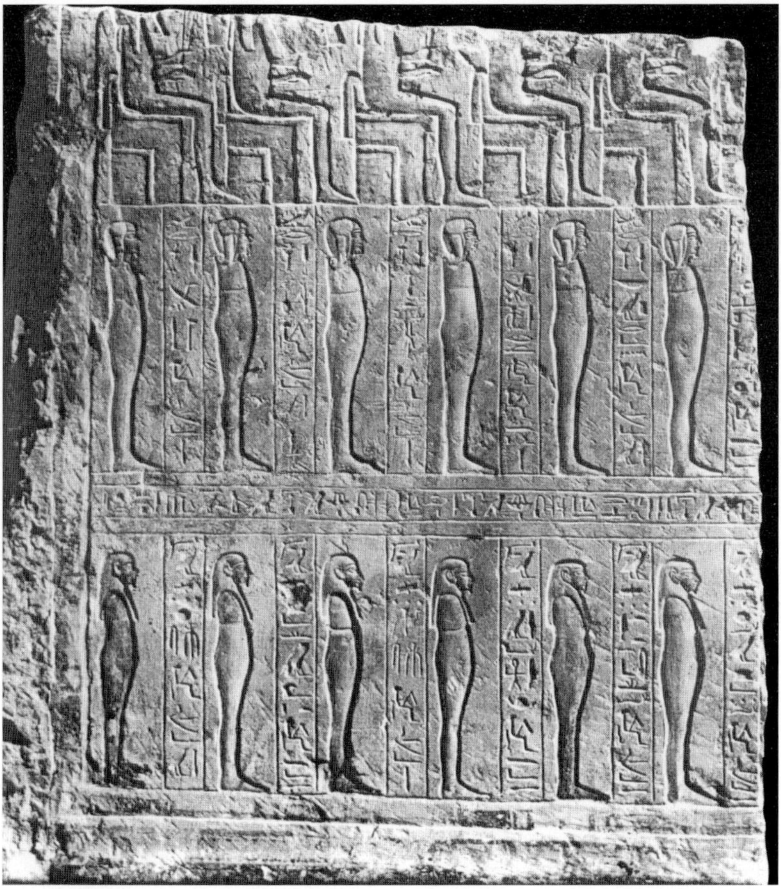

FIGURE 4.14 *Part of the tomb relief (now lost) known as the "Daressy fragment", from Saqqara, 19th Dynasty (c. 1250 B.C.E.). After an archival photograph published in Fischer,* Varia: Egyptian Studies *I, pl. xviii, fig. 3*

The Daressy relief stems from the refined milieu of the important priesthood of Ptah at Memphis, but honoring one's forebears took place on a domestic scale as well, best attested through the so-called ancestor busts from Deir el-Medina and elsewhere, which take the shape of a truncated, wrapped torso with a face framed by the divine wig (Fig. 4.15).[119] Although other interpretations have been proposed, the smooth contours, indication of a neck line, and in some cases white coloring on these figures makes a visual reference to linen wrappings without representing the whole body or its limbs.[120] Most have a three-part head cover and outlined eyes, and some are inscribed for a specific person, male or female. Since the busts were used in domestic contexts, their distinctive form must have suited this setting, bridging aspects of the human and the divine, the specific (a named individual) and the generic (ancestors as a subtype of the venerated dead). Some small examples in clay, stone, wood, or faience were placed in graves, and the bust form also appears on stelae, so that a range of objects in different materials and sizes shared a similar function as, in Meskell's words, "tangible sites of embodied memory that simultaneously operated as a physical channel between worlds."[121]

In the Ptolemaic period, a wrapped figure squatting on the ground was used to represent ancestors on stelae dedicated by their descendants, in one case honoring five generations of male and female progenitors.[122] The

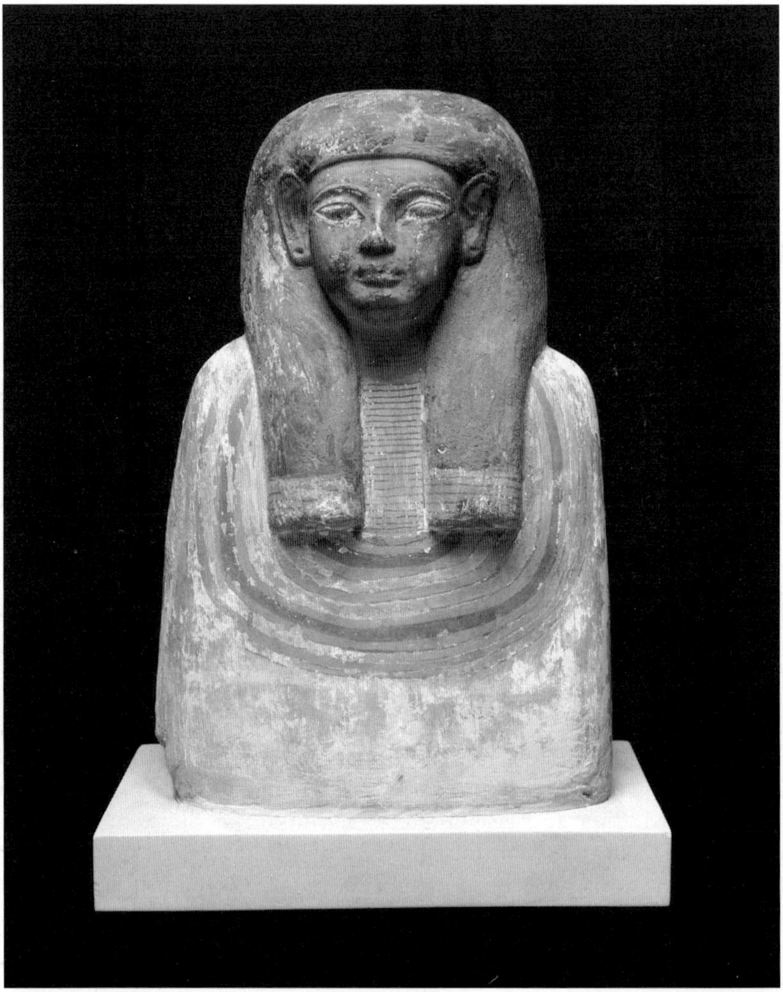

FIGURE 4.15 *Painted limestone object known as an ancestor bust, probably from Thebes, 19th or 20th dynasty (c. 1300–1100 B.C.E.). H. 24.5 cm, W. 15.5 cm. British Museum, EA 61083. Copyright: The Trustees of the British Museum*

squatting figures, seen in profile, resemble a form of sculpture known in Egyptology as a "block" or "Würfelhocker" statue (Fig. 4.16), in which the subject—almost invariably male—squats with his knees tight against his chest and his arms usually crossed on top of them.[123] Often set up in the restricted areas of a temple, this type of statue used the form of a wrapped, cloth-covered body to honor some of the most high-ranking priests and officials of the day. The compact form of the statue lent itself to a number of potential meanings, including the apotropaic role of a liminal guardian: several statues were made in pairs, and a few examples even preserve a wedge-like rear projection used to hold temple doors open on certain occasions.[124] These guardian statues position the honorand in a prominent place and involve the sculpture itself in the act of regulating access to restricted spaces. As with the wooden statuettes of Merer in his short, inscription-covered skirt (see Fig. 4.11), the surface represented as shrouded on block statues frequently became a surface for writing extended, narrative texts in a way that Egyptian art would not have supported on the representation of skin. The multiple layers that wrap the honored individual thus include not only the idea of a textile wrapping but also his scripted identity, from name and lineage to career path and cult loyalties.

One example of a block statue seems a fitting place to end this necessarily brief consideration of the much larger topic of wrapping and art—an example that serves as a segue to the next chapter and as a salient reminder of how crucial linen textiles and wrapping practices were in the imaginative and objective world of ancient Egypt. Carved of fine-grained limestone and standing almost one and a half meters high, the statue is one of a pair dedicated by the high priest of Amun, Bakenkhons, during the reign of Ramses II (see Fig. 4.16). Inscriptions around the back and sides of the body and, in four columns, on the front of the legs present Bakenkhons's illustrious career and the qualities that commend him to the gods and to his fellow priests.[125] Addressing the reader in the first person, Bakenkhons tells us, among other things, that he was a "master of secrets in the sky, earth, and underworld"—and assures us that he was a man who kept his silence.

Among the "secrets" Bakenkhons would have known were the forms of appearance in which gods manifested themselves on earth and the crucial act of wrapping those forms in cloth. Other texts describe this act with the phrase *hebes kheperu* (*ḥbs ḫpr.w*), "clothing the forms of appearance," and classify the word *kheperu,* "forms of appearance," with the mummiform hieroglyph. Thus a wrapped body, not so dissimilar from Bakenkhons's own figure in this block statue, stood for the forms or images that were meant to be wrapped, a fairly straightforward association between word and idea. However, the more common translation of *hebes kheperu* indicated something just as important about the performance of wrapping rituals, for the same phrase meant "to keep a secret"—which is exactly what Bakenkhons did.[126]

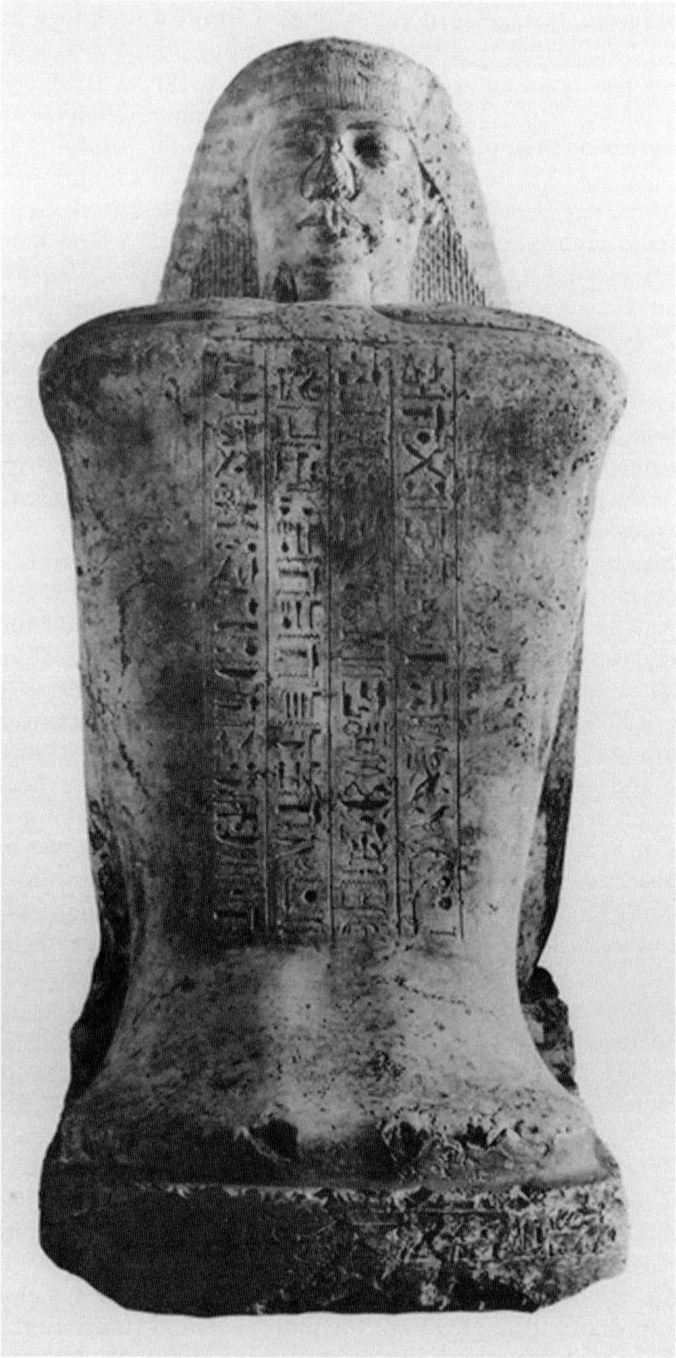

FIGURE 4.16 *Limestone statue of the high priest Bakenkhons, 19th dynasty (c. 1250* B.C.E.*), found in the Karnak cachette. H. 1.5 m. Cairo, Egyptian Museum, CG 42155; after Legrain,* Statues et statuettes de rois, *II, pl. xviii*

In considering the interplay between bodies, textiles, and text, we have moved a long way from the humble flax field. But from the wrapping of embalmed bodies in inscribed linen bandages, to the wrapping of inscribed objects, like a statue or a storage jar, this interplay is persistent in the Egyptian evidence and is enabled by the materiality of linen—especially once we start remembering, rather than forgetting, the textiles involved, in their real as well as represented forms. Channeling between the material and immaterial worlds was accomplished through physical means and actions—linen cloth, circular wrapping, and draping or shrouding an image. The persistence of these concerns in the visual record, and the limited and presumably specific use of wrapped or cloaked figures in art, was meaningful within a cultural system that imbued linen with restorative and life-giving powers and saw clothing and cloth not as two categories, but one. The value of linen went beyond monetary value, for its symbolic significance contributed to the organization of power, gender, and family and household relations in Egyptian society. Textiles, so susceptible to fraying, forged connections between humans, who were similarly prone to decay.

The works of sculpture and painting considered in the second part of this chapter are the artistic expressions of this complex of ideas and likewise helped negotiate relationships among gods, kings, ancestors, and humans. Material derived from the archaeological record or the unwrapping of mummified bodies reinforces the importance ascribed to cloth in the visual and written record, and thus helps link the domestic and mortuary spheres to the elite domains of the temple and the king. Moreover, cloth bound modern and ancient Egypt together through the colonial context of the cotton industry, which became entwined with archaeology through both the developing infrastructure in Egypt and the funding channeled to the field from home. In the nineteenth and early twentieth centuries, Western archaeologists understood cloth in a way later generations, accustomed to synthetic fabrics and overseas outsourcing, do not, and for all that excavators treated textile layers and wrappings as an impediment to be removed, many took such a thorough approach to their discoveries that their reports, measurements, and sometimes photographs give us glimpses of the textiles' transient fate. Through its work of excavation, recording, and study, modern scholarship stepped in to assume the mantle of the ancient priesthood—with an important difference, for like other forms of knowledge construed as scientific, archaeology claims that its goal is not to keep secrets, but to reveal them.

5

Secrecy

Secrets are all around us. They are among the building blocks of society, no less so now than in the reign of Ramses II, when the high priest Bakenkhons declared his knowledge of all the secrets of the sky, the earth, and the underworld—the phrase we saw at the end of the last chapter, carved into the surface of the priest's sculpted and wrapped body (see Fig. 4.16). For Bakenkhons, this knowledge took physical and metonymical form through the wrapping of sacred images in cloth and, crucially, through the display of those wrapped images at carefully orchestrated moments, such as a religious procession or a funeral cortège. This is the paradox of secrecy: the secret must be seen (though not revealed) in order to have its intended effect.

Bakenkhons declared his silence to show that he was in on the secret and worthy of trust. What that secret was scarcely mattered, for secrecy was not so much a matter of hiding what a priest like Bakenkhons knew or did, but of using the claim to hidden knowledge as a basis for the exercise of power—the power of a social elite, of the temple, and, it follows, of the ancient Egyptian state. It is this claim to knowledge as a source of power that links the practice of secrecy *in* ancient Egypt to the practice of secrecy *about* ancient Egypt, which has informed the Western encounter with Egyptian culture from classical Greece to the present day. High priests have more in common with archaeologists or museum curators than any of them might think. This chapter explores that commonality as well as the key differences between the performance of secrecy in the ancient world and in modern times, when secrecy seems to contradict the expectations of a democratic society and the exhortations to transparency in its public institutions.

One such institution is the museum, and over the past twenty to thirty years, many museums have embraced a shift to greater openness in terms of expanding audience engagement, consulting with local and source communities, and facilitating access to their collections and behind-the-scenes operations, often through the use of the web and social media as well as books and television documentaries.[1] Opening access—physical or intellectual—is not giving away a secret, however; it is another way of performing the secrecy that the control of a cultural resource, such as a work of art, so frequently entails. Often mistaken for something secret, what museums keep out of sight is the messy business of organizational life. Spaces like storerooms, conservation labs, and staff kitchens are a backstage to which only performers, rather than the audience, are usually admitted, to use the sociologist Erving Goffman's classic formulation of how individuals and groups present themselves.[2] These spaces may house a group's secrets, but they are not the secret itself.

As a former museum professional, my own analysis of what is and is not a form of secrecy in the museum constitutes part of the ongoing trend towards de-authorizing the institution, here effected through the act of authoring an aspect of its practice in which I was myself involved. A vignette from my own experience helps illustrate this complex relationship and sets the (back)stage for a scene I return to later in this chapter, namely the "mummy store" of the Manchester Museum. At the back of the museum gift shop is an unmarked door that leads to the museum's backstage, where bland corridors and echoing staircases branch off to offices and storerooms. Here, a chilly storeroom dubbed the "mummy store" could be reached only after someone with the appropriate keys had passed through a series of locked fire doors, each of which closed with a solid metal thump. The mummy store itself was a dead end, an oasis of calm with a background hum from the temperamental air-conditioning unit that regulated the humidity. No one went there unless they had a reason, and in any case, few staff had a key—though the number had increased since the days when one curator had insisted on the mummy store having a unique lock. The keys are the key to the secrecy here: it functioned within the organization, not between the museum and its public, who were quite unaware of what lay behind the doors and blacked-out windows. Unlike that which is merely out of sight, secrecy operates where those excluded from the secret are aware of it, for instance, among staff who know who holds which keys. Like Bakenkhons with his pledge of silence, letting yourself through a locked door is a badge of belonging to one group, worn so that those outside the group will see and recognize it. Knowing the secrets of the sky, the earth, and the underworld is all very well, but even better if it offers some advantage in this world, too.

In this chapter, I examine the role of secrecy in ancient Egypt and how the idea of secrecy has influenced the reception of Egypt in the West. I begin by discussing how assumptions made about Egyptian "secrets" have influenced both conventional and alternative approaches to the subject, pitting rationalism (academic Egyptology) against interpretations that it characterizes as esoteric or irrational (theosophy, Freemasonry, Afrocentrism). Anthropological studies of secrecy help move beyond this unhelpful dualism by viewing secrecy in its social context as a form of interaction and organization. Different groups have different reasons for seeking the secrets of Egypt—and even in contemporary society, with its ideals of transparency and of unfettered access to publicly funded institutions like museums and universities, truth claims based on the possession of restricted knowledge have a deep-seated hold. Where the ownership and interpretation of Egyptian antiquities are concerned, what modern scholarship thinks it knows, and doesn't know, too often confuses our own secrets with the secrets of the ancient past, and at the end of the chapter, I return to the question of secrecy in relation to the museum. Every emptied cache, opened tomb, and unwrapped mummy is a mediation between that past and our present in which the present usually wields the upper hand, and that hand is often covered by a curatorial glove.

Secrecy and the Study of Ancient Egypt

> The secret offers, so to speak, the possibility of a second world alongside the manifest world; and the latter is decisively influenced by the former.
>
> Georg Simmel, "The Secret and the Secret Society" (1950 [1908]), p. 330

The sociologist Georg Simmel's 1908 discussion was the first significant, sustained analysis of secrecy as a factor in human sociation. The secret, he asserted, was "one of man's greatest achievements" because it added depth to an individual's inner life and to the structuring of relationships between and among humans, whether for positive or negative effect.[3] He looked in particular at secret societies like the Freemasons, where, he argued, secrecy was both a boundary marker and an organizing principle. Their secrets separated the group and its members from everyone outside the group, while sharing in secrets created a powerful bond among the members that then extended into their activities and interactions in society beyond the group as well. Extrapolating beyond the specific example of Freemasonry, Simmel pointed out that secret knowledge is often passed on in oral form and in heightened circumstances like initiation rites, encouraging personal interaction and further strengthening group bonds.

Anthropologists have used the social implications of Simmel's approach to study secrecy in subjects as diverse as initiation, masquerade, and postcolonial politics (and sometimes all of those together). From this research, two strands of consensus emerge: first, that the form of secrecy matters more than the content of the secrets, and second, that revealing or displaying the secret is integral to secrecy, counterintuitive as that statement may seem.[4] Anything can be a secret, no matter how seemingly banal, and information that would be deemed secret in one situation might be revealed in another because the contexts or the interlocutors are different. Hence secrecy is situational, as well as performative. Since many more people will know the basic content of the secret than are supposed to, it is the "*doing* of secrecy"—by those who are supposed to know it—that matters.[5] Secrets are social by nature, for secrecy requires at least three people: two to know the secret, and a third from whom they can keep it.

Secrecy has sat uncomfortably with the academic study of ancient Egypt, however. A standard reference work compiled in the 1970s and 80s, the *Lexikon der Ägyptologie,* has only a short article on "Geheimnis," and one leading scholar of Egyptian religion, Erik Hornung, has argued that there were no secrets in ancient Egypt because priests brought the statues of the gods out of the temple for public festival days.[6] But the denial of secrecy goes further than questions of theology. From the late nineteenth century to today, denying or minimizing the secret in the Egyptian evidence has been a consistent strategy for distinguishing professionalized work on ancient Egypt from the many popular, "alternative," and mystical studies of ancient Egypt that have always existed alongside it. The tension is over disputed territory—but disputed territory is also common ground.

The extent to which ancient Egypt and secrets go together in the public imagination is easily demonstrated but less easily comprehended on its own terms, rather than through eye-rolling mockery or enthusiastic embrace. The online retailer Amazon can supply readers with dozens of books that fit the words *Egypt* and *secret* comfortably into their titles and subject matter—everything from Zahi Hawass's *Secret Egypt* travel guide, to the *Erotic Secrets of the Forbidden Papyrus.* In early 2012, the first page of Google search results for "secret Egypt" yielded the website Ascending Passage.com, where visitors can "explore Ancient Egypt in a way neglected by conventional archaeology," a phrase that reveals acute awareness of scholarly disbelief.[7] Top of the search results list was a special exhibition held at the Herbert Art Gallery and Museum in Coventry, England, in 2011, featuring more than two hundred objects and curated by a trained Egyptologist.[8] The title, "Secret Egypt," and the accompanying website, with a URL that made no reference to the museum, seem to have been designed to attract an audience leaning towards alternative views, but the exhibition's subtitle, "Unravelling Truth from Myth," clearly assumed that such an unraveling is both possible and desirable. It is a goal held as fervently by the exhibition curators as the goal of spiritual insight—another truth—is held by the creators of Ascending Passage.com, yet the museum exhibition inherently prioritizes its "secret Egypt," and its right to revelation, over others', its "truth" over "myth."

But secrecy is not about truth and myth. It is about people and power—and that is as true for ancient Egypt as it is today, whether it involves the organization of academic disciplines, the museum profession, the Freemasons, or the Kemetic Orthodox Faith association in Chicago, one of a number of contemporary faith practices based on ancient Egyptian religion.[9] As with the claims made by Bakenkhons, secrecy is about who is inside, and who is out, and the interpersonal bonds and boundaries created through the performance of secrecy translate into differentials of power that extend beyond either the form or the content of the secret. Although some of these differentials may be subtle, they are also inevitable. Ultimately, restrictions on knowledge, spaces, and group membership have repercussions throughout a society and are maintained precisely because they produce a desired effect.

The idea of Egypt as a place of secrets is hardly new. The secret source of the Nile was a preoccupation of Greek and Roman authors, which informed imagery of Egypt such as the Palestrina Mosaic and made the river cataracts south of Aswan the subject of works of fiction, not to mention an early version of adventure tourism.[10] Greek and Roman authors also saw in Egyptian religious practice something comparable to the so-called mystery cults (*mysteria*) that featured in their own society, which explicitly involved acts of initiation and levels of revealed knowledge that the initiate was never supposed to repeat—although the initiate could include his experience in a novel, as Apuleius famously did in his *Metamorphoses,* or *The Golden Ass,* a fictionalized account of his loyalty to the cult of Isis and Osiris in Rome.[11] Egyptologists tend to see the mystery cults dedicated to Egyptian gods as alien to the original formulation of Egyptian worship, but to focus on the specifics of different cultic practices misses the larger point that religions are highly adaptable, and most, if not all, have some form of secrecy at their core.[12]

It was this Greek and Roman articulation of an Egyptian secrecy, together with the impenetrability of hieroglyphic writing, that informed Renaissance and early modern ideas about Egypt, as in the work of Athanasius Kircher. Although his work was discredited in the Enlightenment, Kircher's publications had a long reach, not only for his discussions of hieroglyphs, mummification, and obelisks, but also for the illustrations supplied in the volumes, which were fixtures in courtly libraries.[13] Like many seventeenth-century scholars, including Robert Boyle and Isaac Newton, the scope of Kircher's interest in natural philosophy encompassed alchemy and metaphysics, and his studies of Egyptian mythology and monuments should be seen in this context, as should his confident reading of hieroglyphic inscriptions based on what he assumed were their complex, symbolic meanings—inspired in part by reading medieval copies of Horapollo's *Hieroglyphica,* attributed to an Egyptian priest of the fourth century C.E. Champollion's decipherment of hieroglyphs sent Kircher (and Horapollo) back to obscurity, in Egyptological circles at least, but his work retained an appeal for those more interested in the esoteric than the narrowly academic: the poets Ted Hughes and Sylvia Plath had a print of Isis, from Kircher's *Oedipus Aegyptiacus* of 1652, on the walls of their home, in keeping with their interest in Robert Graves's *The White Goddess,* not to mention astrology and Ouija boards (Fig. 5.1).[14]

By the late eighteenth century, the secrets of Egypt were well and truly embedded in the influential sphere of Freemasonry and Rosicrucianism.[15] It was a Masonic tract on Moses and the Egyptian priesthood that inspired Schiller's popular poem "The Veiled Image of Sais," lines of which Beethoven kept in a frame on his piano.[16] The lines quote—or rather, misquote—from Plutarch (*De Iside* 9.354c) and Proclus (*Platonis Timaeum* I.30d–e), each of whom describes a statue of Isis-Athena in the great temple of Sais, in the delta. The goddess is probably a Hellenized version of Neith, who was often equated with Athena and whose temple at Sais was home to Egypt's

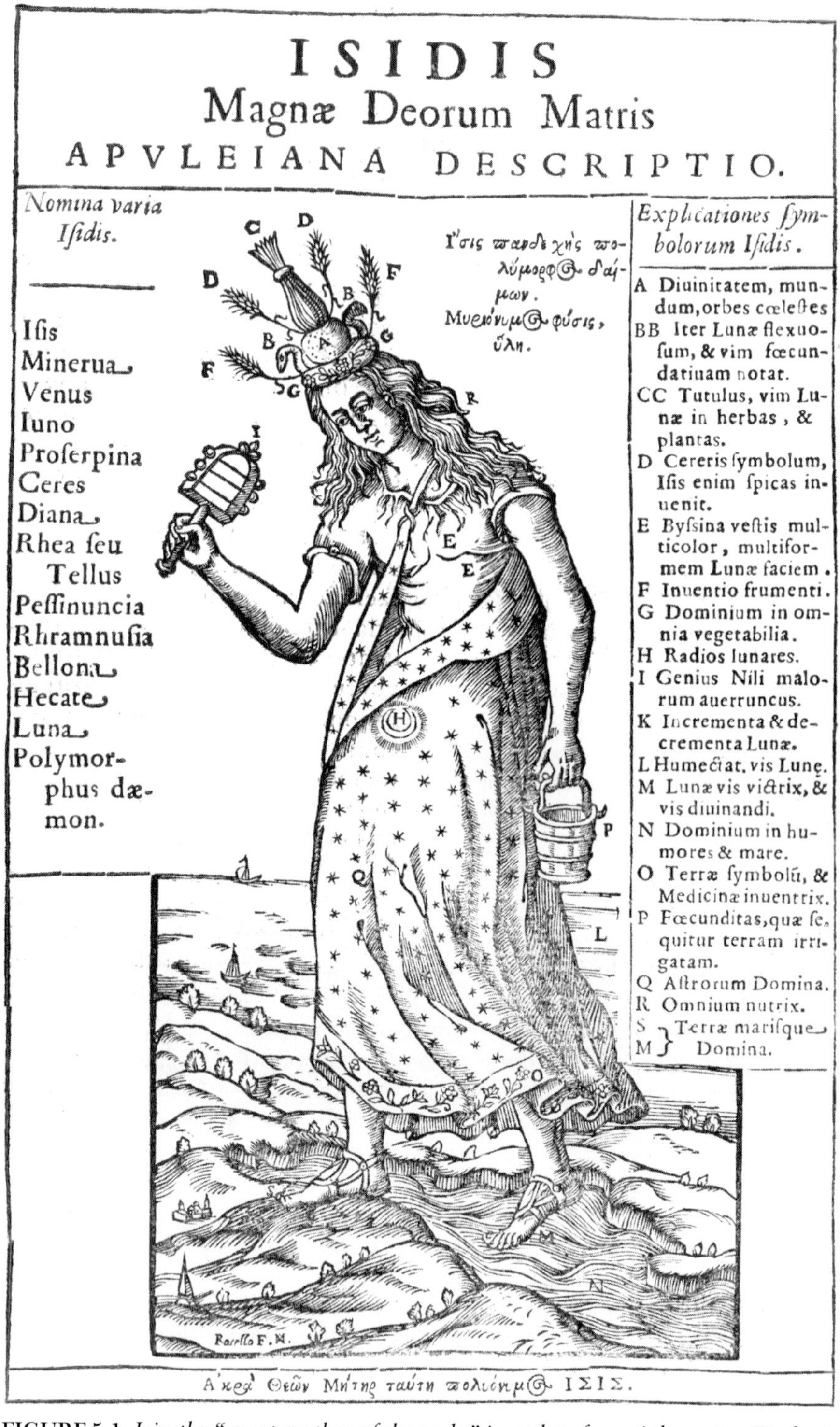

FIGURE 5.1 *Isis, the "great mother of the gods," in a plate from Athanasius Kircher's* Oedipus Aegyptiacus *(1652). Courtesy of the New York Public Library*

finest linen workshops. The statue was said to be inscribed with the words, "I am all that is or was or shall be; no mortal man has ever lifted my veil." In Greek, the words *chiton* and *peplos* referred to the statue's garment, indicating that the goddess was virginal, but a Latin commentary translated the words as *velum,* taking the expression to refer to the ultimate mystery of the divine. The lifting of the veil proved to be a powerful metaphor in the age of Enlightenment, where it came to represent the triumph of European science over Egypt, both modern and ancient.[17] A painting by François-Edouard Picot, entitled *Study and Genius Reveal Ancient Egypt to Greece,* was part of a cycle of themed paintings created for the ceilings of the Egyptian galleries that opened in the Louvre's Musée Charles X in 1827, with Champollion as curator (Fig. 5.2). Picot personified ancient Egypt as a reclining woman in pharaonic-style clothing, the same suppliant figure who had appeared on medals struck to commemorate Napoleon's invasion of the country a generation earlier.[18]

Seeing through secrets was a mark of rationalism, so where the dogged idea that hieroglyphs encoded some secret meaning had thwarted centuries of attempts at decipherment, Champollion "cracked the code" by realizing

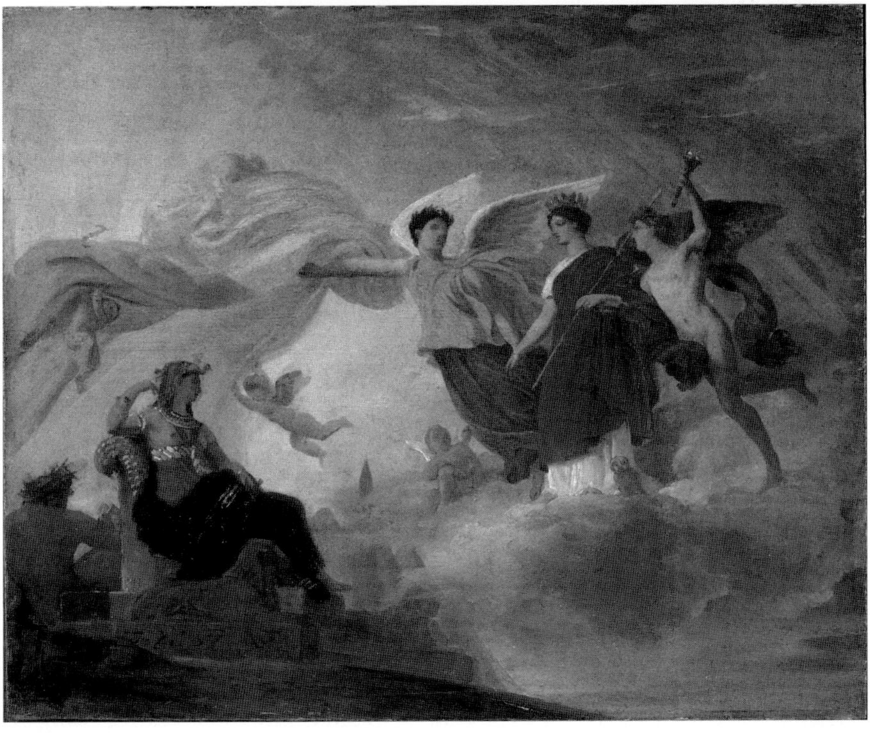

FIGURE 5.2 *François Edouard Picot,* L'Étude et le Génie dévoilent l'antique Égypte à la Grèce, *1826. Copyright: RMN-Grand Palais (musée du Louvre)/René-Gabriel Ojéda*

that they were, by and large, phonetic. The decipherment paved the way for the development of Egyptology as an academic specialism—the term was apparently coined in the 1850s, first in French and then in English[19]—and set a pattern for separating such academic, conventional study from other formulations of the Egyptian past like Freemasonry or, later, the theosophy of H. P. Blavatsky or anthroposophy of Rudolf Steiner. Nonetheless, Freemasonry, Rosicrucianism, and the theosophic movement flourished in the nineteenth and early twentieth centuries, exemplifying what Hornung terms "esoteric" Egyptology.[20] Freemasonry also came to Egypt with Napoleon. It flourished in the late nineteenth century, when there were separate British, French, Italian, and Egyptian lodges in Cairo, although the European lodges began to admit Muslims after 1869.[21] In the wake of the Suez Crisis, Masonic lodges were treated with growing suspicion, and Freemasonry is now banned in most Arab countries, including Egypt, though rumors that Mubarak is a Mason have persisted.

This excursion through Enlightenment ideas of Egypt as a place of secrets has brought us back to Freemasonry, one of the secret societies with which Simmel concerned himself. Part of the ancient inspiration used in Masonry, and similar organizations, is their structure as a hierarchy to which supplicants can only gain access through stages of initiation marked by the gradual revelation of rituals and other kinds of knowledge. These may be quite mundane, since the form is more important than the content of what is conveyed, which is key to the longevity of organizations based on secrecy. Remember Simmel's insight: secrecy is a means of social organization. However, where Simmel focused on secret societies like the Freemasons, and characterized them as setting themselves apart from society at large, anthropological studies have offered an important correction. In his study of the Poro, the largest secret society in West Africa, Beryl Bellman pointed out that the organization sets itself apart only in metaphorical terms, for in fact the Poro was laced through society by its own activities as well as the activities of individual members, with an influence cutting across national and ethnic group boundaries from Liberia to the Ivory Coast.[22] At the same time, as de Jong has argued, secrecy establishes relationships of power, which means it continues to have an important place in modernity, regardless of whether the effects of secrecy might be deemed positive, such as enabling self-assertion by disadvantaged groups, or negative, in terms of the role secrecy plays in the operation of the state.[23]

The appeal of secret societies to groups disadvantaged by the state lies in the protective cloak and camaraderie of the organization, and embracing alternative, rather than mainstream, forms of knowledge may augment the group's sense of separation, reconfigured as a positive act of self-selection. For instance, African American Masonic lodges were well established in the United States in the nineteenth century, encouraged in part by an Africanist identification with ancient Egypt that resonated among blacks seeking to create their own associations in a society where they were free, but hardly equal.[24] Greater influence, however, lies with the mainstream, which is defined by its relationship to institutions of state power and social authority—including the university and the museum. Accordingly, in the remainder of this section, I consider the implications of secrecy for the study of ancient Egypt since the disciplinary formation of Egyptology in the late nineteenth century, including the way in which claims to specialist knowledge continue to define aspects of the discipline as well as its analogues, such as Afrocentrism—all of which in some sense use the "secrets" of Egypt to perform a secrecy of their own by helping define group membership and legitimize interpretations of the ancient past.

Like other academic disciplines, Egyptology itself can be viewed as a closed society through which membership can only be gained by certain stages of attainment, measured in no small part through the mastery of ancient scripts and texts. In Egyptology, the creation of a disciplinary structure has been especially marked precisely because the subject has had a broad and diverse appeal over such a long period of time, with the potential for "contagion" from coeval spheres like Freemasonry or theosophy. Even the "father of Egyptian archaeology," Flinders Petrie, owed the start of his career to an alternative approach, since he and his father first visited Egypt to use their experience as surveyors at the pyramids, hoping to demonstrate the mathematically derived prophesies of British astronomer Charles Piazzi Smyth. Petrie's personal biography thus became a narrative of Egyptology's move away from the esoteric toward the academic. Others have moved in the opposite direction, like his pupil Margaret Murray, who unwrapped the Two Brothers in Manchester and published a number of Egyptological studies but later became as well known for her work on the spirit world and witchcraft (she was alleged to practice Wicca herself) as for her work on ancient Egypt.[25]

There is no single "ancient Egypt" any more than there is a single academic approach. Although a reasonably coherent form of study, organized along disciplinary lines, enjoys the prestige of belonging to universities and museums, other forms of scholarship exist outside of, or adjacent to, this approach and have done so since the establishment of disciplinary apparatuses in the late nineteenth century. There are grey areas as well, such as the numerous amateur Egyptology societies (of which there are more than thirty-five in the UK alone) and a proliferating web and social media presence.[26] The societies regularly host lectures by academics, occupying a fringe that is outside but commingled with the discipline. Many adult and distance learning classes are aimed at the same or similar enthusiasts, who are almost exclusively white, middle class, and either middle-aged and above or else, in some cases, younger people seeking a nontraditional route to education. Excluded from full membership of the academy, amateur Egyptology thus forms its own organization, where belonging is defined through magazine ("journal") subscriptions, annual dues, or the joining of online fora.

An alternative body of scholarship exists in Afrocentric literature, and Afrocentrism too has both professionalized forms and an amateur hinterland, to use the same, somewhat problematic categories adduced for Egyptology. The Afrocentric approach to Egyptian history and culture has been influenced in particular by the work of Senegalese academic Cheikh Anta Diop, whose pan-African interpretation of ancient Egypt resonated not only in postcolonial West Africa, but also in the civil rights–era United States and more recently the UK, France, and beyond.[27] In the late 1980s and early 1990s, Diop and Afrocentrism entered mainstream consciousness with the publication of Martin Bernal's *Black Athena,* which argued that Egypt (and hence Africa) was the point of origin for Greek (and hence European) civilization.[28] *Black Athena* was embraced by Afrocentrists and postcolonial studies even as archaeology, Egyptology, and classical scholarship rejected much of Bernal's evidence and, implicitly or explicitly, his central thesis.[29] This dichotomy mirrors the separate spheres these subjects occupy in professional life, since Afrocentrism and mainstream Egyptology rarely meet, and when they do, tensions can flare.[30] I once spoke to a group of students, alumni, and community members at Manchester Metropolitan University, many of whom self-identified as Afrocentrists. I was surprised at first to be heckled by the audience, but over the course of the discussion after my talk, it transpired that this was not because of anything I had said, but instead due to long-festering anger with the museum where I then worked. According to some of the audience members, a previous curator had also addressed the group and, they said, described Diop's work as "no better than pornography."

The different ways in which ancient Egypt is studied, modeled, and imagined reflect the concerns and objectives of quite disparate groups, whether in different academic subjects or located outside academia, in the realm of "popular" Egyptology (dominated by whites), Africanist or Afrocentric approaches, or New Age, esoteric, or Masonic interests. These groups draw on the same body of evidence; interpret it using similar methodologies, such as physical anthropology (to determine "race"); and may even reach identical conclusions, for instance by asserting, as some proponents of Afrocentrism and theosophy do, that the lost wisdom of the ancient Egyptians can be recovered through secret societies.[31] But whatever truth claims they make, and academic Egyptology is no exception, each group gauges its authority in relation to other groups (academic vs. "lay" participants, a telling choice of words) and its identity in relation to society at large (white vs. black, in particular), which is where dynamics of power come into play. These dynamics leave no doubt that the premise that ancient Egypt is inherently fascinating is a false one, for the fascination with the ancient Egyptian past is rooted in modernity and governed by all that Egypt has represented to others, from the colonial era to the classical past. Multiple "ancient Egypts" arise from the same ground, both literally and figuratively. Scholars or spiritualists, amateur enthusiasts or Afrocentrists, see quite different things in the ancient evidence and have quite different goals in doing so, but all of them assert an authority over the material remains and intellectual heritage of Egyptian antiquity—a secret only they can unlock.

Sacred Secrets

> Did the ghosts of those proud-faced priests and their throngs of devout worshippers still haunt this ancient place and murmur their prayers to Ptah, he who held a symbolled sceptre of power and stability? Did the spirits of vanished priests and departed kings flit to and fro across their ancient haunts, like living shadows without substance?
>
> Paul Brunton, "Karnak Nights," in *A Search in Secret Egypt* (1958 [1935]), p. 227

First published in 1935, *A Search in Secret Egypt* was a best seller for the British theosophist Paul Brunton, whose previous books had seen him meditating in the Himalayas long before the 1960s counterculture "discovered" yoga and Eastern religions. Brunton's journey through Egypt followed a predictable tourist route from Cairo to the archaeological sites of Upper Egypt. Along the way, he met Islamic mystics, witch doctors, and snake charmers—he even learned how to charm a cobra himself—and found a spirit guide from ancient Egypt to lead him toward the universal truths that fakirs, yogis, and other adepts knew, according to the insights nurtured by the theosophical movement. Like others drawn to ancient Egypt explicitly for mystical and religious inspiration, Brunton couched his discoveries in terms of secrets, only some of which he could share with his readership. Such spiritually inflected interpretations of ancient Egypt thus embrace the idea of secrecy in a way that has contributed to scholarly avoidance or misapprehension of the topic. But neither of these approaches, which I characterize here in simplified form as the spiritual and the scholarly, does justice to the operation of secrecy within ancient Egypt. Instead, the social dynamics that emerge from the construction of ancient Egypt *as* a secret have made Egypt a powerful symbol that various groups assert as their exclusive domain.

While spending the night in the king's chamber of the Great Pyramid—with approval granted by the British police staff at Mena—Brunton received a visit from two men with "grave looks" whose white robes, sandals, and "wise aspect" clearly marked them as high priests of an ancient Egyptian cult. Told to stretch himself out in the empty sarcophagus, Brunton did so, entering a trance state in which he felt himself to be floating free of his body. The priests disappeared before the stroke of midnight, but not before the chief priest issued these parting words:

> My son, it matters not whether thou discoverest the door or not. . . . The mystery of the Great Pyramid is the mystery of thine own self. The secret chambers and ancient records are all contained in thine own nature.[32]

The priest's words were prescient, but perhaps not in the way Brunton meant them to be: Brunton's ancient Egypt was, like any modern viewer's, an image of his and history's making. Later in the journey, Brunton came quite literally face to face with his own ancient Egypt when another ancient priest materialized briefly between the looming columns of Karnak temple, his face identical to Brunton's own and thus, inevitably, white. With the howl of a jackal in the distance, and moonlight glinting on ancient stones, Brunton felt himself keeping company with the ghosts of men like Bakenkhons, his nocturnal reverie eliding millennia to join the workaday world of an Egyptian priest.

The white-robed, wide-eyed priests that Brunton encountered in the Great Pyramid and the hypostyle hall of Karnak were immediately recognizable to anyone familiar with Herodotus, who had marveled at the purity restrictions placed on Egyptian priests. Herodotus credits the priests of Memphis, Heliopolis, and Thebes as his sources and as authorities on the ways and histories of Egypt, engaging in a discourse about Egyptian priestly wisdom that in all likelihood was already well established in the mid-fifth century B.C.E., when Herodotus was writing.[33] The conflation of Egyptian religious practices with the mystery cults of the Greek and Roman worlds meant that initiation into the priesthood was not in itself a concern of Herodotus and other classical writers (for whom initiation was for cult membership), but in his account of Egypt, he recognizes the priests as a special, privileged class and refers to knowledge that he, like Brunton, is not at liberty to share with his readers: on the sacred lake of the temple of Athena, or Neith, at Sais, the priests perform a nighttime reenactment of the sufferings of a god whose name cannot be mentioned, clearly Osiris. "I could say more about this, for I know the truth," writes Herodotus, "but let me preserve a discreet silence" (*Histories* II.171). Much like later anthropologists would do, Herodotus used his own initiatory experience to lend authority to his text, an ethnographic trope critiqued by James Clifford that underscores the negotiated nature of the secret.[34]

Many Egyptologists have also maintained a discreet silence when it comes to the role of secrecy in Egyptian religion and initiation rites for the Egyptian priesthood; outright refutation is another stance.[35] But this reluctance to articulate the role of restricted knowledge and the holding of priestly office says more about the distancing strategies of scholarship than it does about the ancient evidence. It is reasonable to expect some test or ritual to accompany movement through the stringently defined hierarchy of the priesthoods that served different gods and temples and that employed multiple ranks and ranges of titles—from first, second, or third prophets down to lowly shrine-bearers. A strongly formulated hierarchy characterized Egyptian society from the period of state formation onward, and hierarchical relationships were created and reinforced through kinship networks, proximity to the king, and membership of groups—priests, scribes, artisans, and other crafts—that organized themselves in part through the performance of secrecy. Group membership required boundaries, and providing stages of induction, training, and mastery of skills and knowledge was one way of creating and replicating those boundaries.

Evidence for the deployment of secrecy as a means of social organization comes from the monuments of the participants themselves, like the biographical inscriptions on statues that priests commissioned for the temples where they served. Secrecy was thus the actors' own category, and knowledge ranging from astronomy and mathematics to the sacred geography of the underworld, and the names of gods and demons, were areas of restricted knowledge, revealed only by progress through certain ranks.[36] Knowing what to know and what not to know was the crux of the matter. As the deceased recites in a passage known as the "negative confession" associated with the judgment scene in the *Book of the Dead,* "I did not know what should not be known."

Derived in part from the earlier *Pyramid Texts* and *Coffin Texts,* the *Book of the Dead,* which first appeared around 1700 B.C.E. and continued in use in some form into the Roman period, makes repeated reference to the secrets that its texts contain—although this aspect of the composition was overlooked in a visually splendid exhibition on the topic staged by the British Museum in 2010.[37] Spells of transformation into an animal form or an *akh*-spirit are among those that make the most explicit avowals of secrecy, and in a somewhat idiosyncratic, and rarely cited, article from 1960, the Austria-born Egyptologist Walter Federn—son of a psychoanalyst, with whom he had fled to the United States before World War II—suggested that such spells had the purpose of enabling senior priests to manifest themselves in supernatural form to initiates, using ethnographic literature on West Africa and Sudan to argue his point.[38] His comparative methodology is open to challenge, but some of the spells Federn used as examples do contain a combination of words and actions that might be part of an initiation performance, and several speak explicitly of initiation or "introduction" to the god. For instance, a recitation to be written on seven eye-of-Horus amulets—possibly linen amulets—went something like, "I have come here, after I have finished the initiation; Anubis is cleansing me." The amulets were then submerged in a solution of beer and natron, and the mixture drunk. The word used for "initiation" or "introduction" in this context, *bes,* can also be translated as "secret" and can refer to the "secret form," or image, of a god. Combined with the most common word for secrets, *seshta* (as in the "master of secrets," *hery-seshta)* or its variant, *sheta,* the phrase *bes sheta* becomes the "secret secrets," often translated in Egyptology as "mysteries."

As a discipline, Egyptology is beginning to question its own categorization of many kinds of evidence as funerary, as if what is preserved in burial contexts could be completely separated from other social practices.[39] Chapter (or spell) 125 of the *Book of the Dead,* which contains the judgment scene and negative confession—so called because the deceased lists all the things he has not done, such as stealing the temple's cattle or having inappropriate sexual relations—is one example of an ancient composition that should be seen in a different light (Fig. 5.3). The judgment is a favorite topic in museum displays and primary school education, especially in the UK, where ancient Egypt has

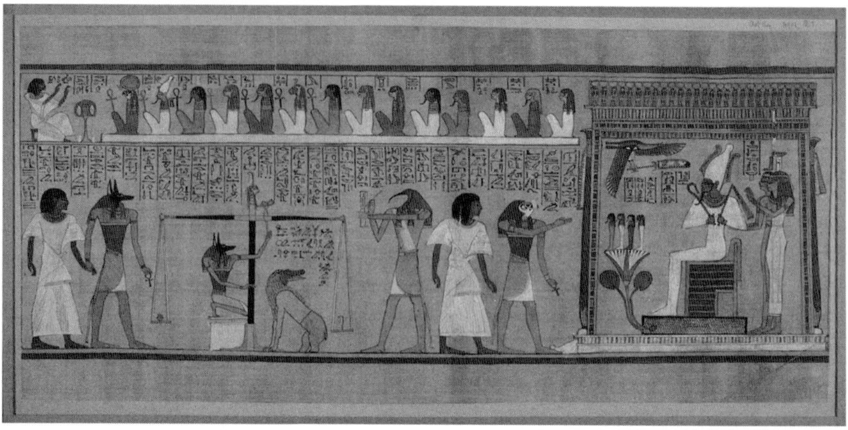

FIGURE 5.3 *Judgment scene in Chapter 125, from the* Book of the Dead *made for Hunefer; from Thebes, 19th Dynasty (c. 1285 B.C.E.). H. 40.0 cm, L. 87.5 cm. British Museum, EA 9901, Sheet 3. Copyright: The Trustees of the British Museum*

formed part of a national curriculum since 1988. Normally presented in these contexts, and in much of the academic and popular literature, as being concerned with the passage of the deceased into the afterlife, the judgment and confession make much more sense in the context of initiation, a sort of ritual trial in which the junior member or supplicant could demonstrate his knowledge and purified state.[40] This is exactly what was done in a Greek papyrus of the Roman period, which translated passages from the *Book of the Dead* for use in the initiation of a stolist, the Greek name for the *hery-seshta* in charge of dressing the statues of the gods.[41] Repurposing texts like these for funerary use is appropriate in that death, like initiation, is a threshold to be crossed over, a *rite de passage* through a liminal state. Moreover, such a secondary use is especially fitting if, like initiation into the priesthood, the "initiation" from death to rebirth was available only to a select few, whether in the Roman period or in earlier periods, since the extant evidence is scattered across time.

Presence and vision were key tropes of knowing. To be initiated was to be "introduced" (the same homonym of *bes,* "secret") into the service of the god, or as other expressions phrase it, "to see the secrets" or "to see the horizon," which may not have been just a metaphor, but a reference to seeing a certain space within the temple, such as a doorway.[42] With its underlying meaning of passing from one milieu to another, especially from a state that is liquid and confined to a state that is airy and luminous, the word *bes* captured well the sense of transcendence and transformation that initiation entailed.[43] Initiation permits the initiated to see what the non-initiated cannot see—or to understand what others may see in a physical sense but that only the initiated can comprehend. Thus priests not only know but discern the secret, which might concern the secrets of a certain god, a sanctuary, or the *akhu,* the *akh*-transfigured spirits created and honored through ritual performances.[44] Being able to enter certain parts of the temple or encounter certain images of the god was probably part of the privileges ascribed to different ranks of priests, and one part of the temple that seems to have been subject to such a restriction was the *akh-menu,* the place of making or maintaining the *akhu.*[45] At Karnak, where Brunton glimpsed his ancient mirror image, inscribed blocks found in fragments near the *akh-menu* recount the "day of initiation" or "day of introduction" (*heru en bes*) of such-and-such a priest, while nearby, but physically isolated from the *akh-menu* and the rest of the temple, a small set of rooms with an elevated, concealed door may have been a setting for initiation, perhaps requiring the initiate to mount a set of stairs the better to see what would be revealed.[46]

Egyptologists uncomfortable with the idea of initiation, or of secrecy in general, have argued that there was no secrecy in Egypt because during religious festivals, grand processions brought the priests and the sacred images out of the restricted space of the temple and along the processional ways that dominated urban space. But that is exactly the point of secrecy: the third person, from whom the secret is kept, needs to know that the other two have a secret, otherwise secrecy is useless. Those outside the secret might even know the basics of what the secret is—the mythology of the god, or the wrapping up of the statue—so long as they also realize their inability to know or understand it fully, and acknowledge that those in possession of the secret are in a position of privilege and power. Hence a public procession or display does not mean that secrecy is not at stake—quite the opposite. Depictions of the god's shrine being carried on its boat, which are a standard part of festival scenes in temples and tombs, give pride of place to the people who were in on the secret, while the crowds lining the streets, feasting, and praying are rarely represented (Fig. 5.4).[47] They are the third party, the people from whom the secret was kept.

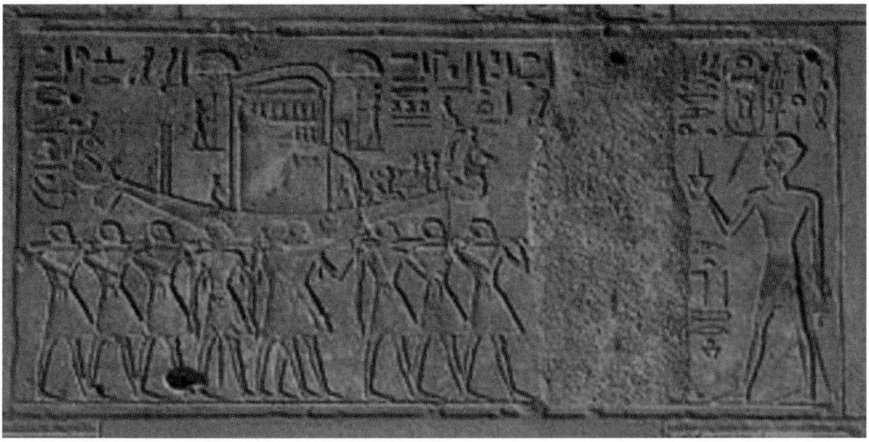

FIGURE 5.4 *The processional bark of Amun carried by priests, with Thutmose III proffering incense at far right. Part of the relief has been chiselled away to remove the figure of the other ruler, Hatshepsut. From the Red Chapel at Karnak, 18th dynasty (c. 1460 B.C.E.). Courtesy of Martin Andreas Stadler*

The language of secrets is visual as well as verbal. Shrines were physical manifestations of secrecy in ancient Egypt and contributed to its performative aspects, since they were simultaneously visible and concealed on festival occasions. Carried aloft on a sacred boat, the shrine containing the god's statue was wrapped or draped in white cloth, just like the image inside it.[48] Some shrines seem to have had small upper doors that could be kept open, in which case the face of the wrapped-up statue would be (just) visible inside, but other shrines, with full-length doors, may have been kept shut and sealed. How much anyone could see of the shrine, or even the face of a statue, in the mêlée of a festival procession was in some ways less important than the fact that the appearance of the wrapped statue and shrine in public served to hide it in full view, signaling the existence of the secret with the secret itself. Certain statues of gods and deified kings seem to have been specially designated for festival processions, although other statues may also have been used in boat shrines. The processional statues were known in Egyptian as *shesemu* and were implicated in the performance of oracles, where the movement of the boat indicated an answer to questions directed to it, either orally or through inscribed chits placed in its path.[49] Selected reliefs on the walls of temples seem to have been veiled as well, through fixings that would allow a textile to be stretched in place, perhaps over images that were the focus of particular kinds of devotion.[50]

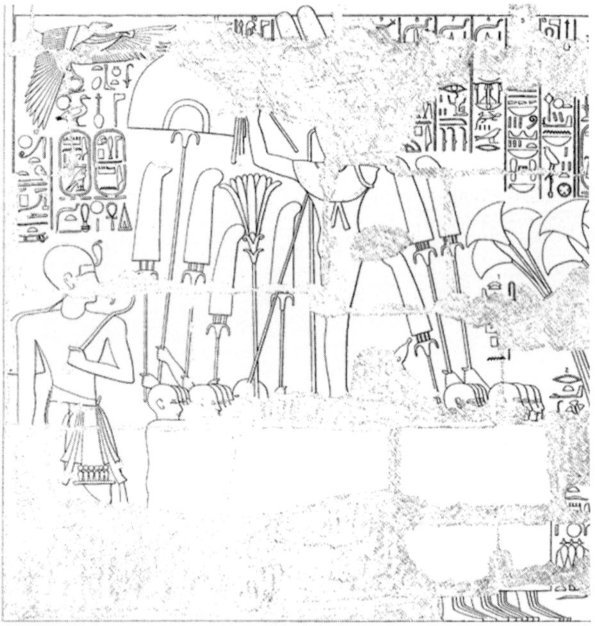

FIGURE 5.5 *Just visible in this drawing of the scene, a large cloth covers the priests carrying the processional bark of Min, from their shoulders to just above their ankles. From the temple of Khonsu, Karnak, under high priest Herihor (c. 1075 B.C.E.). Courtesy of the Oriental Institute of the University of Chicago.*

Layers of wrapping and concealment enhanced the aura already attached to these objects, whose lives were conducted in secret from their inception and creation to their daily care and eventual decline.[51] Not only the statue and shrine, but also the priests who carried the boat, might be draped in a concealing cloth, as represented in a scene at the temple of Khonsu at Karnak (Fig. 5.5).[52] Carrying the boat involved priests of different ranks, although where their titles are stipulated, most are prophets, known in Egyptian as servants of the god (*hem-netjer, ḥm-nṯr*). Boats associated with the cults of dead kings could also be accompanied by *sem*-priests wearing the leopard skin.[53] At the Amun temple at Karnak, one scene of the processional boat of Amun depicts the carriers as jackal-headed humans at the stern end and falcon-headed humans at the prow, a reference to the ancestral *ba*-spirits of Hierakonpolis and Buto (Fig. 5.6). Since Egyptian artistic conventions combine animal heads and human bodies for so many otherworldly figures, these images may refer only to these divine figures, but they could also be interpreted as priests wearing masks, not unlike the jackal-headed figure cradling the wrapped image of Hunefer in his *Book of the Dead* papyrus (see Fig. 3.5). Widely associated with the performative aspect of secrecy by secret societies and religious orders—think of the penitential robes and hoods worn by participants in Spanish Holy Week processions—masking may well have been practiced in ancient Egypt, but the pictorial evidence for it is slim and inconclusive.[54] The technology to make wearable masks existed, given the proliferation of masks made to fit over the heads of mummies, but only two masks survive from outside a burial context: a heavy (eight kilogram), fired clay example in the form of a divine jackal's head, with holes in the neck to allow the wearer to see out, and a plaster-coated linen face mask with a leonine aspect and cut-out eyes, excavated by Petrie at el-Lahun.[55] In written texts, like

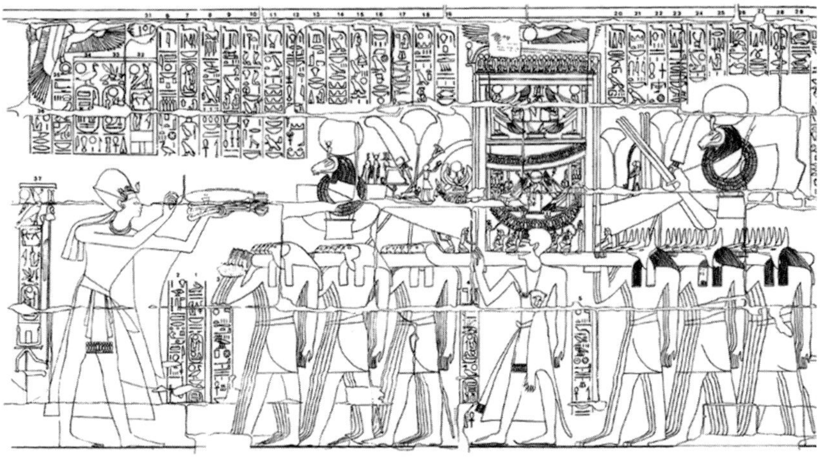

FIGURE 5.6 *Ramses II censing the bark of Amun, from the hypostyle hall, Karnak, 19th dynasty (c. 1290–1224 B.C.E.). Courtesy of the Oriental Institute of the University of Chicago*

the *Coffin Texts* that covered the interior of coffins in the Middle Kingdom, masks associated with the mummified body are called the deceased's "secret face," an expression that elsewhere evokes primeval, regenerative powers.[56]

Concealing the god, its shrine, and its servants when they were put on public view was an act of revelation in the service of power, and in social, rather than theological, terms, the power at stake was the power of the priests over a time period that, the evidence suggests, spanned several hundred years. Revelation is the necessary counterpart of secrecy, establishing the boundaries of what could be heard, or seen, or understood, and hence the boundaries of who could know, act, and speak in Egyptian society. Rites of initiation and bodily disciplines were similarly revealing in the sense of signaling to the excluded who was "in" on the secret. This was especially true since most Egyptian priests, from the Old Kingdom to the Ptolemaic period, served in rotation in set groups, usually four groups per temple; the Rosetta Stone records a Ptolemaic royal decree increasing the number of groups to five.[57] These men lived most of the year as householders in the community, albeit with privileges. A man's household and neighbors knew perfectly well who he was and in what capacity he served the god, and any observant wife would be able to recognize her husband's feet shuffling under the weight of a processional boat, even under a veil or mask. Obscurity had done its job, for the secret—or rather, the existence of the secret—was out.

Secrecy and Social Structure

> They imparted their secret and divine sciences to no one who did not belong to their caste, and it was long impossible for foreigners to learn anything; it was only in later times that a few strangers were permitted to enter the initiation after many severe preparations and trials. Besides this, their functions were hereditary, and the son followed the footsteps of his father.
>
> Joseph Ennemoser, *A History of Magic, Vol. 1* (1854), p. 240

Who were these men who carried the gods on their shoulders, or saw them face to face? In his *History of Magic*, written in 1819 but only translated into English in 1854, the Austrian physician Joseph Ennemoser relied on Greek, Roman, and Biblical sources to draw conclusions about Egyptian magic before the decipherment of hieroglyphs. Decades later, his work was quoted as an authority by the leading theosophist H. P. Blavatsky, who would also have approved of Ennemoser's faithful support of Mesmerism. By 1877, when Blavatsky's treatise *Isis Unveiled* first appeared in print, the discipline of Egyptology was distancing itself from the notion of cult secrets and priestly castes that she and Ennemoser both espoused in different contexts.[58] Egyptology needed Egyptian religion to fit a more rational mold—as rational, at least, as a pagan, polytheistic religion could be. The idea that priests underwent initiation or were part of an endogamous, hereditary system, like the caste system of the Indian subcontinent, was relegated to esotericists like Blavatsky, while academic research got on with the business of classifying texts, enumerating spells and genealogies, and discussing "phyles" of priests, using the ancient Greek word for "tribe" to designate the groups that served within a cult. But if, as I have been arguing, secrecy is a fundamental aspect of the sacred in many religions as well as an effective and adaptable means of group organization, then secrecy is no more irrational than any other social or cultural phenomenon. In that sense, Ennemoser's pre-Champollion venture into Egyptian religion captured the spirit of the system well, for secret knowledge did determine the outside and the inside of the priesthood, and fathers did pass their roles to their sons, and their sons' sons.

A man named Basa, who was a priest at the temple of the goddess Hathor at Dendera around 800 B.C.E., dedicated an image of himself in the form of a limestone block statue where his squatting figure is some forty-one centimeters high (Fig. 5.7).[59] In the long inscription that follows the elegant curves of his wrapped body, Basa recounts his numerous titles and ranks within the priesthood. He was, to name the most important ones, the third prophet of Hathor, lady of Dendera; the master of secrets of all the gods and goddesses of Dendera; the pure one of hands; a temple scribe; an astrologer; and the temple's stolist priest, a translation of the Egyptian phrase, "master of secrets of the gods' clothing"—thus, Basa was the priest responsible for wrapping and unwrapping the statues. This same title appears in the names of Basa's ancestors, which he also lists on his statue: all twenty-six generations of them, on his father's side, a mere four on his mother's, all serving in the priesthood at Dendera. In the reign of Ramses II, his illustrious ancestor Nebwenenef was the high priest of Hathor at Dendera and was chosen by an oracle to be high priest of Amun at Thebes, where he was buried and had the rare distinction of a funerary temple being erected in his honor.[60] An impressive lineage, and reminiscent of Herodotus's account of how Theban priests had shown the historian Hecateus the statues of generations of their predecessors to help reckon time, which they could do with precision through 345 successive statues (*Histories* II.143).

Basa had stepped into a role he was born to fill. His claim to know the details of twenty-six unbroken generations of descent exemplifies the use of genealogical lineage to support claims to status, property, entitlement, or expertise, whether among the European nobility, the Daughters of the American Revolution, or the genealogies of the Old Testament, which are just as long, or longer, than Basa's. What matters most is that this line of ancestral descent mattered to Basa and in the context of his life and work. The upper strata of Egyptian society—the king, his family, and his associates; the priesthoods of large and small temples throughout the country; the literate scribal class; and the officials and leading families at provincial, town, and village levels—are responsible for most of the visual and written culture deemed to represent "ancient Egypt" today, but this exclusivity is downplayed in many popular presentations of the subject. Perhaps it feels alienating in contemporary society, which aspires to

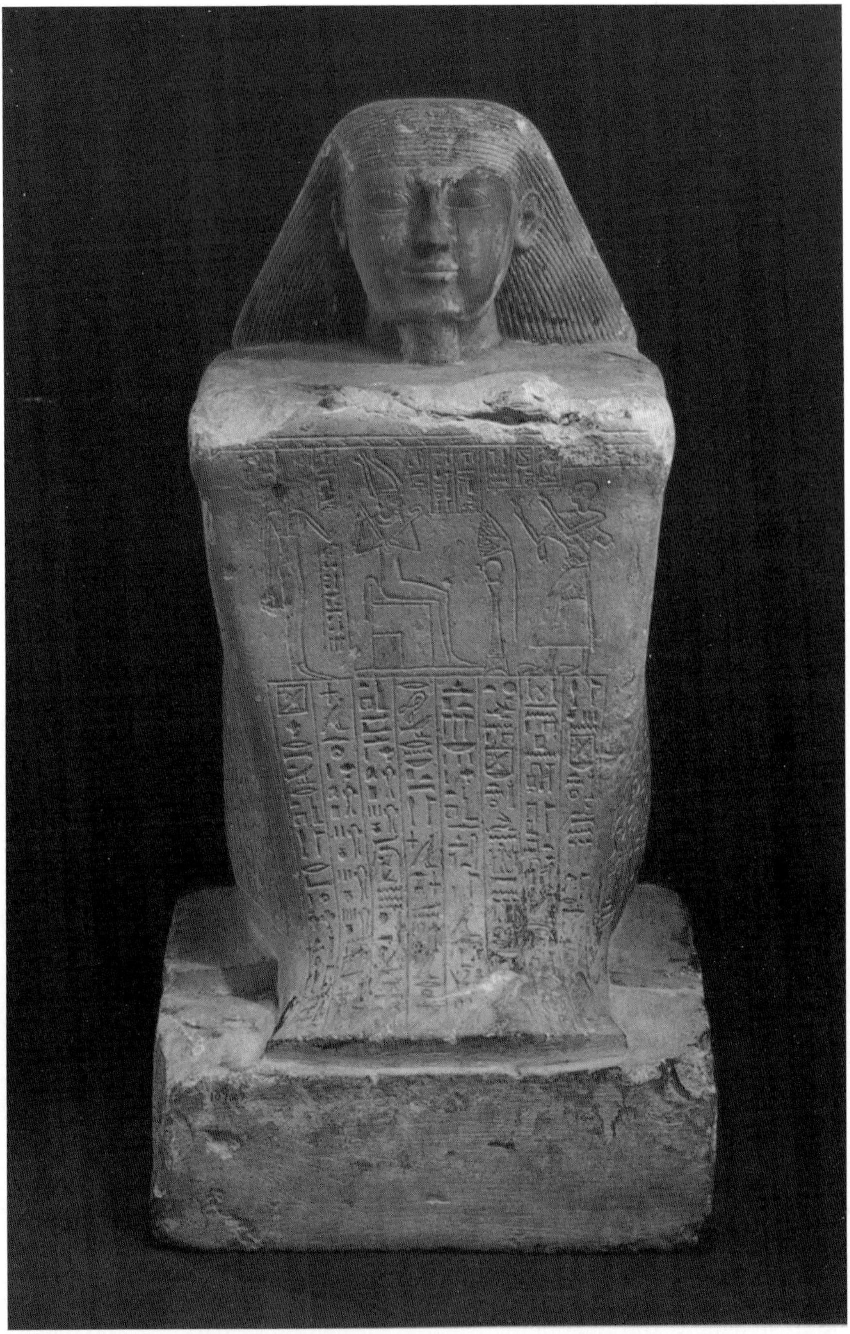

FIGURE 5.7 *Limestone statue of Basa, a priest at the temple of Hathor, Dendera, 22nd dynasty (c. 900–800* B.C.E.*). H. 41.0 cm, W. 23.0 cm, D. 20.0 cm. Oriental Institute Museum 10729. Courtesy of the Oriental Institute of the University of Chicago*

egalitarianism, or in museums where access to Egyptian objects, and bodies, is conceived not as a privilege, but as a right. For an individual like Basa, however, his lineage and titles were a badge of belonging to the select.

In the three tableaux incised around his enveloped body, each of which shows him praying to Osiris, Basa repeats the two titles that seem to have been the most important: third prophet of Hathor and master of the secrets of clothing. How functional such titles were is in many ways as moot a point as the "accuracy" of his genealogy: to take a British example with several hundred years of history behind it, one could argue that "Black Rod" (or "Gentleman Usher of the Black Rod," to give its full expression) is not a very functional title today since the gentleman in question has only a ceremonial role whose chief requirement is to be present one day a year for the state opening of Parliament—but no one could argue that the existence of Black Rod is unimportant. No Black Rod, no Parliament, to put it in succinct terms. Some ancient Egyptian "titles" resemble nothing more than forms of respectful address, as when the personal names of elite married women were prefaced by the phrase "mistress of the house." Others specifically marked an individual's closeness to the king, such as being "the king's seal-bearer" or a "child of the nursery," which was used for members of the king's inner circle who had been adopted, or taken, from other families and ethnic groups and raised alongside him in childhood. The existence of so many epithets, forms of address, and administrative or religious titles, many of which were held concurrently by the same person, only underscores the existence of a stringent hierarchy, which needed such nomenclature to identify, rank, and reward the elite. It also indicates the extent to which the organization of cults and temples seeped into other areas of society.

In temple hierarchies, the stolist, or *hery-seshtạ ab-netjer* (*ḥrj-sštȝ ʿb nṯr*, "the master of secrets who adorns the gods"), ranked lower than prophets but higher than scribes and shrine-bearers. Egyptological literature offers a range of interpretations for the general title *hery-seshta*, from being the most mundane and perfunctory of roles to indicating a level of protected or restricted knowledge based on initiation. Exact functionality and usages undoubtedly varied by time and place.[61] But although *hery-seshta* occurs in many titles connected with the administrative, temple, and funerary spheres, certain associations recur, namely in areas where restricted access and information were at stake. The role of the *hery-seshta* in wrapping a mummy was one such area, and not surprisingly, "master of secrets" was the most common epithet of the god Anubis. In hieroglyphic script, the title could be written with a single sign, representing a recumbent jackal—the animal of Anubis—resting on top of a shrine, a visual pun of the god being "above" (*hery*) the secret represented by the shrine and its contents. In the Ptolemaic and Roman periods, documentary evidence points to the *hery-seshta* of clothing, the stolist, being closely involved with burials and embalming practices, including animal mummification, with the Greek neologism "necrostolist" sometimes applied to these practitioners.[62] Plutarch associated

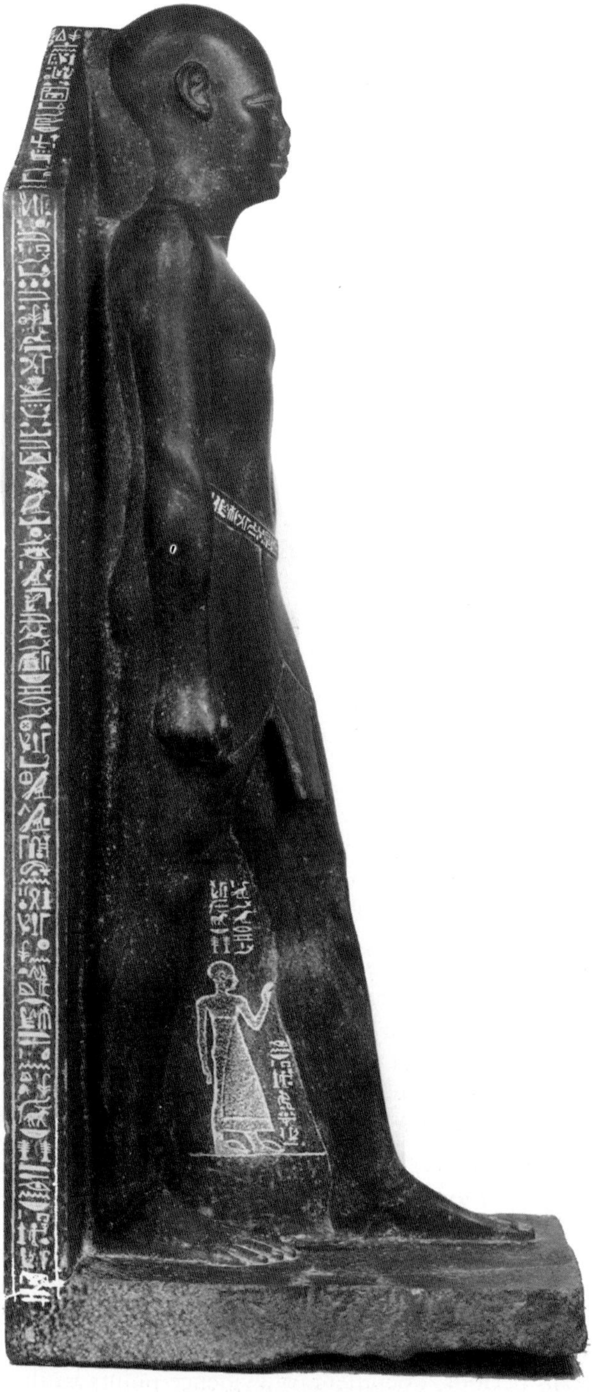

FIGURE 5.8 *Granite statue of Ahmose, son of Smendes, a stolist (wrapping priest) in the cult of king Nectanebo; from Karnak, 4th c.* B.C.E. *H. 95.0 cm. Cairo, Egyptian Museum JE 37075*

stolists with the temple crypts, which fits the function of the crypts as storerooms for statues and their ointments, linen clothing, and adornments.[63]

Like Basa, a number of stolist priests are known through their temple statues, and some of these priests held other high ranks as well, such as Senenmut, one of the highest-ranking administrators under queen Hatshepsut and the man whose mother Hatnofer's burial was so richly supplied with linen, as we saw in Chapter 4. A battered block statue from Karnak, one of several statues that depict Senenmut with Hatshepsut's young daughter Neferure, lists his many titles, which include the "one who veils," "the master of secrets in the House of the Morning," "the one who envelops the two crowns with red cloth," and the "sealer" or "chancellor" (*sematy*) of Horus. *Sematy* was another Egyptian word sometimes translated as stolist, since this functionary could also wrap cloth around images and appeared as the "god's chancellor" or "god's seal-bearer" in the *Ritual of Embalming*. The title could even be written with a hieroglyphic symbol that was itself represented as wrapped in narrow bandages.[64] In the Ptolemaic period, both block statues and striding statues, in which the subject's body is more revealed, commemorate stolists, and the inscriptions on these statues regularly make reference to the intimate contact these ritualists had with sacred images of the gods and to the secrets they knew. Two examples from the Karnak cachette give a sense of the phrasing used. The first, a block statue in hard, dark stone, describes the *hery-seshta* Neferhotep as "the one who enters the sacred place, the *sem*-priest of the one who is at the head of the embalming workshop, the one who knows the unknown place where Sokar is elevated on his barque."[65] The second, a striding statue just under one meter high, is inscribed for Ahmose, son of Smendes, a priest in the cult of the deified king Nectanebo who bore the title "master of secrets and purifier of the god, who revivifies Osiris in the House of Gold" (Fig. 5.8).[66] In a prayer on the statue's back pillar, Ahmose addresses the god he served: "May I not grow tired of seeing your face, well embalmed and adorned excellently in the necropolis beside Medinet Habu." So close in their wording are the titles for an embalmer and a stolist that the first publication of Ahmose's statue translated his title as the former, and his prayer to see the god "well embalmed" shares the same ambiguity. The phrase is perhaps better rendered as well wrapped, for which Ahmose, the stolist, could take credit.

As a "master of secrets" who dressed the god, the stolist had an obvious parallel to the "master of secrets" responsible for the wrapping of both human and animal mummies, and we can imagine that both roles required specialist knowledge revealed through a process of training and initiation. Although any knowledge can be secret, the knowledge that was deemed secret in ancient Egypt shares certain traits. It often has a technical component, like mathematical calculations, astrology, or surgery, and it involves a direct encounter with something potent. Other roles that might seem more mundane, such as animal butchery, could also require the mastery of secrets, not just for the skills required, but for the restricted, ritual context in which they would be put to use.[67]

Art was another secret. On his commemorative limestone stela, dated to the twelfth dynasty (c. 1800 B.C.E.) and now in the Louvre, the artist Irtysen

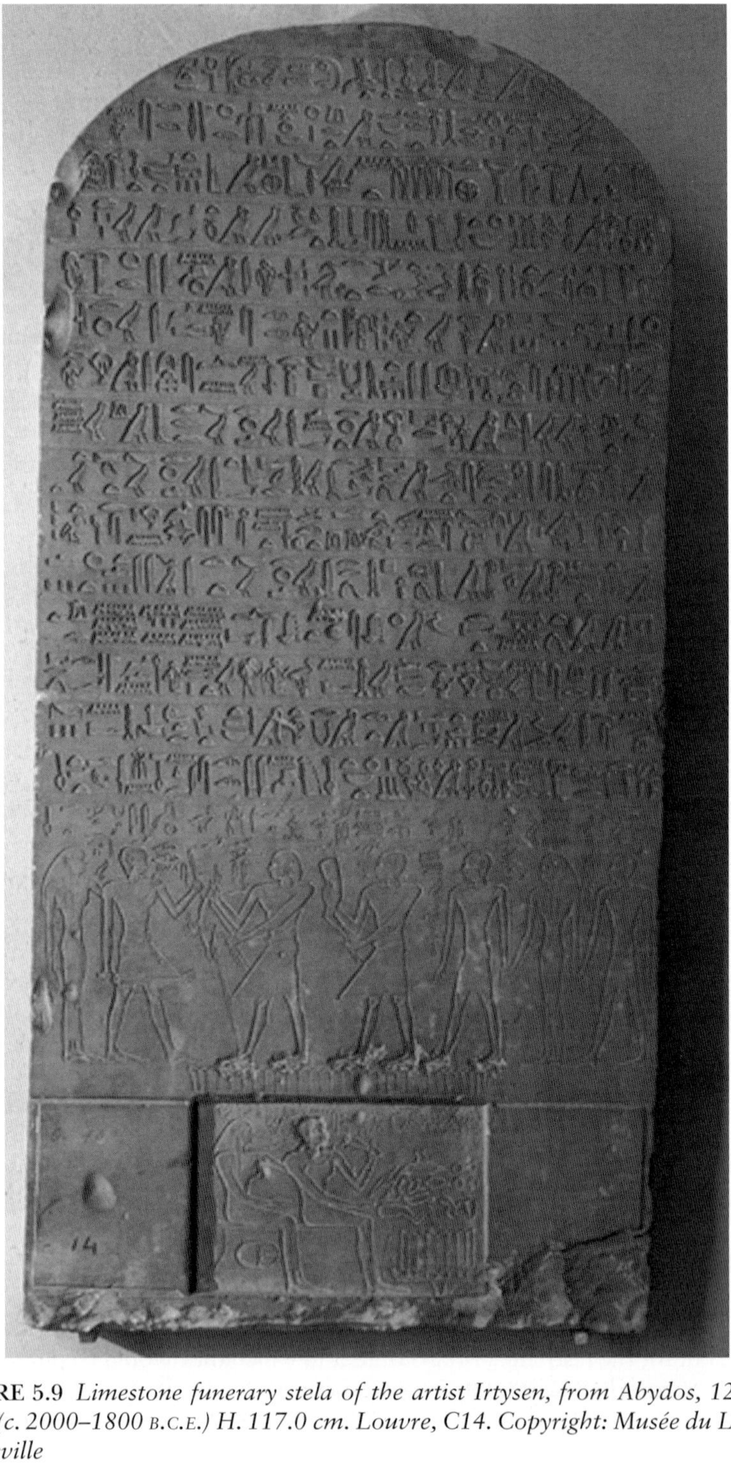

FIGURE 5.9 *Limestone funerary stela of the artist Irtysen, from Abydos, 12th dynasty (c. 2000–1800 B.C.E.) H. 117.0 cm. Louvre, C14. Copyright: Musée du Louvre/ Chuzeville*

offers a unique insight into what an Egyptian artist did and knew—which was, he tells us, secret (Fig. 5.9).[68]

> I know the secret of the divine word [that is, the hieroglyphs], and the composition of ceremonial rituals; I have acquired mastery over all the magical formulae, and there is nothing I don't know about them.
>
> I am a craftsman who excels at his art and has a superior level of knowledge; I know how to estimate dimensions, re-cut and fit until an element is in place.
>
> I know the posture of the male statue and the appearance of the female, the attitude of the eleven birds of prey, the convulsion of the isolated prisoner, how to portray a squint, the enemies' expression of terror, the arm movements of a hippopotamus hunter, and the leg movements of a running man.
>
> I know how to make pigments and products that melt without fire, and that are insoluble in water.

Finally, he says:

> Nobody will know of this except me and my eldest son, the god having ordered that he be initiated, as I have noticed his ability to oversee works in all the precious materials, from silver and gold to ivory and ebony.

Irtysen was a draughtsman, a sculptor, and an overseer of craftsmen, and the secrets he knew including writing, working with precious and difficult materials, and making images, together with the magical and ritual functions associated with them—and he would pass this knowledge, and his job, through his family line, in much the same way that Basa had acquired his priesthoods. An artist's work overlapped with sacred spheres, giving artists access to spaces and acts to which only priests were otherwise meant to be privy. Not every sculptor, draughtsman, or painter would have been as literate as Irtysen claims to be, but the ability to read was not the only critical point. Even seeing or being in the presence of sacred images and compositions, much less creating them, was an exposure to all the powers and mysteries of the divine realm—and of its human representatives on earth. Proclamations of secret knowledge thus functioned on the social level, for to be able to make such a claim was what aligned an individual with his peers and his kin. Secrets were in the blood.

Secret Knowledge and Sacred Space

Irtysen claimed to know the secret of writing, which in Egypt could become part of the secret itself. To write something down did not necessarily make it less secret, given that very few people could read and that texts were inscribed in the most inaccessible places, high up on temple walls or deep inside royal tombs. Legibility was not the point. The pictorial form of hieroglyphs opened up further ways to make a secret writing system even more arcane, for instance through retrograde script that reversed the orientation of the hieroglyphs, or through a form of cryptography, which used the polyvalent phonetic and ideographic values of hieroglyphs to create visually pleasing forms and playful takes on syntax and vocabulary. For instance, a hymn to the creator god Khnum at the temple of Esna was composed entirely of crocodile hieroglyphs repeated more than a hundred times with minor variations, and much the same could be done with hieroglyphs of rams, which framed one of the temple doorways.[69]

Assmann has referred to such cryptic compositions as an "aesthetic of secrets," but this aesthetic is hardly limited to the written word.[70] The material world of objects, bodies, and crafted space also shared an aesthetic of secrets and concealment. Secrecy imbued every aspect of a sacred image, from the selection of materials used to make it, to the facture itself, which took place in an area physically removed from the everyday. In the contexts of the object's use, shrines or cloth coverings helped materialize the secret, heightening the aura of hiddenness and facilitating the ritual performance of concealment and revelation. Arguably, the layering of textiles, adornments, and surface decoration—like the inscriptions on statues—further contributed to making the object "secret," which also made it efficacious.

Egyptian sources reinforce the link between cloth and concealment, and it is worth exploring some of these sources in further detail. Even though they come from the most restricted of contexts—temple complexes and royal tombs—these compositions of intertwined text and image, which are inseparable in hieroglyphic writing, convey cosmological conceptions that resonate with the material and artistic evidence for the use of textile wrappings at various periods. One of the compositions found in New Kingdom royal tombs is variously known as the *Amduat* ("that which is in the *duat*," or underworld) or the *Book of the Hidden Chamber,* a space where the secret images of the gods exist. Like the *Book of Caverns,* its primary concern is the sun god's journey through the night, when his powers must be restored. As the middle of the night approaches, and the sun god prepares to pass by the chest that contains the "secret body" of Osiris, a goddess called "The concealing one" uses her "hidden arms," or cloth, to protect the sun god's eyes from seeing the coffin, a parallel for the Weaver-goddess in the *Book of Caverns,* who gives the sun god his "two arms," or shroud. In the *Book of the Hidden Chamber,* the eighth and ninth hours of the night are explicitly concerned with linen and wrapping. The gods who populate the eighth hour are shown seated on the hieroglyphic symbol for lengths of cloth: two forked "sticks" that represent twisted warp threads forming a fringe on a fine piece of linen (Fig. 5.10). These figures are said to be the secrets or mysteries made by the god Horus, and whoever knows their names "will have clothing in the earth," perhaps a reference to the linen wrappings used in a burial.[71] In the same hour, four goddesses, depicted in

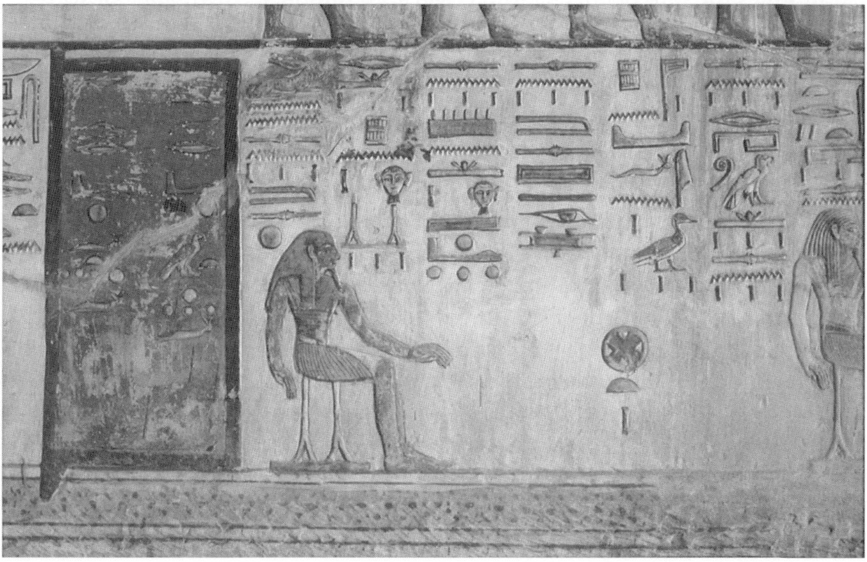

FIGURE 5.10 *An underworld deity in the* Book of the Hidden Chamber, *from the tomb of Seti I (KV17), Valley of the Kings, 19th dynasty (c. 1290 B.C.E.). Photograph by Francis Dzikowski. Copyright: Theban Mapping Project.*

profile as wrapped figures with no arms, occupy a space called "she who envelops her images" and have cloth hieroglyphs at their feet. Accordingly, their names—"She who veils," "The dark one," "She who decorates," and "She who puts together"—seem to refer to the creation, wrapping, and adornment of a sacred image and, in the same vein, a mummified body.[72]

The ninth hour of the *Book of the Hidden Chamber* continues the cloth-related theme, with a divine tribunal of twelve gods squatting on signs for cloth, all wrapped—"with hidden arm," as the text reads. Their names include "He who belongs to clothing" (*menkhet-y*), "He who is clothed" (*hebesu*), and "He who is linen-clothed" (*irty-wy*), and like the twelve fire-spitting cobras at the bottom of the scene, also resting on cloth symbols, they are said to "remain on (in?) their clothes," their mysterious forms illuminating the darkness.[73] The cloth is a form of light so bright that, like the sun, it hides the gods behind it.[74] The reference to having "hidden arms" is both a verbal and pictorial metaphor for being wrapped in cloth, which recurs in another underworld composition called the *Book of Gates*. In this book, the middle of the night, when the bodies of the sun god and Osiris are united, is again the crucial juncture and is populated by white-shrouded figures called the "gods whose arms are hidden." These gods support the joined body of Re-Osiris, which itself is never depicted, and the sun god commands them, "What is in me is hidden from you, it is hidden from the netherworld. Cover up your arms."[75] The mystical climax of the *Book of Gates,* with its depiction of a procession whose sacred image is present through its absence, exemplifies the link between cloth coverings and the performance of secrecy. What is most sacred was not to be seen but could be carried, processed, and displayed—the paradox of the secret.

Sequences of gates were more than metaphors in cryptic compositions like the aforementioned examples. Deeply buried tombs, underground passageways, and temples surrounded by high mud-brick walls are just some of the ways in which the idea of the secret was literally mapped onto the ancient Egyptian landscape and its built environment. The control and concealment of space shaped where people lived and how. Temples and their enclosure walls defined the structure of urban areas, and the processional way leading to and from the temple was the main street of a town or village—wide, paved, and bordered with sculpture.[76] Most members of the populace had little or no access to the temple itself, but the settlement was essentially organized with the shrine at its heart, reached via the temple's central, symmetrical axis through layers of doorways and courtyards, bewildering columned halls, and sequences of closed doors. In the innermost reaches of the temple was the holy of holies in which the shrine containing the wrapped cult statue stood in seclusion, but statues and their shrines existed in multiples, whether in temples or tombs or in locations that offered alternatives to these more formal expressions of piety, such as votive shrines set up outside temple enclosures or domestic spaces reserved for devotional practices.[77] Excavations at North Saqqara, where temple complexes dedicated to a range of cults have yielded an array of votive deposits, archaeologists found caches of objects and shrines located on the borders of the precinct. Most of the shrines were simple wooden constructions; one, with its doors still bolted shut and tied with string, contained multiple objects that hint at a range of depositional practices, in this case relating to Osiris, Isis, and the infant Horus.[78]

As the art historian David Summers has argued, a shrine manifests the idea of the center—the center being what is most valued and most potent in a given society.[79] But it would be a mistake to think that value and power lay within the shrine itself. The shrine was a form of secrecy, and what mattered was not its contents so much as their control. In this way, the physical manipulation of space enforced a network of relationships in ancient Egypt where bolts and seals were bulwarks against the fragile wrappings of providence and time.

Museums and the Public Secret

> As we ponder Georg Simmel's uplifting statement that *secrecy magnifies reality*, creating a world split between a visible exterior and an invisible depth that determines the exterior, it is possible to be assailed by panic; *first*, and worst of all, that if it wasn't for secrecy, reality would be a pretty drab affair....
>
> Michael Taussig, *Defacement* (1999), p. 56

The image of doors shutting the secret away from the outside world brings me back to the stage I set at the beginning of this chapter: the museum storeroom, tended out of public view but for the public good. As Simmel's theory of secrecy asserts, however, what is out of sight is not necessarily a secret because the secret must be signaled to outsiders in order to have its intended effect. It is this understanding of secrecy that I have applied in my analysis of wrapping practices and processions in ancient Egyptian cult, which helped establish bonds and boundaries between the priests and their communities. Jan Assmann has suggested that the ancient Egyptians were in awe of the secret: "To reveal the cult secrets would, in the eyes of the worshippers, unleash a cosmic catastrophe," as he puts it.[80] Pressing this point further, the catastrophe that will result if secrets are revealed without appropriate control is not only a cosmic, but also a social one—and appropriate control is the salient point. The operation of secrecy on a cultic level, such as the levels of knowledge revealed through stages of priestly initiation, is only one aspect of the secret. To borrow an image from the golden age of Hollywood, the risk is not that people will see the man behind the curtain, but that they will no longer be in awe of the great and powerful Wizard of Oz.

In modern times, the museum bears a certain resemblance to institutions that rely on secrecy and ritual, with its concealed spaces, layers of access, and focus on the care of "transcendent treasures" (to use Weiner's phrase again), some of which are revealed to the public through display and other technologies. Moreover, as we have seen, power and secrecy often go together, and the development of museums in the course of the long nineteenth century, in tandem with the rise of industrialized nation-states, situates them within discursive strategies and relationships of power.[81] But it would be erroneous to see museums as fixed entities, mired in the historical contexts in which they were founded (significant as those contexts are) and unresponsive to internal or external pressures to change. Power relations are just that—relational—and over the past twenty to thirty years, many museums have made substantial efforts to change the dynamics of their inward- and outward-facing operations. This has entailed, for instance, expanding and diversifying the visitor base; making stored collections and archives more "accessible" (through the Internet, events, or visible storage); and advocating "transparency" and "accountability," managerial terms that suggest, but do not necessarily facilitate, self-reflective practice.[82] Such an opening up of the museum is incompatible with Simmel's theory of secrecy: museums are not displaying their secrets, but denying that any secrets exist.

My use of "scare quotes" around these expressions—accessibility, transparency, and accountability—points to the fluidity with which the terms are used and to the implication they carry with them, namely that museums have otherwise exemplified the opposite, by being inaccessible, obfuscatory, and unaccountable in ways now considered inappropriate for public institutions. The backstage areas of a museum, including its storerooms, have in many ways become emblematic in debates about access and transparency. These are hidden spaces in the sense that they do not appear on visitor maps, and access to them is restricted to staff and accompanied visitors, who gain entrance through unmarked doors controlled by keys, codes, or cards. Although passing through those doors can elicit a sense of excited anticipation, as Macdonald recounts in her ethnography of the Science Museum, much of the day-to-day work that goes on there is as routine as in any office.[83] In museums, as in other institutions of modernity, this routine includes processes of decision-making that are contingent on many factors, some historical, some external to the institution, and some internal. Goffman referred to Simmel's work on secrecy to characterize behind-the-scenes processes as "secret," regardless of whether these actions and decisions were signaled to the public; some of these secrets were "dark" secrets (Goffman's scare quotes), comprising knowledge that the team conceals because it is "incompatible with the image of self that the team attempts to maintain before its audience."[84] For Simmel, secrecy did raise ethical questions, but his primary concern was secrecy as a tool of social distancing, whether within an organization or between the organization and its outsiders. Writing in 1950s America, however, Goffman suggested that secrets might have a more deceitful, even sinister, potential, presaging the negative qualities now associated with restricted access and absence of accountability. Its hidden storerooms, public mission, and lingering aura of the elite give the museum a marked symbolic potency where issues of institutional openness are concerned.

Rather than the secrecy Simmel adduced, which requires those "in the know" to reveal their possession of the secret but not necessarily the secret itself, the modern museum is meant to demonstrate that it has no secrets. Nonetheless, museums do participate in what Taussig has called the "public secret"—that which everyone in society knows at some level but does not acknowledge.[85] One example of the public secret is how (and whether) contemporary societies address the multiple legacies of slavery and colonialism, effecting an "imperialist amnesia" that overlooks the connections between mummy investigations and racial science or between archaeology, museums, and colonial rule.[86] As Edwards and Mead have recently suggested, museums in the UK struggle to integrate colonial histories into their exhibition narratives, despite the agendas of transparency and inclusivity the museums themselves avow.[87] In characterizing the role of the public secret in modern life, Taussig refers to acts of iconoclasm, vandalism, or defacement as a "wound of sacrilege" that renders the secret more public than it was meant to be—that draws attention to the very thing that was meant to be unspoken or unseen. Museums and the objects they house have repeatedly been subject to such acts, from attacks on the Rokeby Venus or Michelangelo's *Pieta* to the looting of the Iraq Museum in 2003. But vandalizing a painting or ransacking displays and storerooms at most threatens, but does not topple, the status quo, because drawing attention to the public secret reinforces its sway. In fact, Taussig argues, the public secret invites its own revelation for precisely this purpose; such transgressions may thus be acts against the powers that be, enabled by the powers that be.[88] Hence the outcry over the Tutankhamun statues, whose damage during the Egyptian uprising, by hands unknown, revealed not one, but two public secrets: the power Mubarak's regime intended to keep over Egypt's future and the power the West intends to keep over Egypt's past.

Two pieces of legislation exemplify the complex relationship that our own society has with the secret—and both have affected museums, institutions that appear to embody public openness. Although no longer the case, within the past generation, employees of national museums in the UK, such as the British Museum, had to sign a statement agreeing to abide by the Official Secrets Act when handling sensitive information. Signing had no legal effect, and staff were bound by the act whether they signed a statement or not; the point was to remind them that as employees of Her Majesty's government, their role in the museum would bring them into contact with knowledge that could not be revealed. More recently, and to somewhat opposite effect, Freedom of Information legislation has created a framework for public rights of access to information held by public authorities, including not just national museums, but any museum in receipt of public funds. Thus, on the one hand, legislative practice recognized the role of secrecy in museum operations, but on the other, suggested that such secrecy may not be in the public good.

Behind the scenes, like other modern institutions, museums survey themselves, and here, I return to the storerooms of the Manchester Museum, which were not a secret on Simmel's terms but which were sometimes home to secrets, including public ones. While I was working there with a visiting researcher one day, the museum registrar popped his head through the first locked door to tell me that he was dealing with a Freedom of Information request from a journalist who wanted to know if the museum's collection of Egyptian mummies had experienced any damage. The irony, we both knew (a "dark" secret), was that the museum's "mummy store" had only recently sustained a flood, caused by a plumbing leak upstairs, that had meant many fragile objects had to be moved temporarily to adjacent storerooms while the water was mopped up. Furthermore, the museum's collection of ancient Egyptian human remains had been the subject of extensive biomedical research for some thirty years, which had been a recent source of tension within the museum administration.

No human remains had been affected by the flooding, and "mummy store" was in any case something of a misnomer, as if the room had been named for what it did not contain rather than what it did. Most of the museum's two dozen or so human mummies had been on display since the last gallery renovation in the late 1980s, and the space was simply an organic storeroom, the only one in the museum with humidity control. It contained Egyptian antiquities made of wood, ivory, papyrus, leather, basketry, and textile, which require an especially dry environment. There were embalmed bodies, but most of them were animals. The few remaining human mummies included several children's bodies, chiefly intact in their wrappings, and a headless adult of indeterminate sex that had been "autopsied" (another misnomer) a few years before, its abdomen chiseled out to yield a set of miniature amulets that had been embedded in solidified layers of linen, resin, and flesh.

The storeroom also contained fragments of mummies—testaments of colonial-era tourism, when a mummified head, hand, or foot made a suitable souvenir, but also testaments of how heads had been collected for research on race, as Gliddon had done for Morton. Some of the heads had address labels or Blu Tack adhesive putty stuck to the surface from more recent research by students enrolled on degrees in the university. Other human remains in the storeroom included skulls and long bones, internal organs, flakes of skin, fingernails, bits of scalp and hair, at least one penis, and a great deal of powder, such as what was left of the skin and flesh of the Two Brothers unwrapped by Margaret Murray in 1908, stored in three Edwardian glass specimen jars. Once buried in the vicinity of Egypt's first kings, a disarticulated skeleton from the Early Dynastic cemeteries at Abydos lay uncovered in a wooden drawer long separated from its cabinet, the bones coated with a thick layer of black dust from the city's industrial past. And hundreds of plastic bags and cardboard boxes held what was left of a Ptolemaic mummy unwrapped and dissected on BBC television in 1975 and repeatedly divided and sampled ever since. It was this assortment of human remains, of bodies and body parts prised out of coffins, unwrapped, chiseled, snapped off, and scalpeled, that gave the innermost storeroom its name, as if the shelves and drawers of other material it contained—ivory hairpins, wooden spindles, palm leaf baskets, meter after meter of linen—were mere sideshows to the main attraction.

Museums have often been likened to modern temples, sacred spaces that accommodate ritual practice and mediate experiences of enchantment or awe by setting selected objects apart.[89] Objects that had a religious significance in their original context, such as a medieval altarpiece or a statue of the Buddha, are stripped of that sanctity but given a new, differently sanctified meaning within the museum, one that is based on civic rather than religious sentiment. The museum as secular shrine must also accommodate competing claims and negotiated compromises in contemporary museological practice, such as the *puja* rites that have been carried out for some Hindu and Buddhist images displayed in Western museums.[90] One drawback to the interpretation of museums as sites of ritual is that it rests largely on what museums display, rather than the backstage operations and stored collections that are, for many museums, as integral to institutional identity as any public-facing spaces. The inner sanctum is not only what visitors see, but also what they do not, for as both Simmel's and Taussig's theories of secrecy suggest, the fundamental values and assumptions of society lie on the delicate boundary between what is known and unknown, remembered and forgotten, reconfigured and suppressed.

The journalist's question about damage, the flakes of skin and numbered bones in storage behind the locked doors, and the mummified bodies on display upstairs, complete with x-rays and other "facts" for viewers to digest: all these encounters with Egyptian antiquity depended on assumptions—public secrets, perhaps—about the role of museums in the collection, care, and control of cultural objects. In the shrine of modern knowledge, nothing could be more mundane than the ownership (and destruction) of other people's dead bodies, and nothing could be more significant than how easily such assumptions are made, for behind it lay mechanisms of power defined by competing histories and temporalities. The fire door fell shut behind the registrar as he left, the lock tumblers falling back into place. So far as I am aware, the museum responded to the Freedom of Information request with a statement that none of its mummies had suffered any damage at all.

In the context of a Freedom of Information request, my query to the museum registrar—define "damage"—could only be facetious, for the definition at stake was not "damage," as the request put it, but the definition of the sacred itself, which is produced in secret and can be hidden in plain sight: a priestly procession, a mummy unwrapping, or even, if we follow Taussig on the public secret, a museum vitrine. Secrecy purports to set certain objects and individuals apart, like the "masters of secrets" and the cult statues, or embalmed bodies, that they wrapped in ancient Egypt. In reality, however, secrecy is the connective tissue of society, though for whose benefit is another matter.

Secrecy is as present in an egalitarian society as it is in an autocratic one; it simply takes different forms, especially where the public secret is concerned in democratic states. The secret is essential to heightened experience, that deepening of reality Simmel identified as one of its core effects in social relationships. That is why institutions that require a level of mystique and mystification—religions, heads of state, the military, and many cultural, medical, and academic establishments—speak the language of secrets so fluently. Revelation of the secret is not the threat: inappropriate revelation is, hence certain individuals or groups in a society will decide what others are supposed to know, and how, and when. The ancient Egyptians had their secrets, as do we, but there is no "wound of sacrilege" as long as the priests remain in charge.

6

Sanctity

One proposed etymology for the word *sacred,* from the Latin *sacer,* links it to a root meaning to enclose, protect, or bind. It is easily twinned with the word *secret,* since both refer to something set apart and out-of-bounds that only certain people can be entrusted to handle, care for, or begin to comprehend. In a purportedly secular society like our own, there is no shortage of things and places that are deemed sacred, but they are now as likely to be sites of heritage and commemoration as sites of religious worship. As one British undergraduate learned, after his arrest during protests against the UK government's trebling of tuition fees in 2011, you swing from the Cenotaph at your peril.

In this chapter, I explore the ramifications of the ongoing encounter between two differing conceptions of the sacred: that of ancient Egypt, with its emphasis on wrapping, concealment, and seclusion as a means of knowing the divine, and that of the modern university and museum, where unwrapping, visibility, and publicity are the means of procuring and revealing knowledge. Since much of the evidence discussed in this chapter relates directly to museums, and especially their involvement in the study of Egyptian human remains, I begin by considering the museum as an analog of sacred space before revisiting and expanding my discussion in previous chapters about the interrelationship of museums, archaeology, and the materiality of ancient objects, including mummified bodies. Over the course of the nineteenth, twentieth, and now twenty-first centuries, the investigation and display of the ancient Egyptian dead has changed remarkably little, save for the exploitation of new technologies. Science speaks in a voice of infallibility, or at least that is the implication of such investigations, which use technology to legitimize academic and museological control over objects of knowledge like the mummy, whether the setting is Granville's drawing room or a hospital radiology suite.

In Duncan's influential study of museums as places of "civilizing rituals," she draws a number of parallels between museum visits and ritual acts, deriving some of her understanding of ritual from the work of anthropologists like Mary Douglas and Victor Turner—in fact, Turner had specifically used visiting an exhibition as an example of "liminality" in modern life, since it allows individuals to step out of the everyday world and engage differently with their surroundings.[1] Museums are set apart in time and space, not so much timeless as removed from quotidian time. Foucault included museums in his category of heterotopias, institutions in which time is continually collected and stacked up upon itself, with no end in sight.[2] Rituals similarly both sidestep and stack up time, for they are understood to have been performed in the same way over a long period of time, and in perpetuity, while also removing the participants from anything temporally, spatially, or conceptually outside of the ritual performance.

To continue Duncan's argument, rituals progress through a sequence of prescribed spaces, just as the arrangement of public spaces in a museum guides visitors through a route with limited variation. Finally, rituals have a transformative purpose, and museum participation is construed as a transformative experience for visitors, who can improve themselves through learning or aesthetic wonderment and who may confirm, change, or challenge their social identity, such as class, simply by the act of visiting and engaging with a museum. This may sound suspiciously like a feature of late twentieth-century political directives and funding initiatives, aimed at making museums address issues of social cohesion, but the transformative, improving mission of the public museum is embedded in its early history, especially in post-Enlightenment foundations like the Louvre. Purportedly civic and hence secular, the museum's organization of space suggests otherwise, from the temple-like forms of classical architecture adopted in the nineteenth and early twentieth centuries, to the internal fittings, ambience, and expectations of behavior that came to be enshrined.

Sanctioned by the state and often funded by individuals whose wealth largely derived from colonial expansion, museums are not, and cannot, be neutral spaces of display. Moreover, their significance and impact stretches well beyond their galleries, encompassing the space they occupy in the built environment, the professional and governmental bodies dedicated to them, their position in the market economy, and their role as arbiters, and creators, of cultural norms and values. The extent to which the museum speaks to the conditions of modernity is evident in the astonishing growth of museums today—so much so that becoming a museum is now the favored way to counteract the obsolescence of other modern institutions, like power stations, railway terminals, and radar bunkers.

While the interpretation of museums as ritual sites has its limits, as Witcomb and Macdonald have discussed in different ways, the analogy between museums and religious institutions draws attention to an inherent tension that museums face, depending on how they negotiate the boundary between, on the one hand, presenting information that is assumed or expected to be authoritative, and on the other, creating sensory, emotive, even transformative experiences for their visitors.[3] The latter is especially challenging where difficult subjects are at stake, such as the Holocaust, colonialism, and the collection and display of contested objects, from the Parthenon Marbles to human remains. In museums and popular culture alike, Egyptian antiquities, including human remains, are by and large considered uncontentious and, therefore, free of any requirement for museums or their visitors to reflect on how the objects came to be there, what interpretations are created through their display, and whether the fascination with ancient Egypt in the West reveals more about the West than ancient Egypt.

This chapter examines historical and contemporary practices surrounding an object often assumed to be sacred both by its inclusion in museum collections and by its identification as human: the Egyptian mummy. Just as the unwrapping and anatomical examination of mummified bodies depended on the humanity of the remains, so too have debates about their curation revolved around the shifting nature of mummies as human subjects, inert objects, or some uncanny mixture of the two. However, these debates should not be seen in isolation, either as an issue that affects only museums or relates only to human remains, for they raise issues that extend throughout the academic study of Egyptology, its many alternative permutations, and the entirety of object worlds and imaginaries that evoke ancient Egypt in the present day. In antiquity, the treatment of embalmed bodies was part of a nexus of ideas and practices concerned with linen, wrapping, and the sacred, and if the treatment of Egyptian mummies in the modern world demonstrates anything, it is how far removed our own ideas and practices of sanctity position us from a past we claim as ours.

Monuments, Memories, Mummies: Ancient Egypt in the Museum

As early as the Napoleonic invasion, with its prescient collection of antiquities, the study of ancient Egypt depended on the development of the museum as a viable, public institution, as did the entire enterprise of transporting objects and significant fragments to Europe from Ottoman Egypt. Elliot Colla has characterized this as a process of "artifaction," whereby such objects became "artifacts" for serious study rather than the curiosities or country house adornments of earlier generations.[4] Antiquarianism eventually gave way to a form of scholarship that self-consciously conceived of itself as a specialism focused on the physical remains of ancient Egypt and crucially, after Champollion's decipherment, its language and texts.

Already in the age of Champollion, different museums offered different experiences of ancient Egypt, depending not only on the content of their collections but also on the context in which the collection was presented.[5] The Louvre and the British Museum make a convenient contrast, not least because the museums played out their respective countries' conflict over Egypt both during and after the Napoleonic Wars. Under the restored Bourbon monarchy, and in the wake of his triumphant decipherment, Champollion oversaw the 1827 installation of Egyptian antiquities in the luxuriant setting of the Musée Charles X at the Louvre, all gilded wood, marbled walls, parquet floors, and painted ceilings. In their vitrines, the Egyptian objects seemed as splendid as their surroundings, works of art worthy of a former royal palace, and the decorative scheme of the Louvre's rotunda placed Egypt, Greece, and Italy on an equal footing with France, leading visitors down a separate axis to each of these national schools of art.

In London, Napoleonic booty like the Rosetta Stone, and later additions like the "Young Memnon" head (from a colossus of Ramses II at the Ramesseum), sat uncomfortably in the grey-painted, neoclassical rooms created to house Lord Townley's collection of classical marble sculpture.[6] Imposing, dark-stone statues and sarcophagi interrupted a long gallery of graceful white-stone athletes and goddesses, giving way to an aedicule flanked by Doric columns that framed a Roman version of Myron's *Discobolus* at the far end (Fig. 6.1). Unlike its French counterpart, this ancient Egypt was impressive for its vanquished might, a feeling already voiced before the Memnon head arrived in London in the sonnet *Ozymandias,* which Percy

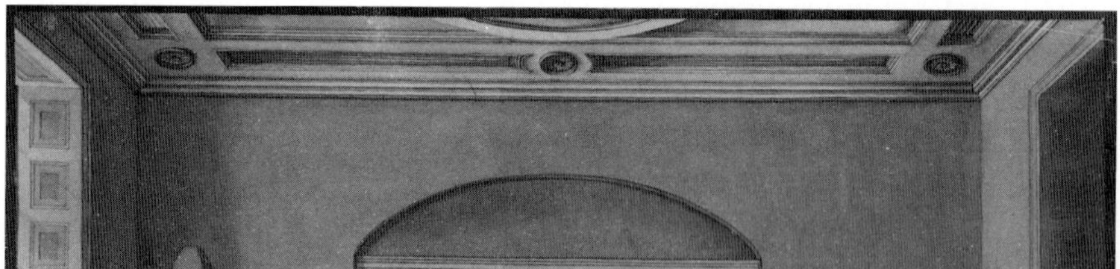

FIGURE 6.1 *Anonymous watercolor entitled 'A room in the sculpture gallery of the British Museum. February 1820. From a sketch taken on the spot in September 1819'. British Museum, Department of Prints and Drawings, no. 1881.11.12.137. Copyright: The Trustees of the British Museum*

Bysshe Shelley wrote and published in the build-up to the sculpture's arrival: "Nothing beside remains." But contemporary observers rarely described the Egyptian works at the British Museum in terms of aesthetic appeal. Impressive, yes, but art, no.

This dichotomy between the French and British installations of Egyptian artifacts still exists and still creates two differing approaches to the ancient past in the modern nation-state. In Paris, visitors move through the same palatial galleries to view a chronological presentation that unabashedly presents the material remains of Egypt as aesthetic material, on par with the winged Nike of Samothrace, the *Mona Lisa,* or any other work presented elsewhere in the Louvre. In London, visitors pass through the Egyptian sculpture gallery, stopping to lean on a colossal sandstone arm to have their picture taken or to stroke the surface of a royal kilt. Art is elsewhere: a few short strides away, among the Parthenon Marbles in the Duveen Gallery, no visitor dares stretch out a hand toward the nose of Selene's panting horse.

Whether ancient Egyptian objects collected in museums were construed as works of art or as archaeological artifacts, they were all sanctified to some extent by virtue of being in a museum, set apart in a space that kept them from other uses and the other lives, or quiet deaths, they might have had. But the sanctity of objects is relational, created and re-created through the interactions that individuals have with the material world, and hence influenced by competing concerns, changing priorities, and differing subjectivities.[7] Similarly, the museum enables not simply one ritual experience, but a diversity of experiences mediated through its space and objects, by its own staff (or ritual experts), and by its visitors and users, who bring with them prior knowledge, assumptions, and expectations.[8]

As the disciplinary formation of archaeology and Egyptology took shape in the second half of the nineteenth century, so too did the professionalization of museum work, beginning with the advent of specialist curators, although exact job titles varied until well into the twentieth century. The growth of museums in the late nineteenth and early twentieth centuries stood in symbiotic relationship to the expansion of archaeology in the colonial era, since museums offered a destination (and justification) for the division of artifacts discovered in Egypt. This altered the way in which museums collected antiquities, as well as the kinds of antiquities they collected. In turn, these trends created the trajectory that shapes the content of Egyptian collections today, and how they are used for research and display.

Archaeologists passed statues, stelae, fragments of temple relief, coffins, mummies, and tomb goods on to their sponsoring museums, as well as more prosaic and plentiful objects like pottery and scarabs, which were newly appreciated for their value within a typology that allowed excavators to date their finds. A brisk tourist trade in coffins, mummies, parts of mummies, and smaller items also added to museum collections over time. Charged with preserving and presenting the physical remains of the past, museums spread from European capitals to regional cities and towns, a pattern replicated in

Australia, Canada, and the United States. The museum model was exported to the colonial setting as well, with European visitors and residents as its primary and target audience. Auguste Mariette, who established an antiquities museum in Cairo, at Boulaq, did accommodate Egyptian visitors with some displays arranged on "useless" aesthetic grounds, he said, because they would not be able to follow the "scientific" arrangement of the other displays, which benefitted from the new knowledge created by archaeology.[9]

The public spaces of the museum, with their ritual semaphores, needed spaces out of public view as well (a vestry and a sacristy, to extend the comparison), where those who tended the objects could do the work of cataloguing, cleaning, numbering, mounting, studying, and of course storing what was not on display. The museum conforms to Derrida's conception of the archive, in which the sacred core of a society consists of the records looked after by officials with public authority, the *archons*.[10] Given its liminal position in relation to the West, for whom it is both origin and Other, ancient Egypt is a particularly apt lens through which to view the museum-as-archive, an external manifestation of internal processes that align the material world with and through cultural memory. Butler and Rowlands have argued that the unstable character of ancient Egypt as a category—an idea explored by Derrida elsewhere in his work as well—means that the entire foundation of Western thought is also unstable, a point of disjuncture, even trauma, which helps account for the multiple imaginings of Egypt to which different interest groups have adhered, and the fervor of interest in antiquities claimed for many, but owned by few.[11] The museum is the site (and sight) where the archival impulse of selecting, collecting, recording, storing, and ordering is brought to bear on material objects, in all their useless, beautiful, and poetic variety.

Whether or not they were attached to universities or had an Egyptologist on staff, museums with sizable Egyptian collections were linked into a network of academic research and professional expertise, especially through the archaeologists who added to the collection. As an institution steeped in cultural probity, the museum lent prestige and authority to any research it conducted as well—not least, research on mummified bodies. As we saw in Chapter 2, the unwrappings of mummies from the Deir el-Bahri cache took place before an invited audience in a gallery of the antiquities museum in Cairo, a setting conveyed in Philippoteaux's painting *Examen d'une momie* (see Fig. 3.3) through the statues and an Old Kingdom relief on display, the suggestion of people milling about in the background, and the Egyptian-style doorway between the two galleries, echoing the fashion in continental museums, such as the Museo Gregoriano in the Vatican and the Neues Museum in Berlin, for Egyptian-themed interior decoration to complement the displays.

When a new antiquities museum in central Cairo opened in 1902, it had abandoned Egyptianizing decor for a bare-walled, Beaux Arts style of classicism (Fig. 6.2).[12] The salmon pink building bordered a public space planned as part of Khedive Ismail's Hausmann-inspired rebuilding of Cairo and thus known as Ismailia Square until it was renamed by Nasser in 1955. On the upper floor, archways and balustrades opened the space to create views into the central court, which supported the weight—in every sense—of stone sculpture and sarcophagi. The French writer Pierre Loti visited not long after it had opened and was unconvinced:

> In the daytime this "Museum of Egyptian Antiquities" is as vulgar a thing as you can conceive, filled though it is with priceless treasures. It is the most pompous, the most outrageous of those buildings, of no style at all, by which each year the new Cairo is enriched; open to all who care to gaze at close quarters, in a light that is almost brutal, upon these august dead, who fondly thought that they had hidden themselves forever.[13]

Loti was the pen name of Julien Viaud, a naval officer whose postings in Southeast Asia and North and West Africa were as representative of French colonial career paths as the India-to-Egypt trajectory was for civil servants and army officers under the British Empire. During his stay in Cairo, Loti was given a personal tour of the museum by Gaston Maspero—at night, which perhaps shielded him from the horror of its architecture. By the light of a lantern, and with the doors "doubly locked" behind them, Maspero and Loti made their way through the museum, which Loti described as "vast," "monumental," and occupied by "mysterious things that are ranged on every side and fill the place with shadows and hiding-places." When at last they reached the first-floor gallery where the bodies from the royal caches were displayed, in air "heavy with the sickly odour of mummies," Loti passed

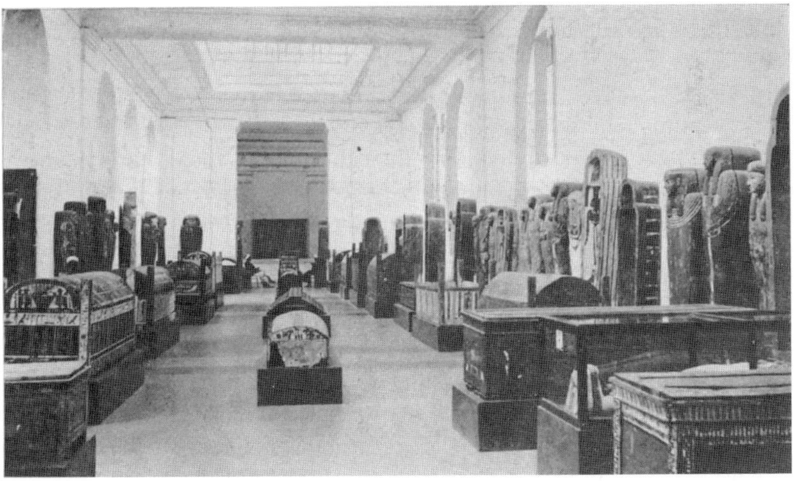

FIGURE 6.2 *Interior view of coffin displays in the Egyptian Museum, Cairo, from an early twentieth-century postcard. Author's photograph*

from case to case, bending over with his lantern to see the faces of the pharaohs. He noted that they were arranged in chronological order and labeled with "common paper tickets," and accounts of the unwrappings some fifteen years earlier were fresh in his mind, such as the near-stampede that accompanied the revelation of the mummy of Ramses II, "wrapped *thousands of times* in a marvellous winding-sheet...finer than the muslin of India, which must have taken years in the making and measured more than 400 yards in length," as he mused hyperbolically.

Its ritual and sanctified character helps make the museum a place of memory formation and accretion: in Loti's account, the memory of the 1880s discovery and unwrapping of the royal mummies was entwined with the imagined memory of their ancient lives and with his own memory-making experience of visiting the building first by day, and then, dramatically, by night. Part of this remembering acknowledged the act of archaeological desecration—the "unswathing" of the "august dead who fondly thought that they had hidden themselves forever." But the remembering also took shape through a range of emotive responses stirred by viewing the mummies: curiosity, dread, calm, and, for one female body in particular, a spectral eroticism. Loti remarked on her "naked shoulders" and "dishevelled hair." His view unobstructed by the glass, the mummy lay revealed and still beneath his gaze, and, he wrote, "straightaway I meet the sidelong glance of her enamelled pupils, shining out of half-closed eyelids, with lashes that are still almost perfect." Loti had seen the sacred object, and revered it.

Revelation, Revisited

In ancient Egypt, the wrapping of objects and bodies in linen marked them as sacred and kept them safe and set apart, holding their divine power securely inside and blocking any potential profanation outside. In contrast, in the museums where Egyptian antiquities are now housed, it is revelation that matters more than concealment, echoing the ideals of a democratic state. Since the Enlightenment, seeing further and further within has been the epistemological basis of knowledge production, epitomized by Schiller's image of the veiled Isis of Sais. What was shrouded or veiled was tantalizing because it hinted at the possibility of revelation and hence the acquisition of more knowledge, especially the forbidden knowledge of the secret. In Schiller's poem, the statue strikes dead the youth who tries to lift its veil, his "sacrilegious gaze" punished (the translation is Bulwer-Lytton's) and the secret truth preserved. In Egyptological practice, a few selected objects, like the mummy of king Amenhotep I, kept their veils, their wraps, in place to tantalize future generations.

In this section, I shift from the historical contexts of mummy unwrappings and museum display considered earlier, to the more recent and contemporary contexts of revelation that form the basis of discussion in the rest of this chapter. The parameters of knowing and not-knowing, seeing and not-seeing, do not arise or exist in isolation. It is significant if a society accepts that only certain individuals can dress, undress, and carry the statue of a god, or hold the keys to storerooms of material collected and conserved for the public good, because such assumptions are the foundations for structures of power. The creation and manipulation of objects is fundamental to how humans create meaning, and potent meanings require potent regulation—hence the value of wrapping, concealment, and secrecy, in ancient society and our own. It would be naive to imagine that museums reveal all, any more than other institutions do. And, like other institutions, museums struggle with irony: an exhibition exploring the relationship between photography and surveillance, held at Tate Modern in 2010, made no reference at all to the security cameras that tracked every gallery.[14]

Just as museums stack up time, they stack up objects as well. Vast collections hold a potential for display, research, education, and so on—a potential that can never be realized and in fact only grows, exponentially, like time. Each unwrapping, each investigation, each identification opens the possibility of further, future, unspecified "research." The museum is a storehouse, an archive, a memory bank; no wonder we fear its violation. It is what we were, what we are, and, in Donald Preziosi's rather teasing formulation, what we will have been.[15]

When new legislation curtailing the division of antiquities came into force in Egypt in the 1920s, post-independence and post-Tutankhamun, museums outside of Egypt began to face a drop-off in the steady supply of objects for their collections. This intensified after Nasser's revolution in the 1950s, by which time Egyptian archaeologists had assumed the leadership of the national antiquities service and its museums. The most stringent legislation banning the export of antiquities from Egypt took effect in 1983, although illicit trade inevitably persists. Their collections may have been more or less complete, at least in terms of finds derived from documented archaeology, but for the purposes of research and knowledge generation, museums needed only to turn to their own back rooms—whose stock included fresh material to unwrap.

The 1960s and 1970s witnessed a spate of studies on mummified human remains using the discursive strategy of that most modern of religions, medical science, to lend gravitas to the participants, the procedure, and the results. In many ways, the sanctification of research on the human corpse was nothing new, if we recall the church setting and religious representation of anatomical theater demonstrations in early modern Europe.[16] Even the language of the new reports, though largely couched in scientific terms, is at times redolent of earlier eras: "The resin burned with a most fragrant odor" is a phrase that would not have been out of place in an ancient Egyptian ritual text, or an 1830s unwrapping, but in fact belongs to the American Midwest of the early 1970s.[17]

In 1973, a medical team from Wayne State University in Detroit resorted to a powered surgical saw to penetrate the resin-soaked linen on a mummy from the University of Pennsylvania's Museum of Archaeology and

Anthropology.[18] As Howard Carter had discovered decades earlier, when dealing with the coffins, mask, and brittle linen wrappings of Tutankhamun, resin could stop an unwrapping in its tracks, and the resin on the Ptolemaic period mummy known as PUM II was typically hard and heavy. The team's first tactic, like Carter's, had been to hammer it away. The surgical saw solved that particular problem, and nine people worked for seven hours to remove twelve layers of linen wrappings. Radiocarbon analysis—then quite a new technique—dated the linen to around 170 B.C.E., as a specialist in styles of funerary art could already have predicted from the appearance of the wrapped mummy, while chemical analysis identified juniper and myrrh among the resin. The scientists also observed that the mummy's exposed skin turned from light to dark brown within twenty-four hours of exposure to air, and to black within a few days. Even if the observation was meant as "objective" description to record an observed phenomenon, it is reminiscent of the fluent Victorian language of race and appears, however unconsciously, to engage with questions of mummies and skin color, as if offering an explanation for why the embalmed bodies of ancient Egyptians may appear "black" or African when, by implication, they were neither. Perhaps tellingly, the mummy unwrapping took place in the center of Detroit, a city that had recently been riven by race riots and split in two along color lines.

Film footage of a CT scan carried out on the same mummy in 2009 shows its present state, including the rectangular section sawed out of the skull at the 1973 "autopsy"—yielding, incidentally, a piece of the *dura mater* membrane that the presiding surgeon gave to a *Detroit News* journalist who was present at the time, and which was recently sold on the Internet in a mocked-up museum "frame," complete with identifying label.[19] The film and photographs of the 2009 scan also illustrate the key accoutrements for handling mummies in the required state of purity: Tyvek wrapping around the body and nitrile gloves on the participants.[20] The wearing of medical gowns, masks, and gloves was a feature of unwrappings and examinations in the 1970s as well, which served to stage these events as scientific research that would yield objective facts and that placed the researchers in a direct line of descent (and evolution) from early nineteenth-century "unrollers" like Granville and Pettigrew. When the Manchester Museum followed suit with its own mummy unwrapping in 1975, all the participants wore full surgical garb, and the hospital clogs and fatigues worn by the lead investigator, assistant curator Rosalie David, were so much a part of the self-presentation and institutional mythologizing of this event that they were kept in the museum's "mummy store" on the same shelves as the fractured linen, splintered bones, and "dust and sweepings" (as the labels on the boxes read) of Mummy 1770 itself (Fig. 6.3).[21]

Ostensibly, gloves and gowns prevent cross-contamination between the mummy and the investigators, for instance if samples are to be taken from the corpse or wrappings for analysis. Conservators, curators, and art

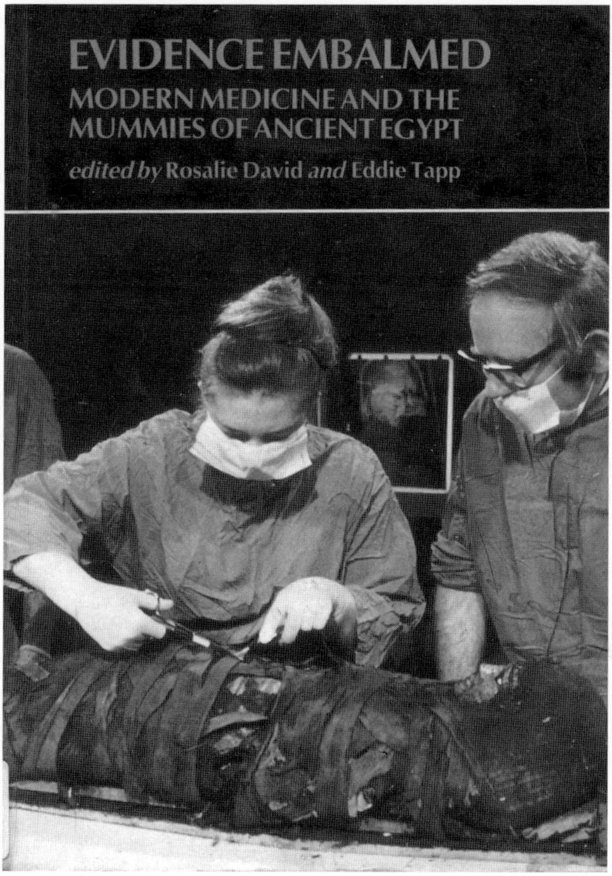

FIGURE 6.3 *Cover of the book* Evidence Embalmed, *featuring the initial stage of unwrapping Manchester Museum "Mummy 1770" in 1975. Courtesy of Manchester University Press*

handlers in museums wear gloves with most objects to prevent oils and sweat on the skin from reacting with the surface of the object, especially if it is made of reactive, fragile, or easily sullied materials. The robing of the participants in mummy examinations owes more to medical practice, however, in keeping with the location of late twentieth-century unwrappings, x-rays, and scans in hospitals due to the equipment required. Discussing the French reinvestigation of the mummy of Ramses II in 1976, Latour also comments on the prominence of white coats and face masks in journalistic coverage of the event, for which the mummy had been flown to Paris and greeted by the Republican Guard. Were the masks, he wonders, to protect the scientists from the dead king, or Ramses from them? The robed performance of the doctors and technicians is one of the supporting and legitimizing structures of science, whose "discoveries" of "facts"—such as the identification in Ramses's body of the bacillus that causes tuberculosis—to be projected backward or forward in time while retaining their authority. The procedures can be endlessly repeated into the future, and each new observation that yields a diagnosis will take precedent over the ancient context of the individual's life and death. In Latour's words, it is "for science, *and for science only,* [that] we forget the local, material, and practical networks that accompany artefacts through the whole duration of their lives."[22] Yet those networks of knowledge production are historically situated, a point underscored by the repetition and refinement of medical investigations of mummified remains over the past two centuries. The technology and the setting of the investigations have changed with the times, but not the core performance of objective, scientific authority or the fact that, in the end, Egyptian mummies almost always returned to the museum, where their status as both corpse and object could be accommodated in boxes, on shelves and trolleys, or, ideally, on display, the subject to which I now turn.

Displaying the Egyptian Dead

> Where does the heart of darkness lie, in the fleshy body-tearing rites of the cannibals or in the photographing eye of the beholder exposing them naked and deformed piece by piece to the world? It is a clinical eye and one never so lewd as in the closeness of the distance it maintains while dissecting the body of the Indian—assessing skin colour, functionalizing, measuring breasts, observing toes, measuring penises. In his fear of the Indians, alone and lost in the jungle, the calming thought came to Captain Whiffen of their proper place: in glass cases in an Anthropological museum.
>
> Michael Taussig, *Shamanism, Colonialism, and the Wild Man* (1987), p. 117

In the context of a museum—which is, after all, an institution predicated on viewing and presence—it is not surprising that mummies have been a central feature of displays for as long as they have been part of institutional collections. Although the practice has varied over time and by institution, from the early nineteenth century onwards mummies that had been unwrapped, dismembered, or dissected were put on display as readily as their wrapped counterparts. As they moved from private collections and domestic settings, which had enabled sensory contact such as touch and smell, into the museum, where they were almost always behind glass, mummies and parts of mummies entered a discourse of vision and visibility, and imaginative fantasy helped pierce the vitrine. The scopophilic charge of seeing the bared bodies, body parts, and faces of the ancient dead fuelled a thousand stories, plays, and novels in which ancient Egyptians came back to life to fall in love, or seek revenge (sometimes both), but rarely was the act of display ever questioned in nineteenth- and twentieth-century scholarship and museological practice.[23] One exception was the display of the royal mummies found in two caches in the late nineteenth century, first at Deir el-Bahri and subsequently in the tomb of Amenhotep II. The discomfiture seemed to stem not from the fact that they were corpses, but from the fact that they were kings.

In 1890, the historical painter and Royal Academician (not to mention Freemason) Edward Poynter wrote a letter to the *Times* in his role as honorary secretary of "The Society for the Preservation of the Monuments of Ancient Egypt," a confederation of British artists, Egyptologists, and political and cultural leaders that was active from 1888 to 1910, and which pressured the British authorities in Egypt over issues like dam construction on the Nile and how badly they thought the French were running the antiquities service. Poynter wrote to the *Times* to express qualms about the display of the unwrapped royal mummies in the Cairo museum, which was then located in an old Khedival palace at Giza. There had been, he said, "in many minds a feeling of regret that the mortal remains of these world-renowned Monarchs, whose exploits had passed into the stage of fable when Herodotus wrote of them, should, after having lain in sacred and undisturbed repose through so many ages, have been finally unearthed by the resistless curiosity of the modern spirit."[24]

Appended to Poynter's letter in support of his case was a missive from Edouard Naville, the Swiss archaeologist who was active on behalf of Britain's Egypt Exploration Fund. Naville had laid the argument out to Sir Colin Scott-Moncrieff of the Egyptian Ministry of Public Works, which had responsibility for the antiquities service. Naville's specific complaint was part of a campaign for a new, purpose-built museum (eventually built a decade later—the Egyptian Museum in Tahrir Square), and it is worth quoting his statement at length:

> The mummies have all been unrolled, and the bodies of the great kings of Egypt are exhibited under glass in one of the upper rooms of the Museum of Ghizeh. You will agree with me that these mummies are not to be considered as ordinary museum objects, and that some special measures must be taken for their preservation. There is no doubt that such as they are now they will not last; they will not stand the changes of temperature and of moisture in the air. One of these, the mummy of Seti I, is quite white now. I thought at first it was from mouldiness; it seems to be salt, which is quite as bad. The mummies have been photographed, studied, measured carefully; it is our duty to transmit them intact to future generations, and not to let them perish for the sake of a few visitors, for whom a well-made cast would answer just as well. I believe it is necessary to remove them from the museum, and to deposit them somewhere out of

> the reach of robbers. My idea is that they should be wrapped up again in silk and put in leaden coffins hermetically closed.

He went on to suggest that, given the museum's proximity to the Giza plateau, the perfect solution would be to rebury the mummies in an unused chamber of the pyramids.

In the 1920s, Egyptian nationalists took up the cause of the royal mummies, who had come to represent a line of indigenous sovereignty. The mummies were moved out of the antiquities museum to a former post office, where they were still on view, and later to the pharaonic-style mausoleum planned for nationalist leader Sa'ad Zaghloul.[25] After World War II, the antiquities museum once again made space for them in a dedicated gallery on the first floor, which opened in 1947. When Jean Cocteau viewed the mummies in 1949, he affirmed that their display was not a sacrilege because, he said, "they did not hide themselves in order to disappear, but in order to await the cue for their entry on stage."[26] In 1981, president Anwar Sadat saw it differently and ordered the mummy room closed.[27] The bodies were placed in storage in the basement of the museum until the Mubarak government reopened the royal mummy room in 1994, refurbished and fitted with high-spec display cases by the Getty Conservation Institute. A second room opened in 2006, and today, visitors purchase an extra ticket to gain admission to these galleries.

The bodies or body parts of allegedly royal mummies have also been the only human remains repatriated to Egypt, usually at the instigation of the then-owners. In 2003, the Michael C. Carlos Museum at Emory University returned a mummy that may be that of Ramses I, which it had acquired in a job lot of antiquities from a museum in Niagara Falls.[28] In 2006, a French postman made headlines, and was at one point under arrest, when he tried to sell samples of hair and linen from the mummy of Ramses II, inherited from his father, who was one of the technicians involved in the 1976 analysis of the mummy in Paris. Sent back to Egypt by French authorities the following year, the fragments were placed on display with the mummy, and culture minister Farouk Hosni used the incident as an example of Egypt's determination to recover all illicitly removed antiquities: "Despite its tiny size," he said, "Ramses II's hair is priceless and forthcoming generations would never forgive us if we neglect its return."[29] A similar scene was played out in 2010, when the phalanx of a large toe (probably the left one, for the curious) was handed over to the head of the Supreme Council of Antiquities by a Swiss scientist, who had apparently acquired it from the University of Liverpool professor of anatomy who x-rayed the mummy of Tutankhamun in 1968. The toe is not from Tutankhamun but from a mummy in another royal tomb, KV55, often argued to be that of the previous king, Akhenaten. At a press conference, the Swiss scientist said,

> I felt touched and honoured to bring back to Egypt the body piece of a supposed royal mummy. From an ethical point of view, it is an important

act. Apart from macroscopic-visual inspection and photographic recording, I have not further examined or sampled the specimen by any invasive method.[30]

The head of the antiquities council, Dr. Zahi Hawass, duly announced that the toe bone, like Ramses II's lock of hair, would go on display in the Cairo museum.

As their century-long history makes clear, the ownership and display of the royal mummies has been a persistent source of concern. But for other ancient Egyptian bodies, such concerns are more rare and couched in quite general terms, for instance about the need to avoid "sensationalist" display. Any question about the ancient actors' intention for the body to remain hidden—which, on the surface, chimes with modern ideas, both Western and Egyptian—is little more than rhetorical, immediately countered by suggestions that mummies are too important, too inherently fascinating, not to be on view or that, as Cocteau asserted about the royal mummies, they were secretly planning their revelation all along.

Many Egyptologists, self-styled mummy experts, and museums follow Cocteau's reasoning in deflecting responsibility for the display of Egyptian mummies onto the mummies themselves, as if these inanimate beings were exerting their will through their appointed ambassadors. One ploy, which seems to be increasingly popular in the twenty-first century, is the assertion that displaying the dead and their burial goods is a way to ensure that their memory—understood in universal, essentializing terms—survives. Museum staff, either in person or through panels and labeling in the display, inform visitors that repeating an individual's name is exactly what the ancient Egyptians wanted, a "fact" derived from Egyptian ritual texts that call for preservation of the name as an aspect of personhood. The museum visitor is invited to perform this ancient rite by reciting a translated Egyptian prayer, repeating what is presumed to be the ancient individual's name, or even, in the case of children in school groups, greeting the mummified body in chorus with a cheerful "good morning, so-and-so." At the Royal Cornwall Museum in Truro, for instance, visitors to a revamped display on ancient Egypt, opened in June 2012, "are encouraged to say the mummy's name with the wish 'May he live forever' out loud in keeping with the ancient Egyptian belief that to remember the deceased's name achieves immortality."[31]

Referring to Egyptian human remains by a personal name purports to emphasize the common humanity of contemporary visitors and the ancient dead, a presumption that can only be maintained by ignoring copious differences between cultures, temporalities, and not least materialities, since the human-ness of the mummy is a function of its reception in the West. Compounding such misguided interpretive efforts is the fact that the names ascribed to the remains are often erroneous, because the name is taken from a coffin that is not original to the mummified body, and inevitably are only approximations of ancient naming practices and pronunciations.[32] An ancient name considered too unwieldy might also be turned into a nickname for the public, as the Ashmolean Museum has done for the coffins, tomb goods, and wrapped mummy inscribed for a priest whose full name was written in hieroglyphs as Djed-djehuty-iwef-ankh, a naming pattern typical of the time this individual lived (around 600 B.C.E.) and which has the meaning "Thoth [the god] says, 'He will live' [or 'May he live']." Refurbished galleries opened in 2011 display the tomb group in a single large case, accompanied by a video of CT scan images of the wrapped mummy, and throughout, the deceased is referred to by the simplified name "Djed."

If ancient Egyptian prayers conveniently lend themselves to performance in the ritual space of the museum gallery, it is in part because museum staff feel able to characterize the gallery itself as a sort of tomb. In the late twentieth century, galleries have been designed to resemble Egyptian tombs, or at least stereotypes of tombs, with dark walls, dim lighting, and passageways and architectural features meant to evoke a descent or a maze-like journey in the footsteps of the archaeologist.[33] Like the recitation of the prayer and presumed personal name, the trope of museum-as-tomb professes to fulfill the intentions of the ancient actors by "preserving" their bodies, grave goods, and, by extension, personal identities. By functioning as a second tomb for mummies and other antiquities, the museum comes to represent the resurrection after death for which the ancient Egyptians had been hoping.[34] In this sense, museum staff and researchers seem confident that they stand on sacred ground.

Different museums in different countries have taken different approaches to the display of Egyptian remains and, in particular, unwrapped bodies and body parts. In the United States, museums of archaeology, like the University of Pennsylvania Museum, or natural history, like the Smithsonian's National Museum of Natural History, are much more likely to incorporate unwrapped bodies in their displays, while art museums, which hold the largest collections of Egyptian antiquities in the United States, restrict themselves to wrapped examples, where the details of wrappings, masks, shrouds, and other adornments are meant to become the viewer's focus. British museums and their visitors are quite accustomed to viewing any kind of mummy, wrapped or unwrapped, whole or in part, while in continental Europe, the practice varies by country and institution.[35] In Germany, a survey conducted by Egyptology students at the 1998 exhibition *Das Geheimnis der Mumien: Ewiges Leben am Nil,* held in the Kulturforum in Berlin, revealed that of more than 1,400 visitors who completed a questionnaire, 89 percent thought it was justifiable to present human corpses in a museum, although 48 percent agreed that ancient Egyptians would not have consented to the practice.[36] But aside from such special exhibitions, which attract an audience interested in the subject matter, human remains from ancient Egypt, especially mummified bodies in fragmentary or unwrapped states, are rarely displayed in German museums. A number of variables are at work here, from the kind of museum, to the nature of the remains (so-called bog bodies are displayed in German museums, for instance), to the interests and expectations of the audience. There is no "natural" reaction to human remains simply because they are human, for such reactions are as much a part of culture as the idea of what a human is.[37]

The past twenty-five years have seen a sea change in the curation of human remains and sacred objects held in ethnographic collections, particularly in North America and Australasia but also in the UK and other former colonial powers. This development has come about partly within the profession, for instance as anthropology addressed its colonial past, and partly in response to activism within source communities whose artifacts, burial goods, and bodies had been acquired under circumstances of, at best, unequal power and, at worst, duplicity and deceit. The shift toward what could be characterized as collaborative curating, whereby museum staff and source communities share in decision-making about the ownership, use, and display of certain objects, has led to a raft of new practices, projects, and areas of research.[38] The repatriation of objects and human remains; requirements for the source community to consent to scientific research on remains; or restrictions on who may handle or view an object, and under what conditions, are examples of the negotiated arrangements anthropology curators can expect to encounter in the course of their professional duties, and guidance on such matters is codified in the ethical tenets adopted by organizations like the Museum Ethnographers Group in the UK.[39] Questions concerning human remains in particular have been taken up by other professional bodies too, as well as governments—an indication of the gravity accorded to these issues in nations shaped by settler colonialism in particular. The Native American Graves Protection and Repatriation Act of 1990 was a watershed in the practice of museum anthropology in the United States, while the Vermillion Accord adopted by the World Archaeological Congress at a meeting in South Dakota in 1989 has arguably had less impact.[40] More recently, the British government's Working Group on Human Remains issued a set of guidelines for museums in 2004, after consultation within the sector, while the Human Tissue Act of 2004 established a Human Tissue Authority to regulate the collection, storage, ownership, research and teaching use, and public display of human tissue less than a hundred years old—requiring, for instance, that individuals give consent while alive for any part of their body to be displayed after death.[41]

The mass of guidelines, ethical statements, and legislation all attempt to codify the relationship between subjects (museum staff, source communities, user groups and visitors) and objects (human remains) who were once subjects themselves. The fraught nature of the task is evident in the language used in much of the documentation, which manages to be both vague and contradictory: the Vermillion Accord would have archaeologists "respect…the wishes of the dead concerning disposition…when they are known or can be reasonably inferred" and "respect…the scientific research value of skeletal, mummified and other human remains (including fossil hominids)…when such value is demonstrated to exist."[42] The Accord and other guidance documents say nothing about what to do when those two tenets directly oppose each other.

Sociologist Tiffany Jenkins has argued that museums' readiness to abrogate their "commitment to an empirical rationale" amounts to a "crisis of cultural authority", and critiques the vague language (such as "respect") some museum professionals and vocal interest groups have used in what are now well-rehearsed debates about the display of human remains in particular.[43] Jenkins seems taken aback that the impetus for change now comes from "cultural authorities"—that is, museum professionals—rather than external pressures, but this is not as new a development as she suggests, given its ultimate roots in postmodern and postcolonial scholarship of the 1970s and '80s. Thus, in anthropological curatorship today, it comes as no particular surprise for museums to seek the advice of Aboriginal Australians about which objects and paintings should have restrictions on viewing, or for an institution like the Tropenmuseum in Amsterdam to critique its own holdings not only of human remains but also of all the related archival matter, such as photographs and records of anthropometry, and to announce that it would be happy to repatriate the material to any relevant source community that will take it.[44]

For most archaeological curators, however, such actions remain unthinkable, especially for archaeological remains deemed to have no source community or where a potential source community, such as contemporary Egyptians, has not conveyed any coordinated opinions or concerns, although this situation may change in the future. The difference is in part one of time-depth: the ancient remains studied by archaeology are so far removed in time that no living descendants are considered, rightly or wrongly, to exist. But the difference is also a product of the stories that museum specialists, archaeologists, and Egyptologists choose to tell and the histories they forget. To associate ancient Egyptian human remains too closely with the population of modern Egypt presses the same nerve as the damaged Tutankhamun statues or requests to return the Rosetta Stone, not to mention all the pained sensitivities surrounding race.

The few attempts known to me where museums have taken the initiative in changing their approach to displaying Egyptian mummies have been scattergun and met with mixed results. In 2010, the Brooklyn Museum of Art rewrapped, in its original linen, the mummified body of a man that had been unwrapped in the 1950s, after it was acquired by transfer from the Metropolitan Museum of Art in 1952.[45] At the time of the transfer, the curator of the Brooklyn Museum's Egyptian collection, John Cooney, opined that mummies had no place in an art museum, and after it was unwrapped, Cooney attempted to arrange for the burial or incineration of the body. This was impossible due to New York state legislation requiring a death certificate for the disposal of a corpse, and in a TV program aired in the United States in 1958, credit was given to a museum technician for saving and storing the mummy when all other avenues had been exhausted. The initiative to rewrap the mummy seems to have come from conservators interested in studying the textiles, and attempts to recreate the original wrapping technique were facilitated by records of the Metropolitan Museum's excavation of the mummy at Deir el-Bahri in the 1920s, coincidentally photographed by Harry Burton, the same photographer who recorded the tomb of Tutankhamun (Fig. 6.4). In an interview with the *New York Times* about the rewrapping, curator Ed Bleiberg categorized wrapped mummies as "artifacts" and said that Brooklyn Museum of Art would not display unwrapped mummies, only wrapped (or rewrapped) bodies. "We display the mummies, and we respect them," he explained. Press coverage persisted, however, in referring to the rewrapped mummy by the nickname "Melvin," which it had previously been given by the museum—and the new arrangement of the wrappings has left off what the excavation photos clearly show: an additional drape of cloth that covered the painted mummy mask as well.[46]

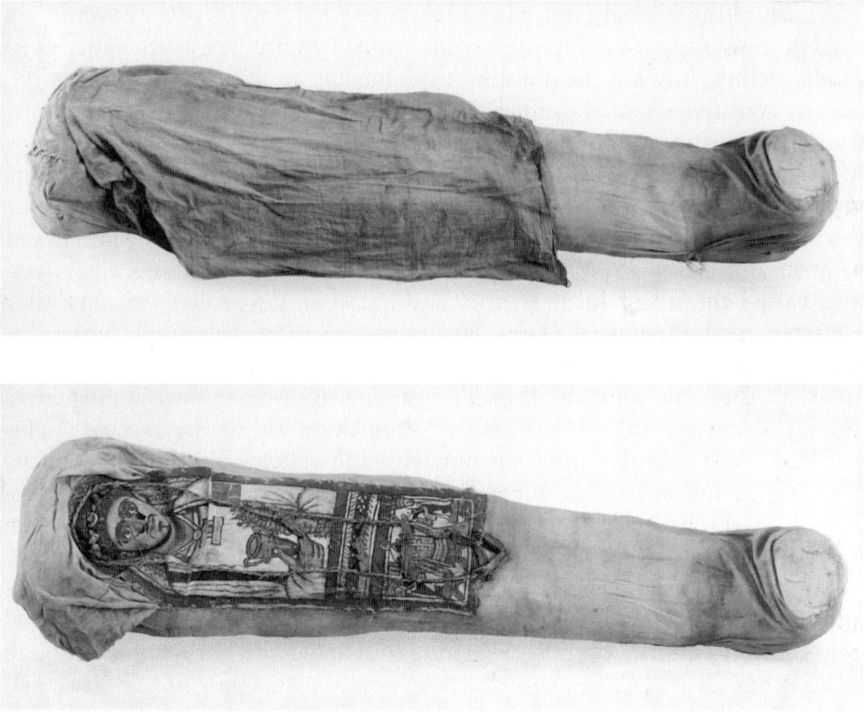

FIGURE 6.4 *Roman period mummy from Deir el-Bahri (burial XL, A), with cloth wrappings and covered mask. The mummy is now Brooklyn Museum of Art 52.128. The Metropolitan Museum of Art, photograph by Egyptian Expedition, 1928–29. Image © The Metropolitan Museum of Art*

Ten years previously, the Archaeological Museum of Kraców also elected to rewrap a mummy in its collection, which it had made the subject of extensive interdisciplinary research after unwrapping it in 1995.[47] The museum justified the project based on the poor condition of the mummy and the information that stood to be gathered by the investigations, taking the ICOM code of ethics as a guide in favor of research. "Mindful of the respect due to the dead woman," the unwrapping and autopsy were carried out with a minimum of press coverage, and in an echo of Maspero's and Elliot Smith's investigations of the royal mummies, the Egyptian ambassador to Poland was invited to attend. Reconstruction and rewrapping of the body was built into the project from the start, and the rewrapping finally took place in January 1999, requiring forty-eight hours of work and thirty extra meters of bandages created from modern fabric. Part of the face was left exposed so that when the mummy was returned to its coffin for display, the coffin lid could be opened slightly to permit visitors the view. As one of the leaders of the project observed, "weighing human curiosity and the demands of science against respect for the bodily remains of a human individual is a difficult matter indeed."[48]

In 2008, the Manchester Museum caused a flurry of press coverage in the UK by wrapping some of the unwrapped mummies in its galleries in modern cloth, in what the museum explained as an attempt to raise awareness of sensitivities surrounding the display of human remains in conjunction with its special exhibition featuring the bog body known as Lindow Man, on loan from the British Museum.[49] Given that the whole focus of the museum's Egyptian gallery, and copious local press coverage, had for some thirty years presented the ancient Egyptian human remains in Manchester as groundbreaking examples of medical and scientific research, the coverings raised the ire of local visitors and amateur Egyptology groups; they were removed a few weeks later. The museum had made a similar intervention in its mammal gallery two years previously, using lengths of cloth to cover all the male animals in order to make the point that the normative animal in natural history displays is often the male of the species.[50] This too had irked visitors, although not with the vehemence that greeted the covering of the mummies. Inconsistencies also plagued the museum's approach to the Egyptian gallery: the skeletons of the Two Brothers, which had been wired together and displayed in an original 1912 vitrine since the 1980s, were left uncovered due to the difficulty of opening and closing the antiquated case, and the covered mummies were referred to by personal names, following the paradigm of individualizing the bodies, even though at least one of the names was derived from a coffin that bore no original relation to the mummy displayed within it. Further, and perhaps most significantly, the temporary changes to the display did not address operations that went on behind-the-scenes, in particular the museum's ongoing collaboration with scientific research on the ancient Egyptian human remains in its collection—those boxed and bagged remnants, bones, and bodies that were, as we saw in the last chapter, considered to be damage-free.

Technologies of Revelation

> The blurring between life and death, objects and subjects, manifests itself everywhere within the discourse of and around forensic anthropology.
>
> Thomas Keenan and Eyal Weizman, *Mengele's Skull* (2012), p. 65

Debates about whether or not to display Egyptian mummies are symptomatic of much larger, but poorly articulated, issues about the intellectual and actual ownership of cultural property; the relative values of research, education, and entertainment; and what responsibilities, if any, the present has towards the past. For a start, the distinction between "human remains" and "sacred objects" is a false one, imposed by the mind/body duality enshrined in Western thought. Likewise, the idea that source communities must demonstrate a link by lineage, geographic fixity, or both reflects a cultural perspective that favors kinship or settled occupation over other modes of social organization. One could envision, for instance, a situation in which followers of faith practices based on ancient Egyptian belief systems would wish to identify themselves as descendants with an interest in what happens to human remains, as some pagan groups have done for archaeological remains found in Britain; Afrocentric groups could make similar claims.[51]

Museums, like people, forget. Watching televised press coverage of the 2011 uprising in Tahrir Square, I was struck by the omnipresence of the antiquities museum in the background, its century-old, stone-carved frills contrasting with the steel and concrete blocks around it, and by its absence in the commentary of reporters, who mentioned other buildings on the Square, such as the burning headquarters of Mubarak's party or the dreaded hulk of the Mugamma administration block, but not the museum itself. It was as if the museum's existence were so obvious that no explanation was needed, and as if its history were so remote that it had contributed nothing to the events taking place or—just as importantly—the reaction to those events in the West. The vandalism and looting that took place in the museum elicited no background account of the pink, European-style elephant in the room, even when the museum's mummies became, briefly, a cause for concern, with news headlines claiming that looters had ransacked cases and ripped the heads off bodies.[52] But once online Egyptology commentators, and Egyptian antiquities officials, had determined that the mummified heads and scattered bones photographed on a floor somewhere in the museum were not royal remains, and had already been in fragments, attention could revert to the damaged Tutankhamun statues and other suitable examples of what is invariably termed, in these contexts, "global" heritage. The reports of damaged mummies, but not the retractions, were eagerly picked up by Islamophobic websites.[53]

That silence and forgetfulness continue to plague museums, archaeology, and Egyptology where mummies are concerned is evident in the work of unwrapping and analysis that continues to take place, both in museums and in the field. The cover story of a 2010 issue of the Egypt Exploration Society's members magazine, *Egyptian Archaeology,* featured Japanese excavations at the site of Dahshur, where a number of intact burials dating

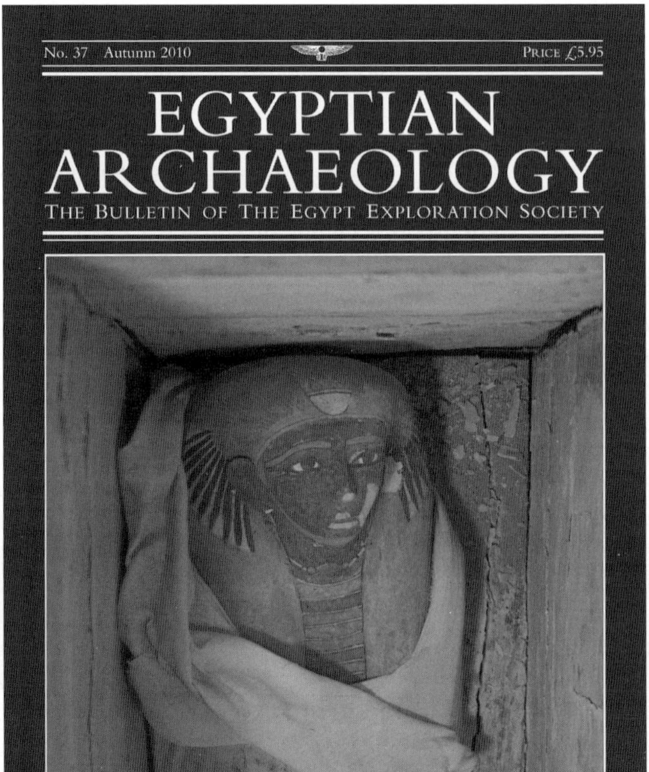

FIGURE 6.5 *Cover of* Egyptian Archaeology *magazine, Autumn 2010 with a photograph of the coffin and mummy of Senu, as found; from Dahshur, 12th dynasty (c. 2000–1800* B.C.E.*). Photograph copyright Waseda University Expedition to Dahshur. Image reproduced courtesy of the Egypt Exploration Society and Waseda University*

to the Middle Kingdom have been discovered (Fig. 6.5).[54] Photographs on the cover of the magazine and inside show the pristine linen shrouds that were gathered around the wrapped mummies, but they also show that the shrouds and masks were then removed; it is unclear whether or not the mummies were further unwrapped as well. Whatever the excavators have done, what is so striking about the article, with its titular reference to "intact coffins" and appearance in a publication meant for both professional and popular audiences, is that it makes no mention at all of the textile wrappings illustrated in its own photographs.

More commonly, the unwrapping of ancient Egypt now takes place through technologies of revelation, such as endoscopy, CT scans, x-rays (still preferred for dental evidence), and facial reconstruction. The mantra is that such technologies are nondestructive and noninvasive, but as with the dichotomy between a body and an object, that distinction is a matter of perspective. Such technologies involve seeing what was only, if ever, meant to be revealed under conditions of purity and ritual control. On a more prosaic level, they also involve a degree of handling and movement that most museum objects are spared, making the unique human quality of mummified remains once again the determining factor in their treatment. Just five weeks into my post as curator of the Manchester Museum's Egyptian collection, I was left speechless while supervising an endoscopy demonstration to which the museum had agreed on the basis that it involved students on a course in the university. The endoscope operator, who had collaborated with the museum's "mummy project" for many years, pulled down the brittle leaves of linen at the hip of the designated mummy (the headless body "autopsied" years earlier), peered at the pubis, and then swung around to poke the thin metal tool into an opening at the neck and shove it back and forth, all without acknowledging my presence, much less the box of nitrile gloves conservators had instructed us to wear.[55] "In the old days," he announced to the assembled students, "we'd have spent the whole afternoon down here and had a good rummage," although he admitted that the body was too packed with resin for much of anything to be seen.

Gloves begin to seem rather futile in the face of such technological advances, but as with the CT scan footage of the University of Pennsylvania mummy known as PUM II, or photographs of Manchester's earlier unwrapping and dissection of Mummy 1770 (see Fig. 6.3), protective gear enforces modern conditions of purity and ritual control. It is part of a discourse of scientific objectivity, which sets "facts," methods, technologies, and deduction into a linear narrative of discovery whose conclusions are irreproachable because they are "scientific."[56] Many scientists would be the first to admit the difficulties with such a narrative, but it is endemic to the presentation of Egyptian mummies in museums and other public fora. Objectivity, and medical gowns, played a prominent role in the CT scanning and DNA sampling of the mummy of Tutankhamun, sponsored by the National Geographic Society and carried out in the Valley of the Kings in 2005.[57] As in previous studies of ancient Egyptian DNA, the identification of diseases and the reconstruction of Tutankhamun's family tree proved highly contentious, since a number of researchers dispute the possibility of obtaining uncontaminated and adequately preserved chains of DNA from mummified remains; media coverage reported only the positive results, however, not the doubts.[58] Another well-publicized outcome of the National Geographic project was a set of facial reconstructions based on the CT scans, made by three different teams of forensic scientists working in Egypt, France, and the United States; the reconstructions accompanied a tour of objects from the tomb at American museum venues.[59] Both the American and French teams commented on what they termed the Caucasoid and North African features of the skull; only the American team had not been told who the subject of their reconstruction was. The French team used a forensic artist to create a lifelike model based on the scans, using silicon "skin," glass eyes, hair, and makeup inspired in part by wooden sculptures of the king. This appealing image was the one preferred by the media and featured on the cover of *National Geographic* magazine in June 2005, although questions of race haunted public reception of the boy-king's reappearance elsewhere, for instance on both Afrocentric and right-wing websites.[60]

Such reconstructions have an immense popular appeal, seeming as they do to bring viewers face to face with the dead, erasing time, distance, and difference. They are also part of the forensic turn, another product of late twentieth-century science, which has manifested in popular culture through detective novels, films, and television programs in which the protagonists are forensic pathologists or crime scene investigators. In a recent essay, two scholars of human rights and visual studies, Thomas Keenan and Eyal Weizman, term the phenomenon of adding flesh to bones a "forensic aesthetics" and identify the turning point in its popular, and legal, acceptance as the 1985 reconstruction of the skull thought to belong to Josef Mengele.[61] Unlike the Nuremberg trials, which had relied on copious archival documentation to convict the architects and agents of the Holocaust, later trials for war crimes relied on the testimony of human witnesses and of human remains—in Mengele's case, unusually, the remains of perpetrator rather than victim. Keenan and Weizman describe techniques of forensic reconstruction as "technologies of persuasion, representation, and power—not of *truth,* but of *truth construction*" (emphasis original).[62] These techniques stretch the limits of what is considered scientific objectivity by bringing imaginative arts to bear on evidence. In the case of Mengele, this was done by overlaying known photographs of him and photographs of the skull believed (and subsequently accepted) to be his, using various angles and combinations to make a visual argument that neither law nor science could refute: Mengele had been found.

Sculpted reconstructions originally relied on plaster casts taken from skulls but now use computerized data to turn a virtual reconstruction into clay, plaster, or cast bronze reality. The science, rather than art, of the process is carefully explained in technical language, supported by copious measurements, statistics, and population data.[63] In museums, texts accompanying the display of reconstructions try to convey certainty while allowing for a margin of error. The pale-skinned, heavily eye-shadowed wax head reconstructed from Mummy 1770 at Manchester "may not be accurate in every detail," one label said, but "represents the type of face that 1770 must have had." Using the inventory number to refer to the deceased asserts a "scientific" way of speaking about the mummified remains, of which only a fragment from the face of the skull had survived.[64] At the National Museum of Scotland, reconstructed heads of two mummies have been cast in the commemorative material of bronze and feature both on display and online. The first, of the mummy of a young royal woman excavated by Petrie at Gurna on the West Bank of Luxor, comes from a burial with a distinctive style of pottery produced in what is now northern Sudan ("Nubia"), which, the museum says, may mean the woman is "ethnically Egyptian or from many other ethnic backgrounds."[65] Drawings represent the reconstructed face tinted with different skin colors, which visitors to the website can toggle between, while the sculpted head, according to the artist responsible for it, wears a "wig" of thin plaits, distancing the mummified body from the possibility of having African hair worn in braids or, in fact, any hair at all.[66] The second reconstruction, based on CT scans of the Third Intermediate Period mummy of a man named Iuefnamun, represents him as having a bald or shaven head without, apparently, considering that the hair had been removed for the purpose of mummification, or that a priest like Iuefnamun would have removed his body hair for a specific reason, at a specific time.[67] The museum does point out Iuefnamun's role in history, though: he is one of the priests responsible for the reburial of royal mummies in the Deir el-Bahri cache, where his name appears in the so-called dockets inscribed on reused coffins.

The persuasiveness of the visual—seeing is believing—is what gives revelatory technology its particular power in the context of museum research and display, especially when combined with modern faith in medicine. Techniques developed for other purposes, such as radiography and scanning, bring the prestige of medical science to the interpretation of archaeological material, yielding results that are presumed to convey objectivity and truth in a way that humanities and the social sciences fail to do. Conceptually, these technologies, as well as the twinning of archaeology and science, have much earlier roots, stretching back to the study of ancient skulls as indices of race. In Margaret Murray's publication of the Two Brothers find, a photograph that accompanied a discussion of the men's physiognomy paired the two skulls with the wooden statuettes found in their coffins, one of which measured 25.4 centimeters tall, the other just 18 centimeters (Fig. 6.6). The skull on the left, from the mummy of Nakht-ankh, had been deemed by medical study to be "caucasoid" and "effeminate," while the skull on the right, from the mummy of Khnum-nakht, had been identified as "negroid" and "robust."[68] Comparison of the skulls to the statuettes led Murray and her coauthors to conclude that the ancient artists had put the wrong inscriptions on the wooden figures, for the skull of each man matched, it was thought, the miniaturized head of the other man's statuette. This conclusion was repeated in the 1970s, when Manchester researchers reconstructed the skulls in plaster and through imaginative drawings.[69] The results also seemed to affirm the supposed racial identification of the bodies, down to the prominent lips recreated for the "negroid" face of Khnum-nakht, whose jaw featured protruding upper and lower teeth. On some occasions, the plaster reconstructions were displayed alongside the wired skeletons, and the drawings

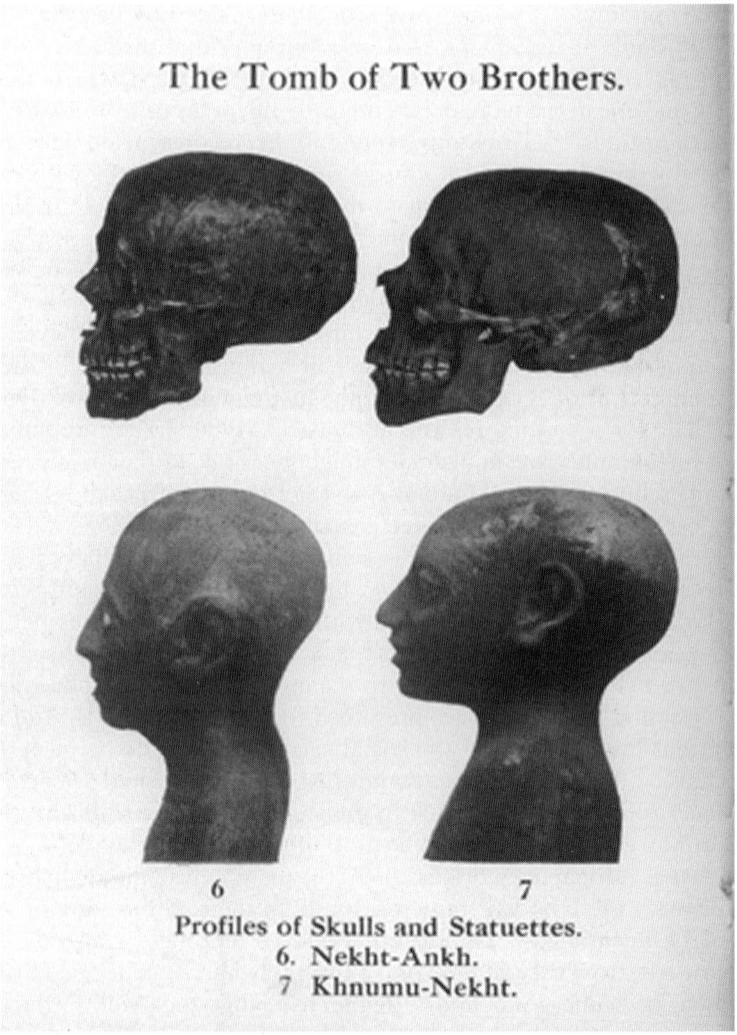

FIGURE 6.6 *Comparison of the skulls and statuettes from the burials of the Two Brothers. After Murray,* The Tomb of Two Brothers, *pl. 17*

were reproduced on interpretation panels as recently as 2006, together with a fictive biography explaining that the men's mother must have had a second marriage to someone of "Nubian" descent, which would explain the racial category assigned to the body of Khnum-nakht.[70]

Science claims to know ancient Egyptian bodies better than the ancient Egyptians did, surpassing Gliddon's claim to Morton in 1841 that "we"—the new Egyptologists—knew Egypt better than any Greek or Roman author had. Countless "mummy projects" have followed in the wake of 1970s efforts like the University of Pennsylvania and Manchester Museum investigations, and as CT scans and related techniques have become widely available, even small museums routinely incorporate such research into the displays of Egyptian mummies, or parts of mummies, that feature in many provincial collections. Technologies of revelation are as ubiquitous as the belief that they are noninvasive and nondestructive, for omniscient sight is a privilege Western modernity has claimed for some two centuries or more. In contemporary museological and Egyptological practice, it seems impossible to imagine *not* carrying out medicalized studies of mummified remains, so potent is the established paradigm that gives mummies this one story (in many permutations) to tell. And tell it they will: like Cocteau's assertion that Egypt's mummies had planned their own discovery and display, technology places credit squarely on the ancient human remains for the conclusions that scholars and scientists draw about their race, deformities, diseases, and demise. The dead bear testimony not against the living, but against themselves.

Revelation, Reborn

> We must lose our childish awe of "treasures" and "wonderful things" in order to replace it with a measured appreciation of the awkwardness, the limitations, the downright intractability of objects that, for whatever reason, we endow with value.
>
> Ludmilla Jordanova, "Objects of Knowledge" (1989), p. 40

The artist Angela Palmer turns bodies into glass. Her work transcribes the data produced by MRI and CT scans into images inked onto the surface of identical glass sheets, which are aligned to form box-like sculptures. Set up parallel to each other, like dominoes, the sandwiched sheets of glass invite the viewer to move around the sculpture because the inked image within changes from every angle. There is no single image at all, but a multitude that move with each shift in vantage point. Technology reveals what is beneath the skin, but it can only do so through an image. Palmer further crafts that image and in doing so brings into question what a body is, especially when that body is relayed in slices of discrete data. How much of the body is present in the image, and how much of what is present can be seen?

In a collaboration with the Ashmolean Museum and the John Radcliffe Infirmary of the University of Oxford in 2008, Palmer created a series of works related to the intact mummy of an approximately eighteen-month-old boy, excavated by Petrie at Hawara and dating to the first or second century C.E. One of the sculptures, *Ashmolean Mummy Boy Lying on His Back,* has been donated to the Ashmolean Museum, where it is now displayed next to the mummy, in identical cases placed side by side in a bay defined by the Roman marble sculptures in the museum's Randolph Gallery, directly behind Cockerell's neoclassical façade (Fig. 6.7). *Mummy Boy* is made up of 111 Mirogard glass sheets that stand in a slotted sycamore plinth, its rectangular shape and wood and glass components creating a new coffin for the boy's body. In the present arrangement, visitors see both the real

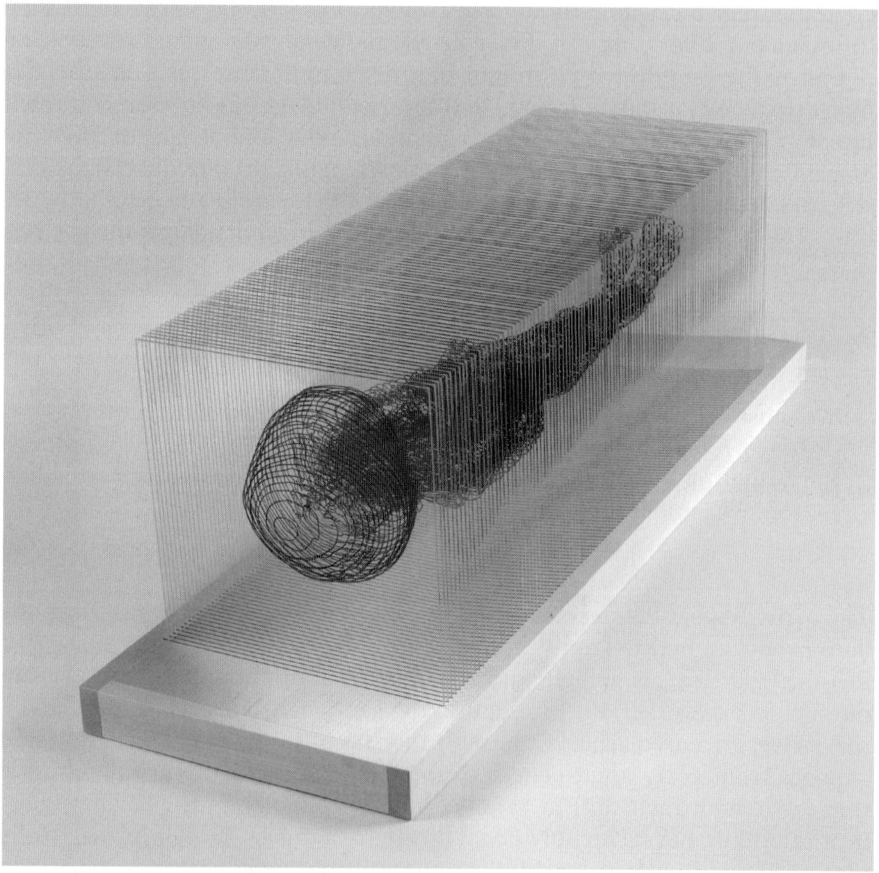

FIGURE 6.7 *Angela Palmer,* Ashmolean Mummy Boy Lying on His Back *(2008). Photograph by Todd-White Art Photography, used by kind permission of the artist*

mummy and the revealed mummy aligned and approached from the head end, setting Palmer's sculpture up as the interior of the wrapped body's exterior. As the viewer moves around *Mummy Boy,* peering over, through, and between the glass panes, the boy's "unravelled" body slips in and out of view, visible and invisible at once.[71] Looking straight on at the sides of the glass panels means that only their smoothed edges are visible, each pane separated by mere millimeters from its neighbor. With the inked image out of sight, concealed by the glass edges and the spaces in between them, the coffin remains shut, the wrapping intact. Like a scientist or an archaeologist, it is the viewer who is responsible for opening the coffin and unwrapping the mummy within.

In Egyptian antiquity, the makers of sacred objects, whether mummies or statues, worked in the same seclusion for which their creations were destined. Artistic creation itself took ritual form, and the *sem*-priest who donned a leopard-skin robe for the *Opening of the Mouth* of a sacred image might also perform a rite to imagine the image into being in the first place, seeing its divine form where there had been nothing but a block of stone or wood.[72] To do this, the *sem* was wrapped in bandages and placed in seclusion in that part of the temple known as the "house of gold," where statues and other works of art were made and where artists who were "masters of secrets" underwent their initiation (Fig. 6.8).[73] The Egyptian text of the rite plays on the similar words for wrapping, *sedjer,* and seclusion, *djeser,* which is also the word for sacred.[74] In order to "see" in his mind an image that was or would be wrapped, the *sem* had to become a wrapped image himself.

There can be little doubt that the treatment afforded to a range of objects from ancient Egypt—human and animal mummies, statues, and votive figures, to name a few—was regarded as sacred and that the act of wrapping and, often, concealing them was what marked, made, and maintained their sacred character. We can certainly infer, in other words, what the "wishes of the dead concerning disposition" were, to use the language of the Vermillion Accord, which urges archaeologists to honor ("respect") those wishes "whenever possible, reasonable and lawful." For the ancient Egyptians whose burial goods and bodies fill museum galleries and storerooms, however, such wish fulfillment is unlikely. They are not so much in the wrong place as in the wrong time.

In their own time, as we saw in Chapter 1, sacred objects like the gilded wooden statues in Tutankhamun's tomb were dressed in linen and shut in shrines, in keeping with the regular, ritual care that such images required because they gave physical presence to the divine (Fig. 6.9). It was the materiality of valued textiles, and the ability to manipulate them in the performance of wrapping, that enabled ancient Egyptian ritualists to access the sacred. Covering or concealing what could be seen, touched, and handled was a way to make manifest what could only be imagined. This is one of the most powerful, and confounding, characteristics of materiality: the material world inevitably refers to the immaterial. The material world also

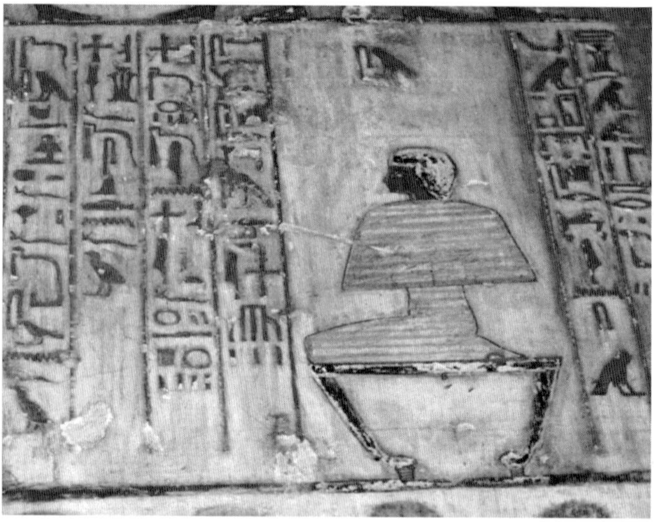

FIGURE 6.8 *The wrapped sem-priest in a scene from the* Opening of the Mouth *ritual, tomb of Rekhmire, Thebes, 18th dynasty (c. 1450 B.C.E.). Courtesy of John Freed*

moderates relationships within society, for people and things are indivisible. Hence the textiles used in mummy wrappings forged figural as well as literal bonds, between the life stages of individuals, between individuals and their households, and between households and the institutions of the state, such as the temples where linen was produced, tallied, stored, and offered up to the gods.

The survival of the material world of ancient Egypt owes much to the Egyptian cultural predilection for seclusion and concealment. The desert edges of the Nile valley have preserved more tombs and temples than urban settlements, and the ancient habit of burying, sealing, and caching everything from mummies, to statues, to papyri in these locations has proved ideal for the investigations of modern archaeologists. But therein lies the proverbial rub: archaeology and museums both depend on revelation, and have been blind to the immateriality that wrapping once engendered. The undoing of all the layers that ancient actors put in place has been the basis of knowledge production, disciplinary formations, and institutional and professional identities, yet it remains a point of silence. Undressed, like a child's doll, the statuettes from the tomb of Tutankhamun glint under photographic arc lights, ready to embark on their journey to the museum (Fig. 6.10). But how different would our imagining of ancient Egypt be if we forgot the sacred aura of their museum destination, or the heroic romance of their archaeological discovery, and instead remembered the materiality

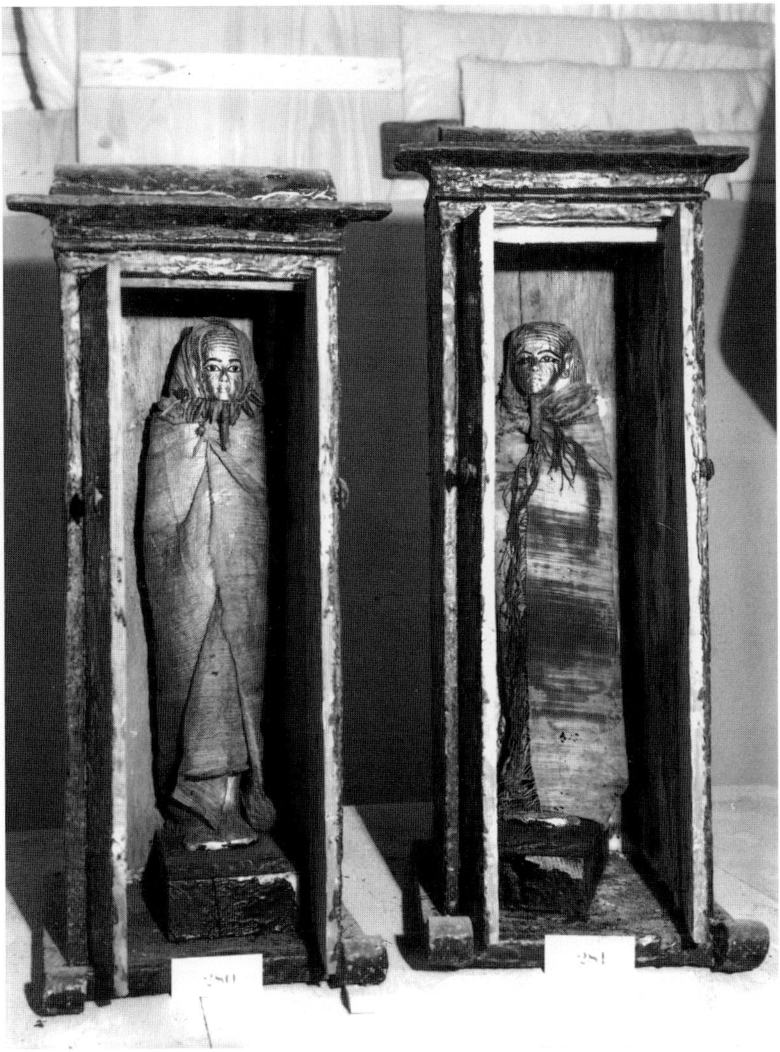

FIGURE 6.9 *Statues of the gods Imsety and Mamu from the tomb of Tutankhamun, wrapped and in their shrines; Carter nos. 280 and 281. Photograph by Harry Burton. Copyright: Griffith Institute, University of Oxford*

of their linen cloths and the sociality of the secret conditions in which they were made and wrapped?

The research questions that Egyptology pursues, and the interpretations that museums with Egyptian collections present, rest on such absences and assumptions, which remain by and large unchallenged. The study of

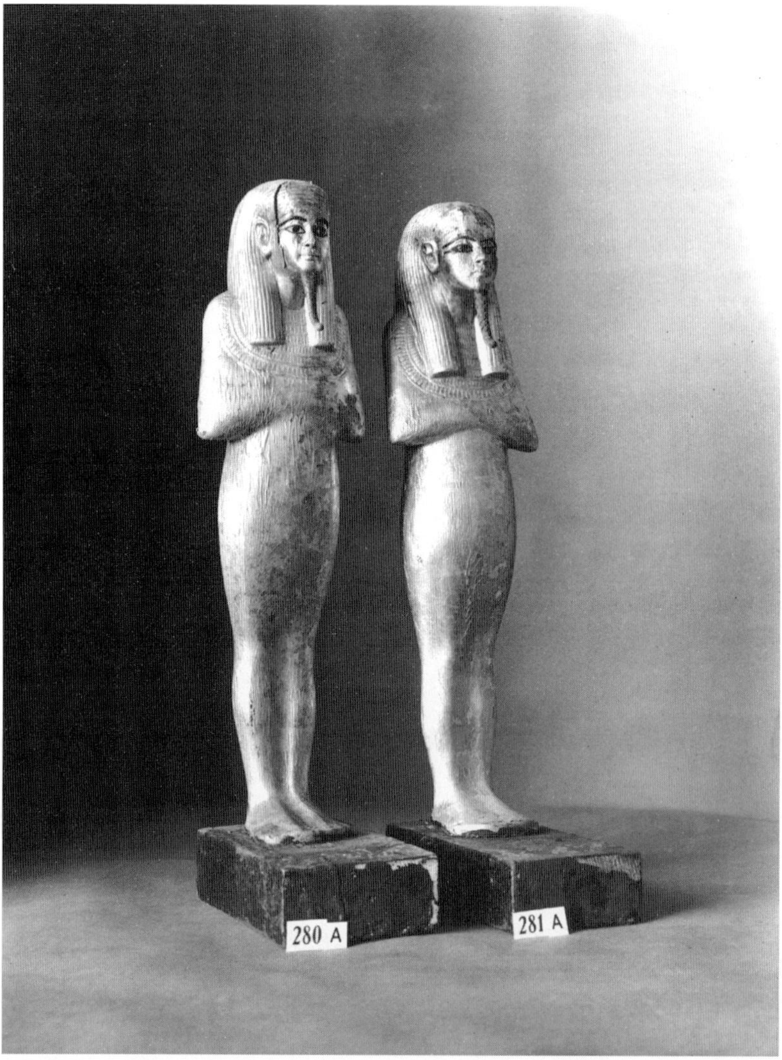

FIGURE 6.10 *The statues from Fig. 6.9, removed from the shrines and unwrapped. Photograph by Harry Burton. Copyright: Griffith Institute, University of Oxford*

archaeologically recovered material is wrongly considered to refer only to dead subjects, with no implications for the living, a point that Lynn Meskell has argued in her essay "Sites of Violence," which informs much of my discussion here.[75] In Egyptology, academics and others have echoed the colonialist stance that Egypt's Islamic population has no relationship with, or interest in, the country's ancient past, which gives Western scholars free rein to excavate, study, and display it as they see fit. Despite the violence that periodically punctures this illusion—the damage to the Egyptian Museum in 2011, or the murder of tourists at Deir el-Bahri in 1997—both professionals and amateurs involved in Egyptology have persisted in seeing heritage and politics as unrelated spheres. Modern Egyptians are made Other by being located in a time and value system different, and more "primitive," than the archaeologist's, the same phenomenon that Fabian characterized as being central to anthropology's creation of its objects of study.[76] The decolonizing of archaeology in Egypt and elsewhere in the Middle East is a fraught and tentative venture, no matter how well-meaning the intentions of Western and autochthonous archaeologists.[77] In the field, where non-Western archaeologists of necessity "confront colonialism not simply as a residual memory but as a daily reality, as a living present as opposed to a historical past," the preservation, recording, and interpretation of a site may allow for negotiation and multivocality in a more open, and even urgent, way than in institutions on the "home ground" of Western scholarship, such as museums.[78] There, the objects of Egyptology—the ancient Egyptians (as they are valorized) and their material and mortal remains—appear coeval with the West, made to answer its own concerns, satisfy its curiosity, and maintain implicit superiority over the Orient and Africa.

As is clear from the Vermillion Accord, the ICOM code of ethics, and other attempts at regulating, or regularizing, professional practices in archaeology and museums, ethical frameworks offer a false sense of doing the right thing, "deceptively positive" when their entire formulation is "neither neutral nor value-free."[79] Most university academics working on ancient Egyptian material do not feel that any particular codes of ethics apply to them, while the codes available to museum professionals have a broader remit, covering such areas as acquisitions and financial probity, and still accommodate destructive analysis of human remains in their care on the presumption that the scientific community has a right to conduct research.[80] In the biological sciences, research on living or recently deceased subjects is governed by informed consent and the anonymization of results. When two Swiss scientists—including the anatomist who returned the KV55 toe to Egyptian authorities—tried to evaluate scientific research on ancient Egyptian mummies in relation to ethical practice, they had to admit that neither informed consent nor anonymity were honored in studies of the ancient dead.[81] Rather than make any recommendations about ethical decision-making in research on Egyptian mummies, the authors restrict their discussion to "moral issues" such as conflicts of interest, excluding what they term "non-moral questions," such as money and politics. This seems an odd choice given the public and private funds expended on such research and on the museum displays concerned with the results, not to mention the political contexts in which the collection and study of Egyptian antiquities has taken place.

We cannot extricate ourselves from the past, but we can change our engagement with it, and this is what I would argue both museums and universities concerned with ancient Egypt must now undertake as a matter of priority. Museums may argue that it is their role in society to present the results of academic and scientific research to the public and to illustrate the traces of the past for the enlightenment of the present.[82] This does not prevent them from incorporating critical histories into their displays, reading "against the grain" of their collections to tell other stories in other ways, much as some historical exhibitions have embraced an expanded, more inclusive, and self-aware presentation of such challenging subjects as Apartheid or the Third Reich.[83] To do so may unsettle both museum staff and museum visitors, because it does not fit the ritual (and fantasy) they have come to expect from exhibitions on ancient Egypt. That is the point. Boris Wastiau recounts how an exhibition of Congolese artworks at the Royal Museum of Central Africa in Tervuren, Belgium, which incorporated the colonial histories of how the objects were collected, left visitors "feeling exposed":

> The museum as "site of memory" and the objects as unexpected pieces of historical evidence about their relationship to the maintenance of the museum's tradition, unsettled them by conjuring up disturbing images of the past.[84]

For a Belgian audience, "disturbing images of the past" include the violent history of Belgian exploitation of the Congo, which is the origin of the Tervuren museum's collection.

The collecting of Egyptian antiquities is no less implicated in colonial histories, as is scholarship that relies on historic collections or ongoing fieldwork for its research. Even more than the arts of sub-Saharan Africa, whose appropriation by the West began in earnest in the late nineteenth and early twentieth centuries, the material remains of ancient Egypt have been incorporated into Western narratives of Self and Other, in varying proportions. As a discipline, Egyptology has heretofore engaged in little self-reflection, relying instead on positivist approaches to its chosen objects. Further, its philological orientation has meant that, more than the cognate discipline of archaeology, Egyptology keeps its objects at a distance, seeing texts instead of the surfaces on which they are written, much less the layers of meaning and materials to which those surfaces belong. Whether through the media or the museum, Egyptology has a certain public presence, but lack of involvement, or even familiarity, with its own history and methods has left it ill-equipped to challenge well-worn narrative tracks ("discovery," "death," "treasures," "eternity").[85] Much the same could be said for amateur and alternative Egyptologies, although arguably, they are more removed from structures of power and from expectations of academic critique.

How museum professionals and academic Egyptologists engage with these varied publics is an area deserving careful consideration, and one that presents both difficulties, since established groups may perceive alternative views as a threat to their interests or expertise, and opportunities, since expanding the range of views and voices present in the public arena is a step towards making fresh tracks. Embracing multiple viewpoints does not mean that all of them are equally valid or viable, and the medicalized stance I have questioned in this chapter is as ripe for inclusion as any other. Unconditional acceptance of each theorem or point of view is not the aim; an explicit awareness of the historically and culturally specific nature of our encounters with ancient Egypt is, on the part of practitioners and publics alike. Today, Egyptian mummies may pull crowds and guarantee column inches, but this is the legacy of some two hundred years of engagement with the ancient unwrapped body—two centuries in which its materiality and its humanity have seen it sacrificed to science, to fantasy, to commerce. No rewrapping—real or metaphorical—can reverse time, but there is the possibility that adding new turns and layers to our stories can foreground it, and in so doing acknowledge the long reach of recent as well as ancient histories.

In the galleries and storerooms of museums, we see many things we were not meant to see. This is all but unavoidable, for we are entangled with the things of ancient Egypt in our world, not in theirs. From the anatomical gaze that greeted Egyptian mummies as crucial evidence for the early nineteenth-century study of race, as I traced in Chapter 2, to the new technologies of the "forensic turn" that have shaped mummy research over the past forty years, wrapped bodies that were sacred to their ancient creators have been put to uses they could not have imagined, and under quite different regimes of value. Parallels between the present and the past may lull us into a sense of safe familiarity, as if the museum really were a temple, and scientists or curators its priests. That sense is false, besides which, parallel lines by definition do not converge.

To impose modern sensibilities onto ancient society implies that shared humanity equates to shared cultural values. It does not: the diversity of experience is one of the wonders that enrich the study of both past and present, and the complexity of how past and present intertwine is one of the legacies with which the object world endows us. Like Palmer's *Mummy Boy*, it exists in the spaces in between: it is what survives, and it is also what time, or human agency, or both have stripped away.

AFTERWORD

In this book, I have traced the significance of wrapping practices in ancient Egypt, drawing out a thread that linked the production and use of linen; ideas about human reproduction, kingship, and the divine; and the performance of secrecy as a marker (and maker) of social organization. Throughout, I have used a critical analysis of historical contexts, together with insights from anthropological and material culture studies, to suggest new ways of understanding archaeological and textual evidence from ancient Egypt. Even the most famous and best-documented discovery in Egyptian archaeology—the tomb of Tutankhamun—appears in quite a different light when viewed through the lens of both its modern afterlives and the ancient actions to which its fragile textile wrappings, caught on camera, attest.

The long time span and diverse identities encompassed by the rubric "ancient Egypt" warns against generalizations or evolutionary narratives, but certain patterns and connections that emerge at different times and places point to the important role played by textiles, wrapping, and concealment in structuring Egyptian society and discourse. In Chapter 3, I argued that wrapping the dead in textiles was the common denominator of a set of practices characterized as mummification, which have many parallels with the treatment of sacred objects. Chapter 4 focused on linen textiles whose use in temple rituals and in the wrapping of the dead took them out of commodity circulation and imbued them with cultural and symbolic values instead—including the value placed on flax as an agricultural product, on the labor of women as spinners and weavers, and on the life histories that cloth and clothing embodied. I also explored the representation of textiles and wrapping in Egyptian art, which suggests a close association between cloth and concealment as well as wrapping and regeneration. Hidden secrets are a well-worn trope where ancient Egypt is concerned, and in defining itself as an academic discipline, Egyptology has tended to reject any hint of mysteries or esoteric knowledge, although alternative interpretations of ancient Egypt often embrace them. As Chapter 5 demonstrated, secrecy cannot be so readily excluded, because in certain contexts, it has offered an effective means of social organization, used to establish and maintain hierarchies. Signaling possession of the secret is essential to the organization of such hierarchies and their operations of influence, a model which fits the ancient Egyptian priesthood well, and extended from there to other social sectors. To be effective, those in possession of the secret must show their hand to those they mean to exclude, and it is this near-revelation, under appropriate controls, that gives secrets such power and makes desecration such a threat.

The two questions with which the book began—why were certain Egyptian bodies and objects wrapped in linen, and why had they been so systematically unwrapped in modern times?—presented a conundrum in that much of what we know about ancient textiles and wrapping techniques derives from the very unwrappings that undid the original practice. That is why it has been so important not to separate the two. Throughout this study, I have tried to demonstrate that the unwrapping of ancient Egypt was, and is, inextricably tied to the West's construction of itself as all-knowing, all-seeing, and all-powerful, implicating Egyptian antiquities—and especially mummified human remains—in a colonial and now postcolonial discourse of bodily paradigms and power. To this end, I have placed particular emphasis on the role of the museum as the institution whose origin, development, and ongoing practices are enmeshed in this discursive strategy, straddling public and academic spheres. This line of argument, supported by historical contextualization, informs each chapter but is especially prominent in Chapters 2 and 6, which bookend my discussion of the ancient evidence. In the nineteenth century, as Chapter 2 discussed, the investigation of Egyptian mummies was part of a discursive strategy that sought to define the alterity (or otherwise) of ancient Egypt and, hence, the place of a "great civilization" in relation to the West. Two centuries later, the technology used in the study of mummified remains has advanced considerably more than the discourse that surrounds it, where questions of race and disease shadow each facial reconstruction, CT scan, and DNA analysis. By considering some contemporary examples of museological practice in relation to Egyptian mummies, Chapter 6 brought out the contradictions that arise through facile, if well-intentioned, efforts to convey "respect" or justify unfettered research and display—contrast, for example, the obsequies and legal actions brought to bear on mere fragments of the royal mummies, and the careless handling, familiar or erroneous naming, and "make it all okay" pronouncement of prayers to which other mummies have been subject.

As I stated at the outset, my purpose has not been to offer museums or academics an instruction manual for changing the foundations of training and research, developing an ethics of twenty-first-century Egyptology, or curating sacred objects and mummified bodies, although on the last point, I have posited that these were one and the same to the ancient actors. The issues surrounding Egyptian mummies and skeletal remains in museums, for instance, should not be reduced to whether or not to reveal them through display or other technologies, although that is one possible question to consider. To my mind, it is instead a matter of using collections and displays in ways that challenge long-standing assumptions and make explicit the interwoven histories of Egypt and the West, which are inscribed, sometimes literally, in the material biographies of so many museum objects. Among other things, this will mean incorporating other and underrepresented voices, including those of modern Egyptians. It is a process that museums and academics can begin unilaterally, however, by disrupting the scientism that has come to dominate displays and press coverage of mummification in recent decades and by grappling with the materiality of collections throughout their life cycles, including their transformation by archaeology and the museum. It is this side-on look that lets the object world revolve, bringing us not the ancient perspective, which is forever just beyond us, but a different and fresh perspective on the archive in which our history tangled itself with theirs.

I realize that many scholars and practitioners might still prefer to separate (somehow) the past and the present, politics and heritage, "facts" and "theories," and will thus reject any approach informed by such concerns. As I write this in the summer of 2013, that is a position that seems increasingly untenable: news this week from Egypt documents the complete ransacking of an antiquities museum at Mallawi, attributed by Egyptian media to supporters of the Muslim Brotherhood. Coverage and reactions in the West have been more subdued this time, perhaps reflecting greater unease and uncertainty, as well as mounting death counts. Nonetheless, for those who see postcolonial theorizing, much less decolonization, as peripheral to archaeologically based research, I hope that at least the following point is clear: without understanding how a discipline such as Egyptology has selected and shaped its objects of study, and the questions it asks of them, it will never be possible to ask anything else. Historical critique helps us see our limitations, while cross-disciplinary engagement shows us new possibilities. It is through this approach that I have found it possible to reassess wrapping practices in ancient Egyptian society alongside the unwrapping of ancient Egypt in our own, and therefore to conclude that within the time and place we know as "ancient Egypt," the making and manipulation of textiles was central to networks of human relationships; economic, social, and cultural exchanges; and the interface between life and death, being and becoming, human and divine.

Wrapping was both the source and the sign of the sacred in this ancient culture. It created an interior and an exterior—that which was wrapped, and that which wrapped—but the relationship between the two was symbiotic, not oppositional. The wrapping transformed what it wrapped and was, itself, transformed. Even if removed at some later point, whether by priests or archaeologists, the textile wrapping is linked inextricably to the object or body that it enclosed.

Likewise, without its wrapping, that object or body will be left undone, incomplete, its visibility negotiated by times and terms that were not its own. The memory of that wrapped state exists in the museum and in the archive, where times and object worlds collide—yet time and again, we have imagined an ancient Egypt devoid of its material meanings and its histories, which now include our own. Someone draped the backcloth, posed the statues, positioned the inventory numbers, and exposed the plate, just as someone had once arranged the cloth, layered the coffins, shut the shrine, and looped the cord around the bolt to seal it, as memorialized in Burton's photographs (Fig. A.1). But the seal is open, and we are still lost in the breach.

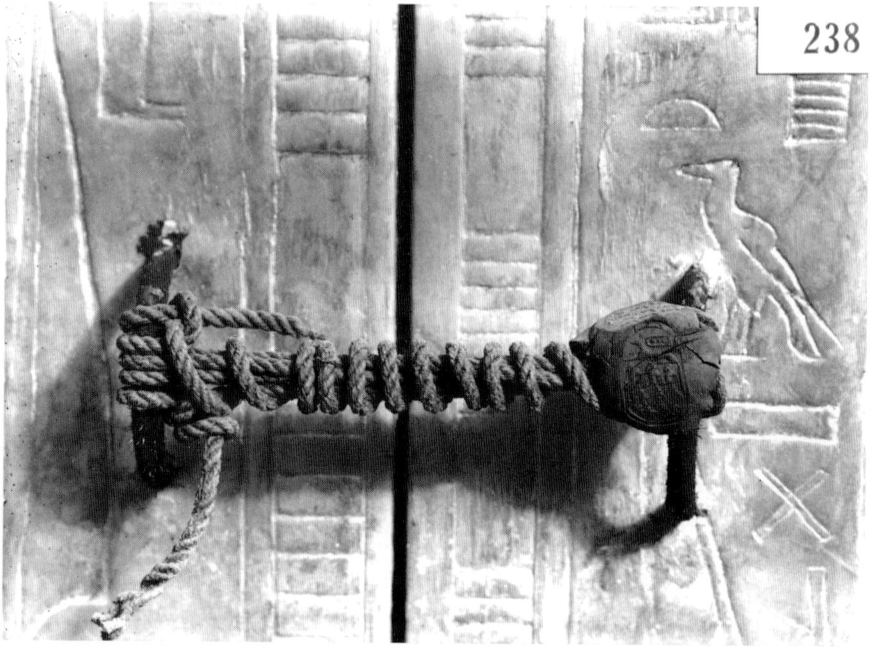

FIGURE A.1 *The seal on the third shrine (of four) surrounding the sarcophagus and nested coffins of Tutankhamun. Photograph by Harry Burton. Copyright: Griffith Institute, University of Oxford*

NOTES

Preface

1 Ancient dates conform to the chronology in J. Baines and J. Malek, *Cultural Atlas of Ancient Egypt*, 2nd rev. ed. (New York: Checkmark Books, 2000).

Chapter 1 Desecration

1 ICOM, "ICOM Urges to Protect Egypt's Cultural Heritage" (February 2011), http://icom.museum/news/news/article/icom-urges-to-protect-egypts-cultural-heritage/; UNESCO, "UNESCO Director-General Launches Heritage and Press Freedom Alert for Egypt" (February 1, 2011), http://www.unesco.org/new/en/media-services/single-view/news/unesco_director_general_launches_heritage_and_press_freedom_alert_for_egypt/; ICBS, "Egypt Statements" (January 31, 2011), http://www.ancbs.org/cms/index.php/en/press-room/archives/egypt; AIA, "Statement from the Archaeological Institute of America Concerning the Looting of Artifacts in Egypt" (January 31, 2011), http://www.archaeological.org/news/aianews/3934; AAA, "AAA Signs Statement of Support for Egypt," http://www.aaanet.org/issues/policy-advocacy/Egypt-Letter.cfm; and WAC, "Egypt Statement" (February 6, 2011), http://www.worldarchaeologicalcongress.org/component/content/article/63-press-releases/518-egypt-statement (all last accessed April 24, 2013).

2 Dissenting voices included archaeologist Neil Asher Silberman blogging at Searching for Authenticity, "Archaeology and the Criminal in Us" (January 28, 2011), http://neilsilberman.wordpress.com/2011/01/28/archaeology-and-the-criminal-in-us/; anthropologist Rosemary Joyce, at The Berkeley Blog, "Of People and Things: Egyptian Protest and Cultural Properties" (February 4, 2011), http://blogs.berkeley.edu/2011/02/04/of-people-and-things-egyptian-protest-and-cultural-properties/; and posts and comments on the Zero Anthropology blog, at "The American Anthropological Association and Egypt: It's Mostly About the Artifacts?" (February 5, 2011), http://zeroanthropology.net/2011/02/05/the-american-anthropological-association-and-egypt-its-mostly-about-the-artifacts/ (all last accessed April 24, 2013). For anthropologists' observations on the events of January–February 2011, see E. Haugerud (ed.), "Egypt Forum: 2011 Revolt. Reflections from Nine Anthropologists" in the special issue of *American Ethnologist* 39 (February 2012), and for a penetrating analysis written in the wake of 9/11 and the "war on terror" in Afghanistan, see L. Meskell, "Negative Heritage and Past Mastering in Archaeology," *Anthropological Quarterly* 75 (2002).

3 M. Taussig, *Defacement: Public Secrecy and the Labor of the Negative* (Stanford, CA: Stanford University Press, 1999), p. 1.

4 "Sad photograph": Egyptology News, "The Tutankhamun Panther Prior to Restoration" (February 17, 2011), http://egyptology.blogspot.com/2011/02/tutankhamun-panther-prior-to.html; "devastating footage": M. Maitland, The Eloquent Peasant, "Statues of Tutankhamun Damaged at the Egyptian Museum" (January 29, 2011), http://www.eloquentpeasant.com/2011/01/29/statues-of-tutankhamun-damagedstolen-from-the-egyptian-museum/ (both last accessed April 24, 2013). Extensive media coverage and public comments in Internet fora also played notable roles in the reception and circulation of news about the looting of the antiquities museum in Baghdad and the destruction of the Bamiyan Buddhas in Afghanistan. See S. Pollock, "The Looting of the Iraq Museum: Thoughts on Archaeology in a Time of Crisis," *Public Archaeology* 3 (2003), and C. Colwell-Chanthaphonh, "Dismembering/Disremembering the Buddhas: Renderings on the Internet during the Afghan Purge of the Past," *Journal of Social Archaeology* 3 (2002).

5 D. M. Reid, "French Egyptology and the Architecture of Orientalism: Deciphering the Façade of Cairo's Egyptian Museum," in L. C. Brown and M. S. Gordon (eds.), *Franco–Arab Encounters: Studies in Memory of David C. Gordon* (Beirut: American University of Beirut, 1996); C. Riggs, "Colonial Visions: Egyptian Antiquities and Contested Histories in the Cairo Museum," *Museum Worlds: Advances in Research* 1 (2013).

6 D. M. Reid, "Indigenous Egyptology: The Decolonization of a Profession?" *Journal of the American Oriental Society* 105 (1985); D. M. Reid, *Whose Pharaohs? Archaeology, Museums, and Egyptian National Identity from Napoleon to World War I* (Berkeley: University of California Press, 2002).

7 See E. Colla, *Conflicted Antiquities: Egyptology, Egyptomania, Egyptian Modernity* (Durham, NC: Duke University Press, 2007), pp. 199–210; B. R. Parkinson, "Tutankhamen on Trial: Egyptian Nationalism and the Court Case for the Pharaoh's Artifacts," *Journal of the American Research Center in Egypt* 44 (2008).

8 For the Metropolitan Museum of Art arrangement, see the November 10, 2010, press release at http://www.metmuseum.org/about-the-museum/press-room/news/2010/metropolitan-museum-and-egyptian-government-announce-initiative-to-recognize-egypts-title-to-19-objects-originally-from-tutankhamuns-tomb (last accessed April 24, 2013); the inquiry to the eighth earl of Carnarvon appeared in various media outlets, based on Zahi Hawass, "Lord Carnarvon's Obsession," *Asharq Alawsat* (January 10, 2011), available online at http://www.aawsat.net/2011/01/article55247959.

9 See Camden Arts Centre, "Never the Same River (Possible Futures, Probable Pasts)," http://www.camdenartscentre.org/whats-on/view/exh11 (last accessed June 26, 2012).

10 Hayward Gallery, *Richard Wentworth's Thinking Aloud* (London: Hayward Gallery, 1998), pp. 40, 54.

11 The Tutankhamun excavation archive is available to search online at The Griffith Institute, "Tutankhamun: Anatomy of an Excavation," http://www.griffith.ox.ac.uk/tutankhamundiscovery.html (last accessed June 26, 2012).

12 D. Miller, "Afterword," in L. Meskell (ed.), *Archaeologies of Materiality* (Malden, MA, and Oxford: Blackwell, 2005).

13 A. Appadurai (ed.), *The Social Life of Things: Commodities in Cultural Perspective* (Cambridge: Cambridge University Press, 1986); I. Kopytoff, "The Cultural Biography of Things: Commoditization as Process," in A. Appadurai (ed.), *The Social Life of Things: Commodities in Cultural Perspective* (Cambridge: Cambridge University Press, 1986); I. Hodder, *Reading the Past: Current Approaches to Interpretation in Archaeology* (Cambridge: Cambridge University Press, 1991); I. Hodder, *Entangled: An Archaeology of the Relationships between Humans and Things* (Malden, MA: Wiley-Blackwell, 2012); L. Meskell, *Object Worlds in Ancient Egypt: Material Biographies Past and Present* (Oxford and New York: Berg, 2004); A. Gell, *Art and Agency: An Anthropological Theory* (Oxford: Clarendon Press, 1998); D. Miller (ed.), *Materiality* (Durham, NC, and London: Duke University Press, 2005). See discussion in R. W. Preucel, *Archaeological Semiotics* (Malden, MA, and Oxford: Blackwell, 2006), pp. 14–16 and *passim*.

14 N. Thomas, "The Case of the Misplaced Ponchos: Speculations Concerning the History of Cloth in Polynesia," *Journal of Material Culture* 4 (1999); W. Keane, "Signs Are Not the Garb of Meaning: On the Social Analysis of Material Things," in D. Miller (ed.), *Materiality* (Durham, NC, and London: Duke University Press, 2005).

15 T. Ingold, "Materials against Materiality," *Archaeological Dialogues* 14 (2007); B. Olsen, *In Defense of Things: Archaeology and the Ontology of Objects* (Lanham, MD, and Plymouth, UK: Altamira Press, 2010).

16 C. Pinney, "Things Happen: Or, from Which Moment Does that Object Come?" in D. Miller (ed.), *Materiality* (Durham, NC, and London: Duke University Press, 2005). For a thoughtful discussion of the challenges the body—and specifically the skeletal remains of the body—also presents to this dichotomy, see J. R. Sofaer, *The Body as Material Culture: A Theoretical Osteoarchaeology* (Cambridge: Cambridge University Press, 2006), especially pp. 62–88.

17 G. Kubler, *The Shape of Time: Remarks on the History of Things* (New Haven, CT: Yale University Press, 1962), p. 1.

18 L. Meskell, "Objects in the Mirror Appear Closer Than They Are," in D. Miller (ed.), *Materiality* (Durham, NC, and London: Duke University Press, 2005); and compare Meskell (ed.), *Archaeologies of Materiality*.

19 Meskell, "Objects in the Mirror."

20 One of the four objects, the *djed*-pillar amulet in the west corner of the south wall (Carter no. 260), had no wrapping preserved. *Book of the Dead* spell 151, which relates to the practice of placing the bricks and objects in the four wall niches of a tomb, specifies that the *djed*-pillar should be wrapped, but not the other three; the spell also indicates different correlations between object and wall (north, south, east, or west) than those found in many tombs, including the tomb of Tutankhamun. Furthermore, the Osiris figure (Carter no. 257) is atypical, and a fifth object—the more usual reed torch (Carter no. 263)—and its brick were found on the floor at the entrance to the Treasury instead of in a wall niche. See A. M. Roth and C. H. Roehrig, "Magical Bricks and Bricks of Birth," *Journal of Egyptian Archaeology* 88 (2002); F. Scalf, "Magical Bricks in

the Oriental Institute Museum of the University of Chicago," *Studien zur Altägyptischen Kultur* 38 (2009); and B. Lüscher, *Untersuchungen zu Totenbuch Spruch 151* (Wiesbaden: Harrassowitz, 1998).

21 Carter no. 261a, with photographs of the draped jackal and the inscription, but not the complete tunic, available in the online archive. For the tunic, see G. Vogelsang-Eastwood, *Tutankhamun's Wardrobe: Garments from the Tomb of Tutankhamun* (Rotterdam: Barjesteh van Waalwijk van Doorn & Co's, 1999), pp. 54–55.

22 H. Carter, *The Tomb of Tut-Ankh-Amen* (London: Sphere, 1972 [1933]), p. 163.

23 Carter no. 288 and 288a: Carter, *The Tomb of Tut-Ankh-Amen,* p. 175.

24 One example: D. Meeks, *Année Lexicographique 2 (1978)* (Paris: Margeride, 1981), 72.2648, on *Coffin Texts* I, 82b.

25 A. Erman and H. Grapow (eds.), *Wörterbuch der ägyptischen Sprache*, Vol. 1 (Berlin: Akademie-Verlag, 1926–61), p. 67.12.

26 W. Wendrich, *The World According to Basketry: An Ethno-Archaeological Interpretation of Basketry Production in Egypt* (Leiden: Research School CNWS, 1999); S. Heslop and A. B. Neto (eds.), *Basketry: Making Human Nature* (Norwich: Sainsbury Centre for Visual Arts, 2011).

27 For the gold-leafed shrine (Carter no. 108), see M. Eaton-Krauss and E. Graefe, *The Small Golden Shrine from the Tomb of Tutankhamun* (Oxford: Griffith Institute, 1985).

28 A. B. Weiner, *Inalienable Possessions: The Paradox of Keeping-While-Giving* (Berkeley and Los Angeles: University of California Press, 1992), especially at pp. 3, 11–13; J. Schneider and A. B. Weiner, "Cloth and the Organization of Human Experience," *Current Anthropology* 27 (1986), pp. 178–79.

29 B. J. Kemp and G. Vogelsang-Eastwood, *The Ancient Textile Industry at Amarna* (London: Egypt Exploration Society, 2001), pp. 168–69; and see discussions in M. Banerjee and D. Miller, *The Sari* (Oxford: Berg, 2003).

30 Mesoamerica: J. Guernsey and F. K. Reilley (eds.), *Sacred Bundles: Ritual Acts of Wrapping and Binding in Mesoamerica* (Barnardsville, NC: Boundary End Archaeology Research Center, 2006). Japan: J. Hendry, *Wrapping Culture: Politeness, Presentation and Power in Japan and Other Societies* (Oxford: Clarendon Press, 1992).

31 A. Gell, *Wrapping in Images: Tattooing in Polynesia* (Oxford: Clarendon Press, 1993), pp. 176–81; A. B. Weiner, "Cultural Difference and the Density of Objects," *American Ethnologist* 21, no. 2 (1994).

32 Gell, *Wrapping in Images,* p. 179.

33 Thus also Hendry, *Wrapping Culture,* especially p. 122.

34 J. Baines, "Restricted Knowledge, Hierarchy, and Decorum: Modern Perceptions and Ancient Institutions," *Journal of the American Research Center in Egypt* 27 (1990).

35 A typical, passing reference is that uses of cloth might include "what could have been a common habit of covering or wrapping furniture, statues and other objects": Kemp and Vogelsang-Eastwood, *The Ancient Textile Industry,* p. 165.

36 E. Hornung, *Conceptions of God in Ancient Egypt: The One and the Many* (Ithaca, NY: Cornell University Press, 1982).

37 A. M. Roth, "Buried Pyramids and Layered Thoughts: The Organisation of Multiple Approaches in Egyptian Religion," in C. J. Eyre (ed.), *Proceedings of the Seventh International Congress of Egyptologists, Cambridge, 3–9 September 1995* (Leuven: Peeters, 1998).

38 J. Assmann, *Das kulturelle Gedächtnis: Schrift, Erinnerung und politische Identität in frühen Hochkulturen* (Munich: Beck, 1992); see also J. Assmann, "Kollektives Gedächtnis und kulturelle Identität," in J. Assmann and T. Hölscher (eds.), *Kultur und Gedächtnis* (Frankfurt: Suhrkamp, 1988), published in English as J. Assmann, "Collective Memory and Cultural Identity," *New German Critique* 65 (1995). Roth does not cite Assmann's work.

39 Roth, "Buried Pyramids and Layered Thoughts," p. 992. For magical techniques, see R. K. Ritner, *The Mechanics of Ancient Egyptian Magical Practice* (Chicago: Oriental Institute of the University of Chicago, 1993), p. 143, and for the schema of "containment" in Egyptian ritual texts, see R. Nyord, *Breathing Flesh: Conceptions of the Body in the Ancient Egyptian Coffin Texts* (Copenhagen: Museum Tusculanum Press, 2009).

40 Carter described the unwrapping in his journal, and see Carter, *The Tomb of Tut-Ankh-Amen,* pp. 140–57, but no study specifically addresses the use of so many containers, shrouds, and layers of wrapping for the mummy.

41 Translated in A. Piankoff and N. Rambova, *The Shrines of Tutankhamon* (New York: Pantheon, 1955).

42 Journal entries dated October 23 and 24, 1925: The Griffith Institute, "Howard Carter's Diaries: The Fourth Excavation Season in the Tomb of Tutankhamun," http://www.griffith.ox.ac.uk/gri/4sea4not.html (last accessed April 24, 2013).

43 The classic account of tomb robberies in the royal cemeteries is T. E. Peet, *The Great Tomb-Robberies of the Twentieth Egyptian Dynasty* (Oxford: Clarendon Press, 1930); see also C. N. Reeves, *Valley of the Kings: The Decline of a Royal Necropolis* (London and New York: Kegan Paul, 1990), and K. Jansen-Winkeln, "Die Plünderung der Königsgräber des Neuen Reiches," *Zeitschrift für Ägyptische Sprache und Altertumskunde* 122 (1995).

44 S. Hooper, "Embodying Divinity: The Life of A'a," *Journal of the Polynesian Society* 116 (2007); see also A. L. Kaeppler, "Containers of Divinity," *Journal of the Polynesian Society* 116 (2007).

45 A typical account derived from medical analysis of the mummy is B. Brier, *The Murder of Tutankhamen: A 3000-year-old Murder Mystery* (London: Weidenfeld & Nicolson, 1998). For an insightful critique of the biographies of Akhenaten, including the emphasis placed on race, see D. Montserrat, *Akhenaten: History, Fantasy, and Ancient Egypt* (London: Routledge, 2003), especially pp. 12–54.

46 The Griffith Institute, "Howard Carter's Diaries," http://www.griffith.ox.ac.uk/gri/4sea4not.html (last accessed April 24, 2013). This is the source of the following quotations as well.

47 The Griffith Institute, "Howard Carter's Account of the Examination of Tutankhamun's Mummy," http://www.griffith.ox.ac.uk/gri/4mummy.html (last accessed April 24, 2013).

48 H. Carter and A. H. Gardiner, "The Tomb of Ramesses IV and the Turin Plan of a Royal Tomb," *Journal of Egyptian Archaeology* 4 (1917). For a diagram of the Ramses IV and Tutankhamun burials, see Roth, "Buried Pyramids and Layered Thoughts," p. 997 fig. 2.

49 Carter, *The Tomb of Tut-Ankh-Amen,* p. 169.

50 The Griffith Institute, "Howard Carter's Diaries: The Fifth Excavation Season in the Tomb of Tutankhamun," http://www.griffith.ox.ac.uk/gri/4sea5not.html (last accessed September 24, 2010).

51 What Colla terms "artifaction": E. Colla, *Conflicted Antiquities: Egyptology, Egyptomania, Egyptian Modernity* (Durham, NC: Duke University Press, 2007), pp. 8–9, 25–29, 60–66.

52 X-rays in 1968: F. F. Leek, *The Human Remains from the Tomb of Tutankhamun* (Oxford: Griffith Institute, 1972); for the 2005 CT scan, which featured in numerous television, news, and magazine reports, see the official Egyptian press release, at http://www.drhawass.com/blog/press-release-tutankhamun-ct-scan (last accessed April 24, 2013).

53 Colla, *Conflicted Antiquities,* p. 16; N. Thomas, *Entangled Objects: Exchange, Material Culture, and Colonialism in the Pacific* (Cambridge, MA: Harvard University Press, 1991).

54 S. Muñoz Viñas, *Contemporary Theory of Conservation* (Oxford and Burlington, MA: Elsevier Butterworth-Heinemann, 2005).

55 B. Butler, "'Taking on a Tradition': African Heritage and the Testimony of Memory," in F. de Jong and M. Rowlands (eds.), *Reclaiming Heritage: Alternative Imaginaries of Memory in West Africa* (Walnut Creek, CA: Left Coast Press, 2007). On cultural memory, both generally and in relation to ancient Egypt, see also Assmann, *Das kulturelle Gedächtnis*; J. Assmann, *Religion and Cultural Memory* (Stanford, CA: Stanford University Press, 2006); Assmann, "Collective Memory and Cultural Identity" (German and English versions).

56 See the cogent discussions in W. Wendrich, "Egyptian Archaeology: From Text to Context," in W. Wendrich (ed.), *Egyptian Archaeology* (Malden, MA, and Oxford: Wiley-Blackwell, 2010), and in J. Baines, "*Egyptology and the Social Sciences:* Thirty Years On," in A. Verbovsek, B. Backes, and C. Jones (eds.), *Methodik und Didaktik in der Ägyptologie: Herausforderungen eines kulturwissenschaftlichen Paradigmenwechsels in den Altertumswissenschaften* (Munich: Wilhelm Fink, 2011), especially at pp. 578–79. Other contributions to the latter volume make more modest claims than its title would suggest.

57 Thus Baines, "*Egyptology and the Social Sciences:* Thirty Years On," pp. 574–75, although the point should be seen in the context of his more wide-ranging argument.

58 Colla, *Conflicted Antiquities,* p. 17; F. N. Bohrer, *Orientalism and Visual Culture: Imagining Mesopotamia in Nineteenth-Century Europe* (Cambridge: Cambridge University Press, 2003), pp. 4–6.

59 Z. Bahrani, *The Graven Image: Representation in Babylonia and Assyria* (Philadelphia: University of Pennsylvania Press, 2003), especially pp. 6–12; quoted text at p. 10.

60 Compare Bennett's discussion of the relationship between anthropological fieldwork and the development of museums such as the Musée de l'Homme, in the

light of French colonial objectives: T. Bennett, "Museum, Field, Colony: Colonial Governmentality and the Circulation of Reference," *Journal of Cultural Economy* 2 (2009).

61 A point Nadia Abu el-Haj has made in regard to Palestine and Israel: N. Abu el-Haj, *Facts on the Ground: Archaeological Practice and Territorial Self-Fashioning in Israeli Society* (Chicago and London: University of Chicago Press, 2001), p. 6; see also M. Díaz-Andreu's wide-ranging study, *A World History of Nineteenth-Century Archaeology: Nationalism, Colonialism, and the Past* (Oxford: Oxford University Press, 2007).

62 The forthcoming *Histories of Egyptology: Interdisciplinary Measures,* edited by William Carruthers, marks a forward step, although histories of the discipline continue to favor descriptive biography over situated critique, e.g., T. Schneider and P. Raulwing (eds.), *Egyptology from the First World War to the Third Reich: Ideology, Scholarship, and Individual Biographies* (Leiden and Boston: Brill, 2013). Compare also D. Gange, *Dialogues with the Dead: Egyptology in British Culture and Religion, 1822–1922* (Oxford: Oxford University Press, 2013), published just as this manuscript went to press.

63 On Grapow, see T. Schneider, "Ägyptologen im Dritten Reich: Biographische Notizen anhand der sogenannten 'Steindorff-Liste,'" in T. Schneider and P. Raulwing (eds.), *Egyptology from the First World War to the Third Reich: Ideology, Scholarship, and Individual Biographies* (Leiden and Boston: Brill, 2013), pp. 157–65; for Fascist interpretations of the reign of Akhenaten, see Montserrat, *Akhenaten,* pp. 106–13.

Chapter 2 Revelation

1 C. N. Reeves and J. H. Taylor, *Howard Carter before Tutankhamun* (London: British Museum Press, 1992), pp. 56–67.

2 On the history of the archaeological service in Egypt, see D. M. Reid, *Whose Pharaohs? Archaeology, Museums, and Egyptian National Identity from Napoleon to World War I* (Berkeley: University of California Press, 2002), esp. pp. 172–77.

3 H. Carter, "Report on the Tomb of Mentuhotep Ist at Deir El-Bahari, known as Bab El-Hoçan," *Annales du Service des Antiquités d'Égypte* 2 (1901), p. 202.

4 Carter, "Report on the Tomb of Mentuhotep Ist," p. 204.

5 Cairo, Egyptian Museum JE 36405: H. R. Hall, "The XIth Dynasty Temple at Deir el-Bahari," *Proceedings of the Society of Biblical Archaeology* 27 (1905); W. L. Nash, "The Tomb of Mentuhetep I (?) at Dêr el Bahri, Thebes," *Proceedings of the Society of Biblical Archaeology* 23 (1901).

6 Letter quoted in Reeves and Taylor, *Howard Carter*, p. 67.

7 Cairo, Egyptian Museum JE 36195, H 138.0 cm, W 47.0 cm: sample publications include J. Malek, *Egypt: 4000 Years of Art* (London: Phaidon, 2003), p. 94; E. Russmann, *Egyptian Sculpture: Cairo and Luxor* (Austin: University of Texas Press, 1989), pp. 49–52; and M. Saleh and H. Sourouzian, *The Egyptian Museum: Official Catalogue* (Mainz: Philipp von Zabern, 1987), no. 67.

8 C. A. Diop, *The African Origin of Civilization: Myth or Reality* (Chicago: Lawrence Hill Books, 1974), p. 17 fig. 9.

9 His drawing of the wrapped statue is replicated in Reeves and Taylor, *Howard Carter*, p. 65.

10 E. Burke III and D. Prochaska, "Introduction: Orientalism from Postcolonial Theory to World Theory," in E. Burke III and D. Prochaska (eds.), *Genealogies of Orientalism: History, Theory, Politics* (Lincoln, NE, and London: University of Nebraska Press, 2008), discussing E. W. Said, *Orientalism* (London: Penguin, 1978), in particular.

11 Other 1970s critiques include T. Asad, *Anthropology and the Colonial Encounter* (London: Ithaca Press, 1973); B. Turner, *Marx and the End of Orientalism* (London: Allen and Unwin, 1978); and see Burke and Prochaska, "Introduction: Orientalism from Postcolonial Theory," especially pp. 12–14.

12 For example, J. M. MacKenzie, *Orientalism: History, Theory and the Arts* (Manchester: Manchester University Press, 1995). A. L. Macfie (ed.), *Orientalism: A Reader* (Edinburgh: Edinburgh University Press, 2000), collects a range of reviews and responses to the work.

13 L. Nochlin, "The Imaginary Orient," *Art in America* (1983), reprinted in L. Nochlin, *The Politics of Vision: Essays on Nineteenth-Century Art and Society* (New York: Harper & Row, 1989); T. Mitchell, *Colonising Egypt* (Cambridge: Cambridge University Press, 1988).

14 T. Porterfield, *The Allure of Empire: Art in the Service of French Imperialism 1798–1836* (Princeton, NJ: Princeton University Press, 1998), p. 156 n. 10.

15 My discussion here owes much to the insightful evaluation in R.J.C. Young, *Colonial Desire: Hybridity in Theory, Culture and Race* (London and New York: Routledge, 1995), pp. 159–63.

16 H. K. Bhabha, *The Location of Culture* (London and New York: Routledge, 1994).

17 Porterfield, *Allure of Empire*, p. 10.

18 In anthropology, exemplified by work such as J. Fabian, *Time and the Other: How Anthropology Makes Its Object* (New York: Columbia University Press, 1983); J. Clifford, *The Predicament of Culture: Twentieth Century Ethnography, Literature and Art* (Cambridge, MA: Harvard University Press, 1988); J. Clifford, "Rearticulating Anthropology," in D. A. Segal and S. J. Yanagisako (eds.), *Unwrapping the Sacred Bundle: Reflections on the Disciplining of Anthropology* (Durham, NC: Duke University Press, 2005); and N. Thomas, *Entangled Objects: Exchange, Material Culture, and Colonialism in the Pacific* (Cambridge, MA: Harvard University Press, 1991). For a consideration of archaeology and postcolonialism, see P. van Dommelen, "Postcolonial Archaeologies between Discourse and Practice," *World Archaeology* 43 (2011), part of a themed issue of *World Archaeology*; C. Gosden, *Archaeology and Colonialism: Cultural Contact from 5000 BC to the Present* (Cambridge: Cambridge University Press, 2004); C. Gosden, "The Past and Foreign Countries: Colonial and Post-Colonial Archaeology and Anthropology," in L. Meskell and R. W. Preucel (eds.), *A Companion to Social Archaeology* (Malden, MA, and Oxford: Blackwell, 2004); M. Liebmann and U. Z. Rizvi (eds.), *Archaeology and the Postcolonial*

Critique (Lanham, MD: AltaMira Press, 2008); and L. Meskell (ed.), *Archaeology under Fire: Nationalism, Politics and Heritage in the Eastern Mediterranean and Middle East* (London and New York: Routledge, 1998).

19 E. Boehmer, *Colonial and Postcolonial Literature*, 2nd edition (Oxford: Oxford University Press, 2005), p. 5.

20 E. W. Said, *Culture and Imperialism* (London: Vintage, 1993), p. 153.

21 There is an extensive critical literature dealing with travelers' accounts, including: J. Barrell, "Death on the Nile: Fantasy and the Literature of Tourism, 1840–1860," *Essays in Criticism* 41 (1991); D. Gregory, "Between the Book and the Lamp: Imaginative Geographies of Egypt, 1849–50," *Transactions of the Institute of British Geographers* NS 20 (1995); D. Gregory, "Colonial Nostalgia and Cultures of Travel: Spaces of Constructed Visibility in Egypt," in N. AlSayyad (ed.), *Consuming Tradition, Manufacturing Heritage: Global Norms and Urban Forms in the Age of Tourism* (London: Routledge, 2001); and D. Gregory, "Scripting Egypt: Orientalism and the Cultures of Travel," in J. Duncan and D. Gregory (eds.), *Writes of Passage: Reading Travel Writing* (London: Routledge, 1999). See also the important discussion of travel writing on Egypt, sub-Saharan Africa, and the Americas, in M. L. Pratt, *Imperial Eyes: Travel Writing and Transculturation* (London and New York: Routledge, 1992).

22 S. MacDonald, "Lost in Time and Space: Ancient Egypt in Museums," in S. MacDonald and M. Rice (eds.), *Consuming Ancient Egypt* (London: University of London Press, Institute of Archaeology, 2003), p. 97.

23 For example, see the history of the Egyptian department provided on the website of the Metropolitan Museum of Art: http://www.metmuseum.org/en/about-the-museum/museum-departments/curatorial-departments/egyptian-art (last accessed April 24, 2013). The British Museum, whose website offers a much longer history of its Egyptian collections, makes no mention of the division of finds or of colonial governance: see http://www.britishmuseum.org/the_museum/departments/ancient_egypt_and_sudan/history_of_the_collection/development_of_the_collection/expansion_of_the_collection.aspx (last accessed April 24, 2013).

24 Thus S. Quirke, "Modern Mummies and Ancient Scarabs: The Egyptian Collection of Sir William Hamilton," *Journal of the History of Collections* 9 (1997), p. 255. K. H. Dannenfeldt, "Egypt and Egyptian Antiquities in the Renaissance," *Studies in the Renaissance* 6 (1959), pp. 16–22, recounts explicit bans on the transport of mummies by ship.

25 For further details, see the fascinating and astute analysis in P. Schwyzer, *Archaeologies of English Renaissance Literature* (Oxford: Oxford University Press, 2007), pp. 151–74, as well as L. Noble, *Medicinal Cannibalism in Early Modern English Literature and Culture* (New York: Palgrave Macmillan, 2011), especially pp. 17–34, and R. Sugg, *Mummies, Cannibals and Vampires: The History of Corpse Medicine from the Renaissance to the Victorians* (Abingdon and New York: Routledge, 2011).

26 P. Della Valle, *The Pilgrim: The Travels of Pietro Della Valle*, transl. G. Bull (London: Hutchinson, 1993). The two wrapped, richly decorated mummies Della Valle shipped back to Rome had quite a different fate and remain intact today in the Albertinum gallery of Dresden.

27 J. Godwin, *Athanasius Kircher's Theatre of the World* (London: Thames and Hudson, 2009), pp. 77–79.

28 T. Greenhill, *[Nekrokedeia]: Or, the Art of Embalming* (London: Printed for the author, 1705), pp. 289–90.

29 J. Sawday, *The Body Emblazoned: Dissection and the Human Body in Renaissance Culture* (London and New York: Routledge, 1995), especially pp. 54–140, and see B. M. Stafford, *Body Criticism: Imaging the Unseen in Enlightenment Art and Medicine* (Cambridge, MA, and London: MIT Press, 1991).

30 M. Foucault, *The Order of Things: An Archaeology of the Human Sciences* (London and New York: Routledge, 2002 [1970]); M. Foucault, *Discipline and Punish: The Birth of the Prison* (London: Penguin, 1991 [1977]); and see A. Butchart, *The Anatomy of Power: European Constructions of the African Body* (London and New York: Zed Books, 1998), pp. 17–24.

31 F. Henniker, *Notes during a Visit to Egypt, Nubia, the Oasis Boeris, Mount Sinai, and Jerusalem* (London: John Murray, 1824), p. 139.

32 Quirke, "Modern Mummies." Three false mummies in the Egyptian collection in Berlin, also of eighteenth-century origin, were never unwrapped: see R. Germer, H. Kischkewitz, and M. Lüning, "Pseudo-mumien der Ägyptischen Sammlung Berlin," *Studien zur Altägyptischen Kultur* 21 (1994), with a list of examples in other museum collections.

33 English translations collected in J. F. Blumenbach, *The Anthropological Treatises of Johann Friedrich Blumenbach* (London: Longman, Green, Longman, Roberts & Green, 1865)—including a memoir by Marx. For a summary of how Blumenbach's categories of race developed over the years, see R. Bhopal, "The Beautiful Skull and Blumenbach's Errors," *British Medical Journal* 335 (2007).

34 O. Moscucci, "Granville, Augustus Bozzi (1783–1872)," *Oxford Dictionary of National Biography*, http://www.oxforddnb.com/index/11/101011299/ (last accessed June 27, 2011), DOI: 10/1093/ref:odnb/11299; A. Sakula, "Augustus Bozzi Granville (1783–1872): London Physician-Accoucheur and Italian Patriot," *Journal of the Royal Society of Medicine* 76 (1983); A. B. Granville, *Autobiography of A. B. Granville, M.D., F.R.S.* (London: Henry S. King, 1874).

35 H. D. Donoghue et al., "Tuberculosis in Dr Granville's Mummy: A Molecular Re-examination of the Earliest Known Egyptian Mummy to be Scientifically Examined and Given a Medical Diagnosis," *Proceedings of the Royal Society B* 277 (2010).

36 A. B. Granville, *An Essay on Egyptian Mummies* (London: W. Nicol, 1825), p. 5.

37 In 1820, Granville had presented a dissected fetus and ovary to the Society to document an unusual, and fatal, ectopic pregnancy: A. B. Granville, "A Case of the Human Foetus Found in the Ovarium, of the Size It Usually Acquires at the End of the Fourth Month," *Proceedings of the Royal Society of London* 110 (1820).

38 A. B. Granville, "An Essay on Egyptian Mummies, with Observations on the Art of Embalming among the Ancient Egyptians," *Proceedings of the Royal Society of London* 115 (1825); Granville, *An Essay on Egyptian Mummies*, pp. 7, 14. In all subsequent references, I cite the latter version, a pamphlet issued by the

prestigious London firm of William Nicol, which is freely available to download through Google Books.

39 Granville, *An Essay on Egyptian Mummies*, p. 5.

40 Granville, *An Essay on Egyptian Mummies*, p. 7.

41 Granville, *An Essay on Egyptian Mummies*, p. 8.

42 Granville, *An Essay on Egyptian Mummies*, pp. 8–9.

43 Granville, *An Essay on Egyptian Mummies*, pp. 11–12.

44 Granville, *An Essay on Egyptian Mummies*, p. 15.

45 Granville, *An Essay on Egyptian Mummies*, p. 29.

46 Granville, *An Essay on Egyptian Mummies*, p. 13.

47 Granville, *An Essay on Egyptian Mummies*, p. 15.

48 Granville, *Autobiography of A. B. Granville*, Vol. 2, 209–11.

49 T. J. Pettigrew, *A History of Egyptian Mummies* (London: Longman, 1834). Susan Pearce considers Pettigrew's mummy unwrappings in some detail, within a broader discussion of early nineteenth-century encounters with Egyptian mummies: see S. M. Pearce, "Bodies in Exile: Egyptian Mummies in the Early Nineteenth Century and Their Cultural Implications," in S. Ouditt (ed.), *Displaced Persons: Conditions of Exile in European Culture* (Aldershot: Ashgate, 2002).

50 The *Times*, September 16, 1844, p. 3, described a Pettigrew mummy unwrapping at the annual meeting of the British Archaeological Association in dismissive terms: "The process, however, has been often described, and the present [mummy] was not possessed of any peculiar feature of novelty."

51 For Gliddon's career, see S. J. Wolfe, *Mummies in Nineteenth Century America: Ancient Egyptians as Artifacts* (Jefferson, NC, and London: McFarland, 2009), pp. 141–67.

52 S. Trafton, *Egypt Land: Race and Nineteenth-Century American Egyptomania* (Durham, NC: Duke University Press, 2004), pp. 123–26; R. Hoberman, "In Quest of a Museal Aura: Turn of the Century Narratives about Museum-Displayed Objects," *Victorian Literature and Culture* 31 (2003); N. Daly, "That Obscure Object of Desire: Victorian Commodity Culture and Fictions of the Mummy," *NOVEL* 28 (1994).

53 Trafton, *Egypt Land*, p. 126.

54 E. A. Poe, "Some Words with a Mummy," in R. W. Griswold and N. P. Willis (eds.), *The Works of the Late Edgar Allan Poe* (New York: Blakeman and Mason, 1850), quoted text at p. 443. See discussion in Trafton, *Egypt Land*, pp. 132–39, especially at pp. 135–36; D. D. Nelson, *National Manhood: Capitalist Citizenship and the Imagined Fraternity of White Men* (Durham, NC, and London: Duke University Press), 1998, pp. 205–16; D. A. Long, "Poe's Political Identity: A Mummy Unswathed," *Poe Studies* 23 (1990); and B. R. Pollin, "Poe's 'Some Words with a Mummy' Reconsidered," *Emerson Society Quarterly* 60 (1970).

55 See also D. Montserrat, "Unidentified Human Remains: Mummies and the Erotics of Biography," in D. Montserrat (ed.), *Changing Bodies, Changing Meanings: Studies on the Human Body in Antiquity* (London and New York: Routledge, 1998).

56 Granville, *An Essay on Egyptian Mummies*, p. 49.

57 Compare Hoberman, "In Quest of a Museal Aura."

58 Recounted in Mitchell, *Colonising Egypt*.

59 See J.R.I. Cole, *Colonialism and Revolution in the Middle East: Social and Cultural Origins of Egypt's Urabi Movement* (Princeton, NJ: Princeton University Press, 1993), p. 192.

60 Cole, *Colonialism and Revolution*, p. 192.

61 An important attempt to recover the indigenous workforce in an excavation archive is S. Quirke, *Hidden Hands: Egyptian Workforces in Petrie Excavation Archives, 1880–1924* (London: Duckworth, 2010).

62 As discussed in Reid, *Whose Pharaohs?*.

63 W.M.F. Petrie and E. Mackay, *Heliopolis, Kafr Ammar and Shurafa* (London: School of Archaeology in Egypt, 1915), pp. 47–48, pl. lvi.

64 D. Challis, *The Archaeology of Race: The Eugenic Ideas of Francis Galton and Flinders Petrie* (London: Bloomsbury Academic, 2013), traces Petrie's friendship and collaboration with the eugenicist Francis Galton, to whom he supplied skulls from numerous excavations. For intact mummies from Petrie's 1888–89 and 1911 seasons at Hawara, see S. Walker and M. L. Bierbrier, *Ancient Faces: Mummy Portraits from Roman Egypt* (London: British Museum Press, 1997), pp. 37–39 (no. 11), 47–48 (no. 22), and 53–54 (no. 29); P. C. Roberts, "'One of Our Mummies Is Missing': Evaluating Petrie's Records from Hawara," in M. L. Bierbrier (ed.), *Portraits and Masks* (London: British Museum Press, 1997); L. Corcoran, *Portrait Mummies from Roman Egypt* (Chicago: University of Chicago Press, 1995), checklist on pp. 9–12; and R. Germer, H. Kischkewitz, and M. Lüning, "Das Grab der Aline und die Untersuchung der darin gefundenen Kindermumien," *Antike Welt* 24 (1993).

65 For corvée and other labor regimes used in Egyptian archaeology, see A. Clément, "Rethinking 'Peasant Consciousness' in Colonial Egypt: An Exploration of the Performance of Folksongs by Upper Egyptian Agricultural Workers on the Archaeological Excavation Sites of Karnak and Dendera at the Turn of the Twentieth Century (1885–1914)," *History and Anthropology* 21 (2010)—a wide-ranging discussion based in part on Maspero's own writings. On the Urabi revolt and its background, see Cole, *Colonialism and Revolution*.

66 Maspero's own account appears in G. Maspero, "Rapport sur la trouvaille de Deir-el-Bahari," *Bulletin de l'Institut d'Égypte (série 2)* 2 (1881), and was reiterated several times, in particular G. Maspero, *Guide du visiteur au Musée de Boulaq* (Boulaq: au Musée, 1883), pp. 314–20.

67 Maspero, "Rapport sur la trouvaille," p. 135 (author's translation).

68 For recent scholarship on the cachette tomb, see E. Graefe and G. Belova (eds.), *Royal Cache TT 320: A Re-examination* (Cairo: Supreme Council of Antiquities, 2010); for the inscriptions ("dockets"), see C. N. Reeves, *Valley of the Kings: The Decline of a Royal Necropolis* (London and New York: Kegan Paul, 1990), pp. 225–43, and J. Černý, "Studies in the Chronology of the Twenty-First Dynasty," *Journal of Egyptian Archaeology* 32 (1946), demonstrating that the mummies of Ramses I, Seti I, and Ramses II were reburied on the day that Pinudjem II was buried.

69 Maspero, *Guide du visiteur*, p. 319 ("fret des rois").

70 Shadi Abd el-Salam's 1969 film *al-Mumiya* (released with the English title *The Night of Counting the Years*) contrasted the destructiveness of the Abd er-Rassuls with the preservationist efforts of Ahmed Kamal, pitting peasant tradition against urban modernism and suggesting that Egypt's national identity lies in its pharaonic past: see E. Colla, "Shadi Abd al-Salam's *al-Mumiya*: Ambivalence and the Egyptian Nation-State," in A. A. Ahmida (ed.), *Beyond Colonialism and Nationalism in the Maghrib: History, Culture, and Politics* (New York: Palgrave Macmillan, 2010).

71 Cole, *Colonialism and Revolution*, p. 263.

72 Thus S. Ikram and A. Dodson, *The Mummy in Ancient Egypt: Equipping the Dead for Eternity* (London: Thames and Hudson, 1998), p. 80, with a plan of the Boulaq Museum indicating the gallery (fig. 77).

73 G. Elliot Smith, *The Royal Mummies,* Catalogue général des antiquités égyptiennes (Cairo: Institut Français d'Archéologie Orientale, 1912), pp. 32–33, pl. xxviii.

74 See G. Maspero, *Les momies royale de Déir el-Baharî* (Paris: Ernest Leroux, 1889), pp. 765–73.

75 See Reeves, *Valley of the Kings*, p. 238, table 10/6, no. 42 for translation and further references.

76 Maspero, *Les momies royale*, pp. 563–66, 767, pl. xvii.

77 G. Maspero, "Procès verbal de l'ouverture des momies de Ramsès II et de Ramsès III," *Revue Archéologique, series 3* 8 (1886), quoted in Elliot Smith, *Royal Mummies*, p. 85.

78 For the importance of physical anthropology in the nineteenth century, see G.W.J. Stocking, *Victorian Anthropology* (New York: The Free Press, 1987); the colonial history of the practice is traced, with particular reference to the Netherlands, in D. van Duuren, *Physical Anthropology Reconsidered: Human Remains at the Tropenmuseum* (Amsterdam: Royal Tropical Institute/KIT, 2007).

79 Elliot Smith, *Royal Mummies*, p. 42, pls. xxix–xxx.

80 Howard Carter helped Elliot Smith transport the mummy across Cairo by cab; see W. R. Dawson (ed.), *Sir Grafton Elliot Smith: A Biographical Record by His Colleagues* (London: Jonathan Cape, 1938), pp. 29–36.

81 G. Daressy and G. Elliot Smith, "Ouverture des momies provenant de la seconde trouvaille de Deir el-Bahari," *Annales du Service des Antiquités d'Égypte* 4 (1903).

82 G. Elliot Smith, "An Account of the Mummy of a Priestess of Amen Supposed to be Ta-Usert-Em-Suten-Pa," *Annales du Service des Antiquités d'Égypte* 7 (1906), quoted text at pp. 155, 157.

83 Elliot Smith, *Royal Mummies*; see Dawson, *Sir Grafton Elliot Smith*, pp. 39–41.

84 Elliot Smith, *Royal Mummies*, pp. 73–80, pls. lxiv–lxvi.

85 Results of the Survey were published in a series of bulletins (1908–11) and reports (1910–27) through the National Printing Department in Cairo. For anatomical specimens that Elliot Smith collected on the Survey, see T. I. Molleson, "The Nubian Pathological Collection in the Natural History Museum, London," in W. V. Davies and R. Walker (eds.), *Biological Anthropology and the Study of Ancient Egypt* (London: British Museum Press, 1993), and H. A. Waldron,

"The Study of Human Remains from Nubia: The Contribution of Grafton Elliot Smith and His Colleagues to Palaeopathology," *Medical History* 44 (2000). Elliot Smith also left skeletal remains from the Survey in the pathology collection at Manchester University; these were accessioned by Manchester Museum in 2000 but deaccessioned in 2006, when they were transferred to a center for "biomedical Egyptology" privately endowed at the university in 2003.

86 D. A. Lorimer, "Race, Science and Culture: Historical Continuities and Discontinuities, 1850–1914," in S. West (ed.), *The Victorians and Race* (Aldershot: Ashgate, 1996), p. 24; D. A. Lorimer, "Theoretical Racism in Late-Victorian Anthropology, 1870–1900," *Victorian Studies* 31 (1988); Stocking, *Victorian Anthropology*, pp. 238–73.

87 See Young, *Colonial Desire*; A. McClintock, *Imperial Leather: Race, Gender and Sexuality in the Colonial Contest* (New York and London: Routledge, 1996).

88 T. Champion, "Beyond Egyptology: Egypt in 19th and 20th Century Archaeology and Anthropology," in P. Ucko and T. Champion (eds.), *The Wisdom of Egypt: Changing Visions through the Ages* (London: University of London Press, Institute of Archaeology, 2003), especially at pp. 163–67. For the influence of Prichard's work, see Young, *Colonial Desire*, and for an overview of the race debate surrounding ancient Egypt in the nineteenth century, see R. Bernasconi, "Black Skin, White Skulls: The Nineteenth Century Debate over the Racial Identity of the Ancient Egyptians," *Parallax* 13 (2007).

89 On Morton, Nott, and Gliddon, see Champion, "Beyond Egyptology"; Nelson, *National Manhood*, pp. 102–104, 109–34, 191–92; R.J.C. Young, "Egypt in America: *Black Athena*, Racism and Colonial Discourse," in A. Rattansi and S. Westwood (eds.), *Racism, Modernity and Identity: On the Western Front* (Cambridge: Polity Press, 1994), especially at pp. 161–63; and Young, *Colonial Desire*, pp. 118–41.

90 See Young, *Colonial Desire*, pp. 126–33.

91 See Young, *Colonial Desire*, pp. 177–78 for examples of color theory applied to identifying people of mixed-race descent, for instance by the color of the scalp or the nail cuticles. On readings of racial physiognomy in literature and art, see M. Hamer, "Black *and* White? Viewing Cleopatra in 1862," in S. West (ed.), *The Victorians and Race* (Aldershot: Ashgate, 1996).

92 Elliot Smith, *Royal Mummies*, p. 9, and Maspero, "Procès verbal," at p. 3 ("la peau est d'un jaune terreux").

93 Elliot Smith, *Royal Mummies*, quoted at pp. 82 and 13, respectively.

94 Elliot Smith, *Royal Mummies*, pp. 60–62.

95 He wrote an essay on the subject for the Royal Anthropological Institute in 1934: see Dawson, *Sir Grafton Elliot Smith*, pp. 105, 257–68.

96 S. L. Gilman, *Difference and Pathology: Stereotypes of Sexuality, Race, and Madness* (Ithaca, NY, and London: Cornell University Press, 1985), pp. 76–108 (hymen claim, from South Carolina, at p. 89). For a critique of how scholarly treatments of Baartman have reinforced stereotypes of African bodies, see Z. Magubane, "Which Bodies Matter? Feminism, Poststructuralism, Race, and the Curious Theoretical Odyssey of the 'Hottentot Venus,'" *Gender and Society* 15 (2001).

97 Maspero, *Les momies royale*, p. 553; Elliot Smith, *Royal Mummies*, p. 10.

98 Quoted in A. M. Lythgoe and D. Dunham, *The Predynastic Cemetery N 7000, Naga–Ed–Dêr Part IV* (Berkeley and Los Angeles: University of California Press, 1965), p. 208 (burial N7346).

99 Elliot Smith, *Royal Mummies*, pp. 12, 108, 100, 13, respectively; see also pp. 14, 82, 97, 103, 110.

100 Elliot Smith, *Royal Mummies*, p. 27.

101 Elliot Smith, *Royal Mummies*, p. 67.

102 Elliot Smith, *Royal Mummies*, p. 89.

103 M. A. Ruffer and R. L. Moodie, *Studies in the Palaeopathology of Egypt* (Chicago: University of Chicago Press, 1921), p. xiv.

104 M. A. Ruffer, "Remarks on the Histology and Pathological Anatomy of Egyptian Mummies," *Cairo Scientific Journal* 40 (1910), p. 2.

105 M. A. Ruffer, "On Arterial Lesions Found in Egyptian Mummies (1580 BC–525 AD)," *Journal of Pathology and Bacteriology* 15 (1911), p. 453.

106 M. A. Ruffer and A. Rietti, "On Osseous Lesions in Ancient Egyptians," *Journal of Pathology and Bacteriology* 16 (1912), pp. 439–40.

107 Ruffer and Rietti, "On Osseous Lesions," p. 440.

Chapter 3 Mummification

1 R. L. Vos, *The Apis Embalming Ritual: P. Vindob.* 3873 (Leuven: Peeters, 1993), with discussion of date, contents, and copying at pp. 41–42; W. Spiegelberg, "Ein Bruchstück des Bestattungsritual der Apisstiere," *Zeitschrift für Ägyptische Sprache und Altertumskunde* 56 (1920).

2 See D. Frankfurter, *Religion in Roman Egypt: Assimilation and Resistance* (Princeton, NJ: Princeton University Press, 1998), especially pp. 198–264; also J. Assmann, *Religion and Cultural Memory* (Stanford, CA: Stanford University Press, 2006), especially at p. 135.

3 A. Mariette and G. Maspero, *Le Sérapeum de Memphis* (Paris: F. Vieweg, 1882); S. Ikram (ed.), *Divine Creatures: Animal Mummies in Ancient Egypt* (Cairo and New York: American University in Cairo Press, 2005), pp. 72–105.

4 Vos, *Apis Embalming Ritual,* p. viii.

5 B. Latour, "On the Partial Existence of Existing and Nonexisting Objects," in L. Daston (ed.), *Biographies of Scientific Objects* (Chicago and London: University of Chicago Press, 2000), p. 248.

6 M. J. Raven, "Egyptian Concepts on the Orientation of the Human Body," *Journal of Egyptian Archaeology* 91 (2005), pp. 49–50; Otto, "Die beiden vogelgestaltigen Seelen vorstellungen der Ägypter," *Zeitschrift für Ägyptische Sprache und Altertumskunde* 77 (1942), p. 82. The dates on mummy labels from Roman Egypt fall seventy days after the date of death: see W. Scheidel, "The Meaning of Dates on Mummy Labels: Seasonal Mortality and Mortuary Practice in Roman Egypt," *Journal of Roman Archaeology* 11 (1998).

7 *Pir* bandages were used in mummy wrapping, were worn by mourners, and designate the bandage-like decoration on some coffins: see P. Collombert, "La bandelette-*pyr* au cou des deuillants," *Revue d'Égyptologie* 57 (2006).

8 *Nemes* is also the word for the cloth head covering worn by Egyptian kings, which was associated with streaming rays of light: K. Goebs, "Untersuchungen zu Funktion und Symbolgehalt des *nms*," *Zeitschrift der Ägyptische Sprache und Altertumskunde* 122 (1995).

9 P. Vindob. 2873, Verso I.4; see Vos, *Apis Embalming Ritual*, p. 196 for commentary.

10 See Vos, *Apis Embalming Ritual*, commentary at pp. 107–13, with a possible reconstruction of the wrapping at pp. 235–40.

11 For the verb *neten*, only attested in this papyrus, see Vos, *Apis Embalming Ritual*, p. 229.

12 S. Sauneron, *Rituel de l'embaumement* (Cairo: Imprimerie Nationale, 1952); M. Smith, *Traversing Eternity: Texts for the Afterlife from Ptolemaic and Roman Egypt* (Oxford: Oxford University Press, 2009), excerpt and discussion at pp. 215–44. The two most complete papyri are P. Louvre 5158, which has ink vignettes depicting gods mentioned in the text, and P. Boulaq III in the Cairo collection, which comes from a Theban tomb and was first published by Auguste Mariette in 1871.

13 For the *wetiu*, see F. Jonckheere, "Considérations sur l'auxiliaire médical pharaonique," *Chronique d'Égypte* 28 (1953), pp. 62–63. F. Janot, *Les instruments d'embaumement de l'Égypte ancienne* (Cairo: Institut Français d'Archéologie Orientale, 2000), pp. 15–23, collects the evidence for different priests and workers mentioned in these texts and other sources.

14 Theban Tomb (TT) 23: see W. R. Dawson, "Making a Mummy," *Journal of Egyptian Archaeology* 13 (1927), at pl. xvii, and see pl. xviii for the other depiction, based on an early nineteenth-century drawing by Ipollito Rosellini. See also S. Ikram and A. Dodson, *The Mummy in Ancient Egypt: Equipping the Dead for Eternity* (London: Thames and Hudson, 1998), p. 107 fig. 108, for an earlier copy of the former scene, made by Champollion in 1845.

15 The Davies drawing suggests that in the top right scene, the *khery-heb* holds an ink palette rather than a scroll, but in the absence of a pen or writing surface in his other hand, a palette would be unusual; this scene was evidently one of the most damaged.

16 Paul Dominique Philippoteaux, *Examen d'une momie*. Private collection. H 183.0 cm, W 275.0 cm. Provenance information courtesy of Peter Nahum at the Leicester Galleries; I have not been able to confirm any details of the painting's history independently. The 1875 date sometimes ascribed to it (for instance on the Leicester Galleries website) cannot be correct given that the date of the unwrapping is March 1891, during Philippoteaux's two-year sojourn in Egypt. For further details and images, see Peter Nahum at the Leicester Galleries, "Paul Dominique Philippoteaux (1845–1924)," http://www.leicestergalleries.com/19th-20th-century-paintings/d/paul-dominique-philippoteaux/21387 (last accessed June 26, 2012), and for analysis of the painting in relation to the antiquities museum in Cairo, see C. Riggs, "Colonial Visions: Egyptian Antiquities

and Contested Histories in the Cairo Museum," *Museum Worlds: Advances in Research* 1 (2013).

17 "Artist Philioppoteaux Here," *New York Times*, November 14, 1892.

18 P. Schwyzer, *Archaeologies of English Renaissance Literature* (Oxford: Oxford University Press, 2007), pp. 151–74; Ikram and Dodson, *The Mummy in Ancient Egypt*, pp. 61–67.

19 For example, S. Ikram, "Mummification," in W. Wendrich (ed.), *UCLA Encyclopedia of Egyptology* (Los Angeles: UCLA, 2010), p. 1 (mummification as dehydration) and p. 2 (mummification as desiccation plus wrapping).

20 E. Hornung, "Fisch und Vogel: Zur altägyptischen Sicht des Menschen," *Eranos Jahrbuch* 52 (1983); E. Meyer-Dietrich, *Senebi und Selbst: Personenkonstituenten zur rituellen Wiedergeburt in einem Frauensarg des Mittleren Reiches* (Fribourg and Göttingen: Academic Press; Vandenhoeck & Ruprecht, 2006), pp. 201–2, 219–20; R. Nyord, *Breathing Flesh: Conceptions of the Body in the Ancient Egyptian Coffin Texts* (Copenhagen: Museum Tusculanum Press, 2009), pp. 342–50.

21 For New Kingdom evidence that may cross a broader social spectrum, see L. Meskell, "Dying Young: The Experience of Death at Deir el-Medina," *Archaeological Review from Cambridge* 13 (1994).

22 See J. Baines and P. Lacovara, "Burial and the Dead in Ancient Egyptian Society: Respect, Formalism, Neglect," *Journal of Social Archaeology* 2 (2002). Even in cemeteries where large numbers of individuals have been found, for instance in Kharga Oasis, differences among the bodies point to social differentiation: compare F. Dunand et al., *Douch I. La Nécropole* (Cairo: Institut Français d'Archéologie Orientale, 1992), and F. Dunand and R. Lichtenberg, "Dix ans d'exploration des nécropoles d'El-Deir (Oasis de Kharga): Un premier bilan," *Chronique d'Égypte* 83 (2008), with further references.

23 One influential anthropological study of the Indian caste system: L. Dumont, *Homo Hierarchicus: The Caste System and Its Implications* (London: Weidenfeld & Nicolson, 1970).

24 Of numerous examples, I mention two widely available English-language publications since the late 1990s: Ikram and Dodson, *The Mummy in Ancient Egypt*, pp. 108–28; and A. R. David, "Mummification," in P. T. Nicholson and I. Shaw (eds.), *Ancient Egyptian Materials and Technology* (Cambridge: Cambridge University Press, 2000). J. H. Taylor, *Death and the Afterlife in Ancient Egypt* (London: British Museum Press, 2000), offers a more nuanced approach to mummification in general, while J. Jones, "New Perspectives on the Development of Mummification and Funerary Practices during the Pre- and Early Dynastic Periods," in J.-C. Goyon and C. Cardin (eds.), *Proceedings of the Ninth International Congress of Egyptologists, Grenoble, 6–12 Septembre 2004*, Vol. 1 (Leuven: Peeters, 2007) casts similar doubt on the idea that observing natural processes of desiccation was the impetus for developing artificial mummification in the Early Dynastic period.

25 On mummification in the Roman period, see B. Gessler-Löhr, "Mummies and Mummification," in C. Riggs (ed.), *The Oxford Handbook of Roman Egypt* (Oxford: Oxford University Press, 2012).

26 Two New Kingdom examples: M. J. Raven, *The Tomb of Iurudef: A Memphite Official in the Reign of Ramesses II* (London: Egypt Exploration Society, 1991), pp. 13–14, 69–71; P. F. Dorman, "Family Burial and Commemoration in the

Theban Necropolis," in N. Strudwick and J. H. Taylor (eds.), *The Theban Necropolis: Past, Present, Future* (London: British Museum Press, 2003).

27 A. T. Sandison, "Balsamierung," in W. Helck and E. Otto (eds.), *Lexikon der Ägyptologie*, Vol. 1 (Wiesbaden: Harrassowitz, 1975); Ikram, "Mummification."

28 D. Wengrow, *The Archaeology of Early Egypt: Social Transformations in North-East Africa, 10,000 to 2650 BC* (Cambridge: Cambridge University Press, 2006), pp. 116–23.

29 Ikram and Dodson, *The Mummy in Ancient Egypt*, pp. 128; for this burial, see H. E. Winlock, "The Museum's Excavations at Thebes," *Bulletin of the Metropolitan Museum of Art*, Part 2, *The Egyptian Expedition 1924–1925 (1926)*, pp. 21–3.

30 See Ikram, *Divine Creatures*, pp. 28–29.

31 M. Taussig, *Mimesis and Alterity: A Particular History of the Senses* (London and New York: Routledge, 1993).

32 E. Hornung, *Conceptions of God in Ancient Egypt: The One and the Many* (Ithaca, NY: Cornell University Press, 1982).

33 M. Douglas, *Purity and Danger* (London: Routledge and Kegan Paul, 1966); V. Valeri, *The Forest of Taboos: Morality, Hunting, and Identity among the Huaulu of the Moluccas* (Madison, WI, and London: University of Wisconsin Press, 1999), especially pp. 69–82; and see discussion in R. Osborne, *The History Written on the Classical Greek Body* (Cambridge: Cambridge University Press, 2011), pp. 162–66.

34 The related *Commiphora gileadensis* is found in Jordan and the Levant and is the "balm of Gilead" of the Bible; on this and related materials, see M. Serpico, "Resins, Amber and Bitumen," in P. T. Nicholson and I. Shaw (eds.), *Ancient Egyptian Materials and Technology* (Cambridge: Cambridge University Press, 2000).

35 F. Colin, "Le parfumeur *(p3 ʿnt)*," *Bulletin de l'Institut Français d'Archéologie Orientale* 103 (2003).

36 N. Baum, "*Sntr*: Une révision," *Revue d'Égyptologie* 45 (1994).

37 H.-H. Münch, "Categorizing Archaeological Finds: The Funerary Material of Queen Hetepheres I at Giza," *Antiquity* 74 (2000); T. I. Rzeuska, "And Where Are the Viscera…? Reassessing the Function of Old Kingdom Canopic Recesses and Pits," in N. Strudwick and H. Strudwick (eds.), *Old Kingdom, New Perspectives: Egyptian Art and Archaeology 2750–2150 BC* (Oxford and Oakville, CT: Oxbow Books, 2011).

38 C. Graves-Brown, "Licking Knives and Stone Snakes: The Ideology of Flint in Ancient Egypt," in M. Martinón-Torres and T. Rehren (eds.), *Archaeology History and Science: Integrating Approaches to Ancient Materials* (Walnut Creek, CA: Left Coast Press, 2008).

39 Raven, "Egyptian Concepts on the Orientation of the Human Body"; see also J.-C. Goyon, "Chiurgie religieuse ou thanatopraxie? Données nouvelles sur la momification en Égypte et réflexions qu'elles impliquent," in *Sesto Congresso Internazionale di Egittologia, Atti*, Vol. 1 (Turin: International Association of Egyptologists, 1992).

40 See M. Pezin and F. Janot, "La 'pustule' et les deux doigts," *Bulletin de l'Institut Français d'Archéologie Orientale* 95 (1995).

41 G. Daressy and G. Elliot Smith, "Ouverture des momies provenant de la seconde trouvaille de Deir el-Bahari," *Annales du Service des Antiquités d'Égypte* 4 (1903), at p. 160, where Elliot Smith observed stitching on the twenty-first-dynasty mummy of a woman named Tau-henet.

42 Vos, *Apis Embalming Ritual*, pp. 45–46, Recto II, lines 10–13. I have used the personal pronouns *it* and *its* rather than *him* and *his* to refer to the bull, for clarity.

43 Vos, *Apis Embalming Ritual*, p. 50, Recto IV, line 1.

44 A. Erman and H. Grapow (eds.), *Wörterbuch der ägyptischen Sprache*, Vol. 1 (Berlin: Akademie-Verlag, 1926–61), pp. 378–80, examples from the New Kingdom. See K. M. Cooney, *The Cost of Death: The Social and Economic Value of Ancient Egyptian Funerary Art in the Ramesside Period* (Leiden: Nederlands Instituut voor het Nabije Oosten, 2007), pp. 18–21, and compare H. E. Winlock, "The Tombs of the Kings of the Seventeenth Dynasty at Thebes," *Journal of Egyptian Archaeology* 10 (1924), p. 239 n. 2, suggesting *wet* as a "covering."

45 Two notable but brief discussions: D. Wengrow, *What Makes Civilization? The Ancient Near East and the Future of the West* (Oxford: Oxford University Press, 2010), pp. 143–44; J. Assmann, *Death and Salvation in Ancient Egypt* (Ithaca, NY, and London: Cornell University Press, 2005), pp. 105–6. On cult statues in ancient Egypt, see D. Lorton, "The Theology of Cult Statues in Ancient Egypt," in M. B. Dick (ed.), *Born in Heaven, Made on Earth: The Making of the Cult Image in the Ancient Near East* (Winona Lake, IN: Eisenbrauns, 1999), and G. Robins, "Cult Statues in Ancient Egypt," in N. H. Walls (ed.), *Cult Image and Divine Representation in the Ancient Near East* (Boston: American Schools of Oriental Research, 2005). For many comparable statue practices in the Ancient Near East, see the recent study by J. M. Evans, *The Lives of Sumerian Sculpture: An Archaeology of the Early Dynastic Temple* (Cambridge: Cambridge University Press, 2012), especially pp. 111–45.

46 The manufacture, installation, and treatment (including eventual disposal) of ancient Egyptian cult statues bears many similarities to the use of statues in Hindu practice from the eleventh century to today: see R. H. Davis, *Lives of Indian Images* (Princeton, NJ: Princeton University Press, 1997), especially pp. 15–50.

47 Compare Davis, *Lives of Indian Images*, pp. 32–33, 49, 205–7, and Wengrow, *What Makes Civilization?*, pp. 109–10, quoting Leo Oppenheim on divine statues in Mesopotamia: "Pro- and anti-iconic tendencies…still linger in the scholar's ambivalent attitude towards 'idols' and taint his approach to all alien religions."

48 Summarized in M. Smith, "Osiris and the Deceased," in W. Wendrich (ed.), *UCLA Encyclopedia of Egyptology* (Los Angeles: UCLA, 2008).

49 Daressy and Elliot Smith, "Ouverture des momies," p. 159.

50 G. Elliot Smith, *The Royal Mummies*, Catalogue général des antiquités égyptiennes (Cairo: Institut Français d'Archéologie Orientale, 1912), pp. 95, 106;

on gilded skin, see F. Dunand, "Les 'têtes dorées' de la nécropole de Douch," *Bulletin de la Societé Française d'Égyptologie* 93 (1982), and discussion in Gessler–Löhr, "Mummies and Mummification," in C. Riggs (ed.), *The Oxford Handbook of Roman Egypt* (Oxford: Oxford University Press, 2012), pp. 675–77.

51 Elliot Smith, *The Royal Mummies*, pp. 49 (Amenhotep III), 70–73 (Siptah), pls. lx–lxiii.

52 C. Riggs, "Gilding the Lily: Shrouds, Sculpture, and the Representation of Women in Ptolemaic and Early Roman Egypt," in P. D. Manuelian and S. E. Thompson (eds.), *Egypt and Beyond: Essays Presented to Leonard H. Lesko* (Providence, RI: Brown University Press, 2008).

53 E. Otto, *Das ägyptische Mundöffnungsritual* (Wiesbaden: Harrassowitz, 1960), is the standard edition and presents early evidence for the rite. Additional discussions include R. B. Finnestad, "The Meaning and Purpose of Opening the Mouth in Mortuary Contexts," *Numen* 25 (1978); A. M. Roth, "The *pšs-kf* and the 'Opening of the Mouth' Ceremony: A Ritual of Birth and Rebirth," *Journal of Egyptian Archaeology* 78 (1992); A. M. Roth, "Fingers, Stars, and the 'Opening of the Mouth': The Nature and Function of the *ntrwj*-blades," *Journal of Egyptian Archaeology* 79 (1993); H. W. Fischer-Elfert, *Die Vision von der Statue im Stein: Studien zum altägyptischen Mundöffnungsritual* (Heidelberg: C. Winter, 1998); Lorton, "The Theology of Cult Statues," pp. 147–79. See also H. Willems, *The Coffin of Heqata (Cairo JdE 36418): A Case Study of Egyptian Funerary Culture of the Early Middle Kingdom* (Leuven: Peeters, 1996).

54 Otto, *Das ägyptische Mundöffnungsritual.* For description and scenes from the tomb of Rekhmire, see N. de Garis Davies, *The Tomb of Rekh-Mi-Re at Thebes* (New York: Metropolitan Museum of Art, 1943).

55 Roth, "The *pšs-kf* and the 'Opening of the Mouth' Ceremony"; Roth, "Fingers, Stars, and the 'Opening of the Mouth.'"

56 Otto, *Das ägyptische Mundöffnungsritual*, pp. 101–19 (Scenes 48–53).

57 See D. Franke, "*Sem*-Priest on Duty," in S. Quirke (ed.), *Discovering Egypt from the Neva: The Egyptological Legacy of Oleg D. Berlev* (Berlin: Achet-Verlag, 2003).

58 U. Rummel, "Das Pantherfell als Kleidungsstück im Kult: Bedeutung, Symbolgehalt und theologische Verortung einer magischen Insignie," *Imago Aegypti* 2 (2007).

59 W. Barta, *Aufbau und Bedeutung der altägyptischen Opferformel* (Glückstadt: J. J. Augustin, 1968), p. 100; see N. de Garis Davies, *The Tomb of Puyemre at Thebes*, Vol. 2, *The Chapels of Hope* (New York: Metropolitan Museum of Art, 1923), pl. 50.

60 On the concept of *akh,* see G. Englund's classic study *Akh: Une notion religieuse dans l'Égypte pharaonique* (Uppsala, Sweden: Uppsala University, 1978), as well as further discussions such as R. J. Demaree, *The 3ḫ ikr n Rʿ Stelae: On Ancestor Worship in Ancient Egypt* (Leiden: Nederlands Instituut voor het Nabije Oosten, 1983); F. Friedman, "The Root Meaning of *3ḫ*: Effectiveness or Luminosity," *Serapis* 8 (1984–1985); T. DuQuesne, "'Effective in Heaven and on Earth': Interpreting Egyptian Religious Practice for Both Worlds," in

J. Assmann and M. Bommas (eds.), *Ägyptische Mysterien?* (Munich: Wilhelm Fink, 2002); and J. Gee, "A New Look at the Conception of the Human Being in Ancient Egypt," in R. Nyord and A. Kjølby (eds.), *"Being in Ancient Egypt": Thoughts on Agency, Materiality and Cognition. Proceedings of the Seminar Held in Copenhagen, September 29–30, 2006* (Oxford: Archaeopress, 2009).

61 G. Lefebvre, "Textes du tombeau de Petosiris," *Annales du Service des Antiquités d'Égypte* 21 (1921), p. 57: 126, lines 3–4 and 137, line 6.

62 M. Burchardt, "Ein saitischer Statuensockel in Stockholm," *Zeitschrift für Ägyptische Sprache und Altertumskunde* 47 (1910), especially commentary no. 25.

63 See discussion in M. Eaton-Krauss, *The Representations of Statuary in Private Tombs of the Old Kingdom* (Wiesbaden: Harrassowitz, 1984), pp. 77–81. The equivalent term for a female statue was *repit* (or *reput*), possibly derived from the word for a carrying-chair: see W. Kaiser, "Zu den [hieroglyphs] der älteren Bilddarstellungen und der Bedeutung von *rpw.t,*" *Mitteilungen des Deutschen Archäologischen Instituts Kairo* 39 (1983).

64 See M. Eaton-Krauss, "Embalming Caches," *Journal of Egyptian Archaeology* 94 (2008); compare M. Müller, "Die Königsplastik des Mittleren Reiches und ihre Schöpfer: Reden über Statuen—Wenn Statuen reden," *Imago Aegypti* 1 (2005), p. 44.

65 All examples date to the Ptolemaic and Roman periods: for *sedjed*, see Erman and Grapow, *Wörterbuch der ägyptischen Sprache*, Vol. 4, p. 396. For *ky* (a concrete image of the king or god) and *ked* (an unknowable form of the god) in the temple of Horus at Edfu, see P. Wilson, *A Ptolemaic Lexicon: A Lexicographical Study of the Texts in the Temple of Edfu* (Leuven: Peeters, 1997), pp. 1047, 1070. For *akh* written with the A53 classifier, see A. B. Kamal, *Stèles ptolémaïques et romaines*, Catalogue général des antiquités égyptiennes (Cairo: Institut Français d'Archéologie Orientale, 1904), pp. 138–40, pl. xlvi (Cairo, Egyptian Museum CG 22151).

66 Erman and Grapow, *Wörterbuch der ägyptischen Sprache,* Vol. 5, pp. 255–59.

67 See A. M. Lythgoe and D. Dunham, *The Predynastic Cemetery N 7000, Naga-Ed-Dêr Part IV* (Berkeley and Los Angeles: University of California Press, 1965), entries on individual graves; J. Jones, "Towards Mummification: New Evidence for Early Developments," *Egyptian Archaeology* 21 (2001); and R. F. Friedman, "The Cemeteries of Hierakonpolis," *Archéo-Nil* 18 (2008).

68 Burial 2172E: J. E. Quibell, *Archaic Mastabas* (Cairo: Institut Français d'Archéologie Orientale, 1923), p. 11, with pl. 29.3; G. Elliot Smith, "Egyptian Mummies," *Journal of Egyptian Archaeology* 1 (1914), p. 192, with pl. 31.1. For natron and other salts present in linen, see M. Stoll and D. Fengel, "Chemical and Structural Studies on Ancient Egyptian Linen," *Berliner Beiträge zur Archäometrie* 10 (1988).

69 W.M.F. Petrie, E. Mackay, and G. A. Wainwright, *Meydum and Memphis (III)* (London: School of Archaeology in Egypt, 1910), p. 12.

70 Petrie et al., *Meydum and Memphis (III)*, pp. 14–16, pl. xi. A few seasons later, Petrie thought he had identified another de-fleshed burial at Tarkhan, where grave 902, of Early Dynastic date, contained a contracted burial with well-preserved linen in direct contact with the bones: W.M.F. Petrie, G. A. Wainwright,

and A. H. Gardiner, *Tarkhan I and Memphis V* (London: School of Archaeology in Egypt, 1913), p. 27, pl. xxvii.

71 G. A. Reisner, *A History of the Giza Necropolis*, Vol. 1 (Cambridge, MA: Harvard University Press, 1942), pp. 450–53, pl. 42. For the Reisner excavations, see the Giza Archives Project website hosted by the Museum of Fine Arts, Boston, at http://www.gizapyramids.org (last accessed March 2, 2013).

72 W.M.F. Petrie, *Medum* (London: David Nutt, 1892), pp. 17–18; Elliot Smith, "Egyptian Mummies," pp. 191–92, pl. 31.2.

73 J.-P. Lauer and D. E. Derry, "Découverte à Saqqarah d'une partie de la momie du roi Zoser," *Annales du Service des Antiquités d'Égypte* 35 (1935), p. 28.

74 On the discovery: C. M. Firth and J. E. Quibell, *The Step Pyramid* (Cairo: Institut Français d'Archéologie Orientale, 1935), pp. 99–102; for the remains, see Lauer and Derry, "Découverte à Saqqarah."

75 See N. Tacke, "Die Entwicklung der Mumienmaske im Alten Reich," *Mitteilungen des Deutschen Archäologischen Instituts Kairo* 52 (1996), and compare earlier discussions of the plaster covers and molded linen structures that interpret them as precursors of portraiture: D. Spanel, *Through Ancient Eyes: Egyptian Portraiture* (Birmingham, AL: Birmingham Museum of Art, 1988), especially at p. 19; W. S. Smith, *A History of Egyptian Sculpture and Painting of the Old Kingdom* (London: For the Boston Museum of Fine Arts, by Oxford University Press, 1949), pp. 23–28.

Chapter 4 Linen

1 W.M.F. Petrie, *Roman Portraits and Memphis (IV)* (London: School of Archaeology in Egypt, 1911), pp. 16–18, pl. xxiii.

2 H. Persson, "Collecting Egypt: The Textile Collection of the Victoria and Albert Museum," *Journal of the History of Collections* 24 (2012).

3 A. B. Weiner, *Inalienable Possessions: The Paradox of Keeping-While-Giving* (Berkeley and Los Angeles: University of California Press, 1992), quoted phrase at p. 3 and p. 33.

4 J. Alvarez-Mon, *The Arjan Tomb: At the Crossroads of the Elamite and the Persian Empires* (Leuven: Peeters, 2010), pp. 30–39, for evidence from Iran. J. P. Wild and F. Wild, "Cotton: The New Wool. Qasr Ibrim Study Season 2008," *Archaeological Textiles Newsletter* 46 (2008), and J. P. Wild, F. Wild, and A. Clapham, "Irrigation and the Spread of Cotton Growing in Roman Times," *Archaeological Textiles Newsletter* 44 (2007) discuss evidence for cotton in the southern reaches of the Nile Valley, at sites such as Qasr Ibrim.

5 G. R. Gliddon, *A Memoir on the Cotton of Egypt* (London: James Madden, 1841).

6 J. H. Hammond, *Selections from the Letters and Speeches of the Hon. James H. Hammond, of South Carolina* (New York: John F. Trow & Co., 1866), pp. 311–22.

7 E.R.J. Owen, *Cotton and the Egyptian Economy 1820–1914: A Study in Trade and Development* (Oxford: Clarendon Press, 1969), pp. 89–121.

8 E. Neuville, "Women, Cloth, Fluff and Dust in Elizabeth Gaskell's *North and South*," *Textile 8* (2010).

9 C. Riggs, "Jesse Haworth and the Manchester Museum," *Bulletin of the Association for the Study of Travel in Egypt and the Near East (ASTENE)* 24 (2005).

10 For an account of the acquisition and unwrapping of the mummies, see S.J.M.M. Alberti, "Molluscs, Mummies and Moon Rock: The Manchester Museum and Manchester Science," *Manchester Region History Review* 18 (2007), and the discussion of Murray's role in K. L. Sheppard, "Between Spectacle and Science: Margaret Murray and the Tomb of the Two Brothers," *Science in Context* 25 (2012).

11 M. A. Murray, *The Tomb of Two Brothers* (Manchester: Sherratt & Hughes, 1910), pp. 7–8.

12 The outermost layer on Khnum-nakht had been placed over the front of the body and laced up the back using a fringe torn from another large cloth and twisted like a cord: Murray, *The Tomb of Two Brothers*, p. 77.

13 A. P. Thomas, "The Midgleys of Bolton and Their Contribution to the Scientific Examination of Ancient Textiles," *Archaeological Textile Newsletter* 45 (2007).

14 J. Garstang, *The Burial Customs of Ancient Egypt* (London: Archibald Constable, 1907), p. 103.

15 My account of flax processing and yarn preparation relies on B. J. Kemp and G. Vogelsang-Eastwood, *The Ancient Textile Industry at Amarna* (London: Egypt Exploration Society, 2001), especially pp. 25–34 and 57–88, here and in the following paragraphs. Accounts of the specific stages and techniques in flax harvesting and preparation vary somewhat by author, and three additional sources are E.J.W. Barber, *Prehistoric Textiles: The Development of Cloth in the Neolithic and Bronze Ages* (Princeton, NJ: Princeton University Press, 1991), pp. 11–15; P. Baines, *Linen: Hand Spinning and Weaving* (London: B. T. Batsford, 1989); and J. Allgrove-McDowell's section on "Ancient Egypt, 5000–332 BC," in D. T. Jenkins (ed.), *The Cambridge History of Western Textiles* (revised by Vogelsang) (Cambridge: Cambridge University Press, 2003). For an overview of flax processing and linen manufacture in Egypt, see also G. Vogelsang-Eastwood, *The Production of Linen in Pharaonic Egypt* (Leiden: Stichting Textile Research Centre, 1992), and G. Vogelsang-Eastwood, "Textiles," in P. T. Nicholson and I. Shaw (eds.), *Ancient Egyptian Materials and Technology* (Cambridge: Cambridge University Press, 2000).

16 Balls of flax excavated at el-Lahun ("Kahun") have been identified as unspun fibers, in keeping with experimental observations of the unretted method: Kemp and Vogelsang-Eastwood, *The Ancient Textile Industry*, p. 33.

17 For splicing and spinning flax, see Kemp and Vogelsang-Eastwood, *The Ancient Textile Industry*, pp. 70–77, and compare Barber, *Prehistoric Textiles*, pp. 44–51.

18 See C. Cartwright, H. Granger-Taylor, and S. Quirke, "Lahun Textile Evidence in London," in S. Quirke (ed.), *Lahun Studies* (Reigate: SIA 1998), with discussion based on evidence from the Middle Kingdom settlement site at el-Lahun; and see Kemp and Vogelsang-Eastwood, *The Ancient Textile Industry*, p. 57.

19 S. J. Allen, "Spinning Bowls: Representation and Reality," in J. Phillips (ed.), *Ancient Egypt, the Aegean, and the Near East: Studies in Honour of Martha Rhoads Bell* (San Antonio, TX: Van Siclen Books, 1997).

20 Kemp and Vogelsang-Eastwood, *The Ancient Textile Industry*, offer extensive discussion of weaving, especially at pp. 307–38. For ground looms, see also J. Picton and J. Mack, *African Textiles* (London: British Museum Press, 1989), pp. 58–65, citing the work of textile expert Grace Crowfoot. Crowfoot recorded her observations on the use of the ground loom in the Anglo-Egyptian Sudan, where she lived for several years because her husband was the assistant director of education in the colony: see G.M. Crowfoot, "Spinning and Weaving in the Sudan," *Sudan Notes and Records* 4 (1921), and her biography and bibliography, available from Brown University, "Breaking Ground: Women in Old World Archaeology," http://www.brown.edu/Research/Breaking_Ground/introduction.php (q.v. "Crowfoot"; last accessed June 12, 2012).

21 Theban Tomb (TT) 20: N. de Garis Davies, *Seven Private Tombs at Kurnah* (London: Egypt Exploration Society, 1948), pp. 49–50, pl. 35.

22 J. de Morgan, *Fouilles à Dahchour en 1894–1895* (Vienna: Adolphe Holzhausen, 1903), p. 74; R. Germer, *Die Textilfärberei und die Verwendung gefärbter Textilien im Alten Ägypten* (Wiesbaden: Harrassowitz, 1992), p. 8.

23 On the linen from the royal mummies, see Germer, *Die Textilfärberei*, pp. 75–82.

24 M. Stoll and D. Fengel, "Chemical and Structural Studies on Ancient Egyptian Linen," *Berliner Beiträge zur Archäometrie* 10 (1988). Ammonia derived from stale urine (human or animal) also has a bleaching effect on cloth left in the sun, but there is no textual or scientific evidence for this process in ancient Egypt.

25 Kemp and Vogelsang-Eastwood, *The Ancient Textile Industry*, p. 26.

26 Mollusk "silk" is discussed in S. Dalley, "Ancient Assyrian Textiles and the Origins of Carpet Design," *Iran* 29 (1991); see also the Muschelseide project of the Naturhistorisches Museum, Basel, at http://www.muschelseide.ch/de.html (last accessed June 12, 2012).

27 C. H. Roehrig, "Egyptian: Sheet of 'Royal Linen,'" *Metropolitan Museum of Art Bulletin* 53 (1995–96).

28 É. Chassinat and C. Palanque, *Une campagne de fouilles dans la nécropole d'Assiout* (Cairo: Institut Français d'Archéologie Orientale, 1911), pp. 162–63, pl. xxxiii, and see J. Malek, *Egypt: 4000 Years of Art* (London: Phaidon, 2003), no. 100.

29 Vogelsang-Eastwood, "Textiles," p. 281.

30 G. Vogelsang-Eastwood, *Pharaonic Egyptian Clothing* (Leiden: E. J. Brill, 1993), pp. 119–22.

31 See Vogelsang-Eastwood, "Textiles," especially pp. 285–86; P. A. Bochi, "Of Lines, Linen, and Language: A Study of a *Patterned* Textile and Its Interweaving with Egyptian Beliefs," *Chronique d'Égypte* 71 (1996).

32 A. Appadurai (ed.), *The Social Life of Things: Commodities in Cultural Perspective* (Cambridge: Cambridge University Press, 1986).

33 Weiner, *Inalienable Possessions*, pp. 58–59.

34 For the Tutankhamun bandages, see H. E. Winlock and D. Arnold, *Tutankhamun's Funeral* (New York: Metropolitan Museum of Art, 2010), pp. 36, 69 (note), and for the Ahmose-Meritamun linen, see H. E. Winlock, *The Tomb of Queen Meryet-Amun at Thebes* (New York: Metropolitan Museum of Art, 1932), especially pp. 11–13. H. H. Nelson, "The Identity of Amon-Re of United-with-Eternity," *Journal of Near Eastern Studies* 1 (1942), p. 135, refers to the weaver credited on the twenty-first-dynasty wrappings of Ramses III.

35 Compare also Tim Ingold's discussion of the relationship between textile production and basketry, "Making Culture and Weaving the World," in P. M. Graves-Brown (ed.), *Matter, Materiality and Modern Culture* (London and New York: Routledge, 2000).

36 J. H. Taylor, *Journey through the Afterlife: Ancient Egyptian Book of the Dead* (London: British Museum Press, 2010), p. 62 fig. 21.

37 H. Kockelmann, *Untersuchungen zu den späten Totenbuch-Handschriften auf Mumienbinden* (Wiesbaden: Harrassowitz, 2008), in two volumes, with the character and history of the Hor bandages at pp. 1–7 in the first volume. For further, in-depth discussion of the use of inscribed bandages and linen amulets on mummies, see the second volume, especially Chapters 4 (textiles), 7 (numbered bandages), and 12 (positioning of bandages on the body).

38 J. Jones, "The 'Linen List' in Early Dynastic and Old Kingdom Egypt: Text and Textile Reconciled," in C. Michel and M.-L. Nusch (eds.), *Textile Terminologies* (Oxford: Oxbow, 2010), lays the issues out clearly. For one model of linen grades, see Kemp and Vogelsang-Eastwood, *The Ancient Textile Industry*, pp. 438–41.

39 See discussion in J. Jones, "The Shroud of *Tny*, R92: A Textile Analysis," in K. Sowada and B. Ockinga (eds.), *Egyptian Art in the Nicholson Museum, Sydney* (Sydney: Mediterranean Archaeology, 2006).

40 H. Junker, *Giza VIII: Der Ostabschnitt des Westfriedhofs, Zweiter Teil* (Vienna and Leipzig: Hölder-Pichler-Tempsky, 1947), pp. 90–108.

41 R. M. Janssen, "The Linens of Idu II," in B. Schmitz (ed.), *Untersuchungen zu Idu II, Giza: Ein interdisziplinäres Projekt* (Hildesheim: Gerstenberg, 1996).

42 W. Helck, "Zur Person des *Jdw II* und des '*nḫ-Pjpj*,'" in B. Schmitz (ed.), *Untersuchungen zu Idu II, Giza: Ein interdisziplinäres Projekt* (Hildesheim: Gerstenberg, 1996).

43 D. Franke, "*Sem*-Priest on Duty," in S. Quirke (ed.), *Discovering Egypt from the Neva: The Egyptological Legacy of Oleg D. Berlev* (Berlin: Achet-Verlag, 2003).

44 Weiner, *Inalienable Possessions*, especially pp. xii, 3, 12–13. For the importance of sisters, daughters, and wives in Egyptian kingship, see L. Troy, *Patterns of Queenship in Ancient Egyptian Myth and History* (Uppsala, Sweden: Uppsala University, 1986).

45 C. H. Roehrig, "Life along the Nile: Three Egyptians of Ancient Thebes," *Metropolitan Museum of Art Bulletin* 60 (2002); and C. H. Roehrig, "The Middle Kingdom Tomb of Wah at Thebes," in N. Strudwick and J. H. Taylor (eds.), *The Theban Necropolis: Past, Present, Future* (London: British Museum Press, 2003), with full references to the earlier excavation reports published by H. E. Winlock.

46 Suggested in P. F. Dorman, "Family Burial and Commemoration in the Theban Necropolis," in N. Strudwick and J. H. Taylor (eds.), *The Theban Necropolis: Past, Present, Future* (London: British Museum Press, 2003).

47 H. E. Winlock, *The Slain Soldiers of Neb-Hepet-Re Mentu-Hotpe* (New York: Metropolitan Museum of Art, 1945); for the date of the burial, and questions about its interpretation, see C. Vogel, "Fallen Heroes?—Winlock's 'Slain Soldiers' Reconsidered," *Journal of Egyptian Archaeology* 89 (2003).

48 On the Egyptian evidence, see B. Haring, *Divine Households: Administrative and Economic Aspects of the New Kingdom Royal Memorial Temples in Western Thebes* (Leiden: Nederlands Instituut voor het Nabije Oosten, 1997).

49 Weiner, *Inalienable Possessions*; see also discussion in D. Wengrow, "Prehistories of Commodity Branding," *Current Anthropology* 49 (2008).

50 Weiner, *Inalienable Possessions*, p. 86.

51 Jones, "The 'Linen List'"; P. Der Manuelian, *Slab Stelae of the Giza Necropolis* (New Haven, CT, and Philadelphia: Peabody Museum of Natural History of Yale University and the University of Pennsylvania Museum of Archaeology and Anthropology, 2003), pp. 153–60. See also E. Edel, "Beiträge zum ägyptischen Lexikon VI: Die Stoffbezeichnungen in den Kleiderlisten des Alten Reiches," *Zeitschrift für Ägyptische Sprache und Altertumskunde* 102 (1975); K. Scheele, *Die Stofflisten des Alten Reiches: Lexikographie, Entwicklung und Gebrauch* (Wiesbaden: Harrassowitz, 2005); and W. S. Smith, "The Old Kingdom Linen List," *Zeitschrift für Ägyptische Sprache und Altertumskunde* 71 (1935).

52 The measuring system is imperfectly understood, but Old Kingdom examples probably combine signs for cloth width and length with signs that indicate multiples of area (in ten square cubits): see discussion of the difficulties in Jones, "The 'Linen List,'" and the classic study by P. Posener-Kriéger, "Les mesures des étoffes à l'Ancien Empire," *Revue d'Égyptologie* 29 (1977).

53 See Kemp and Vogelsang-Eastwood, *The Ancient Textile Industry*, pp. 123–44, and Jones, "The 'Linen List,'" with figs. 6.8–6.10 on p. 92.

54 Manuelian, *Slab Stelae*, p. 157.

55 See Scheele, *Stofflisten*, pp. 10–71 for a lexicographical analysis.

56 Vogelsang-Eastwood, *Pharaonic Egyptian Clothing*, pp. 119–22, and see original publications of the dresses: R. M. Hall, "Garments in the Petrie Museum of Egyptian Archaeology," *Textile History* 13 (1982); R. M. Hall, "Two Linen Dresses from the Fifth Dynasty Site of Deshasheh Now in the Petrie Museum of Egyptian Archaeology, University College London," *Journal of Egyptian Archaeology* 67 (1981); and R. M. Hall and L. Pedrini, "A Pleated Linen Dress from a Sixth Dynasty Tomb at Gebelein Now in the Museo Egizio, Turin," *Journal of Egyptian Archaeology* 70 (1984).

57 E. Schiaparelli, *La tomba intatta dell'architetto Cha nella necropoli di Tebe*, Turin: R. Museo di Antichità, 1927, pp. 90–100; see p. 99 fig. 71 for an example with Kha's name, and L. Meskell, *Archaeologies of Social Life* (Oxford: Blackwell, 1999), for an analysis of the tomb's contents. For clothing in the tomb of Tutankhamun, see G. Vogelsang-Eastwood, *Tutankhamun's Wardrobe: Garments from the Tomb of Tutankhamun* (Rotterdam: Barjesteh van Waalwijk

van Doorn & Co's, 1999). Early publications of the king's tunics: R. Pfister, "Les textiles du tombeau de Toutankhamon," *Revue des Arts Asiatiques* 11 (1937); G. M. Crowfoot and N. de Garis Davies, "The Tunic of Tutankhamun," *Journal of Egyptian Archaeology* 27 (1941).

58 One of the tunics is in the Pitt Rivers Museum, 1890.26.98, W. 117.0 cm (max), L. 135.0 cm (max), and the find is recorded in Petrie's journals (Oxford, Griffith Institute, MSS 1889–1990, p. 29) as taking place in the week of November 28 to December 5, 1889, while he was working in part of the settlement reoccupied during the eighteenth dynasty. I am grateful to Alice Stevenson for this information and for bringing the tunic to my attention.

59 University of Chicago, Oriental Institute Museum 18285, L. 97.0 cm, W. 73.0 cm: see E. Teeter, *Ancient Egypt: Treasures from the Collection of the Oriental Institute, University of Chicago* (Chicago: Oriental Institute, 2003), pp. 44–45, no. 18.

60 S. O. Martin, "Ancient Egyptian Mummy Wrappings from the Mummy '1770': A Technological and Social Study," Ph.D. dissertation, University of Manchester, 2008.

61 B. Bruyère, *Rapport sur les fouilles de Deir el Médineh (1923–1924)* (Cairo: Institut Français d'Archéologie Orientale, 1925), pp. 58–59.

62 Kemp and Vogelsang-Eastwood, *The Ancient Textile Industry*, p. 169. The difficulty of identifying words for clothing is exemplified in J. J. Janssen, *Daily Dress at Deir el-Medina: Words for Clothing* (London: Golden House, 2008).

63 For draped versus cut and tailored cloth, see E. Tarlo, *Clothing Matters: Dress and Identity in India* (London: Hurst, 1996), pp. 27–29; compare M. Banerjee and D. Miller, *The Sari* (Oxford: Berg, 2003), pp. 235–53.

64 A. Erman and H. Grapow (eds.), *Wörterbuch der ägyptischen Sprache*, Vol. 3 (Berlin: Akademie-Verlag, 1926–61), pp. 64–66.

65 Bruyère, *Rapport sur les fouilles*, p. 105; see Erman and Grapow, *Wörterbuch der ägyptischen Sprache*, Vol. 4, p. 449.10–16.

66 See M. Zecchi, "The God Hedjhotep," *Chronique d'Égypte* 76 (2001), p. 11. On the difficulty of transcribing and translating words for linen, the influential Egyptologist Alan H. Gardiner already despaired in 1931: "Perhaps no Egyptologist has been very clear as to what was exactly intended by *šs [sšr]* and by *mnḫt* respectively; something in the clothing line seemed to be meant, but nothing more precise could be said than that." In A. H. Gardiner, "Two Hieroglyphic Signs and the Egyptian Words for 'Alabaster' and 'Linen,' etc.," *Bulletin de l'Institut Français d'Archéologie Orientale* 30 (1931), p. 166.

67 A. Moret, *Le rituel du culte divin journalier en Égypte* (Paris: Ernest Leroux, 1902).

68 See Moret, *Le rituel du culte divin*, pp. 224–27.

69 For the chapels in the Abydos temple, see A. M. Calverley, *The Temple of King Sethos I at Abydos*, Vols. 1–2 (London: Egypt Exploration Society; Chicago: Oriental Institute of the University of Chicago, 1933, 1935). A. R. David, *A Guide to Religious Ritual at Abydos (c. 1300 BC)* (Warminster: Aris and Phillips, 1973), is a convenient compendium of the scenes, though lacking in interpretive

value; it uses the thirty-six scenes in the chapel of Re-Horakhty as a model for the ritual performance.

70 The word the Berlin handbook uses for the fallen clothes of the cult statue is the word for an animal skin, which makes a symbolic link between the wrappings of the statues—certainly linen—and the use of animal skins in other contexts, such as the pied skin that wraps the *tekenu* or the leopard skin worn by *sem*-priests: see D. Lorton, "The Theology of Cult Statues in Ancient Egypt," in M. B. Dick (ed.), *Born in Heaven, Made on Earth: The Making of the Cult Image in the Ancient Near East* (Winona Lake, IN: Eisenbrauns, 1999), pp. 136–38, 160–61 n. 56. Lorton sees the animal skin as perhaps referring to the practice of wrapping the dead in an animal skin, attested in some Predynastic burials.

71 See P. Grandet, *Le Papyrus Harris I (BM 9999)* (Cairo: Institut Français d'Archéologie Orientale, 1994).

72 For example, two pieces with Demotic dedications to Triphis and Osoroeris ("the great Osiris"), preserved in Lille (Institut de Papyrologie et d'Egyptologie 1 and 2) and published by G. Widmer, "A propos de quelques dédicaces sur lin de l'époque romaine: Une pratique votive méconnue?" in E. Frood and A. McDonald (eds.), *Decorum and Experience: Essays in Ancient Culture for John Baines* (2013), and two pieces with hieratic inscriptions now in Brussels (Musées Royaux d'Art et d'Histoire E.7047A and D); for these, see J. Capart, "Bandelettes et linges de momie," *Bulletin des Musées Royaux d'Art et d'Histoire* 13 (1941), and images and entries online at the Global Egyptian Museum, http://www.globalegyptianmuseum.org (last accessed August 19, 2013).

73 Two examples, first, from the Middle Kingdom: "You dress yourself with the garment of Ptah, with the robe which Hathor has taken off" (*Coffin Texts*, Spell 61), in R. O. Faulkner, *The Ancient Egyptian Coffin Texts*, Vol. 1 (Warminster: Aris & Phillips, 1973–78), p. 56; the translation given here is a variant, recorded in A. de Buck and A. H. Gardiner, *The Egyptian Coffin Texts*, Vol. 1 (Chicago: University of Chicago Press, 1935–61), 258f. Second, from the New Kingdom, a prayer to the sun god at the entrance of the tomb of a priest of Amun, Neferhotep, at Thebes (TT 49): "May my body be pure. May I receive the cast-off clothing and see Ptah-Sokar." For these and other examples, see J. Zandee, "Prayers to the Sun-god from Theban Tombs," *Jaarbericht van het vooraziatisch-egyptisch genootschap Ex Oriente Lux (JEOL)* 16 (1959–62), especially at p. 54.

74 J. D. Ray, "An Inscribed Linen Plea from the Sacred Animal Necropolis, North Saqqara," *Journal of Egyptian Archaeology* 91 (2005).

75 M.-L. Ryhiner, *La procession des étoffes et l'union avec Hathor* (Brussels: Fondation Égyptologique Reine Élisabeth, 1995).

76 A. Egberts, *In Quest of Meaning: A Study of the Ancient Egyptian Rites of Consecrating the Meret-Chests and Driving the Calves* (Leiden: Nederlands Instituut voor het Nabije Oosten, 1995). Egberts emphasizes a connection between the linen in the *meret*-chests and the cult of Osiris since the cloth in the chests may represent the mummy bandages of Osiris. If the wrapping of Osiris's body is a parallel for the wrapping of sacred images more generally, however, then Egberts may lay too much stress on the distinctive Osirian character of the *meret*-chests.

77 J. de Morgan et al., *Kom Ombos*, Vol. 2, Part 1 and Vol. 3, Part 2 (Vienna: Adolphe Holzhausen, 1895/1900).

78 A. Aufrère, *Le propylône d'Amon-Rê-Montou à Karnak-Nord* (Cairo: Institut Français d'Archéologie Orientale, 2000), pp. 254–63 (scene 14a). Aufrère translates *djeba* and *sheta* separately, as "wrapping" and "funerary equipment" respectively: see p. 263 (commentary [aa]).

79 See the excellent study by F. Coppens, *The Wabet: Tradition and Innovation in Temples of the Ptolemaic and Roman Period* (Prague: Czech Institute of Egyptology, 2007).

80 Coppens, *The Wabet*, p. 208.

81 Coppens, *The Wabet*, pp. 133–36. On fecundity figures, see J. Baines, *Fecundity Figures* (Oxford: Griffith Institute, 2001 [1985]).

82 See A. M. Blackman and H. W. Fairman, "The Myth of Horus at Edfu—II," *Journal of Egyptian Archaeology* 29 (1943), pp. 34–35; H. Bonnet, *Reallexikon der ägyptischen Religionsgeschichte* (Berlin: De Gruyter, 1952), pp. 764–65; M. Derchain-Urtel, "Tait," in W. Helck and E. Otto (eds.), *Lexikon der Ägyptologie*, Vol. 6 (Wiesbaden: Harrassowitz, 1986); and H. el-Saady, "Reflections on the Goddess Tayt," *Journal of Egyptian Archaeology* 80 (1994).

83 B. Backes, *Rituelle Wirklichkeit: Über Erscheinung und Wirkungsbereich des Webergottes Hedjhotep und den gedanklichen Umgang mit einer Gottes-Konzeption im Alten Ägypten* (Turnhout: Brepols, 2001), pp. 33–39; and Zecchi, "The God Hedjhotep." See also D. Meeks, "Genies, anges, et demons en Égypte," in D. Meeks (ed.), *Genies, anges, et demons: Égypte, Babylone, Israël, Islam, etc.* (Sources Orientales, VIII) (Paris: Édition du Seuil, 1971), pp. 27–28.

84 For swaddling clothes, see P. Wilson, *A Ptolemaic Lexikon: A Lexicographical Study of the Texts in the Temple of Edfu* (Leuven: Peeters, 1997), pp. 500–1.

85 R. el-Sayed, *La déesse Neith de Saïs, I. Importance et rayonnement de son culte* (Cairo: Institut Français d'Archéologie Orientale, 1982), pp. 76–80.

86 S. Schott, "*Rs-n.y und mḥ-n.t* als Häuser der Neith," *Revue d'Égyptologie* 19 (1967). See also C. Sambin and J.-F. Carlotti, "Une porte de fête-sed de Ptolémée II remployée dans le temple de Montou à Médamoud," *Bulletin de l'Institut Français d'Archéologie Orientale* 95 (1995), with further examples linking the crocodiles with textile wrappings.

87 PT 1755 (= 1794). See E. Otto, *Das ägyptische Mundöffnungsritual* (Wiesbaden: Harrassowitz, 1960), pp. 112–14 (scene 50); Backes, *Rituelle Wirklichkeit*, pp. 81–83.

88 Weiner, *Inalienable Possessions*, pp. 72–73.

89 J. F. Borghouts, *Ancient Egyptian Medical Texts* (Leiden: E. J. Brill, 1978), pp. 24–55 (texts 31, 33, 34, 35).

90 *Coffin Texts* Spell 608: Faulkner, *Ancient Egyptian Coffin Texts*, Vol. 2, p. 197, discussed in B. Backes, "Von nun an sollt ihr *Rḫ.ti* heißen: Die 'Beiden Kolleginnen' von Sais," *Göttinger Miszellen* 180 (2001). The translation of the words *sšn* and *msn* as "to twist" and "to spin," as I have done here, is one suggestion for conveying different actions in the process; Faulkner thought netting might be involved instead.

91 H. Whitehouse, *Ancient Egypt and Nubia in the Ashmolean Museum* (Oxford: Ashmolean Museum, 2009), pp. 118–20 (no. 63); C. Riggs, *The Beautiful Burial in Roman Egypt: Art, Identity, and Funerary Religion* (Oxford: Oxford University Press, 2005), pp. 196, 197 fig. 94, 288 (no. 99).

92 Examples include the eighteenth-dynasty temple of Khnum at Kumma, Lower Nubia, reign of Amenhotep II: R. A. Caminos, *Semna-Kumma II: The Temple of Kumma* (London: Egypt Exploration Society, 1998), pls. 69, 73 (scenes 74–75 and 79–80); Luxor temple, reign of Amenhotep III: H. Brunner, *Die südlichen Räume des Tempels von Luxor* (Mainz: Philipp von Zabern, 1977), pl. 135 (Scene XIX/127); Thutmose III: J. Aksamit, "Room C in the Temple of Tuthmosis III at Deir el-Bahari," in B. Haring and A. Klug (eds.), *6. Ägyptologische Tempeltagung: Funktion und Gebrauch Altägyptischer Tempelräume* (Wiesbaden: Harrassowitz, 2007); H. M. Hays, "The Ritual Scenes in the Chapels of Amun," in *The Epigraphic Survey: Medinet Habu*, Vol. 9, *The Eighteenth Dynasty Temple*, Part 1, *The Inner Sanctuaries* (Chicago: Oriental Institute of the University of Chicago, 2009), with pl. 81.

93 *Book of Caverns*, 5th division, Tomb of Ramses VI: translation adapted from A. Piankhoff and N. Rambova, *The Tomb of Ramesses VI* (New York: Pantheon, 1954), p. 100.

94 Schiaparelli, *La tomba intatta,* pp. 136, 137 (fig. 120), 140 (fig. 124), 142. Other sealed jars in the tomb: pp. 155 (fig. 138), 156 (fig. 139), 157 (fig. 140), 158 (fig. 141). For the patterned wrapping of human and animal mummies, see examples in S. Walker and M. L. Bierbrier (eds.), *Ancient Faces: Mummy Portraits from Roman Egypt* (London: British Museum Press, 1997), and S. Ikram (ed.), *Divine Creatures: Animal Mummies in Ancient Egypt* (Cairo and New York: American University in Cairo Press, 2005). For the wrapping of Ptah-Sokar-Osiris figures, with further literature, see M. Minas, "Die ptolemäischen Sokar-Osiris-Mumien: Neue Erkenntnisse zum Ägyptischen Dynastiekult der Ptolemäer," *Mitteilungen des Deutschen Archäologischen Instituts Kairo* 62 (2006).

95 See W. Wendrich, "Entangled, Connected or Protected? The Power of Knots and Knotting in Ancient Egypt," in K. Szpakowska (ed.), *Through a Glass Darkly: Magic, Dreams and Prophecy in Ancient Egypt* (Swansea: Classical Press of Wales, 2006), for knots in ancient Egypt, and for knots, nets, and other patterns as "technologies of enchantment," see A. Gell, "The Technology of Enchantment and the Enchantment of Technology," in J. Coote and A. Shelton (eds.), *Anthropology, Art and Aesthetics* (Oxford: Clarendon, 1992), and A. Gell, "Vogel's Net: Traps as Artworks and Artworks as Traps," *Journal of Material Culture* 1 (1996).

96 A. M. Roth and C. H. Roehrig, "Magical Bricks and the Bricks of Birth," *Journal of Egyptian Archaeology* 88 (2002).

97 For bronze votives with traces of wrappings, see C. I. Green, *The Temple Furniture from the Sacred Animal Necropolis at North Saqqara, 1964–76* (London: Egypt Exploration Society, 1987), p. 2, and discussion in E. A. Hastings, *The Sculpture from the Sacred Animal Necropolis at North Saqqara, 1964–76* (London: Egypt Exploration Society, 1997), especially pp. xxxii–xxxiii.

98 B. Bruyère, *Rapport sur les fouilles de Deir el Médineh* (1928) (Cairo: Institut Français d'Archéologie Orientale, 1929), p. 69, pls. xi–xii. On the use of

shabti-figures in votive contexts, see H. D. Schneider, *Shabtis*, Leiden: Rijksmuseum van Oudheden, 1977, especially Vol. 1, pp. 268–302. Examples of wrapped *shabti*-figures: B. Bruyère, *Rapport sur les fouilles de Deir el Médineh (1934–35)* (Cairo: Institut Français d'Archéologie Orientale, 1937), pp. 130–1; the Earl of Carnarvon and H. Carter, *Five Years' Explorations at Thebes* (London: Henry Frowde, Oxford University Press, 1912), p. 50, pl. xliii; P. E. Newberry, *Funerary Statuettes and Model Sarcophagi*, Vol. 1 (Cairo: Institut Français d'Archéologie Orientale, 1937), pp. 268 (CG 47914), 271–72 (CG 47923); and M. J. Raven, *The Tomb of Pay and Raia at Saqqara* (London: Egypt Exploration Society and the National Museum of Antiquities Leiden, 2005), pp. 76–77, cat. 55a. Often described as the forerunners of *shabti*-figures, wax statuettes wrapped in cloth and placed in miniature coffins were found in the burials of eleventh-dynasty royal females at Deir el-Bahri: Naville, *The XIth Dynasty Temple at Deir el-Bahari*, Part 1 (London: Egypt Exploration Fund, 1907), pp. 49–50.

99 Such as the figures from the Wadi Gabbanet el-Qurud to the west of Thebes, which was also a location for sacred animal burials: C. Lilyquist, *The Tomb of Three Foreign Wives of Tuthmosis III* (New Haven, CT, and London: Yale University Press, 2003), pp. 4–13; C. Ransom Williams, "The Egyptian Collection in the Museum of Art at Cleveland, Ohio," *Journal of Egyptian Archaeology* 5 (1918), p. 174, pl. xxix.

100 G. Castel and G. Soukiassian, "Les mines de galene pharaoniques du Gebel el-Zeit (Égypte)," *Bulletin de la Societé Française d'Égyptologie* 112 (1988).

101 Examples of wrapped statues in tombs: Bruyère, *Rapport sur les fouilles de Deir el Médineh (1934–35)*, pp. 124–30, with figs. 70–71; Chassinat and Palanque, *Une campagne de fouilles*, p. 162, pl. xxxii; E. Delange, *Catalogue des statues égyptiennes du Moyen Empire* (Paris: Réunion des musées nationaux, 1987), pp. 188–89 (E 20576); J. E. Quibell and A.G.K. Hayter, *Teti Pyramid, North Side* (Cairo: Institut Français d'Archéologie Orientale, 1927), p. 37, pl. 20.1–3.

102 K. Price and M. Gleba, "Textiles on Egyptian Mirrors: Pragmatics or Religion?," *Archaeological Textiles Review* 54 (2012), offer the most up-to-date discussion, supported by technical analysis of several examples from the Petrie Museum, University College London; the authors suggest that in addition to a practical function of protecting the reflective surface, wrapping may have helped contain or control the "cosmological power" in the reflective surface. For further examples of wrapped mirrors, see G. Bénédite, *Miroirs*, Catalogue général des antiquités égyptiennes (Cairo: Institut Français d'Archéologie Orientale, 1907), e.g., pp. 14–15 (CG 44209); and G. Brunton, *Qau and Badari I* (London: British School of Archaeology in Egypt, 1927), p. 43 (grave 5311, Dyn. 11); on mirrors in general, see C. Lilyquist, *Ancient Egyptian Mirrors from the Earliest Times through the Middle Kingdom* (Munich: Deutscher Kunstverlag, 1979).

103 J. E. Quibell, *Tomb of Yuaa and Thuiu* (Cairo: Institut Français d'Archéologie Orientale, 1908), p. 35, pl. xvi (CG 51022); T. M. Davis et al., *The Tomb of Iouiya and Touiyou* (London: Archibald Constable, 1907), p. 24, pl. xvii.

104 For the canopic jars of Maiherperi (CG 24006 A–D, travertine, around 28.0 cm H), the original publication is G. Daressy, *Fouilles de la Vallée des Rois (1898–1899)*, Catalogue général des antiquités égyptiennes (Cairo: Institut Français d'Archéologie Orientale, 1902), pp. 11–22. For the canopic jars from the tomb of Sennedjem (CG 4249–4252, painted limestone, H 33.5 to 37.0 cm), see G. A. Reisner and M. H. Abd-ul-Rahman, *Canopics*, Catalogue général des antiquités égyptiennes (Cairo: Institut Français d'Archéologie Orientale, 1967), pp. 173–77, pl. xviii.

105 Metropolitan Museum of Art 10.176.57–60: L. Bull, "Four Egyptian Inscribed Statuettes of the Middle Kingdom," *Journal of the American Oriental Society* 56 (1936).

106 See Vogelsang-Eastwood, *Pharaonic Egyptian Clothing*, pp. 32–33, 53–55.

107 For example, A. Brack and A. Brack, *Das Grab des Haremheb (Theben Nr. 78)* (Mainz: Philipp von Zabern, 1980), p. 53 (scene 13.2), pl. 17a.

108 See J. Baines, *Visual and Written Culture in Ancient Egypt* (Oxford: Oxford University Press, 2007), especially pp. 3–30.

109 E.g., E. Russmann, *Egyptian Sculpture: Cairo and Luxor* (Austin: University of Texas Press, 1989), pp. 70–71.

110 Compare R. Schulz, *Die Entwicklung und Bedeutung des kuboiden Statuentypus: Eine Untersuchung zu den sogenannten "Würfelhockern"* (Hildesheim: Gerstenberg, 1992), especially pp. 736–44.

111 See J. Baines and C. Riggs, "Archaism and Kingship: A Late Royal Statue and Its Early Dynastic Model," *Journal of Egyptian Archaeology* 87 (2001).

112 There is an extensive literature, including the classic study by E. Hornung and E. Staehelin, *Studien zum Sedfest* (Geneva: Éditions de Belles-Lettres, 1974). For a discussion of the *sed* at the Step Pyramid, see F. D. Friedman, "Notions of Cosmos in the Step Pyramid Complex," in P. Der Manuelian (ed.), *Studies in Honor of William Kelly Simpson* (Boston: Museum of Fine Arts, 1996).

113 U. Rummel, "Weihrauch, Salböl und Leinen: Balsamierungsmaterialen als Medium der Erneuerung im Sedfest," *Studien zur Altägyptischen Kultur* 34 (2006). For representations of the *sed* cloak, see H. Sourouzian, "Inventaire iconographique des statues en manteau jubilaire," in C. Berger, G. Clerc, and N. Grimal (eds.), *Hommages à Jean Leclant*, Vol. 1, *Études Pharaoniques* (Cairo: Institut Français d'Archéologie Orientale, 1994). Some examples represent a diamond pattern, perhaps embroidered onto the cloth: see J. Larson, "The Heb-sed Robe and the 'Ceremonial Robe' of Tutankhamun," *Journal of Egyptian Archaeology* 67 (1981).

114 On these rites, with evidence from Karnak, see L. Coulon, "La nécropole osirienne de Karnak sous les Ptolémées," in A. Delattre and P. Heilporn (eds.), *"Et maintenant ce ne sont plus que des villages…": Thèbes et sa région aux époques hellénistique, romaine et byzantine* (Brussels: Association Égyptologique Reine Élisabeth, 2008).

115 For the Ennead, examples include the tomb of Userhet (TT51), in N. de Garis Davies, *Two Ramesside Tombs at Thebes* (New York: Metropolitan Museum of Art, 1927), pl. xi, and the hypostyle hall at Karnak, in H. H. Nelson and W. J. Murnane, *The Great Hypostyle Hall at Karnak*, Vol. 1, Part 1, *The Wall*

Reliefs (Chicago: University of Chicago, 1981), pl. 201. For the Ogdoad, see Aufrère, *Le propylône d'Amon-Rê-Montou*, where the gods receive offerings of linen from a Ptolemaic king.

116 The queen's statue is Cairo, Egyptian Museum, CG 37638 (H 151.0 cm): F. Bisson de la Roque, *Tôd (1934 à 1936)* (Cairo: Institut Français d'Archéologie Orientale, 1937), pp. 130–31 fig. 79. The Kom Ombo scene appears in de Morgan et al., *Kom Ombos*, Vol. 2, Part 1, pp. 186–87 (scenes 244–47). For the tomb of Anherkhawy (TT 359), see N. Cherpion and J.-P. Corteggiai, *La tombe d'Inherkhâouy (TT 359) à Deir el-Medina* (Cairo: Institut Français d'Archéologie Orientale, 2010), especially Vol. 1, pp. 49–50, Vol. 2, pp. 19–25, figs. 30–40; original publication: Bruyère, *Rapport sur les fouilles de Deir el Médineh (1930)* (Cairo: Institut Français d'Archéologie Orientale, 1933), pp. 32–82.

117 For cults associated with deified humans and ancestors, see A. von Lieven, "Deified Humans," in W. Wendrich (ed.), *UCLA Encyclopedia of Egyptology* (Los Angeles: UCLA, 2010); D. Wildung, *Egyptian Saints: Deification in Pharaonic Egypt* (New York: New York University Press, 1977); and D. Wildung, *Imhotep und Amenhotep: Gottwerdung im Alten Ägypten* (Munich and Berlin: Deutscher Kunstverlag, 1977).

118 B. Mathieu, "Réflexions sur le 'fragment Daressy' et ses hommes illustres," in C. Zivie-Coche and I. Guermeur (eds.), "*Parcourir l'éternité*": *Hommages à Jean Yoyotte* (Turnhout: Brepols, 2012), with further references, including J. Yoyotte, "A propos d'un monument copié par G. Daressy (contribution à l'histoire littéraire)," *Bulletin de la Societé Française d'Égyptologie 11* (1952).

119 J. L. Keith, *Anthropoid Busts of Deir el Medineh and Other Sites and Collections* (Cairo: Institut Français d'Archéologie Orientale, 2011), with further references to the extensive literature on these objects. See also L. Meskell, *Object Worlds in Ancient Egypt: Material Biographies Past and Present* (Oxford and New York: Berg, 2004), pp. 73–81; N. Harrington, *Living with the Dead: Ancestor Worship and Mortuary Ritual in Ancient Egypt* (Oxford: Oxbow, 2013), especially pp. 49–59.

120 Friedman's suggestion that the form was inspired by statues holding round-topped stelae is unnecessarily complicated and does not account for the wreaths or collars on several examples: see F. Friedman, "On the Meaning of Some Anthropoid Busts from Deir el-Medina," *Journal of Egyptian Archaeology* 71 (1985), pp. 94–95.

121 Meskell, *Object Worlds*, p. 74. For a stela depicting ancestor busts in *en face* relief (British Museum, EA 270), see her fig. 3.2 on p. 71.

122 Louvre E 25983, H 83.0 cm, from the Fayum: G. Widmer, "La stèle de Paêsis (Louvre E 25983) et quelques formes d'Osiris dans le Fayoum aux époques ptolémaïque et romaine," in L. Coulon (ed.), *Le culte d'Osiris au Ier millénaire av. J.-C.: Découvertes et travaux récents* (Cairo: Institut Français d'Archéologie Orientale, 2010). Compare a stela from Akhmim with the deceased's mother and father shown in block statue form in the lunette: Cairo, Egyptian Museum CG 22054, H 93.0 cm, in A. B. Kamal, *Stèles ptolémaïques et romaines,* Catalogue général des antiquités égyptiennes (Cairo: Institut Français d'Archéologie Orientale, 1904), pp. 51–54, pl. xvii.

123 For block statues, see R. Schultz, *Die Entwicklung und Bedeutung des kuboiden Statuentypus: Eine Untersuchung zu den sogenannten "Würfelhockern"* (Hildesheim: Gerstenberg, 1992), summarized and updated in R. Schultz, "Block Statue," in W. Wendrich (ed.), *UCLA Encyclopedia of Egyptology* (Los Angeles: UCLA, 2008).

124 V. Rondot, "De la fonction des statues-cubes comme cale-porte," *Revue d'Égyptologie* 62 (2011), furthering the discussion in J. J. Clère, "Deux statues 'gardiennes de porte' d'époque ramesside," *Journal of Egyptian Archaeology* 54 (1968).

125 E. Frood, *Biographical Texts from Ramesside Egypt* (Atlanta: Society of Biblical Literature, 2007), pp. 39–46.

126 Erman and Grapow, *Wörterbuch der ägyptischen Sprache*, Vol. 3, p. 65.10–11.

Chapter 5 Secrecy

1 Such as journalist Molly Oldfield's successful book *The Secret Museum* (London: HarperCollins, 2013), about objects rarely on display, and a Canadian television program called *Museum Secrets,* which presents nuggets of information about the highlights of worldwide museums: see http://blog.museumsecrets.tv/ and the website of production company Kensington, http://kensingtontv.com/kensington/index.php (both last accessed April 7, 2013).

2 E. Goffman, *The Presentation of Self in Everyday Life* (London: Penguin, 1969), first published 1959.

3 G. Simmel, "The Secret and the Secret Society," in K. H. Wolff (ed.), *The Sociology of Georg Simmel* (Glencoe, IL: The Free Press, 1950 [1908]), p. 330.

4 See F. de Jong, *Masquerades of Modernity: Power and Secrecy in Casamance, Senegal* (Bloomington: Indiana University Press, 2007), for a sustained engagement with the subject. Other anthropological studies concerned with secrecy include F. Barth, *Ritual and Knowledge among the Baktaman of New Guinea* (New Haven, CT: Yale University Press, 1975); B. Bellman, *The Language of Secrecy: Symbols and Metaphors in Poro Ritual* (New Brunswick, NJ: Rutgers University Press, 1984); S. Brett-Smith, "The Knowledge of Women," in M. Westerman (ed.), *Anthropologies of Art* (Winstown, MA: Sterling and Francine Clark Institute, distributed by Yale University Press, 2005); T. Crook, "Growing Knowledge in Bolivip, Papua New Guinea," *Oceania* 69 (1999); and the exhibition catalogue M. H. Nooter (ed.), *Secrecy: African Art that Conceals and Reveals* (Munich: Prestel, 1993).

5 Bellman, *The Language of Secrecy*, p. 17 (emphasis original), and discussion in de Jong, *Masquerades of Modernity,* pp. 10–14.

6 H. Altenmüller, "Geheimnis," in W. Helck and E. Otto (eds.), *Lexikon der Ägyptologie*, Vol. 2 (Wiesbaden: Harrassowitz, 1977); E. Hornung, *The Secret Lore of Egypt: Its Impact on the West* (Ithaca, NY, and London: Cornell University Press, 2001), p. 13.

7 Ascending Passage: An Alternative Egyptian Mysteries and Science Directory, http://www.ascendingpassage.com/ (last accessed April 8, 2013).

8 "Secret Egypt: Unravelling Myth from Truth," http://secretegypt.org.uk/ (last accessed June 18, 2012). The website closed about a year after the exhibition ended, though the exhibition is available for hire through the Herbert Museum as of this writing: http://www.theherbert.org/index.php/home/whats-on/secret-egypt (last accessed April 8, 2013).

9 The last-named organization maintains a web presence with its own .org URL, as did the Herbert Art Gallery and Museum "Secret Egypt" exhibition: see the House of Netjer, "The Kemetic Orthodox Faith," http://www.kemet.org/ (last accessed June 18, 2012).

10 See I. C. Rutherford, "Travel and Pilgrimage," in C. Riggs (ed.), *The Oxford Handbook of Roman Egypt* (Oxford: Oxford University Press, 2012).

11 On mystery cults in the Hellenistic and Roman worlds, see H. Bowden, *Mystery Cults in the Ancient World* (London: Thames and Hudson, 2010), and with particular reference to ancient Egypt and its classical and European reception, see J. Assmann, "Jehova-Isis: The Mysteries of Egypt and the Quest for Natural Religion in the Age of Enlightenment," in I. A. Bierman (ed.), *Egypt and the Fabrication of European Identity* (Los Angeles: UCLA, Center for Near Eastern Studies, 1995); J. Assmann, *Weisheit und Mysterium: Das Bild der Griechen von Ägypten* (Munich: C. H. Beck, 2000); S. M. Burstein, "Commentary," in I. A. Bierman (ed.), *Egypt and the Fabrication of European Identity* (Los Angeles: UCLA, Center for Near Eastern Studies, 1995); and L. Kákosy, "Tempel und Mysterien," in R. Gundlach and M. Rochholz (eds.), *Ägyptische Tempel—Struktur, Funktion und Programm* (Hildesheim: Gerstenberg, 1994).

12 See H. G. Kippenberg and G. G. Stroumsa, "Introduction: Secrecy and Its Benefits," in H. G. Kippenberg and G. G. Stroumsa (eds.), *Secrecy and Concealment: Studies in the History of Mediterranean and Near Eastern Religions* (Leiden and New York: E. J. Brill, 1995), and K. W. Bolle, "Secrecy in Religion," in K. W. Bolle (ed.), *Secrecy in Religions* (Leiden: Brill, 1987).

13 On Kircher, see P. Findlen (ed.), *Athanasius Kircher: The Last Man Who Knew Everything* (London and New York: Routledge, 2004), and J. Godwin, *Athanasius Kircher's Theatre of the World* (London: Thames and Hudson, 2009).

14 See J. Rose, *The Haunting of Sylvia Plath* (Cambridge, MA: Harvard University Press, 1991), especially pp. 150–55.

15 For an overview, with further references, see Hornung, *The Secret Lore of Egypt*.

16 See J. Assmann, *Das verschleierte Bild zu Sais: Schillers Ballade und ihre griechischen und ägyptischen Hintergründe* (Stuttgart and Leipzig: B. G. Teubner, 1999); J. Assmann, *Religion and Cultural Memory* (Stanford, CA: Stanford University Press, 2006), pp. 187–89; E. Graefe, "Beethoven und die ägyptische Weisheit," *Göttinger Miszellen* 2 (1972); and C. Harrauer, "'Ich bin, was da ist…': Die Göttin von Sais und ihre Deutung von Plutarch bis in die Goethezeit," *Sphairos: Wiener Studien. Zeitschrift für Klassische Philologie und Patristik* 107/108 (1994/1995).

17 Discussed in P. Hadot, *The Veil of Isis: An Essay on the History of the Idea of Nature* (Cambridge, MA, and London: Belknap Press of Harvard University Press, 2006), and see L. Jordanova, *Sexual Visions: Images of Gender in Science and Medicine between the Eighteenth and Twentieth Centuries* (Madison:

University of Wisconsin Press, 1989), pp. 87–89 on the ambivalent relationship between gender and veiling in nineteenth-century metaphors of knowledge.

18 For both the ceiling cycle and the medals, see T. Porterfield, *The Allure of Empire: Art in the Service of French Imperialism 1798–1836* (Princeton, NJ: Princeton University Press, 1998), pp. 81–116, especially at pp. 87–91. On the Napoleonic iconography, and its implications in the study of Egyptian archaeology, see also D. Wengrow, *What Makes Civilization? The Ancient Near East and the Future of the West* (Oxford: Oxford University Press, 2010), pp. 167–68, pl. 18.

19 D. M. Reid, *Whose Pharaohs? Archaeology, Museums, and Egyptian National Identity from Napoleon to World War I* (Berkeley: University of California Press, 2002), p. 113.

20 Hornung, *The Secret Lore of Egypt.*

21 J.R.I. Cole, *Colonialism and Revolution in the Middle East: Social and Cultural Origins of Egypt's Urabi Movement* (Princeton, NJ: Princeton University Press, 1993), pp. 137–53.

22 Bellman, *The Language of Secrecy.*

23 de Jong, *Masquerades of Modernity.*

24 See S. Howe, *Afrocentrism: Mythical Pasts and Imagined Homes* (London and New York: Verso, 1998), pp. 69–72.

25 K. L. Sheppard, "The Lady and the Looking Glass: Margaret Murray's Life in Archaeology," Ph.D. dissertation, University of Oklahoma, 2011.

26 For UK-based societies, see *Ancient Egypt Magazine*, http://ancientegyptmagazine.com/society_contacts.htm; Popular Egyptology websites in English include http://www.egyptology.com; A. Byrnes and K. Phizackerley, "Welcome to Egyptological," http://www.egyptological.com; and J. Hill, "Ancient Egypt Online," http://www.ancientegyptonline.co.uk, none of which is affiliated with universities or museums or operated by individuals with higher degrees in the discipline (all websites last accessed April 8, 2013).

27 A useful survey of the background to Diop's work, and its subsequent impact, can be found in A. Kamugisha, "Finally in Africa? Egypt, from Diop to Celenko," *Race & Class* 45 (2003).

28 In particular, M. Bernal, *Black Athena: The Afroasiatic Roots of Classical Civilization*, Vol. 1, *The Fabrication of Ancient Greece 1785–1985* (New Brunswick, NJ: Rutgers University Press, 1987), Vol. 1, which appeared in 1987. Volumes 2 (1991) and 3 (2006) presented archaeological and linguistic evidence in support of the argument and were not as widely reviewed or discussed.

29 Among the numerous reviews and reactions to *Black Athena,* I single out the following as frequently cited, wide ranging, or (in the case of Young's articles) perceptive: J. L. Berlinerblau, *Heresy in the University: The "Black Athena" Controversy and the Responsibilities of American Intellectuals* (New Brunswick, NJ: Rutgers University Press, 1999); M. R. Lefkowitz, *Not out of Africa: How Afrocentrism Became an Excuse to Teach Myth as History* (New York: Basic Books, 1996); M. R. Lefkowitz and G. M. Rogers (eds.), *Black Athena Revisited* (Chapel Hill and London: University of North Carolina Press, 1996);

J. Peradotto (ed.), Special Issue: The Challenge of *Black Athena, Arethusa* 22 (1989); R.J.C. Young, "*Black Athena*: The Politics of Scholarship," *Science as Culture* 4 (1993); R.J.C. Young, "Egypt in America: *Black Athena*, Racism and Colonial Discourse," in A. Rattansi and S. Westwood (eds.), *Racism, Modernity and Identity: On the Western Front* (Cambridge: Polity Press, 1994); and most recently R.J.C. Young, "The Afterlives of *Black Athena*," in D. Orrells, G. K. Bhambra, and T. Roynon (eds.), *African Athena: New Agendas* (Oxford: Oxford University Press, 2011). Bernal himself responded to several years of ongoing debate in M. Bernal, *Black Athena Writes Back: Martin Bernal Responds to His Critics*, ed. D. C. Moore (Durham, NC: Duke University Press, 2006).

30 For an attempt to bridge the divide, see K. Exell (ed.), *Egypt in Its African Context: Proceedings of the Conference Held at the Manchester Museum, University of Manchester, 2–4 October 2009* (Oxford: Archaeopress, 2011).

31 There is a wide Afrocentric literature on initiation and secret knowledge, including the "negative confession" in *Book of the Dead*, spell 125: for one example, see the website of poet and musician Asar Imhotep, "West Africa and the 42 Declarations of Innocence," January 27, 2012, http://www.asarimhotep.com/index.php/articles/35-west-africa-and-the-42-declarations-of-innocence (last accessed April 8, 2013).

32 P. Brunton, *A Search in Secret Egypt* (London: Rider & Company, 1958 [first edition 1935]), p. 77.

33 See I. S. Moyer, *Egypt and the Limits of Hellenism* (Cambridge: Cambridge University Press, 2011), pp. 42–83.

34 J. Clifford, *The Predicament of Culture: Twentieth Century Ethnography, Literature and Art* (Cambridge, MA: Harvard University Press, 1988), pp. 21–91; de Jong, *Masquerades of Modernity*, pp. 185–94.

35 A notable exception is J. Baines, "Restricted Knowledge, Hierarchy, and Decorum: Modern Perceptions and Ancient Institutions," *Journal of the American Research Center in Egypt* 27 (1990). Opposition to the idea of secrecy or initiation can be found, among others, in S. Morenz, *Egyptian Religion* (Ithaca, NY: Cornell University Press, 1973), and Hornung, *The Secret Lore of Egypt.*

36 On cosmography as an area of priestly knowledge, see A. von Lieven, "Mysterien des Kosmos: Kosmographie und Priesterwissenschaft," in J. Assmann and M. Bommas (eds.), *Ägyptische Mysterien*? (Munich: Wilhelm Fink, 2002), and on the role of apprenticeship and knowledge acquisition in ancient Egypt more broadly, see W. Wendrich, "Introduction. Archaeology and Apprenticeship: Body Knowledge, Identity, and Communities of Practice," in W. Wendrich (ed.), *Archaeology and Apprenticeship: Body Knowledge, Identity, and Communities of Practice* (Tucson: University of Arizona Press, 2013).

37 Initiation rites are briefly mentioned in the catalogue: J. H. Taylor, *Journey through the Afterlife: Ancient Egyptian Book of the Dead* (London: British Museum Press, 2010), no. 209.

38 W. Federn, "The 'Transformations' in the Coffin Texts: A New Approach," *Journal of Near Eastern Studies* 19 (1960); compare T. DuQuesne, " 'Effective in Heaven and on Earth': Interpreting Egyptian Religious Practice for Both Worlds," in J. Assmann and M. Bommas (eds.), *Ägyptische Mysterien*? (Munich:

Wilhelm Fink, 2002). On Federn, see B. V. Bothmer, "A New Fragment of an Old Palette," *Journal of the American Research Center in Egypt* 8 (1969–70).

39 See G. Pinch, "Redefining Funerary Objects," in Z. Hawass (ed.), *Egyptology at the Dawn of the Twenty-First Century, Proceedings of the Eighth International Congress of Egyptologists, Cairo 2000,* Vol. 2, *History, Religion* (Cairo: American University in Cairo Press, 2003), for material evidence, and E. F. Wente, "Mysticism in Pharaonic Egypt?" *Journal of Near Eastern Studies* 41 (1982), for an influential consideration of textual sources; see also J. Assmann, "Death and Initiation in the Funerary Religion of Ancient Egypt," in J. P. Allen (ed.), *Religion and Philosophy in Ancient Egypt* (New Haven, CT: Yale University Press, 1989).

40 Compare R. Grieshammer, "Zum Sitz im Leben des negativen Sündenbekenntnisses," *Zeitschrift der Deutschen Morgenländischen Gesellschaft* Supplement II (1974), with the suggestion that temple gateways were specific locations for the recitation of the confession.

41 R. Merkelbach, "Ein griechisch-ägyptischer Priestereid und das Totenbuch," in *Religions en Égypte Hellénistique et Romaine. Colloque de Strasbourg, 16–18 Mai 1967* (Paris: Presses universitaires de France, 1969).

42 For the expression "to see the secrets," see the block statue of the priest Amenhotep, Cairo, Egyptian Museum CG 583, H 107.0 cm: L. Borchardt, *Statuen und Statuetten von Königen und Privatleuten*, Vol. 2, Catalogue général des antiquités égyptiennes (Berlin: Reichsdruckerei, 1925), pp. 134–39, pl. 100. "To see the horizon" appears on a Ptolemaic period statue of the stolist Wesirwer, Cairo, Egyptian Museum, JE 37134, H 34.0 cm: L. Coulon, "Un serviteur du sanctuaire de Chentayt à Karnak: La statue Caire JE 37134," *Bulletin de l'Institut Français d'Archéologie Orientale* 101 (2001), figs. 1–5.

43 J.-M. Kruchten, *Les annales des prêtres de Karnak* (*XXI–XXIIImes dynasties*) *et autres textes contemporains relatifs a l'initiation des prêtres d'Amon* (Leuven: Departement Oriëntalistiek, 1989), pp. 147–9.

44 See E. Graefe, *Untersuchungen zur Verwaltung und Geschichte der Institution der Gottesgemahlin des Amun vom Beginn des Neuen Reiches bis zur Spätzeit* (Wiesbaden: Harrassowitz, 1981), pp. 60–63.

45 See Kruchten, *Les annales des prêtres de Karnak,* pp. 246–56, who argues that lower ranks of priest, the *wab*-priests, were only admitted to the *akh-menu* on some occasions.

46 D. Laboury, "Archaeological and Textual Evidence for the Function of the 'Botanical Garden' of Karnak in the Initiation Ritual," in P. F. Dorman and B. M. Bryan (eds.), *Sacred Space and Sacred Function in Ancient Thebes* (Chicago: Oriental Institute, 2007); for the *akh-menu* blocks, which were discovered by Legrain in 1898, see Kruchten, *Les annales des prêtres de Karnak.*

47 See M. A. Stadler, "Procession," in W. Wendrich (ed.), *UCLA Encyclopedia of Egyptology* (Los Angeles: UCLA, 2008).

48 Karlshausen's studies of processional barques provide numerous examples, reconstructions, and discussion: C. Karlshausen, "L'évolution de la barque processionelle d'Amon à la 18e dynastie," *Revue d'Égyptologie* 46 (1995); C. Karlshausen, "L'iconographie des barques processionelles divines à la

Basse Epoque: Tradition et innovations," in W. Clarysse, A. Schoors, and H. Willems (eds.), *Egyptian Religion: The Last Thousand Years,* Part 2, *Studies Dedicated to the Memory of Jan Quaegebeur* (Leuven: Peeters, 1998); and C. Karlshausen, *L'iconographie de la barque processionelle divine en Égypte au Nouvel Empire* (Leuven, Paris, and Walpole, MA: Peeters, 2009), especially pp. 211–19 on the veiling of shrines, which she interprets in terms of symbolic protection; p. 284 on textual evidence for the veil, from the New Kingdom; and pp. 296–304 on the visibility (or otherwise) of the statue, with an emphasis on theological, not social, concerns. See also P. J. Brand, "A Graffito of Amen-Re in Luxor Temple Restored by the High Priest Menkheperre," in G. N. Knoppers and A. Hirsch (eds.), *Egypt, Israel, and the Ancient Mediterranean World: Studies in Honor of Donald B. Redford* (Leiden and Boston: Brill, 2004).

49 On *shesemu*: Karlshausen, *L'iconographie de la barque processionelle divine,* pp. 288–304; B. Ockinga, *Die Gottebenbildlichkeit im Alten Ägypten und im Alten Testament* (Wiesbaden: Harrassowitz, 1984), pp. 40–51. For oracles, see J. Černý, "Egyptian Oracles," in R. A. Parker (ed.), *A Saite Oracle Papyrus from Thebes in the Brooklyn Museum (Papyrus Brooklyn 47.218.3)* (Providence, RI: Brown University Press, 1962).

50 See P. J. Brand, "Veils, Votives, and Marginalia: The Use of Sacred Space at Karnak and Luxor," in P. F. Dorman and B. M. Bryan (eds.), *Sacred Space and Sacred Function in Ancient Thebes* (Chicago: Oriental Institute, 2007).

51 The significance of wrapping, layering, and secrecy in a number of west and central African religious traditions may offer useful insights into ancient Egyptian practices: see Nooter, *Secrecy: African Art that Conceals and Reveals,* especially the introductory essay (M. H. Nooter, "Introduction: The Aesthetics and Politics of Things Unseen"), T. O. Beidelman's essay, "Secrecy and Society: The Paradox of Knowing and the Knowing of Paradox," and the editorial discussion at pp. 53–54 and 142–43.

52 The Epigraphic Survey, *Temple of Khonsu,* Vol. 1, *Plates 1–110. Scenes of King Herihor in the Court* (Chicago: Oriental Institute, 1979), pl. 55. At Karnak temple, a patterned textile covers the bearers of a statue of Amun in ithyphallic form, shown standing on its own instead of in a shrine: H. H. Nelson and W. J. Murnane, *The Great Hypostyle Hall at Karnak,* Vol. 1, Part 1, *The Wall Reliefs* (Chicago: University of Chicago, 1981), pl. 159.

53 Karlshausen, *L'iconographie de la barque processionelle divine,* p. 242, citing a relief from Medinet Habu.

54 See T. DuQuesne, "Concealing and Revealing: The Problem of Ritual Masking in Ancient Egypt," *Discussions in Egyptology* 51 (2001); D. Meeks, "Dieu masqué, dieu sans tête," *Archéo-Nil* 1 (1991); D. Sweeney, "Egyptian Masks in Motion," *Göttinger Miszellen* 135 (1993); A. Wolinski, "Ancient Egyptian Ceremonial Masks," *Discussions in Egyptology* 6 (1986); and A. Wolinski, "Egyptian Masks: The Priest and His Role," *Archaeology* 40 (1987).

55 Hildesheim, Roemer-Pelizaeus Museum 1585, H 49.0 cm, W 27.0 cm; Manchester Museum 123, from el-Lahun: W.M.F. Petrie, F. L. Griffith, and P. Newberry, *Kahun, Gurob, and Hawara* (London: Kegan Paul, Trench, Trubner and Co., 1890), p. 28 ("mummers' masks"), pl. viii.27.

56 R. Nyord, *Breathing Flesh: Conceptions of the Body in the Ancient Egyptian Coffin Texts* (Copenhagen: Museum Tusculanum Press, 2009), pp. 157–59.

57 See, for instance, A. M. Roth, *Egyptian Phyles of the Old Kingdom* (Chicago: Oriental Institute of the University of Chicago, 1991), which addresses the Old Kingdom evidence, and for a translation and discussion of the Rosetta Stone decree, see R. B. Parkinson, *The Rosetta Stone* (London: British Museum Press, 2005).

58 H. P. Blavatsky, *Isis Unveiled: A Master-key to the Mysteries of Ancient and Modern Science and Technology* (Los Angeles: The Theosophy Company, 1975 [1877]).

59 Chicago, Oriental Institute Museum 10729: E. Teeter, *Ancient Egypt: Treasures from the Collection of the Oriental Institute, University of Chicago* (Chicago: Oriental Institute, 2003), pp. 71–72 (cat. 35); R. K. Ritner, "Denderite Temple Hierarchy and the Family of Theban High Priest Nebwenenef: Block Statue OIM 10729," in D. P. Silverman (ed.), *For His Ka: Essays Offered in Memory of Klaus Baer* (Chicago: Oriental Institute, 1994).

60 W.M.F. Petrie, *Qurneh* (London: School of Archaeology in Egypt, 1909), p. 114, pl. xlvii. The tomb of Nebwenenef is TT 157, for which see L. Bell, "Dira Abu el-Naga: The Monuments of the Ramesside High Priests of Amun and Some Related Officials," *Mitteilungen des Deutschen Archäologischen Instituts Kairo* 37 (1981); L. Bell, "In the Tombs of the High Priests of Amun," *Expedition* 15 (1973).

61 Compare S. Z. Balanda, "The title ḥry-sšt3 to the End of the New Kingdom," *Journal of the American Research Center in Egypt* 45 (2009); T. DuQuesne, "Anubis Master of Secrets (*ḥrj-sšt3*) and the Egyptian Conception of Mysteries," in A. Assmann and J. Assmann (eds.), *Schleier und Schwelle, II: Geheimnis und Offenbarung* (Munich: Wilhelm Fink, 1998); and K. T. Rydstrom, "ḤRY SŠT3 'in Charge of Secrets': The 3000-Year Evolution of a Title," *Discussions in Egyptology* 28 (1994).

62 See T. Derda, "Necropolis Workers in Graeco-Roman Egypt in the Light of the Greek Papyri," *Journal of Juristic Papyrology* 21 (1991), e.g., p. 21, n. 47, and for a mummy mask inscribed for a *hery-seshta* in the cult of the Buchis bull at Armant, see O. H. Myers and H. W. Fairman, "Excavations at Armant, 1929–31," *Journal of Egyptian Archaeology* 17 (1931), discussing British Museum EA 6969 at pp. 227–28, pls. 55, 57 center.

63 G. Vittmann, "Stolist," in W. Helck and E. Otto (eds.), *Lexikon der Ägyptologie,* Vol. 6 (Wiesbaden: Harrassowitz, 1986); Derda, "Necropolis Workers," pp. 21–22.

64 B. Grdseloff, "Le signe [*sm*] et le titre du stoliste," *Annales du Service des Antiquités d'Égypte* 43 (1943).

65 Cairo, Egyptian Museum JE 36918: R. el-Sayed, "Deux statues inédites du Musée du Caire," *Bulletin de l'Institut Français d'Archéologie Orientale* 84 (1984).

66 Cairo JE 37075, H 95.0 cm: H. W. Fairman, "A Statue from the Karnak Cache," *Journal of Egyptian Archaeology* 20 (1934); further information on the statue is available through the IFAO "Cachette de Karnak" database, http://www.ifao.egnet.net/bases/cachette/ (last accessed April 24, 2013).

67 On the nature of secret knowledge, see H. W. Fischer-Elfert, "Das verschwiegene Wissen des Iritsen (Stele Louvre C14)," in J. Assmann and M. Bommas (eds.), *Ägyptische Mysterien?* (Munich: Wilhelm Fink, 2002), and for a sixth-dynasty example of a priest and butcher who was "master of the secrets of darkness" in the cult of king Khufu, see H. G. Fischer, "Five Inscriptions of the Old Kingdom," *Zeitschrift für Ägyptische Sprache und Altertumskunde* 105 (1978), at pp. 56–57.

68 Louvre C14, probably from Abydos, H 117.0 cm: W. Barta, *Das Selbstzeug. nis eines altägyptischen Kunstlers (Stele Louvre C14)* (Berlin: Bruno Hessling, 1970); Fischer-Elfert, "Das verschwiegene Wissen des Iritsen."

69 C. Leitz, "Die beiden kryptographischen Inschriften aus Esna mit den Widdern und Krokodilen," *Studien zur Altägyptischen Kultur* 29 (2001); L. Morenz, "Schrift-Mysterium: Gottes-Schau in der visuellen Poesie von Esna—insbesondere zu den omnipotenten Widder-Zeichen zwischen Symbolik und Lesbarkeit," in J. Assmann and M. Bommas (eds.), *Ägyptische Mysterien?* (Munich: Wilhelm Fink, 2002).

70 J. Assmann, "Zur Ästhetik des Geheimnisses: Kryptographie als Kalligraphie im Alten Ägypten," in A. Assmann and J. Assmann (eds.), *Schleier und Schwelle, I: Geheimnis und Öffentlichkeit* (Munich: Wilhelm Fink, 1997).

71 E. Hornung and T. Abt, *The Egyptian Amduat: The Book of the Hidden Chamber* (Zurich: Living Human Heritage, 2007), pp. 251–57.

72 Hornung and Abt, *The Egyptian Amduat,* p. 269.

73 Hornung and Abt, *The Egyptian Amduat,* pp. 282–83, 290–91.

74 C. Manassa, "The Judgment Hall of Osiris in the Book of Gates," *Revue d'Égyptologie* 57 (2006), especially at p. 115.

75 After A. Piankhoff and N. Rambova, *The Tomb of Ramesses VI* (New York: Pantheon, 1954), p. 175. For the Book of Gates, see E. Hornung, A. Brodbeck, and E. Staehelin, *Das Buch von den Pforten des Jenseits* (Geneva: Éditions de Belles-Lettres, 1979–80); relevant discussion in J. C. Darnell, *The Enigmatic Netherworld Books of the Solar-Osirian Unity: Cryptographic Compositions in the Tombs of Tutankhamun, Ramesses VI and Ramesses IX* (Göttingen: Vandenhoeck & Ruprecht, 2004); and the detailed critical edition of the extant texts, J. Zeidler, *Pfortenbuchstudien, Teil 1* and *Teil 2* (Wiesbaden: Harrassowitz, 1999).

76 See A. Cabrol, *Les voies processionelles de Thèbes* (Leuven: Peeters, 2001), and Roman period examples in the towns and villages of the Fayum, in P. Davoli, "The Archaeology of the Fayum," in C. Riggs (ed.), *The Oxford Handbook of Roman Egypt* (Oxford: Oxford University Press, 2012).

77 For instance, the elevated, closed-off "beds" (*lits clos*) in the front rooms of houses at Deir el-Medina, discussed in L. Meskell, *Archaeologies of Social Life* (Oxford: Blackwell, 1999), pp. 99–102.

78 See E. A. Hastings, *The Sculpture from the Sacred Animal Necropolis at North Saqqara, 1964–76* (London: Egypt Exploration Society, 1997), pp. xxxii–xxxiv, and C. I. Green, *The Temple Furniture from the Sacred Animal Necropolis at North Saqqara, 1964–76* (London: Egypt Exploration Society, 1987), pp. 5–10 (nos. 1–6), 24–26 (nos. 45–51).

79 D. Summers, *Real Spaces: World Art History and the Rise of Western Modernism* (London: Phaidon, 2003), pp. 139–40.

80 J. Assmann, *Egyptian Solar Religion in the New Kingdom: Re, Amun and the Crisis of Polytheism* (London and New York: Kegan Paul International, 1995), p. 137.

81 T. Bennett, *The Birth of the Museum: History, Theory, Politics* (London: Routledge, 1985), and see discussion in A. Witcomb, *Re-imagining the Museum: Beyond the Mausoleum* (London: Routledge, 2003), pp. 13–18.

82 Thus also S. Macdonald, *Behind the Scenes at the Science Museum* (Oxford: Berg, 2002), pp. 250–53.

83 Macdonald, *Behind the Scenes*, pp. 9–12.

84 Goffman, *The Presentation of Self*, pp. 75–76 (on Simmel), 141 ("dark" secrets).

85 M. Taussig, *Defacement: Public Secrecy and the Labor of the Negative* (Stanford, CA: Stanford University Press, 1999).

86 R. Fletcher, "The Art of Forgetting: Imperialist Amnesia and Public Secrecy," *Third World Quarterly* 33 (2012).

87 E. Edwards and M. Mead, "Absent Histories and Absent Images: Photographs, Museums and the Colonial Past," *Museum & Society* 11 (2013).

88 For a nuanced analysis of Taussig's argument in relation to struggles against oppressive political regimes, see K. Surin, "The Sovereign Individual and Michael Taussig's Politics of Defacement," *Nepantla: Views from the South* 2 (2001).

89 The classic discussion is C. Duncan, *Civilizing Rituals: Inside Public Art Museums* (London and New York: Routledge, 1995), on which see also S. Macdonald, "Enchantment and Its Dilemmas: The Museum as a Ritual Site," in M. Bouquet and N. Porto (eds.), *Science, Magic and Religion: The Ritual Processes of Museum Magic* (New York and Oxford: Berghahn, 2006).

90 T. Guha-Thakurta, " 'Our Gods, Their Museums': The Contrary Careers of India's Art Objects," *Art History* 30 (2007); see also I. Gaskell, "Sacred to Profane and Back Again," in A. McClellan (ed.), *Art and Its Publics: Museum Studies at the Millennium* (Malden, MA, and Oxford: Blackwell, 2003), and C. Wingfield, "Touching the Buddha: Encounters with a Charismatic Object," in S. Dudley, *Museum Materialities: Objects, Engagements, Interpretations* (London and New York: Routledge, 2009).

Chapter 6 Sanctity

1 C. Duncan, *Civilizing Rituals: Inside Public Art Museums* (London and New York: Routledge, 1995).

2 M. Foucault, "Of Other Spaces," J. Miskowiec (trans.), *Diacritics* 16 (Spring 1986); anthologized as M. Foucault, "Texts/Contexts: Of Other Spaces," in D. Preziosi and C. Farago (eds.), *Grasping the World: The Idea of the Museum* (Aldershot: Ashgate, 2004).

3 See A. Witcomb, *Re-imagining the Museum: Beyond the Mausoleum* (London: Routledge, 2003), especially pp. 13–26, and S. Macdonald, "Enchantment and Its Dilemmas: The Museum as a Ritual Site," in M. Bouquet and N. Porto (eds.), *Science, Magic and Religion: The Ritual Processes of Museum Magic* (New York and Oxford: Berghahn, 2006).

4 E. Colla, *Conflicted Antiquities: Egyptology, Egyptomania, Egyptian Modernity* (Durham, NC: Duke University Press, 2007).

5 See C. Riggs, "Ancient Egypt in the Museum: Concepts and Constructions," in A. B. Lloyd (ed.), *A Companion to Ancient Egypt*, Vol. 2 (Oxford and Malden, MA: Wiley-Blackwell, 2010).

6 On the acquisition of the Young Memnon, see Colla, *Conflicted Antiquities*, pp. 24–66, and on the collection and display history of Egyptian antiquities in the British Museum, see S. Moser, *Wondrous Curiosities: Ancient Egypt at the British Museum* (London: Chicago University Press, 2006).

7 N.G.W. Curtis, "Human Remains: The Sacred, Museums, and Archaeology," *Public Archaeology* 3 (2003), offers a thoughtful and thought-provoking discussion that is relevant here and to much of what follows.

8 See M. Bouquet and N. Porto, "Introduction: Science, Magic, and Religion: The Ritual Processes of Museum Magic," in M. Bouquet and N. Porto (eds.), *Science, Magic and Religion: The Ritual Processes of Museum Magic* (New York and Oxford: Berghahn, 2006).

9 D. M. Reid, *Whose Pharaohs? Archaeology, Museums, and Egyptian National Identity from Napoleon to World War I* (Berkeley: University of California Press, 2002), p. 106.

10 J. Derrida, *Archive Fever: A Freudian Impression* (London and Chicago: University of Chicago Press, 1998), with discussion of etymology at p. 2.

11 B. Butler and M. Rowlands, "'The Man Who Would Be Moses,'" in R. Layton, S. Shennan, and P. Stone (eds.), *A Future for Archaeology: The Past in the Present* (Walnut Creek, CA: Left Coast Press, 2006). See also B. Butler, "Egypt: Constructed Exiles of the Imagination," in B. Bender and M. Winer (eds.), *Contested Landscapes: Movement, Exile and Place* (Oxford: Berg, 2001); B. Butler, "'Taking on a Tradition': African Heritage and the Testimony of Memory," in F. de Jong and M. Rowlands (eds.), *Reclaiming Heritage: Alternative Imaginaries of Memory in West Africa* (Walnut Creek, CA: Left Coast Press, 2007); and B. Butler, *Return to Alexandria: An Ethnography of Cultural Heritage Revivalism and Museum Memory* (Walnut Creek, CA: Left Coast Press, 2007).

12 On the design and construction of the museum, see D. M. Reid, "French Egyptology and the Architecture of Orientalism: Deciphering the Façade of Cairo's Egyptian Museum," in L. C. Brown and M. S. Gordon (eds.), *Franco–Arab Encounters: Studies in Memory of David C. Gordon* (Beirut: American University of Beirut, 1996); Reid, *Whose Pharaohs?* pp. 192–95; and C. Riggs, "Colonial Visions: Egyptian Antiquities and Contested Histories in the Cairo Museum," *Museum Worlds: Advances in Research* 1 (2013). The antiquities museum and other museums in Cairo are also discussed in D. Preziosi, *Brain of the Earth's Body: Art, Museums, and the Phantasms of Modernity* (London and Minneapolis: University of Minnesota Press, 2003), pp. 120–32, and W. Doyon,

"The Poetics of Egyptian Museum Practice," *British Museum Studies in Ancient Egypt and Sudan* 10 (2008).

13 P. Loti, *Egypt (La Mort de Philae)*, transl. W. P. Baines (New York: Duffield, 1909), chap. 4 (unpaginated), http://www.gutenberg.org/ebooks/3685 (last accessed June 26, 2012).

14 Tate Modern, *Exposed: Voyeurism, Surveillance and the Camera*, May 18 to October 3, 2010.

15 Preziosi, *Brain of the Earth's Body*, pp. 116–36.

16 Discussed in J. Sawday, *The Body Emblazoned: Dissection and the Human Body in Renaissance Culture* (London and New York: Routledge, 1995).

17 A. Cockburn et al., "A Classic Mummy: PUM II," in A. Cockburn, E. Cockburn, and T. A. Reyman (eds.), *Mummies, Disease and Ancient Cultures*, 2nd edition (Cambridge: Cambridge University Press, 1998 [1980]), pp. 73–74.

18 Cockburn et al., "A Classic Mummy."

19 The video of the 2009 scan is part of the University of Pennsylvania Museum's channel on YouTube, http://www.youtube.com/watch?v=oUaJsHLqMQU; see also Penn Museum "Egypt (Mummies) Gallery," http://www.penn.museum/long-term-exhibits/the-egyptian-mummy.html (both last accessed June 26, 2012). The *dura mater* fragment was sold through the website "Madame Talbot's Victorian and Gothic Lowbrow," which operates through eBay and its own website and is affiliated with an enterprise called Brennan Dalsgard Publishers in Oregon: see http://www.madametalbot.com/pix/exhibits/curio163.htm (last accessed June 26, 2012).

20 For instance, "Museum's Egyptian Mummies: Visit to HUP for CT-Scanning," University of Pennsylvania *Almanac* 55, no. 31, April 28, 2009, http://www.upenn.edu/almanac/volumes/v55/n31/mummies.html (last accessed April 24, 2013).

21 The Manchester unwrapping was filmed for BBC television, and photographs featured in a number of media sources and the publications David subsequently edited: see, for instance, A. R. David (ed.), *Manchester Museum Mummy Project* (Manchester: Manchester Museum, 1979), and A. R. David and E. Tapp (eds.), *Evidence Embalmed: Modern Medicine and the Mummies of Ancient Egypt* (Manchester: Manchester University Press, 1984). For a discussion of the 1970s unwrapping incorporating oral history accounts, see S.J.M.M. Alberti, "Molluscs, Mummies, and Moon Rock: The Manchester Museum and Manchester Science," *Manchester Region History Review* 18 (2007).

22 B. Latour, "On the Partial Existence of Existing and Nonexisting Objects," in L. Daston (ed.), *Biographies of Scientific Objects* (Chicago and London: University of Chicago Press, 2000), pp. 248–51; quoted text at p. 250.

23 On the mummy in popular culture, see J. Day, *The Mummy's Curse: Mummymania in the English-Speaking World* (London and New York: Routledge, 2006), and R. Luckhurst, *The Mummy's Curse: The True History of a Dark Fantasy* (Oxford: Oxford University Press, 2012), the latter with a focus on Victorian and Edwardian literature.

24 *The London Times*, May 29, 1890, p. 12, headed "The New Museum at Cairo."

25 R. M. Coury, "The Politics of the Funereal: The Tomb of Saad Zaghlul," *Journal of the American Research Center in Egypt* 29 (1992).

26 J. Cocteau, *Maalesh: Journal d'une tournée de théâtre* (Paris: Gallimard, 1949), p. 74: "C'est pourquoi un musée ne me semble pas sacrilège.... Ils ne se cachaient pas pour disparaître, mais pour attendre leur entrée en scène."

27 H. Miles, "Mummies at Rest," *The Middle East* 235 (1994), unpaginated.

28 See the museum's dedicated website, http://carlos.emory.edu/RAMESSES/ (last accessed June 26, 2012).

29 Nevine el-Aref, "A Hairy Tale for Ramses II," *Al-Ahram Weekly Online* 840 (April 12–18, 2007), http://weekly.ahram.org.eg/2007/840/eg2.htm (last accessed April 24, 2013). News coverage at the time of the arrest includes "Man Held for 'Pharaoh Relic' Sale," BBC News, November 29, 2006, http://news.bbc.co.uk/1/hi/world/europe/6195646.stm (last accessed April 24, 2013).

30 Rossella Lorenzi, "King Tut's Dad's Toe Returns Home," *Discovery News,* April 15, 2010, http://news.discovery.com/history/king-tuts-dads-toe-returns-home.html (last accessed June 26, 2012).

31 Presentation by Jane Marley of the Royal Cornwall Museum, at a June 2012 gathering of ACCES, the UK's professional association for curators of ancient Egyptian and Sudanese material, held at the Egypt Centre, Swansea, as reported at B. Rogers, Collecting Egypt, "More than Musty Mummies at the Egypt Center," http://collectingegypt.blogspot.co.uk/2012/06/more-than-musty-mummies-at-egypt-centre.html (last accessed June 30, 2012).

32 On these points, see also Day, *The Mummy's Curse,* pp. 34–35.

33 S. MacDonald, "Lost in Time and Space: Ancient Egypt in Museums," in S. MacDonald and M. Rice (eds.), *Consuming Ancient Egypt* (London: University of London Press, Institute of Archaeology, 2003); Day, *The Mummy's Curse,* pp. 78–81, 144–46.

34 Thus D. Wildung, "What Visitors Want to See," *Museum International* 47 (1995).

35 For British attitudes, see H. Kilmister, "Visitor Perceptions of Ancient Egyptian Human Remains in Three United Kingdom Museums," *Papers from the Institute of Archaeology* 14 (2003).

36 M. Fitzenreiter and C. E. Loeben (eds.), "Tote Menschen in einer Mumienausstellung: Was denkt das Publikum darüber? Erste Ergebnisse der Besucherbefragung durch die Ägyptologie-Studierenden der Humboldt-Universität in der Berliner Mumienasstellung," in *Die Ägyptische Mumie: Ein Phänomen der Kulturgeschichte* (Berlin: Seminar für Sudanarchäologie und Ägyptologie, 1998).

37 For discussion of issues relating to the display of human remains in museums, including a small focus group on responses to different kinds of remains, see M. M. Brooks and C. Rumsey, " 'Who Knows the Fate of His Bones?' Rethinking the Body on Display: Object, Art or Human Remains?" in S. J. Knell, S. MacLeod, and S. Watson (eds.), *Museum Revolutions: How Museums Change and Are Changed* (London and New York: Routledge, 2007); see also M. M. Brooks and C. Rumsey, "The Body in the Museum," in V. Cassmann, N. Odegaard, and

L. Powell (eds.), *Human Remains: A Guide for Conservators, Museums, Universities, and Law Enforcement Agencies* (Berkeley, CA: Altamira Press, 2006).

38 See, for instance, L. L. Peers and A. K. Brown (eds.), *Museums and Source Communities: A Routledge Reader* (London and New York: Routledge, 2003), and for issues of reburial and repatriation in particular, see C. Fforde, *Collecting the Dead: Archaeology and the Reburial Issue* (London: Duckworth, 2004); C. Fforde, J. Hubert, and P. Turnbull (eds.), *The Dead and Their Possessions: Repatriation in Principle, Policy and Practice* (London and New York: Routledge, 2004); and C. Fforde and J. Hubert, "Indigenous Human Remains and Changing Museum Ideology," in R. Layton, S. Shennan, and P. Stone (eds.), *A Future for Archaeology: The Past in the Present* (Walnut Creek, CA: Left Coast Press, 2006).

39 Museum Ethnographers Group, *Guidance Notes on Ethical Approaches in Museum Ethnography,* March 2003, and *Guidelines on Management of Human Remains,* first adopted 1991, revised 1994, available to download at the MEG website, http://www.museumethnographersgroup.org.uk/ (last accessed June 28, 2012).

40 Full text available at World Archaeological Congress, "World Archaeological Congress Codes of Ethics," http://www.worldarchaeologicalcongress.org/site/about_ethi.php (last accessed June 28, 2012).

41 The DCMS publication *Guidance for the Care of Human Remains in Museums* is available to download from the National Archives website, http://webarchive.nationalarchives.gov.uk/+/http://www.culture.gov.uk/reference_library/publications/3720.aspx. For the remit of the Human Tissue Authority, see http://www.hta.gov.uk/licensingandinspections/sectorspecificinformation/publicdisplay.cfm (both sites last accessed June 28, 2012).

42 Full text available at World Archaeological Congress, "World Archaeological Congress Codes of Ethics," http://www.worldarchaeologicalcongress.org/site/about_ethi.php.

43 T. Jenkins, *Contesting Human Remains in Museum Collections: The Crisis of Cultural Authority* (New York and London: Routledge, 2011), pp. 108 ("commitment to an empirical rationale"), 129–33 (discussion of "respect").

44 For an example of Aboriginal involvement in a museum exhibition in Geneva, see J. N. Gumbula, "'*Miny'tji waŋawuy Ŋarakawuy*': Paintings Are the Backbone of the Land and Sea," in R. Colombo Dougard and B. Müller (eds.), *Dream Traces: Australian Aboriginal Bark Paintings* (Geneva: Musée d'ethnographie de Genève, 2010) (a reference for which I thank Rachael Murphy), and for the Tropenmuseum, see D. van Duuren, *Physical Anthropology Reconsidered: Human Remains at the Tropenmuseum* (Amsterdam: Royal Tropical Institute/KIT, 2007). M. Bouquet, *Museums: A Visual Anthropology* (London and New York: Berg, 2012), pp. 153–61, discusses this and other examples of human remains repatriation.

45 On this mummy and its excavation, see C. Riggs, "Roman Mummy Masks from Deir el-Bahri," *Journal of Egyptian Archaeology* 86 (2000); C. Riggs, "Forms of the *wesekh* Collar in Funerary Art of the Graeco-Roman Period," *Chronique d'Égypte* 76 (2001); and the Brooklyn Museum of Art online database,

"Cartonnage and Mummy," http://www.brooklynmuseum.org/opencollection/objects/194065/Cartonnage_and_Mummy (last accessed June 30, 2012).

46 Recounted in a *New York Times* article about the rewrapping, in conjunction with the opening of a new gallery called "The Mummy's Chamber" at the Brooklyn Museum of Art in 2010: see T. Loos, "Melvin the Mummy's New Clothes," print edition May 9, 2010, online edition May 6, 2010, at http://www.nytimes.com/2010/05/09/arts/design/09mummies.html?_r=1 (last accessed June 28, 2012).

47 H. Szymańska and K. Babraj (eds.), *Mummy: Results of an Interdisciplinary Examination of the Egyptian Mummy of Aset-Iri-Khet-Es from the Archaeological Museum in Cracow* (Cracow: Polish Academy of Arts and Sciences, 2001); and see discussion in A. Wieczorkiewicz, "Unwrapping Mummies and Telling Their Stories: Egyptian Mummies and Museum Rhetoric," in M. Bouquet and N. Porto (eds.), *Science, Magic and Religion: The Ritual Processes of Museum Magic* (New York and Oxford: Berghahn, 2006), pp. 64–66.

48 K. Babraj, "The Ethics of Research on Mummified Human Remains," in H. Szymańska and K. Babraj (eds.), *Mummy: Results of an Interdisciplinary Examination of the Egyptian Mummy of Aset-Iri-Khet-Es from the Archaeological Museum in Cracow* (Cracow: Polish Academy of Arts and Sciences, 2001), p. 12.

49 The situation is treated in Jenkins, *Contesting Human Remains,* pp. 127–29, and see the museum's blog, Egypt at the Manchester Museum, "Covering the Mummies" (May 6, 2008), http://egyptmanchester.wordpress.com/2008/05/06/covering-the-mummies/. Coverage in the national press included M. Kennedy, "The Great Mummy Cover-Up," *Guardian,* May 23, 2008, http://www.guardian.co.uk/artanddesign/artblog/2008/may/23/maevkennedyfriampic (both sites last accessed June 30, 2012).

50 R. Machin, "Gender Representation in the Natural History Galleries at the Manchester Museum," *Museum & Society* 6 (2008).

51 Compare R. Vaswani, "Remains of the Day," *Museums Journal* 101 (2001).

52 See the summary and critique by T. Jenkins, "Peddling Ancient Prejudices about Egypt," *Spiked,* February 8, 2011, http://www.spiked-online.com/index.php/site/article/10172/ (last accessed June 28, 2012); also C. Riggs, "We've Been Here Before," *Times Higher Education,* February 24, 2011.

53 E.g., a post on January 30, 2011, Islamization Watch, "Egypt Crisis: Looters Destroy Mummies in Cairo Museum," at http://islamizationwatch.blogspot.co.uk/2011/01/egypt-crisis-looters-destroy-mummies-in.html (last accessed April 24, 2013).

54 M. Baba and S. Yoshimura, "Dahshur North: Intact Middle and New Kingdom Coffins," *Egyptian Archaeology* 37 (2010).

55 For the application of this technique at Manchester Museum and the University of Manchester, see K. Wildsmith, "Endoscopy and Mummy Research," in R. David (ed.), *Egyptian Mummies and Modern Science* (Cambridge: Cambridge University Press, 2008).

56 Wieczorkiewicz, "Unwrapping Mummies," especially at pp. 54–56.

57 Photograph: Zahi Hawass, "Dr. Hawass Examines the Mummy of King Tutankhamun," http://www.drhawass.com/photoblog/dr-hawass-examines-mummy-king-tutankhamun; press release: Zahi Hawass, "Press Release—Tutankhamun CT Scan" (March 8, 2005), http://www.drhawass.com/blog/press-release-tutankhamun-ct-scan (last accessed June 26, 2012).

58 J. Marchant, "Ancient DNA: Curse of the Pharaoh's DNA," *Nature* 472 (2011), offers a balanced overview with references to scientific papers.

59 See coverage online at Guardian's Egypt, "Tutankhamun Facial Reconstruction" (May 10, 2005), http://www.guardians.net/hawass/Press_Release_05-05_Tut_Reconstruction.htm, and the National Geographic website, T. Chamberlain, "Photo in the News: King Tut's Face Reconstructed" (May 10, 2005), http://news.nationalgeographic.com/news/2005/05/0510_051005_tutsface.html, with further internal links (both sites last accessed June 28, 2012).

60 For an Afrocentric response, see M. Ampim, Africana Studies, "2005 Update: Tutankhamun Fraud Alert!" (June 2005), http://libtv.com/Manu/king_tut_fraud.htm (last accessed June 28, 2012). Self-identified conservative sites emphasized the "European" results of the DNA profile; see H. Wallace, Occidental Dissent, "Black History Month 2012: DNA Test Results Show King Tut Wasn't Black" (February 1, 2012), http://www.occidentaldissent.com/2012/02/01/black-history-month-2012-king-tut-wasnt-black/ and Council of Conservative Citizens, "Black History Month Myth of the Day: King Tut" (February 2, 2013), http://topconservativenews.com/2013/02/egyptian-minister-of-antiquities-rebukes-american-black-supremacists/ (last accessed April 24, 2013).

61 T. Keenan and E. Weizman, *Mengele's Skull: The Advent of Forensic Aesthetics* (Berlin: Sternberg Press, 2012).

62 Keenan and Weizman, *Mengele's Skull,* p. 67.

63 See C. Wilkinson, *Forensic Facial Reconstruction* (Cambridge: Cambridge University Press, 2008).

64 Quoted and discussed in Wieczorkiewicz, "Unwrapping Mummies," pp. 60–61.

65 See National Museums Scotland, "The Qurna Burial," http://www.nms.ac.uk/highlights/objects_in_focus/qurna_burial.aspx (last accessed June 30, 2012). On the racial or ethnic connotations of the find, see also B. Manley, "Petrie's Revolution: The Case of the Qurneh Queen," in K. Exell (ed.), *Egypt in Its African Context: Proceedings of the Conference Held at the Manchester Museum, University of Manchester, 2–4 October 2009* (Oxford: Archaeopress, 2011). Petrie's report of the burial, and the unwrapping of the mummy: W.M.F. Petrie, *Qurneh* (London: School of Archaeology in Egypt, 1909), pp. 6–10, pls. 22–29.

66 Wilkinson, *Forensic Facial Reconstruction,* p. 198 fig. 6.27.

67 See National Museums Scotland, "Iufenamun, the Mummy Priest," http://www.nms.ac.uk/highlights/objects_in_focus/iufenamun_the_mummy_priest.aspx (last accessed June 30, 2012), and Wilkinson, *Forensic Facial Reconstruction,* p. 198 fig. 6.27.

68 M. A. Murray, *The Tomb of Two Brothers* (Manchester: Sherratt & Hughes, 1910), pp. 15–16 (statuettes), 36–37 (skulls, with "biography" of mother).

69 David (ed.), *Manchester Museum Mummy Project,* pp. 149–57 (reconstructions and discussion by R.A.H. Neave); J. Prag and R. Neave, *Making Faces: Using*

Forensic and Archaeological Evidence (London: British Museum Press, 1997), pp. 41–48.

70 See also Riggs, "Ancient Egypt in the Museum," p. 1147, and Wieczorkiewicz, "Unwrapping Mummies," p. 62.

71 "Unravelled" was the title of the solo exhibition at the Whitechapel and Dodd gallery in London, where the *Mummy Boy* series of works premiered in May 2008: see Angela Spalmer, "Unravelled" (May 21, 2008), http://www.angelaspalmer.com/2008/05/unravelled/. For the museum catalogue of the exhibition, see A. Palmer, *Unravelled: The Journey of an Egyptian Child Mummy and Other Portraits* (London: Waterhouse & Dodd, n.d.), available at http://www.angelaspalmer.com/wp-content/uploads/2011/09/Palmer_unravelled.pdf (both last accessed April 24, 2013). The present Ashmolean display allows visitors to move around the sculpture, but not with as much space as other installations have done, thus diminishing somewhat the effect.

72 H. W. Fischer-Elfert, *Die Vision von der Statue im Stein: Studien zum altägyptischen Mundöffnungsritual* (Heidelberg: C. Winter, 1998).

73 For instance, the stela of the chief sculptor Hatiay from Abydos, from the nineteenth dynasty. Leiden, Rijksmuseum van Oudheden, VI: H. Willems, "The One and the Many in Stela Leiden VI," *Chronique d'Égypte* 73 (1998); J.-M. Kruchten, *Les annales des prêtres de Karnak (XXI–XXIIImes dynasties) et autres textes contemporains relatifs a l'initiation des prêtres d'Amon* (Leuven: Departement Oriëntalistiek, 1989), pp. 192–93. For the House of Gold, see A. von Lieven, "Bemerkungen zum Dekorationsprogramme des Osireion in Abydos," in B. Haring and A. Klug (eds.), *6. Ägyptologische Tempeltagung: Funktion und Gebrauch altägyptischer Tempelräume* (Wiesbaden: Harrassowitz, 2007). L. Coulon, "Le sanctuaire de Chentayt à Karnak," in *Egypt at the Dawn of the Twenty-First Century* (Cairo and New York: American University in Cairo Press, 2002), points out the interchangeability of "House (or Mansion) of Gold" with the "House of Chentayt" (a goddess identified with the mourning Isis), the "House of the Living-of-forms," the "Mansion of Reinvigoration," or the "Secret Chamber." The "House of Gold" was also the name of the quarry that yielded the best quality Egyptian alabaster, a type of travertine valued for its translucence and its luminescent white-gold color—a name that survives today as Hatnub.

74 Fischer-Elfert, *Die Vision von der Statue,* especially pp. 8–16.

75 L. Meskell, "Sites of Violence: Terrorism, Tourism, and Heritage in the Archaeological Present," in L. Meskell and P. Pels (eds.), *Embedding Ethics* (Oxford and New York: Berg, 2005).

76 J. Fabian, *Time and the Other: How Anthropology Makes Its Object* (New York: Columbia University Press, 1983).

77 W. Wendrich, "From Practical Knowledge to Empowered Communication: Field Schools of the Supreme Council of Antiquities in Egypt," in R. Boytner, L. S. Dodd, and B. J. Parker (eds.), *Controlling the Past, Owning the Future: The Political Uses of Archaeology in the Middle East* (Tucson: University of Arizona Press, 2010), and other papers in the same volume: R. Boytner, L. S. Dodd, and B. J. Parker (eds.), *Controlling the Past, Owning the Future: The Political Uses of Archaeology in the Middle East* (Tucson: University of Arizona Press, 2010).

See also M. Liebmann and U. Z. Rizvi (eds.), *Archaeology and the Postcolonial Critique* (Lanham, MD: AltaMira Press, 2008).

78 Y. Hamilakis, "We Are All Middle Easterners Now: Globalization, Immanence, Archaeology," in R. Boytner, L. S. Dodd, and B. J. Parker (eds.), *Controlling the Past, Owning the Future: The Political Uses of Archaeology in the Middle East* (Tucson: University of Arizona Press, 2010), p. 220.

79 Meskell, "Sites of Violence," p. 145.

80 On the rights of scientists, compare J. Marks, "Your Body, My Property: The Problem of Colonial Genetics in a Postcolonial World," in L. Meskell and P. Pels (eds.), *Embedding Ethics* (Oxford and New York: Berg, 2005), especially pp. 38–42.

81 I. M. Kaufmann and F. J. Rühli, "Without 'Informed Consent'? Ethics and Ancient Mummy Research," *Journal of Medical Ethics* 36 (2010).

82 An example specifically concerned with Egyptian mummies: W. Seipel, "Mumien und Ethik im Museum," in W. Seipel (ed.), *Mumien aus dem Alten Ägypten: Zur Mumienforschung im Kunsthistorischen Museum* (Milan: Skira, 1998).

83 See R. Beier-de Haan, "Re-staging Histories and Identities," in S. Macdonald (ed.), *A Companion to Museum Studies* (Malden, MA, and Oxford: Wiley-Blackwell, 2006), and discussion in S. Macdonald, *Difficult Heritage: Negotiating the Nazi Past in Nuremberg and Beyond* (London and New York: Routledge, 2008), pp. 186–92 (especially pp. 191–92). The expression "against the grain" is indebted to A. L. Stoler, *Along the Archival Grain: Epistemic Anxieties and Colonial Common Sense* (Princeton, NJ: Princeton University Press, 2009).

84 B. Wastiau, "The Scourge of Chief Kansabala: The Ritual Life of Two Congolese Masterpieces at the Royal Museum of Central Africa (1884–2001)," in M. Bouquet and N. Porto (eds.), *Science, Magic and Religion: The Ritual Processes of Museum Magic* (New York and Oxford: Berghahn, 2006), quoted text at p. 112.

85 Thus also W. Wendrich, "Epilogue: Eternal Egypt Deconstructed," in W. Wendrich (ed.), *Egyptian Archaeology* (Malden, MA, and Oxford: Wiley-Blackwell, 2010).

REFERENCES

Abu el-Haj, N., *Facts on the Ground: Archaeological Practice and Territorial Self-Fashioning in Israeli Society,* Chicago and London: University of Chicago Press, 2001.

Aksamit, J., "Room C in the Temple of Tuthmosis III at Deir el-Bahari," in B. Haring and A. Klug (eds.), *6. Ägyptologische Tempeltagung: Funktion und Gebrauch Altägyptischer Tempelräume,* Wiesbaden: Harrassowitz, 2007, pp. 1–10.

Alberti, S.J.M.M., "Molluscs, Mummies and Moon Rock: The Manchester Museum and Manchester Science," *Manchester Region History Review* 18 (2007), pp. 130–54.

Allen, S. J., "Spinning Bowls: Representation and Reality," in J. Phillips (ed.), *Ancient Egypt, the Aegean, and the Near East: Studies in Honour of Martha Rhoads Bell,* San Antonio, TX: Van Siclen Books, 1997, pp. 17–38.

Allgrove-McDowell, J., "Ancient Egypt, 5000–332 BC," in D. T. Jenkins (ed.), *The Cambridge History of Western Textiles,* Cambridge: Cambridge University Press, 2003, pp. 30–39.

Altenmüller, H., "Geheimnis," in W. Helck and E. Otto (eds.), *Lexikon der Ägyptologie,* Vol. 2, Wiesbaden: Harrassowitz, 1977, cols. 510–13.

Alvarez-Mon, J., *The Arjan Tomb: At the Crossroads of the Elamite and the Persian Empires,* Leuven: Peeters, 2010.

Appadurai, A. (ed.), *The Social Life of Things: Commodities in Cultural Perspective,* Cambridge: Cambridge University Press, 1986.

Asad, T. (ed.), *Anthropology and the Colonial Encounter,* London: Ithaca Press, 1973.

Assmann, J., "Collective Memory and Cultural Identity," *New German Critique* 65 (1995), pp. 125–31.

Assmann, J., "Death and Initiation in the Funerary Religion of Ancient Egypt," in J. P. Allen (ed.), *Religion and Philosophy in Ancient Egypt,* New Haven, CT: Yale University Press, 1989, pp. 135–59.

Assmann, J., *Death and Salvation in Ancient Egypt,* Ithaca, NY, and London: Cornell University Press, 2005.

Assmann, J., *Egyptian Solar Religion in the New Kingdom: Re, Amun and the Crisis of Polytheism,* London and New York: Kegan Paul International, 1995.

Assmann, J., "Jehova-Isis: The Mysteries of Egypt and the Quest for Natural Religion in the Age of Enlightenment," in I. A. Bierman (ed.), *Egypt and the Fabrication of European Identity,* Los Angeles: UCLA, Center for Near Eastern Studies, 1995, pp. 36–83.

Assmann, J., "Kollektives Gedächtnis und kulturelle Identität," in J. Assmann and T. Hölscher (eds.), *Kultur und Gedächtnis,* Frankfurt: Suhrkamp, 1988, pp. 1–19.

Assmann, J., *Das kulturelle Gedächtnis: Schrift, Erinnerung und politische Identität in frühen Hochkulturen,* Munich: Beck, 1992.

Assmann, J., *Religion and Cultural Memory,* Stanford, CA: Stanford University Press, 2006.

Assmann, J., *Das verschleierte Bild zu Sais: Schillers Ballade und ihre griechischen und ägyptischen Hintergründe,* Stuttgart and Leipzig: B. G. Teubner, 1999.

Assmann, J., *Weisheit und Mysterium: Das Bild der Griechen von Ägypten,* Munich: C. H. Beck, 2000.

Assmann, J., "Zur Ästhetik des Geheimnisses: Kryptographie als Kalligraphie im Alten Ägypten," in A. Assmann and J. Assmann (eds.), *Schleier und Schwelle, I: Geheimnis und Öffentlichkeit,* Munich: Wilhelm Fink, 1997, pp. 313–27.

Aufrère, S., *Le propylône d'Amon-Rê-Montou à Karnak-Nord,* Cairo: Institut Français d'Archéologie Orientale, 2000.

Baba, M., and S. Yoshimura, "Dahshur North: Intact Middle and New Kingdom Coffins," *Egyptian Archaeology* 37 (2010), pp. 9–12.

Babraj, K., "The Ethics of Research on Mummified Human Remains," in H. Szymańska and K. Babraj (eds.), *Mummy: Results of an Interdisciplinary Examination of the Egyptian Mummy of Aset-Iri-Khet-Es from the Archaeological Museum in Cracow,* Cracow: Polish Academy of Arts and Sciences, 2001, pp. 11–21.

Backes, B., *Rituelle Wirklichkeit: Über Erscheinung und Wirkungsbereich des Webergottes Hedjhotep und den gedanklichen Umgang mit einer Gottes-Konzeption im Alten Ägypten,* Turnhout: Brepols, 2001.

Backes, B., "Von nun an sollt ihr *Rḥti* heißen: Die 'Beiden Kolleginnen' von Sais," *Göttinger Miszellen* 180 (2001), pp. 23–28.

Bahrani, Z., *The Graven Image: Representation in Babylonia and Assyria,* Philadelphia: University of Pennsylvania Press, 2003.

Baines, J., "*Egyptology and the Social Sciences:* Thirty Years On," in A. Verbovsek, B. Backes, and C. Jones (eds.), *Methodik und Didaktik in der Ägyptologie: Herausforderungen eines kulturwissenschaftlichen Paradigmenwechsels in den Altertumswissenschaften,* Munich: Wilhelm Fink, 2011, pp. 573–97.

Baines, J., *Fecundity Figures,* Oxford: Griffith Institute, 2001 [1985].

Baines, J., "Restricted Knowledge, Hierarchy, and Decorum: Modern Perceptions and Ancient Institutions," *Journal of the American Research Center in Egypt* 27 (1990), pp. 1–23.

Baines, J., *Visual and Written Culture in Ancient Egypt,* Oxford: Oxford University Press, 2007.

Baines, J., and P. Lacovara, "Burial and the Dead in Ancient Egyptian Society: Respect, Formalism, Neglect," *Journal of Social Archaeology* 2 (2002), pp. 5–36.

Baines, J., and C. Riggs, "Archaism and Kingship: A Late Royal Statue and Its Early Dynastic Model," *Journal of Egyptian Archaeology* 87 (2001), pp. 103–18.

Baines, P., *Linen: Hand Spinning and Weaving,* London: B. T. Batsford, 1989.

Balanda, S. Z., "The Title ḥry-sštꜣ to the End of the New Kingdom," *Journal of the American Research Center in Egypt* 45 (2009), pp. 319–48.

Banerjee, M., and D. Miller, *The Sari,* Oxford: Berg, 2003.

Barber, E.J.W., *Prehistoric Textiles: The Development of Cloth in the Neolithic and Bronze Ages,* Princeton, NJ: Princeton University Press, 1991.

Barrell, J., "Death on the Nile: Fantasy and the Literature of Tourism, 1840–1860," *Essays in Criticism* 41 (1991), pp. 97–127.

Barta, W., *Aufbau und Bedeutung der altägyptischen Opferformel,* Glückstadt: J. J. Augustin, 1968.

Barta, W., *Das Selbstzeugnis eines altägyptischen Kunstlers (Stele Louvre C14)*, Berlin: Bruno Hessling, 1970.

Barth, F., *Ritual and Knowledge among the Baktaman of New Guinea*, New Haven, CT: Yale University Press, 1975.

Baum, N., "*Sntr:* Une révision," *Revue d'Égyptologie* 45 (1994), pp. 17–39.

Beidelman, T. O., "Secrecy and Society: The Paradox of Knowing and the Knowing of Paradox," in M. H. Nooter (ed.), *Secrecy: African Art that Conceals and Reveals*, Munich: Prestel, 1993, pp. 41–47.

Beier-de Haan, R., "Re-staging Histories and Identities," in S. Macdonald (ed.), *A Companion to Museum Studies*, Malden, MA, and Oxford: Wiley-Blackwell, 2006, pp. 186–97.

Bell, L., "Dira Abu el-Naga: The Monuments of the Ramesside High Priests of Amun and Some Related Officials," *Mitteilungen des Deutschen Archäologischen Instituts Kairo* 37 (1981), pp. 51–62.

Bell, L., "In the Tombs of the High Priests of Amun," *Expedition* 15 (1973), pp. 17–27.

Bellman, B., *The Language of Secrecy: Symbols and Metaphors in Poro Ritual*, New Brunswick, NJ: Rutgers University Press, 1984.

Bénédite, G., *Miroirs*, Catalogue général des antiquités égyptiennes, Cairo: Institut Français d'Archéologie Orientale, 1907.

Bennett, T., *The Birth of the Museum: History, Theory, Politics*, London: Routledge, 1985.

Bennett, T., "Museum, Field, Colony: Colonial Governmentality and the Circulation of Reference," *Journal of Cultural Economy* 2 (2009), pp. 99–116.

Berlinerblau, J. T., *Heresy in the University: The "Black Athena" Controversy and the Responsibilities of American Intellectuals*, New Brunswick, NJ: Rutgers University Press, 1999.

Bernal, M., *Black Athena: The Afroasiatic Roots of Classical Civilization*, Vol. 1, *The Fabrication of Ancient Greece 1785–1985*, New Brunswick, NJ: Rutgers University Press, 1987.

Bernal, M., *Black Athena: The Afroasiatic Roots of Classical Civilization*, Vol. 2, *The Archaeological and Documentary Evidence*, New Brunswick, NJ: Rutgers University Press, 1991.

Bernal, M., *Black Athena: The Afroasiatic Roots of Classical Civilization*, Vol. 3, *The Linguistic Evidence*, New Brunswick, NJ: Rutgers University Press, 2006.

Bernal, M., *Black Athena Writes Back: Martin Bernal Responds to His Critics*, ed. D. C. Moore, Durham, NC: Duke University Press, 2006.

Bernasconi, R., "Black Skin, White Skulls: The Nineteenth Century Debate over the Racial Identity of the Ancient Egyptians," *Parallax* 13 (2007), pp. 6–20.

Bhabha, H. K., *The Location of Culture*, London and New York: Routledge, 1994.

Bhopal, R., "The Beautiful Skull and Blumenbach's Errors," *British Medical Journal* 335 (2007), pp. 1308–9.

Bisson de la Roque, F., *Tôd (1934 à 1936)*, Cairo: Institut Français d'Archéologie Orientale, 1937.

Blackman, A. M., and H. W. Fairman, "The Myth of Horus at Edfu—II," *Journal of Egyptian Archaeology* 29 (1943), pp. 2–36.

Blavatsky, H. P., *Isis Unveiled: A Master-key to the Mysteries of Ancient and Modern Science and Technology*, Los Angeles: Theosophy, 1975 [1877].

Blumenbach, J. F., *The Anthropological Treatises of Johann Friedrich Blumenbach*, London: Longman, Green, Longman, Roberts & Green, 1865.

Bochi, P. A., "Of Lines, Linen, and Language: A Study of a *Patterned* Textile and Its Interweaving with Egyptian Beliefs," *Chronique d'Égypte* 71 (1996), pp. 221–53.

Boehmer, E., *Colonial and Postcolonial Literature*, 2nd edition, Oxford: Oxford University Press, 2005.

Bohrer, F. N., *Orientalism and Visual Culture: Imagining Mesopotamia in Nineteenth-Century Europe*, Cambridge: Cambridge University Press, 2003.

Bolle, K. W., "Secrecy in Religion," in K. W. Bolle (ed.), *Secrecy in Religions*, Leiden: E. J. Brill, 1987, pp. 1–24.

Bonnet, H., *Reallexikon der ägyptischen Religionsgeschichte*, Berlin: De Gruyter, 1952.

Borchardt, L., *Statuen und Statuetten von Königen und Privatleuten*, Vol. 2, Catalogue général des antiquités égyptiennes, Berlin: Reichsdruckerei, 1925.

Borghouts, J. F., *Ancient Egyptian Magical Texts*, Leiden: E. J. Brill, 1978.

Bothmer, B. V., "A New Fragment of an Old Palette," *Journal of the American Research Center in Egypt* 8 (1969–70), pp. 5–8.

Bouquet, M., *Museums: A Visual Anthropology*, London and New York: Berg, 2012.

Bouquet, M., and N. Porto, "Introduction: Science, Magic and Religion: The Ritual Processes of Museum Magic," in M. Bouquet and N. Porto (eds.), *Science, Magic and Religion: The Ritual Processes of Museum Magic*, New York and Oxford: Berghahn, 2006, pp. 1–25.

Bowden, H., *Mystery Cults in the Ancient World*, London: Thames and Hudson, 2010.

Boytner, R., L. S. Dodd, and B. J. Parker (eds.), *Controlling the Past, Owning the Future: The Political Uses of Archaeology in the Middle East*, Tucson: University of Arizona Press, 2010.

Brack, A., and A. Brack, *Das Grab des Haremheb (Theben Nr. 78)*, Mainz: Philipp von Zabern, 1980.

Brand, P. J., "A Grafitto of Amen-Re in Luxor Temple Restored by the High Priest Menkheperre," in G. N. Knoppers and A. Hirsch (eds.), *Egypt, Israel, and the Ancient Mediterranean World: Studies in Honor of Donald B. Redford*, Leiden and Boston: Brill, 2004, pp. 257–66.

Brand, P. J., "Veils, Votives, and Marginalia: The Use of Sacred Space at Karnak and Luxor," in P. F. Dorman and B. M. Bryan (eds.), *Sacred Space and Sacred Function in Ancient Thebes*, Chicago: Oriental Institute, 2007, pp. 51–83.

Brett-Smith, S., "The Knowledge of Women," in M. Westerman (ed.), *Anthropologies of Art*, Winstown, MA: Sterling and Francine Clark Institute, distributed by Yale University Press, 2005, pp. 143–63.

Brier, B., *The Murder of Tutankhamen: A 3000-year-old Murder Mystery*, London: Weidenfeld & Nicolson, 1998.

Brooks, M. M., and C. Rumsey, "The Body in the Museum," in V. Cassmann, N. Odegaard, and L. Powell (eds.), *Human Remains: A Guide for Conservators, Museums, Universities, and Law Enforcement Agencies*, Berkeley, CA: Altamira Press, 2006, pp. 261–89.

Brooks, M. M., and C. Rumsey, "'Who Knows the Fate of His Bones?' Rethinking the Body on Display: Object, Art or Human Remains?" in S. J. Knell, S. MacLeod, and S. Watson (eds.), *Museum Revolutions: How Museums Change and Are Changed*, London and New York: Routledge, 2007, pp. 343–54.

Brunner, H., *Die südlichen Räume des Tempels von Luxor*, Mainz: Philipp von Zabern, 1977.

Brunton, G., *Qau and Badari I*, London: British School of Archaeology in Egypt, 1927.

Brunton, P., *A Search in Secret Egypt*, London: Rider, 1958 [first edition 1935].

Bruyère, B., *Rapport sur les fouilles de Deir el Médineh (1923–1924)*, Cairo: Institut Français d'Archéologie Orientale, 1925.

Bruyère, B., *Rapport sur les fouilles de Deir el Médineh (1928)*, Cairo: Institut Français d'Archéologie Orientale, 1929.

Bruyère, B., *Rapport sur les fouilles de Deir el Médineh (1930)*, Cairo: Institut Français d'Archéologie Orientale, 1933.

Bruyère, B., *Rapport sur les fouilles de Deir el Médineh (1934–35)*, Cairo: Institut Français d'Archéologie Orientale, 1937.

Bull, L., "Four Egyptian Inscribed Statuettes of the Middle Kingdom," *Journal of the American Oriental Society* 56 (1936), pp. 166–72.

Burchardt, M., "Ein saitischer Statuensockel in Stockholm," *Zeitschrift für Ägyptische Sprache und Altertumskunde* 47 (1910), pp. 111–15.

Burke III, E., and D. Prochaska, "Introduction: Orientalism from Postcolonial Theory to World Theory," in E. Burke III and D. Prochaska (eds.), *Genealogies of Orientalism: History, Theory, Politics*, Lincoln, NE, and London: University of Nebraska Press, 2008, pp. 1–74.

Burstein, S. M., "Commentary," in I. A. Bierman (ed.), *Egypt and the Fabrication of European Identity*, Los Angeles: UCLA, Center for Near Eastern Studies, 1995, pp. 87–95.

Butchart, A., *The Anatomy of Power: European Constructions of the African Body*, London and New York: Zed Books, 1998.

Butler, B., "Egypt: Constructed Exiles of the Imagination," in B. Bender and M. Winer (eds.), *Contested Landscapes: Movement, Exile and Place*, Oxford: Berg, 2001, pp. 303–18.

Butler, B., *Return to Alexandria: An Ethnography of Cultural Heritage Revivalism and Museum Memory*, Walnut Creek, CA: Left Coast Press, 2007.

Butler, B., "'Taking on a Tradition': African Heritage and the Testimony of Memory," in F. de Jong and M. Rowlands (eds.), *Reclaiming Heritage: Alternative Imaginaries of Memory in West Africa*, Walnut Creek, CA: Left Coast Press, 2007, pp. 31–69.

Butler, B., and M. Rowlands, "'The Man Who Would Be Moses,'" in R. Layton, S. Shennan, and P. Stone (eds.), *A Future for Archaeology: The Past in the Present*, Walnut Creek, CA: Left Coast Press, 2006, pp. 97–105.

Cabrol, A., *Les voies processionnelles de Thèbes*, Leuven: Peeters, 2001.

Calverley, A. M., *The Temple of King Sethos I at Abydos*, Vol. 1, *The Chapels of Osiris, Isis and Horus*, London: Egypt Exploration Society; Chicago: Oriental Institute of the University of Chicago, 1933.

Calverley, A. M., *The Temple of King Sethos I at Abydos*, Vol. 2, *The Chapels of Amun-Re, Re-Harakhti, Ptah, and King Sethos*, London: Egypt Exploration Society; Chicago: Oriental Institute of the University of Chicago, 1935.

Caminos, R. A., *Semna-Kumma II: The Temple of Kumma*, London: Egypt Exploration Society, 1998.

Capart, J., "Bandelettes et linges de momie," *Bulletin des Musées Royaux d'Art et d'Histoire* 13 (1941), pp. 26–27.

Carnarvon, The Earl of, and H. Carter, *Five Years' Explorations at Thebes*, London: Henry Frowde, Oxford University Press, 1912.

Carter, H., "Report on the Tomb of Mentuhotep Ist at Deir El-Bahari, known as Bab El-Hoçan," *Annales du Service des Antiquités d'Égypte* 2 (1901), pp. 201–5.

Carter, H., *The Tomb of Tut-Ankh-Amen,* London: Sphere, 1972 [1933].

Carter, H., and A. H. Gardiner, "The Tomb of Ramesses IV and the Turin Plan of a Royal Tomb," *Journal of Egyptian Archaeology* 4 (1917), pp. 130–58.

Cartwright, C., H. Granger-Taylor, and S. Quirke, "Lahun Textile Evidence in London," in S. Quirke (ed.), *Lahun Studies,* Reigate: SIA, 1998, pp. 92–107.

Castel, G., and G. Soukiassian, "Les mines de galene pharaoniques du Gebel el-Zeit (Égypte)," *Bulletin de la Societé Française d'Égyptologie* 112 (1988), pp. 37–53.

Černý, J., "Egyptian Oracles," in R. A. Parker (ed.), *A Saite Oracle Papyrus from Thebes in the Brooklyn Museum (Papyrus Brooklyn 47.218.3),* Providence, RI: Brown University Press, 1962, pp. 35–48.

Černý, J., "Studies in the Chronology of the Twenty-First Dynasty," *Journal of Egyptian Archaeology* 32 (1946), pp. 24–30.

Challis, D., *The Archaeology of Race: The Eugenic Ideas of Francis Galton and Flinders Petrie,* London: Bloomsbury Academic, 2013.

Champion, T., "Beyond Egyptology: Egypt in 19th and 20th Century Archaeology and Anthropology," in P. Ucko and T. Champion (eds.), *The Wisdom of Egypt: Changing Visions through the Ages,* London: University of London Press, Institute of Archaeology, 2003, pp. 161–85.

Chassinat, É., and C. Palanque, *Une campagne de fouilles dans la nécropole d'Assiout,* Cairo: Institut Français d'Archéologie Orientale, 1911.

Cherpion, N., and J.-P. Corteggiai, *La tombe d'Inherkhâouy (TT 359) à Deir el-Medina,* Cairo: Institut Français d'Archéologie Orientale, 2010.

Clément, A., "Rethinking 'Peasant Consciousness' in Colonial Egypt: An Exploration of the Performance of Folksongs by Upper Egyptian Agricultural Workers on the Archaeological Excavation Sites of Karnak and Dendera at the Turn of the Twentieth Century (1885–1914)," *History and Anthropology* 21 (2010), pp. 73–100.

Clère, J. J., "Deux statues 'gardiennes de porte' d'époque ramesside," *Journal of Egyptian Archaeology* 54 (1968), pp. 135–48.

Clifford, J., *The Predicament of Culture: Twentieth Century Ethnography, Literature and Art,* Cambridge, MA: Harvard University Press, 1988.

Clifford, J., "Rearticulating Anthropology," in D. A. Segal and S. J. Yanagisako (eds.), *Unwrapping the Sacred Bundle: Reflections on the Disciplining of Anthropology,* Durham, NC: Duke University Press, 2005, pp. 24–48.

Cockburn, A., R. A. Barraco, W. H. Peck, and T. A. Reyman, "A Classic Mummy: PUM II," in A. Cockburn, E. Cockburn, and T. A. Reyman (eds.), *Mummies, Disease and Ancient Cultures,* 2nd edition, Cambridge: Cambridge University Press, 1998 [1980], pp. 69–90.

Cocteau, J., *Maalesh: Journal d'une tournée de théâtre,* Paris: Gallimard, 1949.

Cole, J.R.I., *Colonialism and Revolution in the Middle East: Social and Cultural Origins of Egypt's Urabi Movement,* Princeton, NJ: Princeton University Press, 1993.

Colin, F., "Le parfumeur (*p3 'nt*)," *Bulletin de l'Institut Français d'Archéologie Orientale* 103 (2003), pp. 73–109.

Colla, E., *Conflicted Antiquities: Egyptology, Egyptomania, Egyptian Modernity,* Durham, NC: Duke University Press, 2007.

Colla, E., "Shadi Abd al-Salam's *al-Mumiya:* Ambivalence and the Egyptian Nation-State," in A. A. Ahmida (ed.), *Beyond Colonialism and Nationalism in the*

Maghrib: History, Culture, and Politics, New York: Palgrave Macmillan, 2010, pp. 109–43.

Collombert, P., "La bandelette-*pyr* au cou des deuillants," *Revue d'Égyptologie* 57 (2006), pp. 235–38.

Colwell-Chanthaphonh, C., "Dismembering/Disremembering the Buddhas: Renderings on the Internet during the Afghan Purge of the Past," *Journal of Social Archaeology* 3 (2002), pp. 75–98.

Cooney, K. M., *The Cost of Death: The Social and Economic Value of Ancient Egyptian Funerary Art in the Ramesside Period,* Leiden: Nederlands Instituut voor het Nabije Oosten, 2007.

Coppens, F., *The Wabet: Tradition and Innovation in Temples of the Ptolemaic and Roman Period,* Prague: Czech Institute of Egyptology, 2007.

Corcoran, L., *Portrait Mummies from Roman Egypt,* Chicago: University of Chicago Press, 1995.

Coulon, L., "La nécropole osirienne de Karnak sous les Ptolémées," in A. Delattre and P. Heilporn (eds.), *"Et maintenant ce ne sont plus que des villages…": Thèbes et sa région aux époques hellénistique, romaine et byzantine,* Brussels: Association Égyptologique Reine Élisabeth, 2008, pp. 17–32.

Coulon, L., "Le sanctuaire de Chentayt à Karnak," in *Egypt at the Dawn of the Twenty-First Century,* Cairo and New York: American University in Cairo Press, 2002, pp. 138–46.

Coulon, L., "Un serviteur du sanctuaire de Chentayt à Karnak: La statue Caire JE 37134," *Bulletin de l'Institut Français d'Archéologie Orientale* 101 (2001), pp. 137–52.

Coury, R. M., "The Politics of the Funereal: The Tomb of Saad Zaghlul," *Journal of the American Research Center in Egypt* 29 (1992), pp. 191–200.

Crook, T., "Growing Knowledge in Bolivip, Papua New Guinea," *Oceania* 69 (1999), pp. 225–42.

Crowfoot, G. M., "Spinning and Weaving in the Sudan," *Sudan Notes and Records* 4 (1921), pp. 20–39.

Crowfoot, G. M., and N. de Garis Davies, "The Tunic of Tutankhamun," *Journal of Egyptian Archaeology* 27 (1941), pp. 113–30.

Curtis, N.G.W., "Human Remains: The Sacred, Museums and Archaeology," *Public Archaeology* 3 (2003), pp. 21–32.

Dalley, S., "Ancient Assyrian Textiles and the Origins of Carpet Design," *Iran* 29 (1991), pp. 117–35.

Daly, N., "That Obscure Object of Desire: Victorian Commodity Culture and Fictions of the Mummy," *NOVEL* 28 (1994), pp. 24–51.

Dannenfeldt, K. H., "Egypt and Egyptian Antiquities in the Renaissance," *Studies in the Renaissance* 6 (1959), pp. 7–27.

Daressy, G., *Fouilles de la Vallée des Rois (1898–1899),* Catalogue général des antiquités égyptiennes, Cairo: Institut Français d'Archéologie Orientale, 1902.

Daressy, G., and G. Elliot Smith, "Ouverture des momies provenant de la seconde trouvaille de Deir el-Bahari," *Annales du Service des Antiquités d'Égypte* 4 (1903), pp. 150–60.

Darnell, J. C., *The Enigmatic Netherworld Books of the Solar-Osirian Unity: Cryptographic Compositions in the Tombs of Tutankhamun, Ramesses VI and Ramesses IX,* Göttingen: Vandenhoeck & Ruprecht, 2004.

David, A. R., *A Guide to Religious Ritual at Abydos (c. 1300 BC),* Warminster: Aris and Phillips, 1973.

David, A. R., "Mummification," in P. T. Nicholson and I. Shaw (eds.), *Ancient Egyptian Materials and Technology,* Cambridge: Cambridge University Press, 2000, pp. 372–89.

David, A. R. (ed.), *Manchester Museum Mummy Project,* Manchester: Manchester Museum, 1979.

David, A. R., and E. Tapp (eds.), *Evidence Embalmed: Modern Medicine and the Mummies of Ancient Egypt,* Manchester: Manchester University Press, 1984.

Davies, N. de Garis, *Seven Private Tombs at Kurnah,* London: Egypt Exploration Society, 1948.

Davies, N. de Garis, *The Tomb of Puyemre at Thebes,* Vol. 2, *The Chapels of Hope,* New York: Metropolitan Museum of Art, 1923.

Davies, N. de Garis, *The Tomb of Rekh-Mi-Re at Thebes,* New York: Metropolitan Museum of Art, 1943.

Davies, N. de Garis, *Two Ramesside Tombs at Thebes,* New York: Metropolitan Museum of Art, 1927.

Davis, R. H., *Lives of Indian Images,* Princeton, NJ: Princeton University Press, 1997.

Davis, T. M., G. Maspero, P. E. Newberry, and H. Carter, *The Tomb of Iouiya and Touiyou,* London: Archibald Constable, 1907.

Davoli, P., "The Archaeology of the Fayum," in C. Riggs (ed.), *The Oxford Handbook of Roman Egypt,* Oxford: Oxford University Press, 2012, pp. 152–70.

Dawson, W. R., "Making a Mummy," *Journal of Egyptian Archaeology* 13 (1927), pp. 40–49.

Dawson, W. R. (ed.), *Sir Grafton Elliot Smith: A Biographical Record by His Colleagues,* London: Jonathan Cape, 1938.

Day, J., *The Mummy's Curse: Mummymania in the English-Speaking World,* London and New York: Routledge, 2006.

de Buck, A., and A. H. Gardiner, *The Egyptian Coffin Texts,* 8 vols., Chicago: University of Chicago Press, 1935–61.

de Jong, F., *Masquerades of Modernity: Power and Secrecy in Casamance, Senegal,* Bloomington: Indiana University Press, 2007.

Delange, E., *Catalogue des statues égyptiennes du Moyen Empire,* Paris: Réunion des musées nationaux, 1987.

Della Valle, P., *The Pilgrim: The Travels of Pietro Della Valle,* transl. G. Bull, London: Hutchinson, 1993.

Demaree, R. J., *The ꜣḫ ikr n Rꜥ Stelae: On Ancestor Worship in Ancient Egypt,* Leiden: Nederlands Instituut voor het Nabije Oosten, 1983.

Derchain-Urtel, M., "Tait," in W. Helck and E. Otto (eds.), *Lexikon der Ägyptologie,* Vol. 6, Wiesbaden: Harrassowitz, 1986, cols. 185–86.

Derda, T., "Necropolis Workers in Graeco-Roman Egypt in the Light of the Greek Papyri," *Journal of Juristic Papyrology* 21 (1991), pp. 13–36.

Derrida, J., *Archive Fever: A Freudian Impression,* London and Chicago: University of Chicago Press, 1998.

Díaz-Andreu, M., *A World History of Nineteenth-Century Archaeology: Nationalism, Colonialism, and the Past,* Oxford: Oxford University Press, 2007.

Diop, C. A., *The African Origin of Civilization: Myth or Reality,* Chicago: Lawrence Hill Books, 1974.

Donoghue, H. D., O. Y.-C. Lee, D. E. Minnikin, G. S. Besra, J. H. Taylor, and M. Spigelman, "Tuberculosis in Dr Granville's Mummy: A Molecular

Re-examination of the Earliest Known Egyptian Mummy to be Scientifically Examined and Given a Medical Diagnosis," *Proceedings of the Royal Society B* 277 (2010), pp. 51–56.

Dorman, P. F., "Family Burial and Commemoration in the Theban Necropolis," in N. Strudwick and J. H. Taylor (eds.), *The Theban Necropolis: Past, Present, Future,* London: British Museum Press, 2003, pp. 30–45.

Douglas, M., *Purity and Danger,* London: Routledge and Kegan Paul, 1966.

Doyon, W., "The Poetics of Egyptian Museum Practice," *British Museum Studies in Ancient Egypt and Sudan* 10 (2008), pp. 1–37.

Dumont, L., *Homo Hierarchicus: The Caste System and Its Implications,* London: Weidenfeld & Nicolson, 1970.

Dunand, F., "Les 'têtes dorées' de la nécropole de Douch," *Bulletin de la Societé Française d'Égyptologie* 93 (1982), pp. 26–46.

Dunand, F., J.-L. Heim, N. Henein, and R. Lichtenberg, *Douch I. La Nécropole,* Cairo: Institut Français d'Archéologie Orientale, 1992.

Dunand, F., and R. Lichtenberg, "Dix ans d'exploration des nécropoles d'El-Deir (Oasis de Kharga): Un premier bilan," *Chronique d'Égypte* 83 (2008), pp. 258–88.

Duncan, C., *Civilizing Rituals: Inside Public Art Museums,* London and New York: Routledge, 1995.

DuQuesne, T., "Anubis Master of Secrets (*ḥrj-sštȝ*) and the Egyptian Conception of Mysteries," in A. Assmann and J. Assmann (eds.), *Schleier und Schwelle, II: Geheimnis und Offenbarung,* Munich: Wilhelm Fink, 1998, pp. 105–21.

DuQuesne, T., "Concealing and Revealing: The Problem of Ritual Masking in Ancient Egypt," *Discussions in Egyptology* 51 (2001), pp. 5–31.

DuQuesne, T., "'Effective in Heaven and on Earth': Interpreting Egyptian Religious Practice for Both Worlds," in J. Assmann and M. Bommas (eds.), *Ägyptische Mysterien?* Munich: Wilhelm Fink, 2002, pp. 37–46.

Eaton-Krauss, M., "Embalming Caches," *Journal of Egyptian Archaeology* 94 (2008), pp. 288–93.

Eaton-Krauss, M., *The Representations of Statuary in Private Tombs of the Old Kingdom,* Wiesbaden: Harrassowitz, 1984.

Eaton-Krauss, M., and E. Graefe, *The Small Golden Shrine from the Tomb of Tutankhamun,* Oxford: Griffith Institute, 1985.

Edel, E., "Beiträge zum Ägyptischen Lexikon VI: Die Stoffbezeichnungen in den Kleiderlisten des Alten Reiches," *Zeitschrift für Ägyptische Sprache und Altertumskunde* 102 (1975), pp. 13–30.

Edwards, E., and M. Mead, "Absent Histories and Absent Images: Photographs, Museums and the Colonial Past," *Museum & Society* 11 (2013), pp. 19–38.

Egberts, A., *In Quest of Meaning: A Study of the Ancient Egyptian Rites of Consecrating the Meret-Chests and Driving the Calves,* Leiden: Nederlands Instituut voor het Nabije Oosten, 1995.

Elliot Smith, G., "An Account of the Mummy of a Priestess of Amen Supposed to be Ta-Usert-Em-Suten-Pa," *Annales du Service des Antiquités d'Égypte* 7 (1906), pp. 155–82.

Elliot Smith, G., "Egyptian Mummies," *Journal of Egyptian Archaeology* 1 (1914), pp. 189–96.

Elliot Smith, G., *The Royal Mummies,* Catalogue général des antiquités égyptiennes, Cairo: Institut Français d'Archéologie Orientale, 1912.

Englund, G., *Akh: Une notion religieuse dans l'Égypte pharaonique,* Uppsala, Sweden: Uppsala University, 1978.

Ennemoser, J., *The History of Magic,* London: Henry G. Bohn, 1854.

The Epigraphic Survey, *The Temple of Khonsu,* Vol. 1, *Plates 1–110. Scenes of King Herihor in the Court,* Chicago: Oriental Institute, 1979.

Erman, A., and H. Grapow (eds.), *Wörterbuch der ägyptischen Sprache,* 5 vols., Berlin: Akademie-Verlag, 1926–61.

Evans, J. M., *The Lives of Sumerian Sculpture: An Archaeology of the Early Dynastic Temple,* Cambridge: Cambridge University Press, 2012.

Exell, K. (ed.), *Egypt in Its African Context: Proceedings of the Conference Held at the Manchester Museum, University of Manchester, 2–4 October 2009,* Oxford: Archaeopress, 2011.

Fabian, J., *Time and the Other: How Anthropology Makes Its Object,* New York: Columbia University Press, 1983.

Fairman, H. W., "A Statue from the Karnak Cache," *Journal of Egyptian Archaeology* 20 (1934), pp. 1–4.

Faulkner, R. O., *The Ancient Egyptian Coffin Texts,* 3 vols., Warminster: Aris & Phillips, 1973–78.

Federn, W., "The 'Transformations' in the Coffin Texts: A New Approach," *Journal of Near Eastern Studies* 19 (1960), pp. 241–57.

Fforde, C., *Collecting the Dead: Archaeology and the Reburial Issue,* London: Duckworth, 2004.

Fforde, C., and J. Hubert, "Indigenous Human Remains and Changing Museum Ideology," in R. Layton, S. Shennan, and P. Stone (eds.), *A Future for Archaeology: The Past in the Present,* Walnut Creek, CA: Left Coast Press, 2006, pp. 83–96.

Fforde, C., J. Hubert, and P. Turnbull (eds.), *The Dead and Their Possessions: Repatriation in Principle, Policy and Practice,* London and New York: Routledge, 2004.

Findlen, P. (ed.), *Athanasius Kircher: The Last Man Who Knew Everything,* London and New York: Routledge, 2004.

Finnestad, R. B., "The Meaning and Purpose of Opening the Mouth in Mortuary Contexts," *Numen* 25 (1978), pp. 118–34.

Firth, C. M., and J. E. Quibell, *The Step Pyramid,* Cairo: Institut Français d'Archéologie Orientale, 1935.

Fischer, H. G., "Five Inscriptions of the Old Kingdom," *Zeitschrift für Ägyptische Sprache und Altertumskunde* 105 (1978), pp. 42–59.

Fischer, H. G., *Varia: Egyptian Studies I,* New York: Metropolitan Museum of Art, 1976.

Fischer-Elfert, H. W., "Das verschwiegene Wissen des Iritsen (Stele Louvre C14)," in J. Assmann and M. Bommas (eds.), *Ägyptische Mysterien?* Munich: Wilhelm Fink, 2002, pp. 27–35.

Fischer-Elfert, H. W., *Die Vision von der Statue im Stein: Studien zum altägyptischen Mundöffnungsritual,* Heidelberg: C. Winter, 1998.

Fitzenreiter, M., and C. E. Loeben (eds.),"Tote Menschen in einer Mumienausstellung: Was denkt das Publikum darüber? Erste Ergebnisse der Besucherbefragung durch die Ägyptologie-Studierenden der Humboldt-Universität in der Berliner Mumienasstellung," in *Die ägyptische Mumie: Ein Phänomen der Kulturgeschichte,* Berlin: Seminar für Sudanarchäologie und Ägyptologie, 1998, pp. 131–32.

Fletcher, R., "The Art of Forgetting: Imperialist Amnesia and Public Secrecy," *Third World Quarterly* 33 (2012), pp. 423–39.

Foucault, M., *Discipline and Punish: The Birth of the Prison,* London: Penguin, 1991 [1977].

Foucault, M., "Of Other Spaces," J. Miskowiec (trans.), *Diacritics* 16 (Spring 1986), pp. 22–27.

Foucault, M., *The Order of Things: An Archaeology of the Human Sciences,* London and New York: Routledge, 2002 [1970].

Foucault, M., "Texts/Contexts: Of Other Spaces," in D. Preziosi and C. Farago (eds.), *Grasping the World: The Idea of the Museum,* Aldershot: Ashgate, 2004, pp. 371–79.

Franke, D., "*Sem*-Priest on Duty," in S. Quirke (ed.), *Discovering Egypt from the Neva: The Egyptological Legacy of Oleg D. Berlev,* Berlin: Achet-Verlag, 2003, pp. 65–78.

Frankfurter, D., *Religion in Roman Egypt: Assimilation and Resistance,* Princeton, NJ: Princeton University Press, 1998.

Friedman, F. D., "Notions of Cosmos in the Step Pyramid Complex," in P. Der Manuelian (ed.), *Studies in Honor of William Kelly Simpson,* Boston: Museum of Fine Arts, 1996, pp. 337–51.

Friedman, F., "On the Meaning of Some Anthropoid Busts from Deir el-Medina," *Journal of Egyptian Archaeology* 71 (1985), pp. 82–97.

Friedman, F., "The Root Meaning of *3ḫ*: Effectiveness or Luminosity," *Serapis* 8 (1984–1985), pp. 39–46.

Friedman, R. F., "The Cemeteries of Hierakonpolis," *Archéo-Nil* 18 (2008), pp. 9–29.

Frood, E., *Biographical Texts from Ramesside Egypt,* Atlanta: Society of Biblical Literature, 2007.

Gange, D., *Dialogues with the Dead: Egyptology in British Culture and Religion, 1822–1922,* Oxford: Oxford University Press, 2013.

Gardiner, A. H., "Two Hieroglyphic Signs and the Egyptian Words for 'Alabaster' and 'Linen,' etc.," *Bulletin de l'Institut Français d'Archéologie Orientale* 30 (1931), pp. 161–83.

Garstang, J., *The Burial Customs of Ancient Egypt,* London: Archibald Constable, 1907.

Gaskell, I., "Sacred to Profane and Back Again," in A. McClellan (ed.), *Art and Its Publics: Museum Studies at the Millennium,* Malden, MA, and Oxford: Blackwell, 2003, pp. 149–62.

Gee, J., "A New Look at the Conception of the Human Being in Ancient Egypt," in R. Nyord and A. Kjølby (eds.), *"Being in Ancient Egypt": Thoughts on Agency, Materiality and Cognition. Proceedings of the Seminar Held in Copenhagen, September 29–30, 2006,* Oxford: Archaeopress, 2009, pp. 1–14.

Gell, A., *Art and Agency: An Anthropological Theory,* Oxford: Clarendon Press, 1998.

Gell, A., "The Technology of Enchantment and the Enchantment of Technology," in J. Coote and A. Shelton (eds.), *Anthropology, Art and Aesthetics,* Oxford: Clarendon, 1992, pp. 40–66.

Gell, A., "Vogel's Net: Traps as Artworks and Artworks as Traps," *Journal of Material Culture* 1 (1996), pp. 15–38.

Gell, A., *Wrapping in Images: Tattooing in Polynesia,* Oxford: Clarendon Press, 1993.

Germer, R., *Die Textilfärberei und die Verwendung gefärbter Textilien im Alten Ägypten,* Wiesbaden: Harrassowitz, 1992.

Germer, R., H. Kischkewitz, and M. Lüning, "Das Grab der Aline und die Untersuchung der darin gefundenen Kindermumien," *Antike Welt* 24 (1993), pp. 186–96.

Germer, R., H. Kischkewitz, and M. Lüning, "Pseudo-mumien der Ägyptischen Sammlung Berlin," *Studien zur Altäygptischen Kultur* 21 (1994), pp. 81–94.

Gessler-Löhr, B., "Mummies and Mummification," in C. Riggs (ed.), *The Oxford Handbook of Roman Egypt,* Oxford: Oxford University Press, 2012, pp. 664–83.

Gilman, S. L., *Difference and Pathology: Stereotypes of Sexuality, Race, and Madness,* Ithaca, NY, and London: Cornell University Press, 1985.

Gliddon, G. R., *A Memoir on the Cotton of Egypt,* London: James Madden, 1841.

Godwin, J., *Athanasius Kircher's Theatre of the World,* London: Thames and Hudson, 2009.

Goebs, K., "Untersuchungen zu Funktion und Symbolgehalt des *nms,*" *Zeitschrift der Ägyptische Sprache und Altertumskunde* 122 (1995), pp. 154–81.

Goffman, E., *The Presentation of Self in Everyday Life,* London: Penguin, 1969 [1959].

Gosden, C., *Archaeology and Colonialism: Cultural Contact from 5000 BC to the Present,* Cambridge: Cambridge University Press, 2004.

Gosden, C., "The Past and Foreign Countries: Colonial and Post-Colonial Archaeology and Anthropology," in L. Meskell and R. W. Preucel (eds.), *A Companion to Social Archaeology,* Malden, MA, and Oxford: Blackwell, 2004, pp. 161–78.

Goyon, J.-C., "Chiurgie religieuse ou thanatopraxie? Données nouvelles sur la momification en Égypte et réflexions qu'elles impliquent," in *Sesto Congresso Internazionale di Egittologia, Atti,* Vol. 1, Turin: International Association of Egyptologists, 1992, pp. 215–25.

Graefe, E., "Beethoven und die ägyptische Weisheit," *Göttinger Miszellen* 2 (1972), pp. 19–21.

Graefe, E., *Untersuchungen zur Verwaltung und Geschichte der Institution der Gottesgemahlin des Amun vom Beginn des Neuen Reiches bis zur Spätzeit,* Wiesbaden: Harrassowitz, 1981.

Graefe, E., and G. Belova (eds.), *The Royal Cache TT 320: A Re-examination,* Cairo: Supreme Council of Antiquities, 2010.

Grandet, P., *Le Papyrus Harris I (BM 9999),* Cairo: Institut Français d'Archéologie Orientale, 1994.

Granville, A. B., *Autobiography of A.B. Granville, M.D., F.R.S.,* London: Henry S. King, 1874.

Granville, A. B., "A Case of the Human Foetus Found in the Ovarium, of the Size It Usually Acquires at the End of the Fourth Month," *Proceedings of the Royal Society of London* 110 (1820), pp. 101–7.

Granville, A. B., *An Essay on Egyptian Mummies,* London: W. Nicol, 1825.

Granville, A. B., "An Essay on Egyptian Mummies, with Observations on the Art of Embalming among the Ancient Egyptians," *Proceedings of the Royal Society of London* 115 (1825), pp. 269–316.

Graves-Brown, C., "Licking Knives and Stone Snakes: The Ideology of Flint in Ancient Egypt," in M. Martinón-Torres and T. Rehren (eds.), *Archaeology, History and Science: Integrating Approaches to Ancient Materials,* Walnut Creek, CA: Left Coast Press, 2008, pp. 37–60.

Grdseloff, B., "Le signe [*sm*] et le titre du stoliste," *Annales du Service des Antiquités d'Égypte* 43 (1943), pp. 357–66.

Green, C. I., *The Temple Furniture from the Sacred Animal Necropolis at North Saqqara, 1964–76,* London: Egypt Exploration Society, 1987.

Greenhill, T., *[Nekrokedeia]: Or, the Art of Embalming,* London: Printed for the author, 1705.

Gregory, D., "Between the Book and the Lamp: Imaginative Geographies of Egypt, 1849–50," *Transactions of the Institute of British Geographers* NS 20 (1995), pp. 29–57.

Gregory, D., "Colonial Nostalgia and Cultures of Travel: Spaces of Constructed Visibility in Egypt," in N. AlSayyad (ed.), *Consuming Tradition, Manufacturing Heritage: Global Norms and Urban Forms in the Age of Tourism,* London: Routledge, 2001, pp. 212–39.

Gregory, D., "Scripting Egypt: Orientalism and the Cultures of Travel," in J. Duncan and D. Gregory (eds.), *Writes of Passage: Reading Travel Writing,* London: Routledge, 1999, pp. 114–50.

Grieshammer, R., "Zum Sitz im Leben des negativen Sündenbekenntnisses," *Zeitschrift der Deutschen Morgenländischen Gesellschaft* Supplement II (1974), pp. 19–25.

Guernsey, J., and F. K. Reilly (eds.), *Sacred Bundles: Ritual Acts of Wrapping and Binding in Mesoamerica,* Barnardsville, NC: Boundary End Archaeology Research Center, 2006.

Guha-Thakurta, T., "'Our Gods, Their Museums': The Contrary Careers of India's Art Objects," *Art History* 30 (2007), pp. 628–57.

Gumbula, J. N., "*'Miny'tji waŋawuy Ŋarakawuy':* Paintings Are the Backbone of the Land and Sea," in R. Colombo Dougard and B. Müller (eds.), *Dream Traces: Australian Aboriginal Bark Paintings,* Geneva: Musée d'ethnographie de Genève, 2010, pp. 9–11.

Hadot, P., *The Veil of Isis: An Essay on the History of the Idea of Nature,* Cambridge, MA, and London: Belknap Press of Harvard University Press, 2006.

Haugerud, E. (ed.), Special Issue: Egypt Forum: 2011 Revolt. Reflections from Nine Anthropologists, *American Ethnologist* 39 (February 2012).

Hall, H. R., "The XIth Dynasty Temple at Deir el-Bahari," *Proceedings of the Society of Biblical Archaeology* 27 (1905), pp. 173–83.

Hall, R. M., "Garments in the Petrie Museum of Egyptian Archaeology," *Textile History* 13 (1982), pp. 27–45.

Hall, R. M., "Two Linen Dresses from the Fifth Dynasty Site of Deshasheh Now in the Petrie Museum of Egyptian Archaeology, University College London," *Journal of Egyptian Archaeology* 67 (1981), pp. 168–71.

Hall, R. M., and L. Pedrini, "A Pleated Linen Dress from a Sixth Dynasty Tomb at Gebelein Now in the Museo Egizio, Turin," *Journal of Egyptian Archaeology* 70 (1984), pp. 136–39.

Hamer, M., "Black *and* White? Viewing Cleopatra in 1862," in S. West (ed.), *The Victorians and Race,* Aldershot: Ashgate, 1996, pp. 53–67.

Hamilakis, Y., "We Are All Middle Easterners Now: Globalization, Immanence, Archaeology," in R. Boytner, L. S. Dodd, and B. J. Parker (eds.), *Controlling the Past, Owning the Future: The Political Uses of Archaeology in the Middle East,* Tucson: University of Arizona Press, 2010, pp. 217–29.

Hammond, J. H., *Selections from the Letters and Speeches of the Hon. James H. Hammond, of South Carolina,* New York: John F. Trow & Co., 1866.

Haring, B., *Divine Households: Administrative and Economic Aspects of the New Kingdom Royal Memorial Temples in Western Thebes,* Leiden: Nederlands Instituut voor het Nabije Oosten, 1997.

Harrauer, C., "'Ich bin, was da ist...': Die Göttin von Sais und ihre Deutung von Plutarch bis in die Goethezeit," *Sphairos: Wiener Studien. Zeitschrift für Klassische Philologie und Patristik* 107/108 (1994/1995), pp. 337–55.

Harrington, N., *Living with the Dead: Ancestor Worship and Mortuary Ritual in Ancient Egypt,* Oxford: Oxbow, 2013.

Hastings, E. A., *The Sculpture from the Sacred Animal Necropolis at North Saqqara, 1964–76,* London: Egypt Exploration Society, 1997.

Hayward Gallery, *Richard Wentworth's Thinking Aloud,* London: Hayward Gallery, 1998.

Hays, H. M., "The Ritual Scenes in the Chapels of Amun," in *The Epigraphic Survey: Medinet Habu,* Vol. 9, *The Eighteenth Dynasty Temple,* Part 1, *The Inner Sanctuaries,* Chicago: Oriental Institute of the University of Chicago, 2009, pp. 1–14.

Helck, W., "Zur Person des *Jdw II* und des '*nḫ-Pjpj,*'" in B. Schmitz (ed.), *Untersuchungen zu Idu II, Giza: Ein interdisziplinäres Projekt,* Hildesheim: Gerstenberg, 1996, pp. 43–45.

Hendry, J., *Wrapping Culture: Politeness, Presentation and Power in Japan and Other Societies,* Oxford: Clarendon Press, 1992.

Henniker, F., *Notes during a Visit to Egypt, Nubia, the Oasis Boeris, Mount Sinai, and Jerusalem,* London: John Murray, 1824.

Heslop, S., and A. B. Neto (eds.), *Basketry: Making Human Nature,* Norwich: Sainsbury Centre for Visual Arts, 2011.

Hoberman, R., "In Quest of a Museal Aura: Turn of the Century Narratives about Museum-Displayed Objects," *Victorian Literature and Culture* 31 (2003), pp. 467–82.

Hodder, I., *Entangled: An Archaeology of the Relationships between Humans and Things,* Malden, MA: Wiley-Blackwell, 2012.

Hodder, I., *Reading the Past: Current Approaches to Interpretation in Archaeology,* Cambridge: Cambridge University Press, 1991.

Hooper, S., "Embodying Divinity: The Life of A'a," *Journal of the Polynesian Society* 116 (2007), pp. 131–79.

Hornung, E., *Conceptions of God in Ancient Egypt: The One and the Many,* Ithaca, NY: Cornell University Press, 1982.

Hornung, E., "Fisch und Vogel: Zur altägyptischen Sicht des Menschen," *Eranos Jahrbuch* 52 (1983), pp. 455–96.

Hornung, E., *The Secret Lore of Egypt: Its Impact on the West,* Ithaca, NY, and London: Cornell University Press, 2001.

Hornung, E., and T. Abt, *The Egyptian Amduat: The Book of the Hidden Chamber,* Zurich: Living Human Heritage, 2007.

Hornung, E., A. Brodbeck, and E. Staehelin, *Das Buch von den Pforten des Jenseits,* Geneva: Éditions de Belles-Lettres, 1979–80.

Hornung, E., and E. Staehelin, *Studien zum Sedfest,* Geneva: Éditions de Belles-Lettres, 1974.

Howe, S., *Afrocentrism: Mythical Pasts and Imagined Homes,* London and New York: Verso, 1998.

Ikram, S., "Mummification," in W. Wendrich (ed.), *UCLA Encyclopedia of Egyptology*, Los Angeles: UCLA, 2010, http://escholarship.org/uc/item/0gn7x3ff.

Ikram, S. (ed.), *Divine Creatures: Animal Mummies in Ancient Egypt*, Cairo and New York: American University in Cairo Press, 2005.

Ikram, S., and A. Dodson, *The Mummy in Ancient Egypt: Equipping the Dead for Eternity*, London: Thames and Hudson, 1998.

Ingold, T., "Making Culture and Weaving the World," in P. M. Graves-Brown (ed.), *Matter, Materiality and Modern Culture*, London and New York: Routledge, 2000, pp. 50–71.

Ingold, T., "Materials against Materiality," *Archaeological Dialogues* 14 (2007), pp. 1–16.

Janot, F., *Les instruments d'embaumement de l'Égypte ancienne*, Cairo: Institut Français d'Archéologie Orientale, 2000.

Jansen-Winkeln, K., "Die Plünderung der Königsgräber des Neuen Reiches," *Zeitschrift für Ägyptische Sprache und Altertumskunde* 122 (1995), pp. 67–78.

Janssen, J. J., *Daily Dress at Deir el-Medina: Words for Clothing*, London: Golden House, 2008.

Janssen, R. M., "The Linens of Idu II," in B. Schmitz (ed.), *Untersuchungen zu Idu II, Giza: Ein interdisziplinäres Projekt*, Hildesheim: Gerstenberg, 1996, pp. 47–56.

Jenkins, T., *Contesting Human Remains in Museum Collections: The Crisis of Cultural Authority*, New York and London: Routledge, 2011.

Jonckheere, F., "Considérations sur l'auxiliaire médical pharaonique," *Chronique d'Égypte* 28 (1953), pp. 60–76.

Jones, J., "The 'Linen List' in Early Dynastic and Old Kingdom Egypt: Text and Textile Reconciled," in C. Michel and M.-L. Nusch (eds.), *Textile Terminologies*, Oxford: Oxbow, 2010, pp. 81–109.

Jones, J., "New Perspectives on the Development of Mummification and Funerary Practices during the Pre- and Early Dynastic Periods," in J.-C. Goyon and C. Cardin (eds.), *Proceedings of the Ninth International Congress of Egyptologists, Grenoble, 6–12 Septembre 2004*, Vol. 1, Leuven: Peeters, 2007, pp. 979–89.

Jones, J., "The Shroud of *Tny*, R92: A Textile Analysis," in K. Sowada and B. Ockinga (eds.), *Egyptian Art in the Nicholson Museum, Sydney*, Sydney: Mediterranean Archaeology, 2006, pp. 135–45.

Jones, J., "Towards Mummification: New Evidence for Early Developments," *Egyptian Archaeology* 21 (2001), pp. 5–7.

Jordanova, L., "Objects of Knowledge: A Historical Perspective on Museums," in P. Vergo (ed.), *The New Museology*, London: Reaktion, 1989, pp. 21–40.

Jordanova, L., *Sexual Visions: Images of Gender in Science and Medicine between the Eighteenth and Twentieth Centuries*, Madison: University of Wisconsin Press, 1989.

Junker, H., *Giza VIII: Der Ostabschnitt des Westfriedhofs, Zweiter Teil*, Vienna and Leipzig: Hölder-Pichler-Tempsky, 1947.

Kaeppler, A. L., "Containers of Divinity," *Journal of the Polynesian Society* 116 (2007), pp. 97–130.

Kaiser, W., "Zu den [hieroglyphs] der älteren Bilddarstellungen und der Bedeutung von *rpw.t*," *Mitteilungen des Deutschen Archäologischen Instituts Kairo* 39 (1983), pp. 261–96.

Kákosy, L., "Tempel und Mysterien," in R. Gundlach and M. Rochholz (eds.), *Ägyptische Tempel—Struktur, Funktion und Programm,* Hildesheim: Gerstenberg, 1994, pp. 165–73.

Kamal, A. B., *Stèles ptolémaïques et romaines,* Catalogue général des antiquités égyptiennes, Cairo: Institut Français d'Archéologie Orientale, 1904.

Kamugisha, A., "Finally in Africa? Egypt, from Diop to Celenko," *Race & Class* 45 (2003), pp. 31–60.

Karlshausen, C., "L'évolution de la barque processionnelle d'Amon à la 18e dynastie," *Revue d'Égyptologie* 46 (1995), pp. 119–37.

Karlshausen, C., *L'iconographie de la barque processionelle divine en Égypte au Nouvel Empire,* Leuven, Paris, and Walpole, MA: Peeters, 2009.

Karlshausen, C., "L'iconographie des barques processionelles divines à la Basse Epoque: Tradition et innovations," in W. Clarysse, A. Schoors, and H. Willems (eds.), *Egyptian Religion: The Last Thousand Years,* Part 2, *Studies Dedicated to the Memory of Jan Quaegebeur,* Leuven: Peeters, 1998, pp. 859–73.

Kaufmann, I. M., and F. J. Rühli, "Without 'Informed Consent'? Ethics and Ancient Mummy Research," *Journal of Medical Ethics* 36 (2010), pp. 608–13.

Keane, W., "Signs Are Not the Garb of Meaning: On the Social Analysis of Material Things," in D. Miller (ed.), *Materiality,* Durham, NC, and London: Duke University Press, 2005, pp. 182–205.

Keenan, T., and E. Weizman, *Mengele's Skull: The Advent of Forensic Aesthetics,* Berlin: Sternberg Press, 2012.

Keith, J. L., *Anthropoid Busts of Deir el Medineh and Other Sites and Collections,* Cairo: Institut Français d'Archéologie Orientale, 2011.

Kemp, B. J., and G. Vogelsang-Eastwood, *The Ancient Textile Industry at Amarna,* London: Egypt Exploration Society, 2001.

Kilmister, H., "Visitor Perceptions of Ancient Egyptian Human Remains in Three United Kingdom Museums," *Papers from the Institute of Archaeology* 14 (2003), pp. 57–69.

Kippenberg, H. G., and G. G. Stroumsa, "Introduction: Secrecy and Its Benefits," in H. G. Kippenberg and G. G. Stroumsa (eds.), *Secrecy and Concealment: Studies in the History of Mediterranean and Near Eastern Religions,* Leiden and New York: E. J. Brill, 1995, pp. xiii–xxiv.

Kockelmann, H., *Untersuchungen zu den späten Totenbuch-Handschriften auf Mumienbinden, Band I.1–2: Die Mumienbinden und Leinenamuletten des Memphitischen Priesters Hor,* Wiesbaden: Harrassowitz, 2008.

Kockelmann, H., *Untersuchungen zu den späten Totenbuch-Handschriften auf Mumienbinden, Band II: Handbuch zu den Mumienbinden und Leinenamuletten,* Wiesbaden: Harrassowitz, 2008.

Kopytoff, I., "The Cultural Biography of Things: Commoditization as Process," in A. Appadurai (ed.), *The Social Life of Things: Commodities in Cultural Perspective,* Cambridge: Cambridge University Press, 1986, pp. 64–91.

Kruchten, J.-M., *Les annales des prêtres de Karnak (XXI–XXIIImes dynasties) et autres textes contemporains relatifs a l'initiation des prêtres d'Amon,* Leuven: Departement Oriëntalistiek, 1989.

Kubler, G., *The Shape of Time: Remarks on the History of Things,* New Haven, CT: Yale University Press, 1962.

Laboury, D., "Archaeological and Textual Evidence for the Function of the 'Botanical Garden' of Karnak in the Initiation Ritual," in P. F. Dorman and B. M. Bryan (eds.), *Sacred Space and Sacred Function in Ancient Thebes,* Chicago: Oriental Institute, 2007, pp. 27–34.

Larson, J., "The Heb-sed Robe and the 'Ceremonial Robe' of Tutankhamun," *Journal of Egyptian Archaeology* 67 (1981), pp. 180–81.
Latour, B., "On the Partial Existence of Existing and Nonexisting Objects," in L. Daston (ed.), *Biographies of Scientific Objects,* Chicago and London: University of Chicago Press, 2000, pp. 247–69.
Lauer, J.-P., and D. E. Derry, "Découverte à Saqqarah d'une partie de la momie du roi Zoser," *Annales du Service des Antiquités d'Égypte* 35 (1935), pp. 25–30.
Leek, F. F., *The Human Remains from the Tomb of Tutankhamun,* Oxford: Griffith Institute, 1972.
Lefebvre, G., "Textes du tombeau de Petosiris," *Annales du Service des Antiquités d'Égypte* 21 (1921), pp. 40–59.
Lefkowitz, M. R., *Not out of Africa: How Afrocentrism Became an Excuse to Teach Myth as History,* New York: Basic Books, 1996.
Lefkowitz, M. R., and G. M. Rogers (eds.), *Black Athena Revisited,* Chapel Hill and London: University of North Carolina Press, 1996.
Legrain, G., *Statues et statuettes des rois et des particuliers,* Vol. 1, Catalogue général des antiquités égyptiennes, Cairo: Institut Français d'Archéologie Orientale, 1909.
Leitz, C., "Die beiden kryptographischen Inschriften aus Esna mit den Widdern und Krokodilen," *Studien zur Altägyptischen Kultur* 29 (2001), pp. 251–76.
Liebmann, M., and U. Z. Rizvi (eds.), *Archaeology and the Postcolonial Critique,* Lanham, MD: AltaMira Press, 2008.
Lilyquist, C., *Ancient Egyptian Mirrors from the Earliest Times through the Middle Kingdom,* Munich: Deutscher Kunstverlag, 1979.
Lilyquist, C., *The Tomb of Three Foreign Wives of Tuthmosis III,* New Haven, CT, and London: Yale University Press, 2003.
Long, D. A., "Poe's Political Identity: A Mummy Unswathed," *Poe Studies* 23 (1990), pp. 1–22.
Lorimer, D. A., "Race, Science and Culture: Historical Continuities and Discontinuities, 1850–1914," in S. West (ed.), *The Victorians and Race,* Aldershot: Ashgate, 1996, pp. 12–33.
Lorimer, D. A., "Theoretical Racism in Late-Victorian Anthropology, 1870–1900," *Victorian Studies* 31 (1988), pp. 405–30.
Lorton, D., "The Theology of Cult Statues in Ancient Egypt," in M. B. Dick (ed.), *Born in Heaven, Made on Earth: The Making of the Cult Image in the Ancient Near East,* Winona Lake, IN: Eisenbrauns, 1999, pp. 123–210.
Loti, P., *Egypt (La Mort de Philae),* transl. W. P. Baines, New York: Duffield, 1909.
Luckhurst, R., *The Mummy's Curse: The True History of a Dark Fantasy,* Oxford: Oxford University Press, 2012.
Lüscher, B., *Untersuchungen zu Totenbuch Spruch 151,* Wiesbaden: Harrassowitz, 1998.
Lythgoe, A. M., and D. Dunham, *The Predynastic Cemetery N 7000, Naga-Ed-Dêr Part IV,* Berkeley and Los Angeles: University of California Press, 1965.
McClintock, A., *Imperial Leather: Race, Gender and Sexuality in the Colonial Contest,* New York and London: Routledge, 1996.
Macdonald, S., *Behind the Scenes at the Science Museum,* Oxford: Berg, 2002.
Macdonald, S., *Difficult Heritage: Negotiating the Nazi Past in Nuremberg and Beyond,* London and New York: Routledge, 2008.
Macdonald, S., "Enchantment and Its Dilemmas: The Museum as a Ritual Site," in M. Bouquet and N. Porto (eds.), *Science, Magic and Religion: The*

Ritual Processes of Museum Magic, New York and Oxford: Berghahn, 2006, pp. 209–27.

MacDonald, S., "Lost in Time and Space: Ancient Egypt in Museums," in S. MacDonald and M. Rice (eds.), *Consuming Ancient Egypt*, London: University of London Press, Institute of Archaeology, 2003, pp. 87–99.

Macfie, A. L. (ed.), *Orientalism: A Reader*, Edinburgh: Edinburgh University Press, 2000.

Machin, R., "Gender Representation in the Natural History Galleries at the Manchester Museum," *Museum & Society* 6 (2008), pp. 54–67.

MacKenzie, J. M., *Orientalism: History, Theory and the Arts*, Manchester: Manchester University Press, 1995.

Magubane, Z., "Which Bodies Matter? Feminism, Poststructuralism, Race, and the Curious Theoretical Odyssey of the 'Hottentot Venus,'" *Gender and Society* 15 (2001), pp. 816–34.

Malek, J., *Egypt: 4000 Years of Art*, London: Phaidon, 2003.

Manassa, C., "The Judgment Hall of Osiris in the Book of Gates," *Revue d'Égyptologie* 57 (2006), pp. 109–50.

Manley, B., "Petrie's Revolution: The Case of the Qurneh Queen," in K. Exell (ed.), *Egypt in Its African Context: Proceedings of the Conference Held at the Manchester Museum, University of Manchester, 2–4 October 2009*, Oxford: Archaeopress, 2011, pp. 92–97.

Manuelian, P. Der, *Slab Stelae of the Giza Necropolis*, New Haven, CT, and Philadelphia: Peabody Museum of Natural History of Yale University and the University of Pennsylvania Museum of Archaeology and Anthropology, 2003.

Marchant, J., "Ancient DNA: Curse of the Pharaoh's DNA," *Nature* 472 (2011), pp. 404–6.

Mariette, A., and G. Maspero, *Le Sérapeum de Memphis*, Paris: F. Vieweg, 1882.

Marks, J., "Your Body, My Property: The Problem of Colonial Genetics in a Postcolonial World," in L. Meskell and P. Pels (eds.), *Embedding Ethics*, Oxford and New York: Berg, 2005, pp. 29–45.

Martin, S. O., "Ancient Egyptian Mummy Wrappings from the Mummy '1770': A Technological and Social Study," Ph.D. dissertation, University of Manchester, 2008.

Maspero, G., *Guide du visiteur au Musée de Boulaq*, Boulaq: au Musée, 1883.

Maspero, G., *Les momies royale de Déir el-Baharî*, Paris: Ernest Leroux, 1889.

Maspero, G., *Le Musée Égyptien: Recueil de monuments et de notices sur les fouilles d'Égypte*, Vol. 2, Cairo: Institut français d'archéologie orientale, 1904.

Maspero, G., "Procès verbal de l'ouverture des momies de Ramsès II et de Ramsès III," *Revue Archéologique, series 3* 8 (1886), pp. 1–7.

Maspero, G., "Rapport sur la trouvaille de Deir-el-Bahari," *Bulletin de l'Institut d'Égypte (série 2)* 2 (1881), pp. 129–69.

Mathieu, B., "Réflexions sur le 'fragment Daressy' et ses hommes illustres," in C. Zivie-Coche and I. Guermeur (eds.), *"Parcourir l'éternité": Hommages à Jean Yoyotte*, Turnhout: Brepols, 2012, pp. 819–52.

Meeks, D., *Année Lexicographique 2 (1978)*, Paris: Margeride, 1981.

Meeks, D., "Dieu masqué, dieu sans tête," *Archéo-Nil* 1 (1991), pp. 5–15.

Meeks, D., "Genies, anges, et demons en Égypte," in D. Meeks (ed.), *Genies, anges, et demons: Égypte, Babylone, Israël, Islam, etc.* (Sources Orientales, VIII), Paris: Édition du Seuil, 1971, pp. 19–84.

Merkelbach, R., "Ein griechisch-ägyptischer Priestereid und das Totenbuch," in *Religions en Égypte Hellénistique et Romaine. Colloque de Strasbourg, 16–18 Mai 1967,* Paris: Presses universitaires de France, 1969, pp. 69–74.
Meskell, L., *Archaeologies of Social Life,* Oxford: Blackwell, 1999.
Meskell, L. (ed.), *Archaeology under Fire: Nationalism, Politics and Heritage in the Eastern Mediterranean and Middle East,* London and New York: Routledge, 1998.
Meskell, L., "Dying Young: The Experience of Death at Deir el-Medina," *Archaeological Review from Cambridge* 13 (1994), pp. 35–45.
Meskell, L., "Negative Heritage and Past Mastering in Archaeology," *Anthropological Quarterly* 75 (2002), pp. 557–74.
Meskell, L., *Object Worlds in Ancient Egypt: Material Biographies Past and Present,* Oxford and New York: Berg, 2004.
Meskell, L., "Objects in the Mirror Appear Closer Than They Are," in D. Miller (ed.), *Materiality,* Durham, NC, and London: Duke University Press, 2005, pp. 51–71.
Meskell, L., "Sites of Violence: Terrorism, Tourism, and Heritage in the Archaeological Present," in L. Meskell and P. Pels (eds.), *Embedding Ethics,* Oxford and New York: Berg, 2005, pp. 123–46.
Meyer-Dietrich, E., *Senebi und Selbst: Personenkonstituenten zur rituellen Wiedergeburt in einem Frauensarg des Mittleren Reiches,* Fribourg and Göttingen: Academic Press; Vandenhoeck & Ruprecht, 2006.
Miles, H., "Mummies at Rest," *The Middle East* 235 (1994), unpaginated.
Miller, D., "Afterword," in L. Meskell (ed.), *Archaeologies of Materiality,* Malden, MA, and Oxford: Blackwell, 2005, pp. 212–19.
Miller, D. (ed.), *Materiality,* Durham, NC, and London: Duke University Press, 2005.
Minas, M., "Die ptolemäischen Sokar-Osiris-Mumien: Neue Erkenntnisse zum ägyptischen Dynastiekult der Ptolemäer," *Mitteilungen des Deutschen Archäologischen Instituts Kairo* 62 (2006), pp. 197–213.
Mitchell, T., *Colonising Egypt,* Cambridge: Cambridge University Press, 1988.
Molleson, T. I., "The Nubian Pathological Collection in the Natural History Museum, London," in W. V. Davies and R. Walker (eds.), *Biological Anthropology and the Study of Ancient Egypt,* London: British Museum Press, 1993, pp. 136–43.
Montserrat, D., *Akhenaten: History, Fantasy, and Ancient Egypt,* London: Routledge, 2003.
Montserrat, D., "Unidentified Human Remains: Mummies and the Erotics of Biography," in D. Montserrat (ed.), *Changing Bodies, Changing Meanings: Studies on the Human Body in Antiquity,* London and New York: Routledge, 1998, pp. 162–97.
Morenz, L., "Schrift-Mysterium: Gottes-Schau in der visuellen Poesie von Esna—insbesondere zu den omnipotenten Widder-Zeichen zwischen Symbolik und Lesbarkeit," in J. Assmann and M. Bommas (eds.), *Ägyptische Mysterien?* Munich: Wilhelm Fink, 2002, pp. 77–94.
Morenz, S., *Egyptian Religion,* Ithaca, NY: Cornell University Press, 1973.
Moret, A., *Le rituel du culte divin journalier en Égypte,* Paris: Ernest Leroux, 1902.
de Morgan, J., *Fouilles à Dahchour en 1894–1895,* Vienna: Adolphe Holzhausen, 1903.
de Morgan, J., U. Bouriant, G. Legrain, G. Jéquier, and A. Barsanti, *Kom Ombos,* Vol. 2, Part 1, Vienna: Adolphe Holzhausen, 1895.
de Morgan, J., U. Bouriant, G. Legrain, G. Jéquier, and A. Barsanti, *Kom Ombos,* Vol. 3, Part 2, Vienna: Adolphe Holzhausen, 1900.

Moscucci, O., "Granville, Augustus Bozzi (1783–1872)," *Oxford Dictionary of National Biography*, http://www.oxforddnb.com/index/11/101011299/ (last accessed June 27, 2011), DOI: 10/1093/ref:odnb/11299.

Moser, S., *Wondrous Curiosities: Ancient Egypt at the British Museum*, London: Chicago University Press, 2006.

Moyer, I. S., *Egypt and the Limits of Hellenism*, Cambridge: Cambridge University Press, 2011.

Müller, M., "Die Königsplastik des Mittleren Reiches und ihre Schöpfer: Reden über Statuen—Wenn Statuen reden," *Imago Aegypti* 1 (2005), pp. 27–78.

Münch, H.-H., "Categorizing Archaeological Finds: The Funerary Material of Queen Hetepheres I at Giza," *Antiquity* 74, no. 286 (2000), pp. 898–908.

Muñoz Viñas, S., *Contemporary Theory of Conservation*, Oxford and Burlington, MA: Elsevier Butterworth-Heinemann, 2005.

Murray, M. A., *The Tomb of Two Brothers*, Manchester: Sherratt & Hughes, 1910.

Myers, O. H., and H. W. Fairman, "Excavations at Armant, 1929–31," *Journal of Egyptian Archaeology* 17 (1931), pp. 223–32.

Nash, W. L., "The Tomb of Mentuhetep I (?) at Dêr el Bahri, Thebes," *Proceedings of the Society of Biblical Archaeology* 23 (1901), pp. 291–3.

Naville, E., *The XIth Dynasty Temple at Deir el-Bahari*, Part 1, London: Egypt Exploration Fund, 1907.

Nelson, D. D., *National Manhood: Capitalist Citizenship and the Imagined Fraternity of White Men*, Durham, NC, and London: Duke University Press, 1998.

Nelson, H. H., "The Identity of Amon-Re of United-with-Eternity," *Journal of Near Eastern Studies* 1 (1942), pp. 127–52.

Nelson, H. H., and W. J. Murnane, *The Great Hypostyle Hall at Karnak*, Vol. 1, Part 1, *The Wall Reliefs*, Chicago: University of Chicago, 1981.

Neuville, E., "Women, Cloth, Fluff and Dust in Elizabeth Gaskell's *North and South*," *Textile* 8 (2010), pp. 274–85.

Newberry, P. E., *El Bersheh, Part I: The Tomb of Tehuti-Hetep*, London: Egypt Exploration Fund, 1893–4.

Newberry, P. E., *Funerary Statuettes and Model Sarcophagi*, Catalogue général des antiquités égyptiennes, Cairo: Institut Français d'Archéologie Orientale, 1937.

Noble, L., *Medicinal Cannibalism in Early Modern English Literature and Culture*, New York: Palgrave Macmillan, 2011.

Nochlin, L., "The Imaginary Orient," *Art in America* (1983), pp. 118–31, 187–91.

Nochlin, L., *The Politics of Vision: Essays on Nineteenth-Century Art and Society*, New York: Harper & Row, 1989.

Nooter, M. H., "Introduction: The Aesthetics and Politics of Things Unseen," in M. H. Nooter (ed.), *Secrecy: African Art that Conceals and Reveals*, Munich: Prestel, 1993, pp. 23–33.

Nooter, M. H. (ed.), *Secrecy: African Art that Conceals and Reveals*, Munich: Prestel, 1993.

Nyord, R., *Breathing Flesh: Conceptions of the Body in the Ancient Egyptian Coffin Texts*, Copenhagen: Museum Tusculanum Press, 2009.

Ockinga, B., *Die Gottebenbildlichkeit im Alten Ägypten und im Alten Testament*, Wiesbaden: Harrassowitz, 1984.

Oldfield, M., *The Secret Museum*, London: HarperCollins, 2013.

Olsen, B., *In Defense of Things: Archaeology and the Ontology of Objects*, Lanham, MD, and Plymouth, UK: Altamira Press, 2010.

Osborne, R., *The History Written on the Classical Greek Body,* Cambridge: Cambridge University Press, 2011.
Otto, E., *Das ägyptische Mundöffnungsritual,* Wiesbaden: Harrassowitz, 1960.
Otto, E., "Die beiden vogelgestaltigen Seelen vorstellungen der Ägypter," *Zeitschrift der Ägyptische Sprache und Altertumskunde* 77 (1942), pp. 78–91.
Owen, E.R.J., *Cotton and the Egyptian Economy 1820–1914: A Study in Trade and Development,* Oxford: Clarendon Press, 1969.
Palmer, A., *Unravelled: The Journey of an Egyptian Child Mummy and Other Portraits,* London: Waterhouse & Dodd, n.d., http://www.angelaspalmer.com/wpcontent/uploads/2011/09/Palmer_unravelled.pdf.
Parkinson, B. R., "Tutankhamen on Trial: Egyptian Nationalism and the Court Case for the Pharaoh's Artifacts," *Journal of the American Research Center in Egypt* 44 (2008), pp. 1–8.
Parkinson, R. B., *The Rosetta Stone,* London: British Museum Press, 2005.
Pearce, S. M., "Bodies in Exile: Egyptian Mummies in the Early Nineteenth Century and Their Cultural Implications," in S. Ouditt (ed.), *Displaced Persons: Conditions of Exile in European Culture,* Aldershot: Ashgate, 2002, pp. 54–71.
Peers, L. L., and A. K. Brown (eds.), *Museums and Source Communities: A Routledge Reader,* London and New York: Routledge, 2003.
Peet, T. E., *The Great Tomb-Robberies of the Twentieth Egyptian Dynasty,* Oxford: Clarendon Press, 1930.
Peradotto, J. (ed.), Special Issue: The Challenge of *Black Athena, Arethusa* 22 (1989).
Persson, H., "Collecting Egypt: The Textile Collection of the Victoria and Albert Museum," *Journal of the History of Collections* 24 (2012), pp. 3–13.
Petrie, W.M.F., *Medum,* London: David Nutt, 1892.
Petrie, W.M.F., *Qurneh,* London: School of Archaeology in Egypt, 1909.
Petrie, W.M.F., *Roman Portraits and Memphis (IV),* London: School of Archaeology in Egypt, 1911.
Petrie, W.M.F., F. L. Griffith, and P. Newberry, *Kahun, Gurob, and Hawara,* London: Kegan Paul, Trench, Trubner and Co., 1890.
Petrie, W.M.F., and E. Mackay, *Heliopolis, Kafr Ammar and Shurafa,* London: School of Archaeology in Egypt, 1915.
Petrie, W.M.F., E. Mackay, and G. A. Wainwright, *Meydum and Memphis (III),* London: School of Archaeology in Egypt, 1910.
Petrie, W.M.F., G. A. Wainwright, and A. H. Gardiner, *Tarkhan I and Memphis V,* London: School of Archaeology in Egypt, 1913.
Pettigrew, T. J., *A History of Egyptian Mummies,* London: Longman, 1834.
Pezin, M., and F. Janot, "La 'pustule' et les deux doigts," *Bulletin de l'Institut Français d'Archéologie Orientale* 95 (1995), pp. 361–65.
Pfister, R., "Les textiles du tombeau de Toutankhamon," *Revue des Arts Asiatiques* 11 (1937), pp. 207–18.
Piankoff, A., and N. Rambova, *The Shrines of Tutankhamon,* New York: Pantheon, 1955.
Piankoff, A., and N. Rambova, *The Tomb of Ramesses VI,* New York: Pantheon, 1954.
Picton, J., and J. Mack, *African Textiles,* London: British Museum Press, 1989.
Pinch, G., "Redefining Funerary Objects," in Z. Hawass (ed.), *Egyptology at the Dawn of the Twenty-First Century, Proceedings of the Eighth International Congress of Egyptologists, Cairo 2000,* Vol. 2, *History, Religion,* Cairo: American University in Cairo Press, 2003, pp. 443–47.

Pinney, C., "Things Happen: Or, from Which Moment Does That Object Come?" in D. Miller (ed.), *Materiality*, Durham, NC, and London: Duke University Press, 2005, pp. 256–72.

Poe, E. A., "Some Words with a Mummy," in R. W. Griswold and N. P. Willis (eds.), *The Works of the Late Edgar Allan Poe*, New York: Blakeman and Mason, 1850, pp. 438–54.

Pollin, B. R., "Poe's 'Some Words with a Mummy' Reconsidered," *Emerson Society Quarterly* 60 (1970), pp. 60–67.

Pollock, S., "The Looting of the Iraq Museum: Thoughts on Archaeology in a Time of Crisis," *Public Archaeology* 3 (2003), pp. 117–24.

Porterfield, T., *The Allure of Empire: Art in the Service of French Imperialism 1798–1836*, Princeton, NJ: Princeton University Press, 1998.

Posener-Kriéger, P., "Les mesures des étoffes à l'Ancien Empire," *Revue d'Égyptologie* 29 (1977), pp. 86–96.

Prag, J., and R. Neave, *Making Faces: Using Forensic and Archaeological Evidence*, London: British Museum Press, 1997.

Pratt, M. L., *Imperial Eyes: Travel Writing and Transculturation*, London and New York: Routledge, 1992.

Preucel, R. W., *Archaeological Semiotics*, Malden, MA, and Oxford: Blackwell, 2006.

Preziosi, D., *Brain of the Earth's Body: Art, Museums, and the Phantasms of Modernity*, London and Minneapolis: University of Minnesota Press, 2003.

Price, K., and M. Gleba, "Textiles on Egyptian Mirrors: Pragmatics or Religion?," *Archaeological Textiles Review* 54 (2012), pp. 2–13.

Quack, J. F., "Fragmente des Mundöffnungsrituals aus Tebtynis," In K. Ryholt (ed.), *The Carlsberg Papyri, 7: Hieratic Texts from the Collection*, Copenhagen, Museum Tusculanum Press, 2006, pp. 69–150.

Quibell, J. E., *Archaic Mastabas*, Cairo: Institut Français d'Archéologie Orientale, 1923.

Quibell, J. E., *Tomb of Yuaa and Thuiu*, Cairo: Institut Français d'Archéologie Orientale, 1908.

Quibell, J. E., and A.G.K. Hayter, *Teti Pyramid, North Side*, Cairo: Institut Français d'Archéologie Orientale, 1927.

Quirke, S., *Hidden Hands: Egyptian Workforces in Petrie Excavation Archives, 1880–1924*, London: Duckworth, 2010.

Quirke, S., "Modern Mummies and Ancient Scarabs: The Egyptian Collection of Sir William Hamilton," *Journal of the History of Collections* 9 (1997), pp. 253–62.

Ransom Williams, C., "The Egyptian Collection in the Museum of Art at Cleveland, Ohio," *Journal of Egyptian Archaeology* 5 (1918), pp. 166–78.

Raven, M. J., "Egyptian Concepts on the Orientation of the Human Body," *Journal of Egyptian Archaeology* 91 (2005), pp. 37–53.

Raven, M. J., *The Tomb of Iurudef: A Memphite Official in the Reign of Ramesses II*, London: Egypt Exploration Society, 1991.

Raven, M. J., *The Tomb of Pay and Raia at Saqqara*, London: Egypt Exploration Society and the National Museum of Antiquities Leiden, 2005.

Ray, J. D., "An Inscribed Linen Plea from the Sacred Animal Necropolis, North Saqqara," *Journal of Egyptian Archaeology* 91 (2005), pp. 171–9.

Reeves, C. N., *Valley of the Kings: The Decline of a Royal Necropolis*, London and New York: Kegan Paul, 1990.

Reeves, C. N., and J. H. Taylor, *Howard Carter before Tutankhamun*, London: British Museum Press, 1992.

Reid, D. M., "French Egyptology and the Architecture of Orientalism: Deciphering the Façade of Cairo's Egyptian Museum," in L. C. Brown and M. S. Gordon (eds.), *Franco–Arab Encounters: Studies in Memory of David C. Gordon,* Beirut: American University of Beirut, 1996, pp. 35–69.

Reid, D. M., "Indigenous Egyptology: The Decolonization of a Profession?" *Journal of the American Oriental Society* 105 (1985), pp. 233–46.

Reid, D. M., *Whose Pharaohs? Archaeology, Museums, and Egyptian National Identity from Napoleon to World War I,* Berkeley: University of California Press, 2002.

Reisner, G. A., *A History of the Giza Necropolis,* Vol. 1, Cambridge, MA: Harvard University Press, 1942.

Reisner, G. A., and M. H. Abd-ul-Rahman, *Canopics,* Catalogue général des antiquités égyptiennes, Cairo: Institut Français d'Archéologie Orientale, 1967.

Riggs, C., "Ancient Egypt in the Museum: Concepts and Constructions," in A. B. Lloyd (ed.), *A Companion to Ancient Egypt,* Vol. 2, Oxford and Malden, MA: Wiley-Blackwell, 2010, pp. 1129–53.

Riggs, C., *The Beautiful Burial in Roman Egypt: Art, Identity, and Funerary Religion,* Oxford: Oxford University Press, 2005.

Riggs, C. "Colonial Visions: Egyptian Antiquities and Contested Histories in the Cairo Museum," *Museum Worlds: Advances in Research* 1 (2013), pp. 65–84.

Riggs, C., "Forms of the *wesekh* Collar in Funerary Art of the Graeco-Roman Period," *Chronique d'Égypte* 76 (2001), pp. 57–68.

Riggs, C., "Gilding the Lily: Shrouds, Sculpture, and the Representation of Women in Ptolemaic and Early Roman Egypt," in P. D. Manuelian and S. E. Thompson (eds.), *Egypt and Beyond: Essays Presented to Leonard H. Lesko,* Providence, RI: Brown University Press, 2008, pp. 285–304.

Riggs, C., "Jesse Haworth and the Manchester Museum," *Bulletin of the Association for the Study of Travel in Egypt and the Near East (ASTENE)* 24 (2005), pp. 11–12.

Riggs, C., "Roman Mummy Masks from Deir el-Bahri," *Journal of Egyptian Archaeology* 86 (2000), pp. 121–44.

Riggs, C., "We've Been Here Before," *Times Higher Education,* February 24, 2011, p. 28.

Ritner, R. K., "Denderite Temple Hierarchy and the Family of Theban High Priest Nebwenenef: Block Statue OIM 10729," in D. P. Silverman (ed.), *For His Ka: Essays Offered in Memory of Klaus Baer,* Chicago: Oriental Institute, 1994, pp. 205–26.

Ritner, R. K., *The Mechanics of Ancient Egyptian Magical Practice,* Chicago: Oriental Institute of the University of Chicago, 1993.

Roberts, P. C., "'One of Our Mummies Is Missing': Evaluating Petrie's Records from Hawara," in M. L. Bierbrier (ed.), *Portraits and Masks,* London: British Museum Press, 1997, pp. 19–25.

Robins, G., "Cult Statues in Ancient Egypt," in N. H. Walls (ed.), *Cult Image and Divine Representation in the Ancient Near East,* Boston: American Schools of Oriental Research, 2005, pp. 1–12.

Roehrig, C. H., "Egyptian: Sheet of 'Royal Linen,'" *Metropolitan Museum of Art Bulletin* 53 (1995–96), pp. 22.

Roehrig, C. H., "Life along the Nile: Three Egyptians of Ancient Thebes," *Metropolitan Museum of Art Bulletin* 60 (2002), pp. 1–56.

Roehrig, C. H., "The Middle Kingdom Tomb of Wah at Thebes," in N. Strudwick and J. H. Taylor (eds.), *The Theban Necropolis: Past, Present, Future,* London: British Museum Press, 2003, pp. 11–13.

Rondot, V., "De la fonction des statues-cubes comme cale-porte," *Revue d'Égyptologie* 62 (2011), pp. 141–57.

Rose, J., *The Haunting of Sylvia Plath,* Cambridge, MA: Harvard University Press, 1991.

Roth, A. M., "Buried Pyramids and Layered Thoughts: The Organisation of Multiple Approaches in Egyptian Religion," in C. J. Eyre (ed.), *Proceedings of the Seventh International Congress of Egyptologists, Cambridge, 3–9 September 1995,* Leuven: Peeters, 1998, pp. 991–1003.

Roth, A. M., *Egyptian Phyles of the Old Kingdom,* Chicago: Oriental Institute of the University of Chicago, 1991.

Roth, A. M., "Fingers, Stars, and the 'Opening of the Mouth': The Nature and Function of the *ntrwj*-blades," *Journal of Egyptian Archaeology* 79 (1993), pp. 57–79.

Roth, A. M., "The *pšs-kf* and the 'Opening of the Mouth' Ceremony: A Ritual of Birth and Rebirth," *Journal of Egyptian Archaeology* 78 (1992), pp. 113–47.

Roth, A. M., and C. H. Roehrig, "Magical Bricks and the Bricks of Birth," *Journal of Egyptian Archaeology* 88 (2002), pp. 121–39.

Ruffer, M. A., "On Arterial Lesions Found in Egyptian Mummies (1580 BC–525 AD)," *Journal of Pathology and Bacteriology* 15 (1911), pp. 453–62.

Ruffer, M. A., "Remarks on the Histology and Pathological Anatomy of Egyptian Mummies," *Cairo Scientific Journal* 40 (1910), pp. 1–5.

Ruffer, M. A., and R. L. Moodie, *Studies in the Palaeopathology of Egypt,* Chicago: University of Chicago Press, 1921.

Ruffer, M. A., and A. Rietti, "On Osseous Lesions in Ancient Egyptians," *Journal of Pathology and Bacteriology* 16 (1912), pp. 439–65.

Rummel, U., "Das Pantherfell als Kleidungsstück im Kult: Bedeutung, Symbolgehalt und theologische Verortung einer magischen Insignie," *Imago Aegypti* 2 (2007), pp. 109–52.

Rummel, U., "Weihrauch, Salböl und Leinen: Balsamierungsmaterialen als Medium der Erneuerung im Sedfest," *Studien zur Altägyptischen Kultur* 34 (2006), pp. 381–407.

Russmann, E., *Egyptian Sculpture: Cairo and Luxor,* Austin: University of Texas Press, 1989.

Rutherford, I. C., "Travel and Pilgrimage," in C. Riggs (ed.), *The Oxford Handbook of Roman Egypt,* Oxford: Oxford University Press, 2012, pp. 701–16.

Rydstrom, K. T., "ḤRY SŠT3 'in Charge of Secrets': The 3000-Year Evolution of a Title," *Discussions in Egyptology* 28 (1994), pp. 53–91.

Ryhiner, M.-L., *La procession des étoffes et l'union avec Hathor,* Brussels: Fondation Égyptologique Reine Élisabeth, 1995.

Rzeuska, T. I., "And Where Are the Viscera…? Reassessing the Function of Old Kingdom Canopic Recesses and Pits," in N. Strudwick and H. Strudwick (eds.), *Old Kingdom, New Perspectives: Egyptian Art and Archaeology 2750–2150 BC,* Oxford and Oakville, CT: Oxbow Books, 2011, pp. 244–55.

el-Saady, H., "Reflections on the Goddess Tayet," *Journal of Egyptian Archaeology* 80 (1994), pp. 213–17.

Said, E. W., *Culture and Imperialism,* London: Vintage, 1993.

Said, E. W., *Orientalism,* London: Penguin, 1978.

Sakula, A., "Augustus Bozzi Granville (1783–1872): London Physician-Accoucheur and Italian Patriot," *Journal of the Royal Society of Medicine* 76 (1983), pp. 876–82.

Saleh, M., and H. Sourouzian, *The Egyptian Museum: Official Catalogue,* Mainz: Philipp von Zabern, 1987.

Sambin, C., and J.-F. Carlotti, "Une porte de fête-sed de Ptolémée II remployée dans le temple de Montou à Médamoud," *Bulletin de l'Institut Français d'Archéologie Orientale* 95 (1995), pp. 383–457.

Sandison, A. T., "Balsamierung," in W. Helck and E. Otto (eds.), *Lexikon der Ägyptologie,* Vol. 1, Wiesbaden: Harrassowitz, 1975, cols. 610–14.

Sauneron, S., *Rituel de l'embaumement,* Cairo: Imprimerie Nationale, 1952.

Sawday, J., *The Body Emblazoned: Dissection and the Human Body in Renaissance Culture,* London and New York: Routledge, 1995.

el-Sayed, R., *La déesse Neith de Saïs, I. Importance et rayonnement de son culte,* Cairo: Institut Français d'Archéologie Orientale, 1982.

el-Sayed, R., "Deux statues inédites du Musée du Caire," *Bulletin de l'Institut Français d'Archéologie Orientale* 84 (1984), pp. 127–53.

Scalf, F., "Magical Bricks in the Oriental Institute Museum of the University of Chicago," *Studien zur altägyptischen Kultur* 38 (2009), pp. 275–95.

Scheele, K., *Die Stofflisten des Alten Reiches: Lexikographie, Entwicklung und Gebrauch,* Wiesbaden: Harrassowitz, 2005.

Scheidel, W., "The Meaning of Dates on Mummy Labels: Seasonal Mortality and Mortuary Practice in Roman Egypt," *Journal of Roman Archaeology* 11 (1998), pp. 285–92.

Schiaparelli, E., *La tomba intatta dell'architetto Cha nella necropoli di Tebe,* Turin: R. Museo di Antichità, 1927.

Schneider, H. D., *Shabtis,* Leiden: Rijksmuseum van Oudheden, 1977.

Schneider, J., and A. B. Weiner, "Cloth and the Organization of Human Experience," *Current Anthropology* 27 (1986), pp. 178–84.

Schneider, T., "Ägyptologen im Dritten Reich: Biographische Notizen anhand der sogenannten 'Steindorff–Liste,'" in T. Schneider and P. Raulwing (eds.), *Egyptology from the First World War to the Third Reich: Ideology, Scholarship, and Individual Biographies,* Leiden and Boston: Brill, 2013, pp. 120–247.

Schneider, T., and P. Raulwing (eds.), *Egyptology from the First World War to the Third Reich: Ideology, Scholarship, and Individual Biographies,* Leiden and Boston: Brill, 2013.

Schott, S., "*Rs-n.y* und *mḥ-n.t* als Häuser der Neith," *Revue d'Égyptologie* 19 (1967), pp. 99–110.

Schulz, R., "Block Statue," in W. Wendrich (ed.), *UCLA Encyclopedia of Egyptology,* Los Angeles: UCLA, 2008, http://www.escholarship.org/uc/item/3f23c0q9.

Schulz, R., *Die Entwicklung und Bedeutung des kuboiden Statuentypus: Eine Untersuchung zu den sogenannten "Würfelhockern,"* Hildesheim: Gerstenberg, 1992.

Schwyzer, P., *Archaeologies of English Renaissance Literature,* Oxford: Oxford University Press, 2007.

Seipel, W., "Mumien und Ethik im Museum," in W. Seipel (ed.), *Mumien aus dem Alten Ägypten: Zur Mumienforschung im Kunsthistorischen Museum,* Milan: Skira, 1998, pp. 7–11.

Serpico, M., "Resins, Amber and Bitumen," in P. T. Nicholson and I. Shaw (eds.), *Ancient Egyptian Materials and Technology,* Cambridge: Cambridge University Press, 2000, pp. 430–74.

Sheppard, K. L., "Between Spectacle and Science: Margaret Murray and the Tomb of the Two Brothers," *Science in Context* 25 (2012), pp. 525–49.

Sheppard, K. L., "The Lady and the Looking Glass: Margaret Murray's Life in Archaeology," Ph.D. dissertation, University of Oklahoma, 2011.

Simmel, G., "The Secret and the Secret Society," in K. H. Wolff (ed.), *The Sociology of Georg Simmel*, Glencoe, IL: The Free Press, 1950 [1908], pp. 307–76.

Smith, M., "Osiris and the Deceased," in W. Wendrich (ed.), *UCLA Encyclopedia of Egyptology*, Los Angeles: UCLA, 2008, http://www.escholarship.org/uc/item/29r70244.

Smith, M., *Traversing Eternity: Texts for the Afterlife from Ptolemaic and Roman Egypt*, Oxford: Oxford University Press, 2009.

Smith, W. S., *A History of Egyptian Sculpture and Painting of the Old Kingdom*, London: For the Boston Museum of Fine Arts, by Oxford University Press, 1949.

Smith, W. S., "The Old Kingdom Linen List," *Zeitschrift für Ägyptische Sprache und Altertumskunde* 71 (1935), pp. 134–49.

Sofaer, J. R., *The Body as Material Culture: A Theoretical Osteoarchaeology*, Cambridge: Cambridge University Press, 2006.

Sourouzian, H., "Inventaire iconographique des statues en manteau jubilaire," in C. Berger, G. Clerc, and N. Grimal (eds.), *Hommages à Jean Leclant*, Vol. 1, *Études Pharaoniques*, Cairo: Institut Français d'Archéologie Orientale, 1994, pp. 499–530.

Spanel, D., *Through Ancient Eyes: Egyptian Portraiture*, Birmingham, AL: Birmingham Museum of Art, 1988.

Spiegelberg, W., "Ein Bruchstück des Bestattungsrituals der Apisstiere," *Zeitschrift für Ägyptische Sprache und Altertumskunde* 56 (1920), pp. 1–33.

Stadler, M. A., "Procession," in W. Wendrich (ed.), *UCLA Encyclopedia of Egyptology*, Los Angeles: UCLA, 2008, http://escholarship.org.uc/item/679146w5.

Stafford, B. M., *Body Criticism: Imaging the Unseen in Enlightenment Art and Medicine*, Cambridge, MA and London: MIT Press, 1991.

Stocking, G.W.J., *Victorian Anthropology*, New York: Free Press, 1987.

Stoler, A. L., *Along the Archival Grain: Epistemic Anxieties and Colonial Common Sense*, Princeton, NJ: Princeton University Press, 2009.

Stoll, M., and D. Fengel, "Chemical and Structural Studies on Ancient Egyptian Linen," *Berliner Beiträge zur Archäometrie* 10 (1988), pp. 151–72.

Sugg, R., *Mummies, Cannibals and Vampires: The History of Corpse Medicine from the Renaissance to the Victorians*, Abingdon and New York: Routledge, 2011.

Summers, D., *Real Spaces: World Art History and the Rise of Western Modernism*, London: Phaidon, 2003.

Surin, K., "The Sovereign Individual and Michael Taussig's Politics of Defacement," *Nepantla: Views from the South* 2 (2001), pp. 205–19.

Sweeney, D., "Egyptian Masks in Motion," *Göttinger Miszellen* 135 (1993), pp. 101–4.

Szymańska, H., and K. Babraj (eds.), *Mummy: Results of an Interdisciplinary Examination of the Egyptian Mummy of Aset-Iri-Khet-Es from the Archaeological Museum in Cracow*, Cracow: Polish Academy of Arts and Sciences, 2001.

Tacke, N., "Die Entwicklung der Mumienmaske im Alten Reich," *Mitteilungen des Deutschen Archäologischen Instituts Kairo* 52 (1996), pp. 307–36.

Tarlo, E., *Clothing Matters: Dress and Identity in India*, London: Hurst, 1996.

Taussig, M., *Defacement: Public Secrecy and the Labor of the Negative*, Stanford, CA: Stanford University Press, 1999.

Taussig, M., *Mimesis and Alterity: A Particular History of the Senses,* London and New York: Routledge, 1993.

Taussig, M., *Shamanism, Colonialism, and the Wild Man: A Study in Terror and Healing,* Chicago and London: University of Chicago Press, 1987.

Taylor, J. H., *Death and the Afterlife in Ancient Egypt,* London: British Museum Press, 2000.

Taylor, J. H., *Journey through the Afterlife: Ancient Egyptian Book of the Dead,* London: British Museum Press, 2010.

Teeter, E., *Ancient Egypt: Treasures from the Collection of the Oriental Institute, University of Chicago,* Chicago: Oriental Institute, 2003.

Thomas, A. P., "The Midgleys of Bolton and Their Contribution to the Scientific Examination of Ancient Textiles," *Archaeological Textile Newsletter* 45 (2007), pp. 21–25.

Thomas, N., "The Case of the Misplaced Ponchos: Speculations Concerning the History of Cloth in Polynesia," *Journal of Material Culture* 4 (1999), pp. 5–20.

Thomas, N., *Entangled Objects: Exchange, Material Culture, and Colonialism in the Pacific,* Cambridge, MA: Harvard University Press, 1991.

Trafton, S., *Egypt Land: Race and Nineteenth-Century American Egyptomania,* Durham, NC: Duke University Press, 2004.

Troy, L., *Patterns of Queenship in Ancient Egyptian Myth and History,* Uppsala, Sweden: Uppsala University, 1986.

Turner, B., *Marx and the End of Orientalism,* London: Allen and Unwin, 1978.

Valeri, V., *The Forest of Taboos: Morality, Hunting, and Identity among the Huaulu of the Moluccas,* Madison, WI, and London: University of Wisconsin Press, 1999.

van Dommelen, P., "Postcolonial Archaeologies between Discourse and Practice," *World Archaeology* 43 (2011), pp. 1–6.

van Duuren, D., *Physical Anthropology Reconsidered: Human Remains at the Tropenmuseum,* Amsterdam: Royal Tropical Institute/KIT, 2007.

Vaswani, R., "Remains of the Day," *Museums Journal* 101 (2001), pp. 34–35.

Vittmann, G., "Stolist," in W. Helck and E. Otto (eds.), *Lexikon der Ägyptologie,* Vol. 6, Wiesbaden: Harrassowitz, 1986, cols. 63–5.

Vogel, C., "Fallen Heroes?—Winlock's 'Slain Soldiers' Reconsidered," *Journal of Egyptian Archaeology* 89 (2003), pp. 239–45.

Vogelsang-Eastwood, G., *Pharaonic Egyptian Clothing,* Leiden: E. J. Brill, 1993.

Vogelsang-Eastwood, G., *The Production of Linen in Pharaonic Egypt,* Leiden: Stichting Textile Research Centre, 1992.

Vogelsang-Eastwood, G., "Textiles," in P. T. Nicholson and I. Shaw (eds.), *Ancient Egyptian Materials and Technology,* Cambridge: Cambridge University Press, 2000, pp. 268–98.

Vogelsang-Eastwood, G., *Tutankhamun's Wardrobe: Garments from the Tomb of Tutankhamun,* Rotterdam: Barjesteh van Waalwijk van Doorn & Co's, 1999.

von Lieven, A., "Bemerkungen zum Dekorationsprogramm des Osireion in Abydos," in B. Haring and A. Klug (eds.), *6. Ägyptologische Tempeltagung: Funktion und Gebrauch altägyptischer Tempelräume,* Wiesbaden: Harrassowitz, 2007, pp. 167–86.

von Lieven, A., "Deified Humans," in W. Wendrich (ed.), *UCLA Encyclopedia of Egyptology,* Los Angeles: UCLA, 2010, http://escholarship.org.uc/item/3kk97509.

von Lieven, A., "Mysterien des Kosmos: Kosmographie und Priesterwissenschaft," in J. Assmann and M. Bommas (eds.), *Ägyptische Mysterien?* Munich: Wilhelm Fink, 2002, pp. 47–58.

Vos, R. L., *The Apis Embalming Ritual: P. Vindob. 3873,* Leuven: Peeters, 1993.

Waldron, H. A., "The Study of Human Remains from Nubia: The Contribution of Grafton Elliot Smith and His Colleagues to Palaeopathology," *Medical History* 44 (2000), pp. 363–88.

Walker, S., and M. L. Bierbrier (eds.), *Ancient Faces: Mummy Portraits from Roman Egypt*, London: British Museum Press, 1997.

Wastiau, B., "The Scourge of Chief Kansabala: The Ritual Life of Two Congolese Masterpieces at the Royal Museum of Central Africa (1884–2001)," in M. Bouquet and N. Porto (eds.), *Science, Magic and Religion: The Ritual Processes of Museum Magic*, New York and Oxford: Berghahn, 2006, pp. 95–115.

Weiner, A. B., "Cultural Difference and the Density of Objects," *American Ethnologist* 21 (1994), pp. 391–403.

Weiner, A. B., *Inalienable Possessions: The Paradox of Keeping-While-Giving*, Berkeley and Los Angeles: University of California Press, 1992.

Wendrich, W., "Egyptian Archaeology: From Text to Context," in W. Wendrich (ed.), *Egyptian Archaeology*, Malden, MA, and Oxford: Wiley-Blackwell, 2010, pp. 1–14.

Wendrich, W., "Entangled, Connected or Protected? The Power of Knots and Knotting in Ancient Egypt," in K. Szpakowska (ed.), *Through a Glass Darkly: Magic, Dreams and Prophecy in Ancient Egypt*, Swansea: Classical Press of Wales, 2006, pp. 243–69.

Wendrich, W., "Epilogue: Eternal Egypt Deconstructed," in W. Wendrich (ed.), *Egyptian Archaeology*, Malden, MA, and Oxford: Wiley-Blackwell, 2010, pp. 274–78.

Wendrich, W., "From Practical Knowledge to Empowered Communication: Field Schools of the Supreme Council of Antiquities in Egypt," in R. Boytner, L. S. Dodd, and B. J. Parker (eds.), *Controlling the Past, Owning the Future: The Political Uses of Archaeology in the Middle East*, Tucson: University of Arizona Press, 2010, pp. 178–95.

Wendrich, W., "Introduction. Archaeology and Apprenticeship: Body Knowledge, Identity, and Communities of Practice," in W. Wendrich (ed.), *Archaeology and Apprenticeship: Body Knowledge, Identity, and Communities of Practice*, Tucson: University of Arizona Press, 2013, pp. 1–19.

Wendrich, W., *The World According to Basketry: An Ethno-Archaeological Interpretation of Basketry Production in Egypt*, Leiden: Research School CNWS, 1999.

Wengrow, D., *The Archaeology of Early Egypt: Social Transformations in North-East Africa, 10,000 to 2650 BC*, Cambridge: Cambridge University Press, 2006.

Wengrow, D., "Prehistories of Commodity Branding," *Current Anthropology* 49 (2008), pp. 7–34.

Wengrow, D., *What Makes Civilization? The Ancient Near East and the Future of the West*, Oxford: Oxford University Press, 2010.

Wente, E. F., "Mysticism in Pharaonic Egypt?" *Journal of Near Eastern Studies* 41 (1982), pp. 161–79.

Whitehouse, H., *Ancient Egypt and Nubia in the Ashmolean Museum*, Oxford: Ashmolean Museum, 2009.

Widmer, G., "A propos de quelques dédicaces sur lin de l'époque romaine: Une pratique votive méconnue?" in E. Frood and A. McDonald (eds.), *Decorum and Experience: Essays in Ancient Culture for John Baines*, Oxford: Griffith Institute, 2013, pp. 185–92.

Widmer, G., "La stèle de Paêsis (Louvre E 25983) et quelques formes d'Osiris dans le Fayoum aux époques ptolémaïque et romaine," in L. Coulon (ed.), *Le culte d'Osiris au Ier millénaire av. J.-C.: Découvertes et travaux récents,* Cairo: Institut Français d'Archéologie Orientale, 2010, pp. 63–97.

Wieczorkiewicz, A., "Unwrapping Mummies and Telling Their Stories: Egyptian Mummies and Museum Rhetoric," in M. Bouquet and N. Porto (eds.), *Science, Magic and Religion: The Ritual Processes of Museum Magic,* New York and Oxford: Berghahn, 2006, pp. 51–71.

Wild, J. P., and F. Wild, "Cotton: The New Wool. Qasr Ibrim Study Season 2008," *Archaeological Textiles Newsletter* 46 (2008), pp. 3–6.

Wild, J. P., F. Wild, and A. Clapham, "Irrigation and the Spread of Cotton Growing in Roman Times," *Archaeological Textiles Newsletter* 44 (2007), pp. 16–18.

Wildsmith, K., "Endoscopy and Mummy Research," in R. David (ed.), *Egyptian Mummies and Modern Science,* Cambridge: Cambridge University Press, 2008, pp. 43–51.

Wildung, D., *Egyptian Saints: Deification in Pharaonic Egypt,* New York: New York University Press, 1977.

Wildung, D., *Imhotep und Amenhotep: Gottwerdung im Alten Ägypten,* Munich and Berlin: Deutscher Kunstverlag, 1977.

Wildung, D., "What Visitors Want to See," *Museum International* 47 (1995),pp. 4–8.

Wilkinson, C., *Forensic Facial Reconstruction,* Cambridge: Cambridge University Press, 2008.

Willems, H., *The Coffin of Heqata (Cairo JdE 36418): A Case Study of Egyptian Funerary Culture of the Early Middle Kingdom,* Leuven: Peeters, 1996.

Willems, H., "The One and the Many in Stela Leiden VI," *Chronique d'Égypte* 73 (1998), pp. 231–43.

Wilson, P., *A Ptolemaic Lexikon: A Lexicographical Study of the Texts in the Temple of Edfu,* Leuven: Peeters, 1997.

Wingfield, C., "Touching the Buddha: Encounters with a Charismatic Object," in S. Dudley, *Museum Materialities: Objects, Engagements, Interpretations,* London and New York: Routledge, 2009, pp. 53–70.

Winlock, H. E., "The Museum's Excavations at Thebes," *Bulletin of the Metropolitan Museum of Art,* Part 2, *The Egyptian Expedition 1924–1925* (1926), pp. 5–32.

Winlock, H. E., *The Slain Soldiers of Neb-Hepet-Re Mentu-Hotpe,* New York: Metropolitan Museum of Art, 1945.

Winlock, H. E., *The Tomb of Queen Meryet-Amun at Thebes,* New York: Metropolitan Museum of Art, 1932.

Winlock, H. E., "The Tombs of the Kings of the Seventeenth Dynasty at Thebes," *Journal of Egyptian Archaeology* 10 (1924), pp. 217–77.

Winlock, H. E., and D. Arnold, *Tutankhamun's Funeral,* New York: Metropolitan Museum of Art, 2010.

Witcomb, A., *Re-imagining the Museum: Beyond the Mausoleum,* London: Routledge, 2003.

Wolfe, S. J., *Mummies in Nineteenth Century America: Ancient Egyptians as Artifacts,* Jefferson, NC, and London: McFarland and Company, 2009.

Wolinski, A., "Ancient Egyptian Ceremonial Masks," *Discussions in Egyptology* 6 (1986), pp. 47–53.

Wolinski, A., "Egyptian Masks: The Priest and His Role," *Archaeology* 40 (1987), pp. 22–29.

Young, R.J.C., "The Afterlives of *Black Athena*," in D. Orrells, G. K. Bhambra, and T. Roynon (eds.), *African Athena: New Agendas*, Oxford: Oxford University Press, 2011, pp. 174–88.

Young, R.J.C., "*Black Athena:* The Politics of Scholarship," *Science as Culture* 4 (1993), pp. 274–81.

Young, R.J.C., *Colonial Desire: Hybridity in Theory, Culture and Race*, London and New York: Routledge, 1995.

Young, R.J.C., "Egypt in America: *Black Athena*, Racism and Colonial Discourse," in A. Rattansi and S. Westwood (eds.), *Racism, Modernity and Identity: On the Western Front*, Cambridge: Polity Press, 1994, pp. 150–69.

Yoyotte, J., "A propos d'un monument copié par G. Daressy (contribution à l'histoire littéraire)," *Bulletin de la Societé Française d'Égyptologie* 11 (1952), pp. 67–72.

Zandee, J., "Prayers to the Sun-god from Theban Tombs," *Jaarbericht van het vooraziatisch-egyptisch genootschap Ex Oriente Lux (JEOL)* 16 (1959–62), pp. 48–71.

Zecchi, M., "The God Hedjhotep," *Chronique d'Égypte* 76 (2001), pp. 5–19.

Zeidler, J., *Pfortenbuchstudien, Teil 1: Textkritik und Textgeschichte des Pfortenbuches*, Wiesbaden: Harrassowitz, 1999.

Zeidler, J., *Pfortenbuchstudien, Teil 2: Kritische Edition des Pfortenbuches nach den Versiones des Neuen Reiches*, Wiesbaden: Harrassowitz, 1999.

INDEX

Numerals set in *italic* refer to illustrations in the text.